More Praise for
Render to God

"Theology, the study of God, traditionally deals with questions such as: What is God like? What does God do? How does God relate to creation, human and non-human? All too often, books dealing with 'New Testament theology' simply bypass questions of theology in favor of descriptions of the life and teaching of Jesus, of themes such as redemption, salvation, sin, justification, ethics, and the like. The essential questions of theology are left out of consideration. Neyrey has written a book that is remarkable in that it is, in fact, about New Testament theology: the understanding of God presented in an array of New Testament documents. His historical and social understanding of the New Testament is of the highest caliber. His style is crisp, clear, and reader-sensitive. With Neyrey's book and a Bible in hand, a reader can actually develop a deeper understanding of the theologies of New Testament authors, their similarities and differences, and curiously enough, their relevance for the twenty-first-century believer. For many readers it will mark the meeting of the God of our New Testament ancestors in faith for the first time. Close study of this book will prove most rewarding for professional and nonprofessional students of the New Testament."

—Bruce J. Malina
Professor of Biblical Studies, Creighton University

"In vintage fashion, Neyrey filters verses and pericopes from a sequence of Gospels and Epistles through the binary schemes that he and others have constructed from anthropological studies of modern Mediterranean peoples. But this time he also juxtaposes those interpretive schemes with traditional theology or simply replaces the latter with the former. The result is a provocative array of concepts for God-in-relation that will challenge standard biblical theology."

—Richard Horsley
Distinguished Professor of Liberal Arts and the Study of Religion, University of Massachusetts, Boston

Render to God

NEW TESTAMENT UNDERSTANDINGS OF THE DIVINE

JEROME H. NEYREY

FORTRESS PRESS
MINNEAPOLIS

RENDER TO GOD

New Testament Understandings of the Divine

Cover and interior design: Zan Ceeley

Library of Congress Cataloging-in-Publication Data

Neyrey, Jerome H.

Render to God : New Testament understandings of the divine / by Jerome H. Neyrey.

p. cm.

Includes bibliographical references and index.

ISBN 0-8006-3648-1 (pbk : alk. paper)

1. God—Biblical teaching. 2. Bible. N.T.—Theology. 3. Bible. N.T.—Social scientific criticism. I. Title.

BS2398.N49 2004

231—dc22

2004008042

The paper used in this publication meets the minimum requirements of American National Standard for Information Sciences — Permanence of Paper for Printed Library Materials, ANSI Z329.48-1984.

Manufactured in the U.S.A.

08 07 06 05 04 1 2 3 4 5 6 7 8 9 10

CONTENTS

ABBREVIATIONS

Ancient

Abr.	Philo, *On Abraham* (*De Abrahamo*)
Adv. Col.	Plutarch, *Against Colotes* (*Adversus Colotem*)
Adv. Mar.	Tertullian, *Against Marcion* (*Adversus Marcionem*)
Ag. Ap.	Josephus, *Against Apion* (*Contra Apionem*)
Alleg. Interp.	Philo, *Allegorical Interpretation* (*Legum allegoriae*)
Ant.	Josephus, *Judean Antiquities* (*Antiquitates iudaicae*)
Autol.	Theophilus, *To Autolycus* (*Ad Autolycum*)
b.	Babylonian Talmud (Babli)
Ben.	Seneca, *On Benefits* (*De beneficiis*)
Cael.	Aristotle, *On the Heavens* (*De Caelo*)
Cels.	Origen, *Against Celsus* (*Contra Celsum*)
Cher.	Philo, *On the Cherubim* (*De cherubim*)
1 Clem.	*1 Clement*
Cohort.	Justin Martyr, *Exhortation to the Greeks* (*Cohort. ad Graecos*)
Cor.	Plutarch, *Coriolanus*
Creation	Philo, *On the Creation of the World* (*De opificio mundi*)
Decalogue	Philo, *On the Decalogue* (*De decalogo*)
De or.	Cicero, *On Oratory* (*De oratore*)
Descr.	Pausanius, *Description of Greece* (*Graeciae description*)
Dial.	Justin Martyr, *Dialogue with Trypho*
Div. Inst.	Lactantius, *Divine Institutions* (*Divinae Institutiones*)
Dreams	Philo, *On Dreams* (*De somniis*)
Eccles. Rab.	*Ecclesiastes Rabbah*
Ep.	Seneca, *Epistulae morales*
Eternity	Philo, *On the Eternity of the World* (*De aeternitate mundi*)
Exod. Rab.	*Exodus Rabbah*
Flight	Philo, *On Flight and Finding* (*De fuga et inventione*)
Gen. Rab.	*Genesis Rabbah*
Haer.	Irenaeus, *Against Heresies* (*Adversus Haereses*)
Her.	*Rhetoric Ad Herennium*
Inst.	Quintilian, *Instruction in Oratory* (*Institutio oratoria*)

Inv.	Cicero, *On the Invention of Rhetoric* (*De Inventionae Rhetorica*)
Is. Os.	Plutarch, *On Isis and Osiris* (*De Iside et Osiride*)
Joseph	Philo, *On Joseph* (*De Iosepho*)
Jub.	*Jubilees*
Leg.	Athenagorus, *Appeal regarding Christians* (*Legatio pro Christianis*)
Lev. Rab.	*Leviticus Rabbah*
LXX	Septuagint
m.	*Mishnah*
Meg.	*Megillah*
Mem.	Xenophon, *Memorabilia*
Migr.	Philo, *On the Migration of Abraham (De migratione Abrahami)*
Mos.	Philo, *On the Life of Moses* (*De vita Mosis*)
MT	Masoretic text
Names	Philo, *On the Change of Names* (*De mutatione nominum*)
Nid.	*Niddah*
Onom.	Pollux, *Onomasticon*
Or.	Dio Chrysostom, *Orations* (*Orationes*)
Pel.	Plutarch, *Pelopidas*
Pes. Rab Kah.	*Pesiqta de Rab Kahana*
Plant.	Philo, *On Planting* (*De plantatione*)
Pol.	Aristotle, *Politics* (*Politica*)
Pss. Sol.	*Psalms of Solomon*
Q	Sayings Source Q
Q. Ex.	Philo, *Questions and Answers on Exodus* (*Quaestiones et solutiones in Exodum*)
QG	Philo, *Questions and Answers on Genesis* (*Quaestiones et solutiones in Genesin*)
Quaest. conv.	Plutarch, *Convivial Questions* (*Quaestiones convivales*)
Quaest. rom.	Plutarch, *Roman Questions* (*Quaestiones Romanae*)
Rhet.	Aristotle, *Rhetoric* (*Rhetorica*)
Sacr.	Lucian, *On Sacrifices* (*De sacrificiis*)
Sifre Num.	*Sifre Numbers*
Spec. Laws	Philo, *On the Special Laws* (*De specialibus legibus*)
Stoic. rep.	Plutarch, *Replies to the Stoics* (*De stoicorum repugnantiis*)
Strom.	Clement of Alexandria, *Stromata*
Sym.	Plato, *Symposium*
t.	Tosefta
Tg. Neof.	*Targum Neofiti*
Tg. Yer.	*Targum Yerushalmi*
Tim.	Plato, *Timaeus*
Unchangeable	Philo, *That God is Unchangeable* (*Quod Deus sit immutabilis*)
Virt.	Pseudo-Aristotle, *Virtues and Vices*
War	Josephus, *Judean War*
Worse	Philo, *That the Worse Attacks the Better* (*Quod deterius potiori insidari soleat*)
Yeb.	*Yebamot*

Modern

AB	Anchor Bible
ABD	*Anchor Bible Dictionary,* edited by David Noel Freedman, 1992
ABRL	Anchor Bible Reference Library
AGAJU	Arbeiten zur Geschichte des antiken Judentum und des Urchristentums
AJA	American Journal of Archaeology
AJP	*American Journal of Philology*
AnBib	Analecta biblica
ANRW	*Aufstieg und Niedergang der römischen Welt*
ASNU	Acta seminarii neotestamentici upsaliensis
AUSTR	American University Studies; Theology and Religion
BAK	Beiträge zur Altertumskunde
BAR	*Biblical Archaeology Review*
BETL	Bibliotheca ephemeridum theologicarum lovaniensium
Bib	*Biblica*
BibIntSer	Biblical Interpretation Series
BJRL	*Bulletin of the John Rylands Library*
BJS	Brown Judaic Studies
BT	*Bible Translator*
BTB	*Biblical Theology Bulletin*
BZNW	Beihefte zur Zeitschrift für die neutestamentliche Wissenschaft
ConBOT	Coniectanea biblica. Old Testament series
CBQ	*Catholic Biblical Quarterly*
CQ	*Classical Quarterly*
CRBS	*Currents in Research: Biblical Studies*
CurTM	*Currents in Theology and Mission*
EPROER	*Etudes préliminaire aux religions orientales dans l'empire romain*
ETL	*Ephemerides theologicae lovanienses*
EvQ	*Evangelical Quarterly*
EvT	*Evangelische Theologie*
FRLANT	Forschungen zur Religion und Literatur des Alten und Neuen Testaments
HBD	*HarperCollins Bible Dictionary,* edited by Paul J. Achtemeier, 1996
HBT	*Horizons in Biblical Theology*
HR	*History of Religion*
HTR	*Harvard Theological Review*
HUCA	*Hebrew Union College Annual*
IDB	*Interpreter's Dictionary of the Bible,* edited by George A. Buttrick, 1962
IJT	*Indian Journal of Theology*
Int	*Interpretation*
IRT	Issues in Religion and Theology
JAAR	*Journal of the American Academy of Religion*

JAOS	*Journal of the American Oriental Society*
JBL	*Journal of Biblical Literature*
JETS	*Journal of the Evangelical Theological Society*
JHS	*Journal of Hellenic Studies*
JJS	*Journal of Jewish Studies*
JQR	*Jewish Quarterly Review*
JR	*Journal of Religion*
JSJ	*Journal for the Study of Judaism*
JSNT	*Journal for the Study of the New Testament*
JSP	*Journal for the Study of the Pseudepigrapha*
JTS	*Journal of Theological Studies*
LD	Lectio divina
LEC	Library of Early Christianity
LNSAS	Leicester-Nottingham Studies in Ancient Society
LXX	Septuagint
MT	Masoretic text
NovT	*Novum Testamentum*
NovTSup	Novum Testamentum Supplements
NTS	*New Testament Studies*
OBT	Overtures to Biblical Theology
OtSt	Oudtestamentische Studiën
PBGALT	Paradosis: Beiträge zur Geschichte der altchristlichen Literatur und Theologie
PMS	Patristic Monograph Series
POT	Princeton Oriental Texts
RB	*Revue biblique*
RSR	*Recherches de science religieuse*
RSV	Revised Standard Version
SBEC	Studies in the Bible and Early Christianity
SBL	Society of Biblical Literature
SBLDS	SBL Dissertation Series
SBLMS	SBL Monograph Series
SBLSP	*SBL Seminar Papers*
SBLSBS	SBL Sources for Biblical Study
SBLWAW	SBL Writings from the Ancient World
SBT	Studies in Biblical Theology
SE	*Studia evangelica*
SGRR	Studies in Greek and Roman Religion
SHR	Studies in the History of Religions
SIDIC	Service international de documentation judéo-chrétienne
SJLA	Studies in Judaism in Late Antiquity
SJT	*Scottish Journal of Theology*
SNTSMS	Society for New Testament Study Monograph Series

StPB	Studia Post-Biblica
ST	*Studia theologica*
SUNT	Studien zur Umwelt des Neuen Testaments
TBT	*The Bible Today*
TDNT	*Theological Dictionary of the New Testament,* edited by Gerhard Kittel and Gerhard Friedrich, 1964–76
ThTo	*Theology Today*
TLZ	*Theologische Literaturzeitung*
TS	*Theological Studies*
TSAJ	Texte und Studien zum Antiken Judentum
TU	*Texte und Untersuchungen*
TynB	*Tyndale Bulletin*
VC	*Vigiliae christianae*
VCSup	Vigiliae cristianae Supplements
VT	*Vetus Testamentum*
WBC	Word Biblical Commentary
WUNT	Wissenschaftliche Untersuchungen zum Neuen Testament
WW	*Word & World*
ZAW	*Zeitschrift für die alttestamentliche Wissenschaft*
ZNW	*Zeitschrift für die neutestamentliche Wissenschaft*

PREFACE

I worship the God of our fathers . . . having a hope in God that there will be a resurrection of both the just and the unjust.
—Acts 24:14-15

The genesis of this book goes back to the evening that Professor Nils A. Dahl delivered a lecture to the graduate faculty and students at the Yale Divinity School entitled, "The Neglected Factor in New Testament Study" (Dahl 1975). As earnestly as I desired to start writing then and there, I first had to learn my craft and my literature, which has taken thirty years. Seated with me at Dahl's lecture were classmates who indeed wrote their dissertations on the "neglected factor," God: Jouette Bassler, *Divine Impartiality: Paul and a Theological Axiom* (1982); Halvor Moxnes, *Theology in Conflict: Studies in Paul's Understanding of God in Romans* (1980); and Stanley K. Stowers, *The Diatribe and Paul's Letter to the Romans* (1981). My own dissertation dealt with the debate over theodicy in the Greco-Roman world as the relevant background for the controversy in 2 Peter, "The Form and Background of the Polemic in 2 Peter" (cf. Neyrey 1980). But to my knowledge, none of us imagined that we were directly responding to Dahl's challenge.

Over the next several decades, various aspects of the "Neglected Factor" caught my attention, such as the background for theodicy debates in Acts 17 and 23–24 (1990a), the midrash for Ps 82:6 ("I said, 'You are gods'") in

John 10 (1989), the two powers and the correlative two names of God in John 5:19-29 (1986), the topos on God's eternity in Heb 7:3 (1991), and research both on prayer (2001) and then worship. Also, it has been my good fortune to be able to offer graduate seminars on God, which brought me in touch with ancient writers and their God-talk.

In the process of becoming equipped to write a monograph on God, I found certain elements of Judean and Greco-Roman background to be of exceptional worth. As regards Judean background, these topics and themes have proved the most helpful: the rabbinic commonplace of four questions (*b. Nid.* 69b-70a; see Mark 12:13-36); the contrast between the covenants of promise and the covenant of Moses (see Gal 3:6-14); the "kingdom of God," especially in Matthew; the two attributes of God, mercy and just judgment (Exod 34:6-7; see Romans 1–8); the two powers of God, creative and executive (see John 5:19-29; Rom 4:17); the correlation of the names "God" and "Lord" with creative and executive power, respectively. All of these play a significant role in this monograph.

Authors of Greco-Roman God-talk also contributed important materials to this inquiry. First and foremost is the systematic discussion of God in terms of three related philosophical categories: epistemology (What do we know about God and how do we know it?), physics (What is the nature of the Deity?), and ethics (What behavior necessarily follows from the nature of God?). This system, drawn from diverse authors such as Diogenes Laertius and Cicero, is quite evident in Romans and to a lesser extent in Galatians. Second, one of the most contested topics in ancient philosophy was theodicy: does God judge or not? Luke celebrates this debate first between the Stoics and Epicureans in Paul's Areopagus speech in Acts 17 and then between Pharisees and Sadducees in Acts 23–24. Third, according to orthodox Israelites and Stoics, God is supremely a provident Deity, discussion of which Luke highlights throughout the Acts of the Apostles. Finally, the ancients offer a nearly unanimous consensus on the chief characteristic of God in antiquity, namely, God's full eternity: uncreated and ungenerated in the past, and imperishable and without end in the future. This constitutes the primary argument for the divinity of Jesus in Hebrews.

But this study, enriched as it is with Judean and Greco-Roman background materials, would still lack one of the significant contributions of modern New Testament scholarship: the use of the social sciences for interpretation of the documents. Certain concepts and models drawn from cultural anthropology have been accepted with profit by students of Greece and Israel, and I find these particularly productive in this inquiry, both for gathering data and for assessing it responsibly in regard to its cultural context. Three social-science models proved particularly helpful in redressing this neglect of God: (1) patron and benefactor, that is, God-in-relationship; (2) honor, praise, and glory; (3) purity and holiness. These models are foundational for all the book's chapters, but because they might be familiar to many readers and because it seemed unnecessary to repeat the materials again in each chapter, I have positioned them as three appendices at the end of the book. Readers unfamiliar with them are urged to read them first, as use of them occurs in the exposition.

A complete study of God in the New Testament would attempt to interpret all twenty-seven documents, which is neither feasible nor desirable. Instead, a sample of six documents should introduce readers to the diverse ways in which New Testament authors "render to God the things that are God's." I begin with two Gospels, Mark and Matthew, which, without disparaging the christological focus of them, contain as much wonderful materials about God as about Jesus. Second, Luke's Acts of the Apostles provides a systematic view of the Christian God, presented in such a way as to argue that Christian faith is orthodox both to Israel and to the Greco-Roman world. Then three of Paul's letters (Romans, 1 Corinthians, and Galatians) invite a careful study of God, a topic that more recent commentators on Paul argue is the central focus of the letters.

Is anyone else called "God" in the New Testament? Jesus, of course, clearly in John and Hebrews. Study of this point would be worthwhile in and of itself, but I consider an investigation of the formal and precise ways in which Jesus is called "God" (John 1:1-2), "Lord and God" (20:28), and "equal to God" (5:17; 10:33) to be important statements also about God. In Heb 7:3 a figure is said to be "without beginning and without ending"; we learn that this "eternity" is a premier characteristic that identifies true gods and distinguishes them from mortals. "Eternity," then, is a fundamental concept for understanding God.

We are not the first to take up the challenge of Nils Dahl over the "neglected factor" in New Testament studies. A recent Festschrift for Paul Achtemeier, appropriately called *The Forgotten God* (Das and Matera 2002), contains articles on Old and New Testaments. The documents seem chosen as much for the contributor's convenience as for their innate quality. As valuable as the articles are in their own right, one finds no sense that the authors are laboring to uncover the major issues or ways of describing God. Many practice the traditional data gathering of names and attributes; little serious background of the Greco-Roman world inspires and shapes the argument. Much more, then, remains to be done. God is still "neglected" by scholars.

1

PATRON AND VINDICATOR
GOD IN MARK

Render to God the things that are God's.
—Mark 12:17

FOCUS AND PLAN OF INVESTIGATION

Whereas Paul in his letters formally argues theoretical God-talk about the Deity's impartiality or faithfulness, Mark tells a narrative in which all characters are known by their actions, including God. Since gospel writers presume that readers have a clear appreciation of the God of Israel, they do not tend to engage in formal, thematic discussions about God. This is, not surprisingly, a feature of "high-context" societies where much information and understanding is presumed (Hall 1976:105–16). When Jesus states that God is "the God of Abraham, Isaac, and Jacob" (12:26), all hearers know the stories of the covenants of promise made to the oldest patriarchs of Israel. We do not expect, then, a formal discussion of God's nature in Mark's Gospel. In a search for God-talk in Mark, the difficulty is compounded by the fact that all of us read this Gospel with a univocal focus on Jesus as the central figure in the story, such that God might seem like a minor character or merely as legitimating background to the career of Jesus (e.g., Kingsbury 2002:76–83). My task, then, is to find ways to make God's words and actions in this Gospel stand out, which materials can become the data for the investigation of God in Mark's Gospel.

To this end I propose the following three areas of investigation. First, among the names of God, the three most significant are "God" (*theos*), "Father/Abba" (*pater*), and "Lord" (*kyrios*). As we shall see in chapter 7, some Israelite authors distinguish these names in terms of God's actions or functions; thus "God" means Creator and "Lord" refers to God as lawmaker and judge. Is that the case in Mark? Is there specific content to each title? Second, studies of antiquity increasingly urge us to consider God's relationship to Jesus as that of patron to client. Moreover, God has another relationship, this time as patron to Israel through Jesus, which patron-client relationship now envisions Jesus as broker or mediator between God and the people. This will greatly aid in our understanding of God's benefactions and the role Jesus plays in their distribution. In the context of patron-client relationships, I will give special attention to Mark 11–12, of which John Donahue said: "The *didache* [i.e., instruction] of 12:13-34 comes precisely at that time when a positive theology is needed as a replacement for older theology" (1982:581). At this point we will be able to discern Mark's conscious articulation that God is vindicator of those who have been rejected. That is, God's plan and power is to raise those rejected and killed on earth and enthrone them in heaven. At heart, then, we confront a theodicy question about God's presence and power in a world over which it *seems* God has little control. Third, I will sketch the symbolic universe of Mark to understand God in relation to the holiness system of Israel and Mark's understanding of what God authorizes Jesus to do or do differently via-à-vis that system.

WHAT'S IN A NAME? THE NAMES OF GOD IN MARK

When Adam named the various creatures brought to him (Gen 2:19-20), his ability to name indicates both an understanding of the creature and Adam's power over it. Moreover, mortals tend to begin relationships with other persons by learning their name, which may communicate indications of their place in the cosmos in terms of gender, generation, and geography (Malina and Neyrey 1996:92–93, 102–5, 113–25). Human naming, however, does not apply readily to the Deity. Some ancients argued that the Deity was ineffable, unknowable, and unnameable (Young 1979; Runia 1988). No name, then, could describe God's essence; names may describe the Deity's actions, but not his nature or character. But these thinkers were generally elite philosophers, not the authors of the type of writings found in the New Testament. Indeed, it was a mark of honor for a Greco-Roman deity to be "many-named." For example, Cleanthes' Hymn to Zeus begins: "Most glorious of immortals, honored under many names." In a Hellenistic poem, Artemis as a little girl sat on her father's lap and asked for a special gift that would put her on a par with her brother: "Give me many-namedness" (Bremer 1981:194–95). Thus the God of Jesus Christ is "many-named" in Mark's narrative. But how can we appreciate these names of God?

What do names mean? What do they signify? Let us take advantage of Plutarch's remarkable—indeed, unique—summary of what names signify. He provides the best, most comprehensive, native discussion of names in antiquity. Because of its aptness for understanding how names functioned in the ancient world, I cite it in full.

> From this it is perfectly clear that Caius was the proper name; that the second name, in this case Marcius, was the common name of family or clan; and that the third name was adopted subsequently, and bestowed because of some exploit, or fortune, or bodily feature, or special excellence in a man. So the Greeks used to give surnames from an exploit, as for instance, Soter (Savior), and Callinicus (Winner); or from a bodily feature, as Physcon (Fat-paunch) and Grypus (Hook-nose); or from a special excellence, as Euergetes (Benefactor) and Philadelphus (Generous); or from some good fortune, as Eudaemon (Prospero), the surname of the second Battus. And some of their kings have actually had surnames given them in mockery, as Antigonus Doson (Always Promising) and Ptolemy Lathyrus (Lentils). (Plutarch, *Cor.* 11.2-3)

Anthropologists provide a way to decode Plutarch's remarks when they distinguish four kinds of names and what such names tell us about the persons so named (Eickelman 1989:181–87; Neyrey 1998a:55–59). There are (1) personal names; (2) nicknames (James and John = "Boanerges/Sons of Thunder," 3:17); (3) names derived from occupation, origin, and affiliation (Simon of Cyrene, 15:21; Joseph of Arimathea, 15:43); and (4) names embodying one's parents and clan (James and John = "sons of Zebedee,"

1:19; Jesus = "son of Mary," 6:3; Bartimaeus = "Son of Timaeus," 10:46). But what of God? Do any of these classifications apply to Israel's Deity?

Commentators regularly survey the names and features of God that Mark uses (Donahue 1982:565–70). The following chart summarizes the most frequently used names or titles used of God in Mark, the interpretation of which becomes our next task:

"God" (*theos*)	"kingdom of God" (1:15; 4:11) "son of God"/"holy one of God" (1:11, 24; 9:7) "only God can forgive or is good" (2:7) "God of the living" (12:27) "word or command of God" (7:8, 9) "house of God" (11:17) "Lord your God . . . is one" (12:29, 32)
"Father" (*pater*)	"when he comes in the glory of his Father" (8:38) "Your Father who is in heaven may forgive you your trespasses" (11:25) "No one knows . . . but only the Father" (13:32) "Abba, Father . . . thy will be done" (14:36)
"Lord" (*kyrios*)	"Prepare the way of the Lord" (1:3; cf. Isa 40:3) "Blessed . . . who comes in the name of the Lord" (11:9-10; cf. Ps 118:36) "This is the Lord's doing" (12:11; cf. Ps 118:22-23) "The Lord our God, the Lord is one" (12:29; cf. Deut 6:4) "The Lord said to my Lord" (12:36; cf. Ps 110:1) "If the Lord had not shortened the days" (13:20)

Calling the Deity "God"

In regard to the frequent title "God," most of its usages occur in the third category, which has to do with occupation or actions, the most common function of names of a deity in Israel and the Greco-Roman world. Among the Greeks, we know of "Zeus *Polieus*, the Guardian of the City," and "Poseidon *Asphaleios*, the Guardian from Earthquakes" (Burkert 1985:184). Indeed, Quintilian, the Roman rhetorician, instructs students on how to praise the gods in virtue of their deeds:

> In praising the gods . . . we shall proceed to praise the special power of the individual god and the discoveries whereby he has benefited the human race. For example, in the case of Jupiter, we shall extol his power as manifested in the governance of all things, with Mars we shall praise his power in war, with Neptune his power over the sea; as regards inventions we shall celebrate Minerva's discovery of the arts, Mercury's discovery of letters, Apollo's of medicine, Ceres' of the fruits of the earth, Bacchus's of wine. (*Inst.* 3.7.6-8)

Comparably, some Israelites distinguished the titles "God" and "Lord" in terms of functions. The title "God" was associated with creation, since it was thought that the word *theos,* "God," came from the verb *tithēmi,* which means to order or to place. Alternately, the title "Lord" was associated with God's executive functions: to make laws, to rule, and to judge (Neyrey 1988a:25–29). For example, Philo states that God has two powers:

> I should myself say that they [the cherubim] are representations of the two most august and highest potencies of Him, that is, the creative and the kingly. His creative potency is called God (*theos*), because through it He placed and made and ordered this universe, and the kingly is called Lord (*kyrios*), being that with which He governs what has come into being and rules it steadfastly with justice. (*Mos.* 2.99)

Yet I mention this only to note that Mark does *not* follow this usage. Although he refers twice to creation (13:19; see 10:9), he does not make this a formal part of his God-talk or relate it specifically to the name "God." Similarly, Mark's use of "Lord" does not describe the functions of the Deity to rule, judge, and requite. We know of God's actions and operations in Mark, but they are not attached to a particular title.

Eickelman's other source of names has to do with origins, either generation or geography. As regards geography, many deities in Greece were attached to certain shrines, mountains, and temples, such as Apollos Pythias and Zeus Olympios (Burkert 1985:184). According to Mark, God is not from any place or attached to any place; so God has no name that indicates geographical or ethnic roots, such as Jesus is identified with Nazareth or Paul with Tarsus.

But what does Mark signal when he calls the Deity "God"? What actions are in view? As noted, Mark places no emphasis on God as creator or as guardian of Israel. Yet "God" forgives sins (2:7; 11:25) and gives life to the dead. God speaks, authorizes (1:9-11; 11:30-31), commands (7:8, 9, 13), and has a clearly articulated "will" that must be obeyed (14:36). God alone is "good" and "one." Moreover, "God" has a kingdom (1:15; 4:11, 26, 30) and is all powerful, for what is impossible to mortals is possible to God (10:27; 14:36). As we shall see, the bulk of God's actions surround the figure of Jesus, as his patron and benefactor, such that most claims about or confessions of Jesus are equivalently remarks about his patron God. Moreover, as a high-context document, Mark's Gospel presumes that his readers know the story of Israel in its Scriptures and thus know God's relationship with it at least in broad patterns.

Finally, among the Greeks and Romans, it was standard fare to praise a god for either parentage or offspring. For example, Quintilian instructs orators on the praise of gods by means of genealogy: "Even gods may derive honor from their descent, as for instance is the case with the sons of Jupiter, or from their antiquity, as in the case of the children of Chaos, or from their offspring, as in the case of Latona, the mother of Apollo and Diana" (*Inst.* 3.7.8-9). God in Israel cannot have a name derived from parents or clan. God generates, but is not generated; hence God has no genealogy or ancestors. Without father or mother or genealogy, God does not have the same role or trade or craft of his father, nor any other skill or virtue of his clan. God is not like "Jesus, son of Joseph, the carpenter," or "Simon, son of Jonah, the fisherman."

Abba/Father

Like many New Testament documents, Mark's Gospel names the Deity "Father" and even "Abba." "Father" signals a role that I will explore shortly, namely, "patron." Fathers-as-patrons provide power, protection, commitment, material goods, and knowledge, just as fathers labor to provide the same for their households and offspring. In addition to this general understanding of the role of "father," scholars have begun to show that it also expresses certain meanings in Mark's Gospel. Mary Rose D'Angelo argues that "Father" was used in Second Temple Israel to express three aspects of divine power: (1) petition by afflicted and persecuted Israelites (e.g., 3 Macc 6:3-8); (2) appeal for mercy and forgiveness (e.g., Tob 13:4-6), and (3) acknowledgment of God as wise provider of all good (e.g., Wis 14:1-4; D'Angelo 1992b:151–53). Focusing on two texts about prayer, she goes on to show that Jesus' prayer in 14:36 corresponds to the first aspect, namely, the relationship of martyrs suffering persecution for God-Father, whereas the injunction to forgive and receive forgiveness in 11:25 parallels the second usage, namely, appeal for mercy and forgiveness. Mark contains no remarks on God-Father as providential provider. D'Angelo summarizes her exposition of God-Father in Mark: "Thus in Mark, the word 'father' evokes the . . . traditional uses of father for God as the refuge of the persecuted and the giver of forgiveness" (1992b:161). Finally, one must take into account Barr's revisionist argument that "Abba" is not baby talk for father, but rather contains the formal respect adult sons owed their fathers (Barr 1988).

God: Sovereign and Judge

Examining the title "Lord," one notes that Mark gives special attention to one aspect of God's sovereignty and power: God's eschatological power that raises the dead and judges them. Mark repeatedly states that God's providence for Jesus encompasses both Jesus' rejection on earth and his vindication in heaven. Although in both Israelite and Greco-Roman theology the sovereign God rendered just judgment, rewarding the faithful (see Mark 10:30) and punishing the wicked (8:38), Mark's version indicates that the "Lord's" favor and power extend especially to righteous individuals like John the Baptizer, Jesus, and the prophets. In loyalty to God, all were rejected, shamed, and killed. Jesus is the chief figure whom the "Lord" vindicates and raises up; after all, it was Jesus himself who defended the Deity's power to raise the dead (12:24-27). In two places Mark cites a psalm that describes the action of "the Lord" to vindicate and exalt someone. First, in the parable in 12:1ff., after the beloved son is killed by the wicked tenants, Mark cites Ps 118:22-23 to indicate how the Deity undoes the shame done by the builders who rejected the stone and elevates it as the cornerstone. This "Lord," then, raises Jesus from shame and death and exalts him on high. Similarly, Jesus puts a conundrum to the scribes about the "son of David." How can the Messiah be David's son when Psalm 110 calls him David's "Lord"? "The Lord said to my Lord: 'Sit at my right hand'" (12:36). When the Jesus movement uses this psalm, it is in reference to his resurrection (Acts 2:34-35; Heb 1:13). Thus "the Lord," who is the Deity, says to David's sovereign, who is the Christ, to ascend his throne at God's right hand, which is part of Mark's full understanding of Jesus' resurrection.

Although examination of the names of God does not bring to light either original titles or distinctive functions and actions, Mark's names for God are typical of both Israelite and Christian traditions. From this survey we learn of a wide range of activities of the Deity: creator at the beginning and judge at the end, sovereign with a kingdom and entourage, a just sovereign who decrees laws for his people and rewards and punishments for compliance or noncompliance, and a faithful and all-powerful God who manifests loyalty by vindicating his servants. None of this is unique to Mark, since the actions and functions of God here are typical of so many writings of the period. But it should be noted that the bulk of Mark's God-talk centers on eschatological issues: survival of death and reward/punishment.

Circumlocutions

Over twenty-five times Mark uses the passive voice as a circumlocution for the workings of God, thus expressing a sense of divine involvement in and control of human affairs, as well as a cultural respect for God's name. One particular expression dominates this category, namely, that something "is given": all sins are forgiven (2:7); "to you is given to know the mysteries" (4:11); "the measure you give will be the measure given to you" (4:24); "to him who has, more will be given" (4:25); "say whatever is given you to say" (13:11). God, then, remits debts but also acts as benefactor and just judge.

God's Uniqueness

According to the rhetorical rules for praising someone, it is a singular mark of honor to be the first to do something, the only one ever to do it, or the one who most does it. For example, in Aristotle's treatment of the rhetoric of praise, he cites as a way to amplify a grant of honor calling attention to a person's "uniqueness": "One should also use many kinds of amplification, for example if the subject [of praise] is the *only* one or the *first* or *one of a few* or the one who *most* has done something; for all these things are honorable" (*Rhet.* 1.9.38, emphasis added; see also *Rhet.* 2.7.2). Centuries later, Cicero articulated the same principle of uniqueness for the praise of a person's virtue, beneficent deeds, endurance of misfortune, and unique deeds: "And one must select achievements that are of outstanding importance or unprecedented or unparalleled in their actual character" (*De or.* 2.85.347).

Uniqueness had many forms. Although at one time Israel expressed a special formula of loyalty, the Shema of Deut 6:4, "Hear, O Israel, the Lord your God is one," this did not signal uniqueness. Rather, scholars call it an example of *henotheism,* that is, while other gods exist, Israel accepts a covenant with only one deity, God. But centuries later in the time of Jesus and Mark, Israel had come to profess *monotheism,* which denied existence to all gods other than the God of Israel; thus uniqueness belongs to the character of the only God. In this light, note Jesus' remark about God in 10:18, that "only God is good." Similarly, certain scribes object to Jesus' forgiveness of sins, commenting, "Only God can forgive sins" (2:7), implying that Jesus encroaches on God's uniqueness, thus dishonoring God. Moreover, only God knows the day and the hour of the end (13:32)—another uniqueness. Whereas mortals find certain teachings impossible, "all things are possible with God" (10:27). Thus "uniqueness" directs us to Mark's appreciation of the nature of God and God's actions, which are the grounds for praise.

PATRON-CLIENT: GOD-IN-RELATIONSHIP

Given the prevalence and importance of patron-client relationships in antiquity, I suggest that Mark's Gospel be read in that light. Readers familiar with the model of patron-client relations should read on. But readers not familiar with this cultural model are asked to consult appendix one at the end of the book, where they may find a crisp summary of the material. Since one key element of the model needs to be clearly in focus, namely, what goods and services are exchanged between patron and client, I briefly summarize it here. If a detailed list were made of all goods and services that patrons and clients exchange, the list might run on endlessly. In an effort to rationalize and thus abstract the types of goods and services exchanged, I rely on the model of Talcott Parsons, which reduces them to four general symbolic media (Malina 1986a:77–87). Parsons observes that people are always trying to have an effect on someone, for which purpose they may employ four different classifications of goods and services. Thus a benefactor seeking to have an effect on a client might employ: (1) power, (2) commitment, (3) inducement, and (4) influence. These four summary categories, I argue, adequately describe the relation of God, who is father and patron, and Jesus, who is client and broker.

God as Patron

In regard to what the evangelist has to say about God, who is patron and father, Mark first announces a special relationship of God with Jesus in the Jordan theophany (1:9-11). This event, apparently the first of its kind for Jesus, functions as a status transformation ritual in which God selects Jesus and elevates him to the role and status of "beloved son," the one who enjoys God's particular favor, for he is the man "in whom I am well pleased." These declarations about Jesus serve as marks of God's extraordinary and particular *commitment* toward Jesus. God judges that Jesus is a holy person, both loyal to God and now favored by God. This commitment crystallizes Mark's appreciation of Jesus' worthiness of God's favor for reasons such as his faithfulness, obedience, and honoring of God. Thus the patron's commitment is met with the client's commitment. Furthermore, most theophanies in the Bible function as commissionings, that is, patronal investment of a role in a favored client, for example, Moses at the burning bush, Gideon at the threshing floor, Elijah on the mountain, Isaiah in the temple (Habel 1965). Such "call narratives" are rightly understood as the establishment of patron-client relationships. Thus I understand Mark's baptismal account to function as God's commissioning of Jesus to a unique and favored role and status. For Luke's interpretation of this in similar terms, see Rohrbaugh (1995:186–92).

Divine *power* is bestowed when God causes "the Spirit" to descend on Jesus. While this "Spirit" is holy, since it descends from heaven, it particularly expresses God's power. Mark quickly narrates that Jesus' holy Spirit is at war with "unclean spirits" (1:12-13, 23-24). Since a major taxonomy of illness in the New Testament indicates that many illnesses were thought to be the result of "spirit aggression" (Pilch 2000:68–70), we are not surprised that Mark quickly informs us that Jesus has *power* over "disease" and "demons" (1:32-34; 3:10-12). For their part, unclean spirits and demons overpower and subjugate people, the remedy for which is to "destroy" them (1:24) or drive them out (5:2-13), for which power is required.

At one point we hear that Jesus is accused of having an evil spirit: "He is possessed by Beelzebul, and by the prince of demons he casts out demons" (3:22). Because this statement claims that Jesus is not God's loyal client but God's enemy, it touches upon both commitment and power in the God-Jesus relationship. Mark answers this charge with a bold defense. First, readers know that Jesus is not God's enemy, for God said of him, "my beloved Son, with you I am well pleased" (1:11), and God cannot be deceived. Second, the spirit given Jesus as a benefaction is God's "holy" Spirit, not the power of the enemy. Moreover, Jesus proves his commitment and faithfulness to God first in the desert temptations by God's enemy (1:13), and when as God's agent he went about driving out evil and unclean spirits. The apology in 3:23-27 finally removes any possible ambiguity about Jesus as faithful client of God and wielder of God's powerful Spirit. Jesus and Satan cannot be allies, for allies do not fight. Should civil war break out, the house would collapse. Rather, Jesus is the "stronger one" (3:27; cf. 1:7), who as God's client wages war on Satan, Beelzebul, and all demons. As patron, God's power uniquely resides in Jesus, as does God's commitment to him.

God's declaration of Jesus as "beloved Son" and thus client recurs in the theophany called the transfiguration (9:2-9). Commentators point out how similar this second theophany is to that at the Jordan. If, as we saw, theophanies generally function as commissionings, it appears that the Jordan theophany ascribed to Jesus a special status ("beloved Son") and task (to war on Satan with the "holy Spirit"). As a special act of patronage by God, it validated the subsequent actions of Jesus, either to heal diseases and cast out demons or to determine a new way of piety vis-à-vis Sabbath observance, fasting, forgiving sins, and so on. Similarly, the mountain theophany occurs as Jesus leaves Galilee and begins his journey to Jerusalem, at which time powerful healings yield to predictions of controversy, rejection, and death. Commitment is called for now, while power is less evidently in play. When Peter objects to this new direction, Jesus calls him "Satan" and criticizes him for "thinking the thoughts of man, not God" (8:33). The will of the Patron, then, has changed and fresh commitment is called for in the face of new tasks. In this crisis, God acts as patron by declaring again—this time to select disciples—that Jesus remains "my beloved Son" (9:7) and by commanding Peter, James, and John to "listen to him" as he describes the will and plan of his Patron-God. Thus God-Patron once more legitimates Jesus, but no longer for deeds of power and success in Galilee. Rather the faithful Patron now calls forth obedience to all teachings on the way and in the midst of all controversies, betrayals, and sufferings ahead in Jerusalem. Even if success does not continue, God is no less the patron to Jesus, the client. Jesus remains the "beloved Son." The ultimate loyalty of God the Patron to Jesus the client is God's raising of Jesus, not simply to life but to God's right hand. Vindication, then, is the ultimate power and commitment shown by the Patron.

Jesus as Client

How do clients respond to patrons? How do we understand Jesus' response to his Patron? This, too, can tell us much about God, Patron and Father, if God is treated honorably. The bestowal of patronage in antiquity always entailed a strong sense of obligation or duty on the one so favored. As we saw above, four types of "goods" were exchanged. If God is bestowing commitment and power on Jesus, what has Mark to say about Jesus' use of the same media to affect his patron? What does Jesus owe his patron? The answer lies in the way the ancients discoursed on four cardinal virtues: prudence, justice, fortitude, and temperance. Justice best describes the reciprocal duties that clients have toward patrons and vice versa.

> To justice it belongs to be ready to distribute according to desert, and to preserve ancestral customs and institutions and the established laws. First among the claims of righteousness are our duties to the gods, then our duties to the spirits, then those to country and parents. Justice is also accompanied by holiness and truth and loyalty and hatred of wickedness. (Ps.-Aristotle, *Virt.* 5.2-3; see also Cicero, *Inv.* 2.160-61; Menander Rhetor 1.361.17-25)

Justice, then, expresses the duty that those who have received benefaction owe to their patrons and benefactors, especially the gods. Justice is manifested especially by commitment, that is, by the faithfulness, loyalty, and obedience of the client (i.e., "truth and loyalty"). Let us look now at four places in Mark that express Jesus' response to his Patron-Father in terms of justice, commitment, and their parts: 8:31—10:52; 11:15—12:12; 12:13-37; and 14:1—15:39.

Death and Vindication: 8:31—10:52

After Norman Perrin isolated the three rejection/vindication predictions in 8:31; 9:31; and 10:33-34, he indicated how they form a pattern: (1) a statement by Jesus, (2) misunderstanding by the disciples, and (3) Jesus' clarification (1969:40–56). This pattern organizes into three blocks of material the teaching of Jesus on his way from Caesarea Philippi to Jerusalem:

Prediction	Misunderstanding	Clarification
8:31	8:32	8:33—9:29
9:31	9:32	9:33—10:31
10:33-34	10:35-40	10:45-52

Our attention focuses on the predictions, for in them we find expressed the relationship between God-Patron and his client-Son. According to Mark, Jesus understands the predictions as the will of his Patron, which is phrased in a circumlocution generally agreed to express God's plan and purpose: "the Son of man *must* be handed over. . . ." "Must" here equals the divine will. In clarification of his initial remark, Jesus scolds Peter for not accepting his prediction of death/vindication as "the thoughts of God" (8:33). Jesus' justice here means two things: first, accepting God's will for himself and so progressing on his way to Jerusalem; second, teaching a particular "way" of discipleship that reflects this Patron's will for all disciples (8:34-38). That Jesus continues his journey and explains this teaching serves as clear evidence of his justice/commitment to his Patron. The same pattern of faithfulness is attached to the next two predictions of Jesus' rejection and vindication (9:31; 10:33-34).

The New Client versus the Old Ones: 11:15—12:12

Jesus was not God's first client; before him there were kings, such as David and Solomon; prophets, such as Moses and Elijah; and others, such as Israel's high priestly clan. All these figures served as mediators of God's benefaction: power (David, Moses, Elijah), influence (Isaiah, Solomon, Moses), commitment/covenant (David, Moses, high priests). But not all kings and high priests were faithful clients/brokers of God. Jesus' actions in Jerusalem criticize the failure of other brokers, namely the Jerusalem elites, and thus he defends the honor and interests of God-Patron.

At first glance, the incident in the temple (11:15-19) does not appear to fulfill a duty to God, because the story indicates that Jesus interrupted the sacrificial system by upsetting the tables of those who sold the bird offerings of the poor and did not allow anyone to carry anything (i.e., libations, grain offerings, etc.) through the temple (Bauckham 1988). To observant Israelites this would surely offend God by stopping the sacrifices that honored God and by profaning God's dwelling. Subsequently the temple elites demand that Jesus justify his actions (11:27-33). How can Jesus be God's loyal client and offend his Patron? Jesus' clever response ties his authorization with the legitimacy of John's baptism; in short, the answer to both is the same. The person who authorized Jesus' actions via-à-vis the temple is the same figure who authorized John's baptism. Moreover, God-Patron authorized John to baptize Jesus, the event that marked the beginning of a patron-client relationship between God and the "beloved Son" (1:9). As a result of this multistranded bond between God-Patron and Jesus-client, Jesus acts faithfully in all he does and says. Thus Mark argues that in 11:15-19 God continues to be well pleased with his Son-client who now begins to replace temple sacrifice with prayer and fixed sacred space with fluid sacred space. Far from being acts of impiety and disloyalty to his Patron, Jesus' actions reflect loyalty and faithfulness, that is, commitment, even if judged hostilely by others (11:27-33).

The parable that Jesus tells in 12:1-12 confirms his justice/commitment to God, his Patron. A wealthy landlord plants a vineyard, leases it out, but like many absentee owners he lives elsewhere. Even in the basic narrative we see a typical patron-client relationship: the owner = patron, the tenants = clients. At harvest time, this patron expects his clients to fulfill their duty and send him "some of the fruit of the vineyard." To this end he dispenses three waves of servants to collect what is his due, only to have them beaten, wounded, treated shamefully, and finally killed. His clients, then, completely fail in their duty of justice/commitment. The owner-patron then sends the tenants a new person, "a beloved son"; but they show maximum contempt for the owner by killing this son. The client-son obeyed his patron-father and went, thus showing commitment, even if he did not succeed in his dealings with the tenants. The patron-father, then, has two types of clients, disloyal tenants and an obedient son. But thus far the story tells of failed patron-client relationships because the tenants refuse any reciprocity with their patron. The patron's commitment evokes no faithfulness or loyalty on their part, only shame and scorn; inducement due him, that is, the produce of the vineyard that the patron-client contracted for, is not payed, but he is treated with contempt. The patron then cancels the agreement and takes just vengeance on the upstart clients, which action is the use of power. Afterward the patron forms a new patron-client relationship: "He will destroy the tenants and give the vineyard to others" (12:9), that is, a benefaction of commitment. But what of the "beloved son," the patron's loyal client?

To the parable Mark appends Ps 118:22-23, which tells of the patron's faithfulness to his "beloved son" who was killed. The faithful client-son, while rejected by the builders, becomes the cornerstone, and so is honored by his patron. All agree that this speaks about Jesus, who, although rejected on earth by mortals, was posthumously exalted by his Patron ("it is the Lord's doing," 12:11). Thus the faithful client-son, who obeyed his Patron-Father by going to his death at the hands of the Patron's enemies, is granted the Patron's new favor. Commitment is reciprocated by commitment, but of an exalted kind; and the Patron's power over death is exercised on behalf of his client, Jesus. Thus 11:15—12:12 tells about Jesus-the-client's faithfulness to God in his actions and controversies, as well as his Patron's faithfulness to him and his judgment on unfaithful clients. God-Patron, then, acts in judgment on wicked clients and brokers, even as he responds in commitment and power toward his new client/broker, Jesus.

"Render to the Patron the Things That Are the Patron's": 12:13-37

Immediately groups of Jerusalem elites, Pharisees and Herodians (12:13-17), Sadducees (12:18-27), and scribes (12:28-34) challenge Jesus in a series of verbal contests, both cynical and subversive. David Daube once suggested a pattern from the Babylonian Talmud as a template for interpreting the types of questions asked Jesus in 12:13-37 (Daube 1973:158–63; Neyrey 1998a:47–49). He cites a text in which rabbinic elites test another rabbi by means of four questions: "Our Rabbis taught: Twelve questions did the Alexandrians address to R. Joshua b. Hananiah. Three were of a scientific nature, three were matters of *haggadah*, three were nonsense and three were matters of conduct" (*b. Nid.* 69b-70a). Twelve questions, but four categories: (1) "conduct," that is, questions about specific application of the law; (2) "haggadah," that is, questions concerning contradictions in the Scriptures; (3) "nonsense," that is, mocking questions intended to ridicule a teacher's beliefs; and (4) "scientific," that is, questions concerning the theory of the law. Daube argues the following correspondence between these four questions and the controversies in 12:13-37.

Type of Question	Episode	Provoking Question	Theological Response
Conduct	Mark 12:13-17	"Is it lawful to pay tribute to Caesar?"	"Render to God the things that are God's" (12:17)
Nonsense	Mark 12:18-27	the story of the widow and the seven brothers: "whose wife will she be in the resurrection"?	"You know not the power of God" (12:24); and "He is not the God of the dead but of the living" (12:27)
Scientific	Mark 12:28-34	"Which commandment is the first of all?"	"The Lord our God, the Lord is one; you shall love the Lord your God with your whole heart" (12:29-30)
Haggadah	Mark 12:35-37	"The Lord [God] said to my Lord . . ." (12:36); how can David have a son whom he also calls "Lord"?	Implied: God's patronage is not bound to bloodlines or social patterns

The first three episodes pose questions to Jesus, testing his knowledge of and loyalty to God. In the eyes of his questioners, Jesus cannot be God's client. As we shall see, all of the questions in 12:13-37 affirm and celebrate some aspect of God's plan and purpose, which Jesus endorses. God is owed much, just as Caesar is owed taxes; God has power to raise the dead; God, who is one, deserves undivided loyalty; and God is free to elevate David's son higher than his father. In each case, then, Jesus, the client, loyally defends the interests of his Patron.

The theological focus of 12:13-34 has been noted by John Donahue (1982:572–81; see Giblin 1971), to whose study we are indebted. But we can take his analysis several steps further. First, Daube's reference to "four rabbinic questions" urges us to examine all the discussions in Mark 12, including 12:34-37; in the first three episodes, Judean elites ask Jesus questions, whereas in the fourth, Jesus asks them a question. Nevertheless, the four types of questions asked by the rabbis are all asked in 12:13-37; and they constitute a structural and thematic unit. Second, I consider the remark in 12:17 to be the theme of all four questions: "Render to God the things that are God's" (12:17). Donahue and others give a strictly christological reading of "rendering to God" as accepting Jesus as truly deserving of the epithets in 12:14 and honoring him as God's agent/client. For, says Donahue, Jesus is himself "the prime example of one who renders 'to God the things of God'" (Donahue 1982:574). But Donahue and most commentators focus on Jesus, God's client, and have little to say about this God, to whom Jesus says we should render what is due. In contrast to this typical interpretation, I argue that 12:17 be interpreted in its full context, not just in 12:13-17, but within 12:1-12 and 18-37. God, the Patron, is Mark's focus, to whom all should render what is God's. Let us now render to God what Jesus claims for God in 12:13-37.

The previous story (12:1-12) told us that the patron was owed his due by both his tenants and his "beloved son." All of us know the ancient principle of agency: "Who receives me, receives not me but him who sent me" (Mark 9:37), and "who rejects you, rejects me, and who rejects me, rejects him who sent me" (Luke 10:16). Who rejects the messengers, then, rejects their sender. Thus the murder of the "beloved son" is an incalculable insult to the patron, who, like Hallmark cards, sent "the very best." The patron, then, is due inducement, his share of the vineyard's produce, and commitment. When denied these, the patron recovers his due honor and respect by "destroying the tenants." All would render him this right. It belongs to the patron, too, to redress the shame of his "beloved son," which the story says that he does. Mark cites Ps 118:22-23 as a scriptural way of expressing how the patron posthumously honored his loyal client. The "rejected stone," a metaphor for the "beloved son," was subsequently vindicated as "head of the corner." As most people read the story, the Father of the son is God-Patron, who raised the rejected stone to an exalted position (12:11). Thus to "render to God what is God's" in 12:1-12 includes authority and sovereignty (commitment, inducement) to make covenant contracts with vineyard tenants; the authority (commitment) to send even the client-son into danger, with the firm expectation of obedience; the just expectation of the patron to receive the commitment and inducement from his clients; power, shown in retribution toward ungrateful and murderous clients; a new commitment in the offering of the vineyard to new clients; and finally a new commitment and a new act of power in the posthumous honoring of the loyal son. Jesus, the client, declares that all this is due God. All this we should "render to God."

The story in 12:18-27 should also be read in terms of Jesus' demand that Jerusalem "render to God what is God's." Certain Jewish elites step forth who were notorious in first-century Israel for disbelief in the resurrection (see Acts 23:7-8; Josephus, *War* 2.164-65; *Ant.* 13.297; 18.16; Isenberg 1970). Because Sadducees rejected survival after death, for them God does not raise the dead, which is the point they argue in their "nonsense" question. Their case of a woman who married seven brothers functions as an argument that there cannot be survival after death, since the woman married to all seven bothers can be the wife of only one in the afterlife—if there is an afterlife. In short, they refuse to "render to God" the power to raise the dead. Mark portrays Jesus as indignant at this question: "You know neither the scriptures nor the power of God" (12:24). Although Jesus does not cite any particular Scripture, he refers to God's relationship to Moses and to the patriarchs, Abraham, Isaac, and Jacob. The patriarchs "live" before God, at least in the sense that God's promise to them lives. That promise was a type of immortality in that their offspring would continue and multiply and fill the earth. Thus the patriarchs live because their progeny live. With God, then, past promises continue to be alive today and indefinitely into the future. Hence "God is the God of the living." "Render to God," then, must include God's plan and power to raise the dead. "Rendering to God" power to raise the dead was also a chief point in 12:1-12, here, and will be in 12:34-37; we might call this the chief thing that we must "render to God."

A scribe asks the third question, which concerns a principle of the Torah (12:28-34). Whereas 12:13-17 was concerned with a specific application of the law (i.e., "taxes to Caesar"), this scribe asks a theoretical question: "Which commandment is the first of all?" (12:28). Jesus responds by quoting the most fundamental confession of Israel's worship of God, the Shema (Deut 6:4). His recitation of monotheistic faith functions as commitment and loyalty to his Patron. It serves to bind him to that Patron and to declare to scribes, Sadducees, Pharisees, and chief priests his orthodoxy. All Israelites would "render to God" this belief. Moreover, Jesus "renders to God" his duties, first to his Patron, "You shall love the Lord you God with your whole heart . . . mind . . . soul and strength" and then to God's client people, "You shall love your neighbor as yourself." Wholeness is also due God; priests in God's temple must be bodily whole to sacrifice, and animals sacrificed to God must be whole and unblemished (Neyrey 1998c:204–8). Jesus' response is itself "whole." Thus "Render to God the things that are God's" must surely include the fullness of duty and commitment (12:29-31) owed God by Israel's clients.

Mark narrates that the scribe repeats Jesus' answer in full, his commitment, monotheistic faith, wholeness of loyalty to God, and covenant love of fellow Israelites (12:32-33). This repetition serves several purposes. The scribe, presumably informed about the law, canonizes Jesus' remark, "You are right, teacher; you have truly said. . . ." The scribe, who honors all parts of Jesus' statement, takes the discussion one step further by evaluating what Jesus has just declared: "[this] is worth more than all whole burnt offerings and sacrifices" (12:33). This relativizes the commitment and inducement connected with worship in the central shrine of Israel, the temple. The scribe's remark compares two things, both good in themselves; but he values and honors one ("love of God . . . love of neighbor") above the other ("whole burnt offerings and sacrifices"). In doing so, it appears that Jesus' actions toward the temple in 11:15-17 are correspondingly vindicated, for in that episode Jesus downgraded sacrifice but elevated "prayer" as the temple's chief function. Thus if one "renders to God the things that are God's," then monotheistic loyalty, wholeness of commitment to God, and covenant faithfulness to neighbor are precisely the things that should be "rendered to God." Correspondingly, "whole burnt offerings and sacrifices" should *not* be "rendered to God."

Finally, a fourth question, about "contradictions" in Scripture, is asked in 12:35-37 (Dahl 1977b). Unlike the other three, Jesus takes the offensive and asks this one. The question has to do with the interpretation of Ps 110:1, "The Lord said to my Lord, 'Sit at my right hand until I put your enemies under your feet.'" Who are the figures in the citation? "How can the scribes say that the Christ is the son of David?" David calls this "son" "my Lord." How, then, can the Christ be both son of David (inferior) and David's lord (superior)? In a proper patron-client relationship, David's son is also his client and should pay homage to his father-patron, and not assume airs and honors above the greatest of Israel's kings. On the other hand, Psalm 110 describes another type of patron-client relationship: patron: "the Lord," that is, God-Patron, who made David's son his client by naming him David's "lord"; client: the Christ, who is son and client of David, is also the patron of his own royal father. Thus the Christ, son of David, is both "son" and "lord," that is, both David's client and his patron. This is, then, a remarkable description of patronage, which includes at least commitment and power, and probably some forms of influence and inducement. "Render to God," then, means crediting God with making the Christ, son of David, "my Lord."

Inasmuch as we are privy to an academic exercise of scriptural interpretation, we need to ask how Mark is understanding Psalm 110. Throughout the New Testament, Christian authors regularly cite and explain Ps 110:1 in reference to Jesus' being "raised." The clearest example of this comes in Peter's Pentecost address, where he proclaims that "you killed him, God raised him." But God's "raising" is twofold, first "raising" to life and then "raising" to God's right hand. Hence Peter declares about the risen Jesus: "The Lord said to my Lord, 'Sit at my right hand, till I make your enemies a stool for your feet.' Let the house of Israel therefore know assuredly that God has made him both Lord and Christ, this Jesus whom you crucified" (Acts 2:34-36). Does Mark understand Ps 110:1 as a statement of God's raising of Jesus? This meaning certainly fits with several other items we have recently seen. First, in 12:11-12 the patron vindicates his "beloved son" killed by the wicked tenants: the Lord exalts the stone rejected by the builders into the cornerstone. Second, contrary to what the Sadducees say, it belongs to the God of the living to raise the dead (12:24-27). A third and compelling argument comes from a later episode where Jesus uses Ps 110:1 as a claim for God-Patron's commitment. During his trial, Jesus' relationship with God is questioned: "Are you the Christ, the son of the Blessed?" (14:61). The loyal client honors God as his Patron, but expresses this in a combination of references from Scripture: "I am; and you will see the Son of man seated at the right hand of Power and coming with the clouds of heaven" (14:62). The fortunes of this Son-client are plummeting; God-Patron will not prevent Jesus' death, any more than the father protected his "beloved son" from the wicked tenants. Then Jesus' remarks must refer to another time when God-Patron shall have acted to vindicate his Son-client. "Seated at the right hand of Power" refers to God-Patron's raising of Jesus, both to life and then to an exalted role. "Coming with the clouds" indicates that God-Patron will endow his Son-client with executive, judgmental powers whereby he will judge the world, enemies included. Therefore, 12:11-12 along with 18-27 and 35-37 all "render to God" the power and plan to raise the dead, Jesus in particular.

In sum, we know that the evangelist structured the core argument of Mark 12 around the tradition of testing a rabbi with four types of questions. Of specific interest to us is Mark's adaptation of this to focus on God and on Jesus' orthodoxy and faithfulness in relationship to God-Patron. Therefore I read the general statement of Jesus to "render to God the things that are God's" (12:17) as the topic statement to which Mark gives specificity: God's power to raise the dead, God as the God of the living, God as the unique one who must be worshiped with wholeness, and God as the one who vindicates and exalts the Christ, the son of David. All of this shows that Jesus the client manifests exemplary commitment and loyalty to his Patron, but also that God-Patron shows commitment and power to his clients, especially in raising them from the dead.

Prayer: How Clients Relate to Patrons

We have seen how the client-son, Jesus, "rendered to God the things that are God's" in three sections of the narrative, 8:31—10:52; 11:15—12:12; and 12:13-37. But it is in the Passion Narrative that the evangelist describes Jesus accepting his betrayal and death as instances of "thinking the thoughts of God" (8:33), and so the most formal demonstration of his commitment to his God-Patron. The will and plan of God-Patron is known to Jesus, which knowledge is a mark of favor to Jesus. For example, when Jesus says: "The Son of man goes as it is written of him . . ." (14:21), Jesus knows that "goes" means rejection and death (see 8:31; 9:31), his destiny as found in God's Scriptures. On the way to the Mount of Olives, Jesus quotes from Zech 13:7 to the effect that God will "strike the shepherd and the sheep will be scattered" (14:27). At his arrest, Jesus says, "But let the Scriptures be fulfilled" (14:50). In each of these, Jesus, the client, knows what God-Patron expects of him and he faithfully accepts it. What remains unclear is why God-Patron wishes this. Jesus' approaching dishonor and death, however, are by no means the displeasure of his God-Patron.

Two more incidents in the Passion Narrative dramatically display the ideal patron-client relationship between God and Jesus, and both have to do with prayer. In Gethsemane Jesus withdraws to pray: "Sit here while I pray" (14:36). Taking the inner circle of his disciples, he begins quoting snatches of Ps 42:5, 11, and 43:5. Inasmuch as these psalms are themselves prayers, Mark would have us appreciate that these troubling words are the form and text of Jesus' relationship with God at this point. Finally, Jesus "fell to the ground and prayed" a prayer that all disciples would recognize, namely, the Our Father. Jesus addresses God: "Abba, Father," and then petitions "not what I will, but what you will" (14:36). A third fragment of the prayer occurs in Jesus' exhortation to Peter: "pray that you not enter into temptation" (14:38). Mark next tells us that Jesus went away and "prayed, saying the same words" (14:39) not just twice but three times (14:41). This narrative, then, has much to tell us about Jesus' relationship to God, which directly relates to a client-patron relationship.

First, Mark portrays Jesus as a man of great loyalty and faithfulness to God, as witnessed by the fact that Jesus formally prays and continues in prayer. As I understand this scene, Jesus' prayers honor God ("Abba, Father"), in petition to his Patron to act with power to spare him ("remove this cup from me"), and in full-throated obedience and commitment ("not what I will, but what you will"). The text of Jesus' prayer, then, manifests commitment to God, even as it asks that God in his commitment exercise power to save Jesus and his disciples ("pray that you not enter into temptation"). Thus Jesus totally and faithfully declares his commitment to God.

Second, although Mark portrays Jesus as silent when others taunt and mock him, he records Jesus' dying words. In antiquity dying words were treated with great seriousness, which is the case with all four evangelists. At the ninth hour Jesus cried out "Eloi, Eloi, lama sabachthani" (15:34). What is he saying? What language is this? And how do people understand it? Many Semitic words spoken by Jesus in the Gospel are immediately translated into Greek: *talitha koum* = "Little girl, arise" (5:41); *korban* = "given to God" (7:11); *ephphata* = "Be opened" (7:34); *Abba* = "Father" (14:36); *Golgotha* = "the place of a skull" (15:22); and finally *Eloi* . . . = "My God. . . ." But Mark tells us that the bystanders misunderstand Jesus entirely, for they think that he calls "Elijah" to rescue him (15:35-36). Like so many of Jesus' sayings and parables, the spectator crowd never understands, but in private the disciples are given to know the mysteries of the kingdom of God. What is opaque to outsiders becomes clear to insiders. Thus Jesus' executioners—certainly outsiders—do not understand Jesus' last words, but what clues does Mark give the insiders to understand them?

We saw in the case of Jesus' remarks in 14:34 that he spoke words that were sanctioned as appropriate speech with which to address God (Douglas

1982:28–33, 157–60), namely, Israel's sacred psalms. Jesus' last words likewise belong to a psalm, indeed a psalm that functions to give significance to various events in Jesus' passion. Commentators regularly inform us of scriptural allusions in the Markan Passion Narrative, most of which are based on Psalm 22: "drugged wine" (Mark 15:23) = Ps 69:21; "clothes divided" (15:24) = Ps 22:18; "mockery" (15:29) = Ps 22:7; and "My God, my God . . ." (15:34) = Ps 22:1 (Reumann 1974). Mark is not simply arguing that ancient prophecies are fulfilled and thus God's ancient plan is trustworthy. The dying words of Jesus are more significant than mere details about various incidents. I argue that Jesus prays sanctioned words that belong once more to a psalm from Israel's book of prayers. But what kind of psalm? What kind of prayer?

Psalm 22 is regularly classified as a "lament" or "complaint" (P. D. Miller 1994:69–86; Westermann 1980:29–70; Balentine 1993:146–98). But in investigating the lament/complaint, let us not lose focus on patron-client relations; for this type of psalm directly embodies these social relations and operates out of them. Patrick Miller provides a crisp analysis of this type of psalm that highlights its social dynamic:

> The questions of complaint are varied, but all of them are a direct challenge to the way God has acted or threatened to act. . . . The present circumstances of distress seem to indicate to the ones praying a terrible inconsistency on the part of God. The Lord seems to have caused or allowed things to happen in a way inappropriate to the faithfulness and compassion that are characteristic of the Lord of Israel. The fundamental query of all these complaining questions is: Why are you doing this or allowing this to happen? *They are a protest, not a request for information.* (1994:71, emphasis added)

The client, then, declares his commitment and complains that his Patron does not manifest the same. The issue is mutual commitment between client and patron. Moreover, Miller notes that "complaints" in the psalms are phrased in terms of questions, as is Psalm 22:

> Why, O Lord, do you stand far off?
> Why do you hide yourself in times of trouble? (Pss 10:1; 13:1; 89:46)
>
> How long, O God, is the foe to scoff?
> Is the enemy to revile your name forever?

> Why do you hold back your hand;
> Why do you keep your hand in your bosom? (Ps 74:10-11)

These complaint-protests point in two directions, both to the situation of the person praying and to the seeming unresponsiveness of God. At a certain level of abstraction, these complaint questions express the same thing: "God's inability or disinterest in helping a faithful but suffering member of the community articulate the psalmist's predicament, that he or she has trusted in the Lord but to no avail in time of trouble" (Miller 1994:74). In terms of content and tone, these psalms register a similar complaint, namely, that "God is hiding the face, forgetting, abandoning, being far off, rejecting and casting off" (Miller 1994:75). Psalms of lament/complaint, then, declare that the Patron is failing in his duties, primarily commitment; and the person complaining, on the other hand, declares commitment that seems unrequited or ignored.

What type of prayer is this? Students of the New Testament are indebted to Bruce Malina for his study on prayer in terms of social-science models of communication. As an act of communication, prayer contains four basic elements: a sender (the person praying), a medium (in this case, words), a receiver (God), and the purpose and results desired from the communication. Prayer is "a socially meaningful symbolic act of communication, bearing directly upon persons perceived as somehow supporting, maintaining, and controlling the order of existence of the one praying, and performed for the purpose of getting results from or in the interaction of communication" (Malina 1980:215). In terms of the results sought in a communication, clients might seek from their patrons commitment (loyalty), power (escape from enemies), inducement (food in times of famine; money to pay taxes), or influence (information). Psalms of lament/complaint, however, focus on commitment, both declaring the client's loyalty and petitioning the Patron to be faithful too. If the prayer is successful, the Patron's commitment will be activated and his power will likely be exercised.

Based on his insight that prayer is speech "for the purpose of getting results from or in the interaction of communication," Malina differentiates several types of prayer, of which I consider the following relevant for this study: petitionary ("I want . . ."), interactional (maintaining emotional ties: "how lovely is your dwelling place, Lord, mighty God"), self-focused (identification of the self to God: "I have glorified you on earth, having accomplished the work you gave me to do," John 17:4), heuristic ("tell me why"), and informative (confession, praise, and thanksgiving) (Malina 1980:217–18; see also Neyrey 2001:351–53). As we consider Psalm 22 in terms of these types of prayer, we see that it is not heuristic; Jesus is not asking for information. Nor is it instrumental, for Jesus is not asking for a favor, that is, escape from death, which is how his executioners misunderstand him. Nor is it imaginative or informative. Rather, Psalm 22 is primarily interactional, in that Jesus is portrayed as seeking to maintain emotional ties with God; that is, it is about commitment. This type of prayer arises from a sense that God is not living up to his duties in a patron-client relationship, implying that the client has fulfilled his duty and maintains loyalty and faithfulness in the relationship. Perhaps more examples from Miller's treatment of this type of psalm can make this clearer:

> People say to me continually, "Where is your God?" (Ps 42:3)
>
> As with a deadly wound in my body, my adversaries taunt me,
> while they say to me continually, "Where is your God?" (Ps 42:10)

The complaint, then, appeals to God in a situation where the pray-er finds him- or herself shamed and mocked by others. At issue are God's loyalty and faithfulness, which seem totally absent. Thus by his lament/complaint, Jesus calls upon God to honor God's patronal commitment to him. The purpose of this type of prayer is the activation and maintenance of ties, bonds, loyalties—the basic patron-client relationship.

The Patron's Commitment and Power

This reading of Mark 15:34 tells us much about Jesus' faithfulness as client, but what can be said about his patron, God? Does Mark record that Jesus' lament/complaint was heard? Was the patron-client commitment that Jesus saw as lacking finally activated? Yes, and immediately. First, Mark narrates that "the temple veil was torn in two, from top to bottom" (15:38). Mortals might tear the veil in two, but only from bottom to top; the agent of this act must be heavenly, so as to rend it from top to bottom. Mark 15:38 then states that God acts immediately upon the death of Jesus to affirm the patron-client relationship. Why the temple veil? Why not a city wall or major building? We recall the remarks of Jesus about the temple (14:58; 15:29), how he was accused and mocked for them. Inasmuch as the temple was popularly considered the place where God made his name to dwell, it was treated as sacred space. And its system of sacrifice and worship was considered God-mandated, and thus sacred. Jesus' actions in the temple (11:15-17), his defense of them (11:27-33), his remarks about the temple (13:4), and the subsequent use of these remarks both to condemn him (14:58) and mock him (15:29) suggest that in Mark's account considerable importance is placed on whether Jesus is right or wrong, saint or sinner, loyal or disloyal client (Bauckham 1988:86–89). God's tearing of the veil serves to vindicate Jesus' words and actions as genuine commitment to God, his patron. God did not spare his client Jesus from death (see 8:33), but nevertheless honored Jesus by an action immediately bespeaking patronal loyalty, faithfulness, and respect. God-Patron, then, maintains commitment with his client, vindicating his words and actions toward Israel's sacred place. God, indeed, is a faithful patron.

Mark next tells his audience that Jesus' executioner reappraised Jesus' status. The Passion Narrative contains numerous instances when people mock Jesus: the title over the cross, "King of the Jews" (15:26); the taunt, "he saved others; he cannot save himself" (15:31); and the mockery, "let the Christ, the king of Israel, come down from the cross" (15:32). In another context, statements such as these would acknowledge Jesus' role and status, and so honor him (8:29; 11:9-10). But these clearly ridicule Jesus and mock his alleged relationship with God. The executioner, however, declares: "Truly this man was the Son of God" (15:39). His acknowledgment contrasts sharply with previous insults, for the centurion now affirms Jesus' special relationship to God. Jesus' shameful crucifixion and death, then, are not a punishment from God for wickedness, but must be seen in an entirely different light: as obedience, faithfulness, and loyalty to God. The client has not abandoned the Patron, nor has the Patron forsaken the client.

The Patron himself has the last word. Mark's narrative ends with the announcement of glorious news: "You seek Jesus of Nazareth, who was crucified. He has been raised, he is not here" (16:6). Readers know that the person dressed in white belongs to the heavenly realm; he is an official messenger from that realm with a message no less significant than that which Jesus declared at the start of his career (1:15). Now there is a gospel about the beloved Son, as the Proclaimer has become the Proclaimed. The messenger's proclamation is a highly compressed statement of God's vindication of Jesus, and by the end of the story Mark's audience already knows this.

We examined earlier the triple prediction Jesus made on his way to Jerusalem, focusing on Jesus' obedience to the will of his Patron that means "suffer . . . be delivered." Let us consider now the second part of the triple prediction, ". . . and be raised."

8:31	the Son of man must suffer . . . and after three days be raised
9:31	the Son of man will be delivered . . . and after three days be raised
10:33-35	the Son of man will be delivered . . . and after three days be raised

In the light of the relationship between Jesus-client and God-Patron, we learn the following. First, Jesus himself speaks these words, and in doing so he declares his obedience and faithfulness to his Patron. His suffering, then, is not retribution from his Patron for disloyalty, but of a different order, namely, a client's act of obedience fully pleasing to his Patron. More to the point of this study, the three predictions contain the promise that God-Patron will be loyal to Jesus and vindicate him, for so I read the phrase ". . . be raised up." Thus we see commitment on both sides: the client will show obedience and loyalty to the Patron, and the Patron will acknowledge the client's loyalty and vindicate him beyond his earthly shame. This very theme of the Patron's vindication of his client can be found repeatedly in the rest of Mark's narrative, thus highlighting the most important thing Mark has to say about God: the Patron's ultimate commitment and supreme power.

Finally, because of his obedience to his Patron-God, Jesus finds himself on trial before the temple elites, who cannot accept that this troublemaker and deceiver could be the faithful client of God. Because the trial began with the comment that "the chief priests and the whole council sought testimony against Jesus to put him to death" (14:55), most interpreters do not take the high priest's question as a search for information (Neyrey 1998b:658–64). Thus when asked if he is "the Christ, the son of the Blessed," Jesus' response both states his own commitment to God and appeals to the commitment of his Patron. For his consummate loyalty and faithfulness even unto death, Jesus will experience God's vindication of him and enthronement at his Patron's right hand (14:62a). Again commitment by one partner of this patron-client relationship evokes commitment by the other. Moreover, by referring to himself as the "Son of man," Jesus evokes the figure in Daniel 7, which states that what mortals reject and scorn on earth, God will vindicate and honor him in heaven by endowing the "Son of man" with great powers, even power to judge and do justice to his enemies.

In conclusion, by using a patron-client relationship model, we can surface and highlight Mark's understanding of God. We are able now to give greater definition to Jesus' command, "render to God the things that are God's." God-Patron bestows generous blessings as a generous patron. This might include inducement (food), power (victory over evil, raising the dead), and influence (the "gospel" that Jesus preached, 1:15; "the secret of the mysteries of the kingdom," 4:11; "the thoughts of God," 8:33). But God's patronage especially consists of commitment (loyalty and faithfulness). Although the adjective "just" is not used of God in Mark, still God is faithful to his duties, especially his faithfulness to his client Jesus. God gives and also seeks a corresponding commitment from Jesus and other clients. Thus all of God's clients owe faithfulness to God, even as God-Patron is faithful to his clients. The pervasive declaration that all that happens to Jesus is already planned and inscribed in the Scriptures indicates that God's commitment impregnates all the events of Jesus' fate.

It is in Mark 11–12 that the evangelist presents his special information about Jesus' God-Patron, amply filling out what was cryptically said by Jesus, "render to God the things that are God's." The following chart systematizes that material:

1. The power of the living God to raise the dead: 12:11-12 (Ps 118:22-23); 12:18-27; 12:35-37 (Ps 110:1); 14:62
2. Worship of God in prayer preferable to sacrifice: 11:15-19; 12:33; 13:4; 14:58; 15:29
3. Exclusive worship of God: 12:24, 26-27, 29, 32
4. God-Patron's authorization of Jesus-client: 11:27-33

In contrast, clients who are mortals cannot offer God power, inasmuch as they are always subject to disease and death, the workings of the evil one. Nor does God seek inducement (i.e., sacrifice) from his clients, for we learn that love of God and neighbor is "worth more than all whole burnt offerings and sacrifices." In place of sacrifice, God authorizes prayer, a type of commitment, as the formal mode of honoring the Deity. Jesus himself models this most clearly for the disciples (14:36; 15:34).

God-Patron, Jesus-Mediator, and Israel-Client

We should widen the patron-client model to accommodate another figure in the relationship, the mediator or broker (Malina and Rohrbaugh 1992: 235–37, 326–29). In social or commercial terms, a broker places various people in touch with one another, such as a real estate broker linking home sellers and home buyers, a stock broker joining those selling and buying stocks, or a marriage broker arranging for potential brides and grooms to meet (Malina 1996:149–57). A broker must be suitably placed to be accessible both to clients seeking aid and patrons who might provide assistance. Thus a broker is a bridge or link or mediator between patrons and clients.

Albert Oepke listed the following social roles in the ancient world that exemplify the working of brokers or mediators. A mediator is a person who is "neutral" to two parties and negotiates peace or guarantees agreements, arranges business deals, founds a new cult or religion, as king receives divine laws and offers sacrifice for the people, as priest offers prayers and sacrifice to God on behalf of individuals and the people, as prophet brings a teaching or mighty work from God, and as angels deliver communication from God (Oepke 1967). He further notes that the New Testament calls Jesus a mediator or broker in many ways. Jesus serves as the one or unique mediator between the God and humankind (1 Tim 2:5) and the mediator of the new covenant (Heb 8:6; 9:15; 12:24). In Hebrews the author celebrates Jesus' superior priesthood, because Jesus "is able for all time to save those who draw near to God through him, since he always lives to make intercession for them" (Heb 7:25; see 9:24). Other documents speak of him mediating the fullness of God's blessings on the church: "He [God] has put all things under his [Jesus'] feet and made him the head of all things for the church, which is his body, the fullness of him who fills all in all" (Eph 1:22-23). Thus the model of Patron-God and client-Jesus should be nuanced to include patron-mediator-client, a relationship in which God bestows benefaction uniquely through Jesus and Jesus mediates prayer and petitions to God.

I focus here on how Mark presents God-Patron, not simply in relationship to Jesus but especially how God-Patron channels the four classes of benefaction to Israel through Jesus. Mark leaves no doubt that whatever benefaction

Jesus bestows on people is given him by God for this very purpose. The various benefactions which God gives Jesus include:

1. Power: God gives Jesus holy Spirit to war on all demons and unclean spirits (1:12-13, 21-28; 3:22-27; 5:1-20); power over storm demons (4:35-41; 6:45-52); power over death (5:35-43); and if illness is classified as spirit aggression, healings are also acts of power (1:32-34; 7:31-37; 8:22-26).

2. Commitment: Jesus' first act is to herald: "The kingdom of God is at hand; repent, and believe in the gospel" (1:15), which is a major benefaction to Israel. God provides Jesus as well with authority to declare sins forgiven, thus reconciling those whose commitment was in decay (2:1-12). Moreover, God gathers a new family around loyalty to Jesus (3:31-35), and extends the circle of covenant benefaction to include non-Judeans (3:7-10; 5:1-20; 6:53-56; 7:24-31, 31-37).

3. Inducement: God empowers Jesus to multiply foods, first for 5,000 and then for 4,000 people (6:30-41; 8:1-10).

4. Influence: As well as two theophanies, God reveals to Jesus the mysteries of God's kingdom, which he shares with his disciples (4:11). Jesus is likewise given to understand the secret of the Scriptures that tell of the rejection and vindication of the Son of man (12:10, 36; 14:21, 34, 49). Jesus, rabbi and teacher, tells his special teaching on the "way" of the Son of man (8:31—10:45).

We recall that Mark twice narrates that God declares Jesus as God's "beloved Son" (1:11; 9:7). Other characters in the story effectively concur with this, such as the unclean spirit who affirms that in his show of power Jesus demonstrates that he is "the Holy One of God" (1:24). Other spirits too declare the same relationship of Jesus with God, for example, "the Son of God" (3:11). One particularly violent demon, actually a legion of demons, acknowledges Jesus' agency from God: "Jesus, Son of the Most High God" (5:7). Thus the cosmos of spirits hostile to God's clients acknowledges Jesus as broker of this Patron-God. Similarly, Mark records that earthly figures likewise hostile to Jesus acknowledge him as mediator-prophet: "Elijah . . . a prophet, like one of the prophets of old" (6:15). Similarly, at Caesarea Philippi, the disciples repeat the same popular judgment about Jesus' role as broker: "John the Baptist . . . Elijah . . . one of the prophets" (8:28). As Oepke reminded us above, "prophets" are mediators between God and Israel, who dispense God's power, commitment, inducement, and influence. "Prophet," therefore, means "mediator."

Insiders in the story also affirm that Jesus acts as mediator of God-Patron. For example, Jesus forgives the paralytic's sins, an act that some scribes consider a blasphemous usurpation of God's unique powers. To prove them wrong, Jesus then heals the physical body of the man, a sign that cannot be denied. He does it for the express purpose of confirming the mediational role he enjoys between God and the people: "That you may know that the Son of man has authority on earth to forgive sins" (2:10). The crowds then applaud this and affirm his relationship to God: "They were all amazed and glorified God" (2:12). Other people seeking God's benefaction recognize Jesus as mediator of divine patronage; the blind beggar, Bartimaeus, addressed Jesus as "son of David," thus identifying Jesus with Solomon, the son of David, legendary for his wisdom and magic (Duling 1975, 1978); as we know, kings were also mediator figures in Israel. Finally, Jesus' executioner switches his judgment of Jesus from that of a criminal who received just punishment to one that affirms Jesus as a holy man close to God: "Truly this man was the Son of God" (15:39). Thus both God's enemies and God's friends concede Jesus' relationship to God. They agree that his power, as well as the food with which they are fed and the wisdom that enlightens them, comes from God. Thus whatever we learn of Jesus as mediator and broker is also knowledge of his Patron. Indeed, God cannot be honored without honoring the mediator whom God sent.

The full patron-broker-client model, then, surfaces not only the particular relationship of God-Father and Jesus-Son, but also the way in which God-Father bestows on Judeans the full complement of general symbolic media, power, commitment, inducement, and influence. Thus Mark's audience always knows that all that Jesus says and does is from God and for God's people. God alone is Patron, and Jesus is the unique mediator and broker.

REDEFINING GOD'S HOLINESS

Mark narrates that observant Israelites criticized Jesus for various practices, such as how his disciples observed the Sabbath, with whom he ate, whether his disciples fasted, why his disciples ignored washing rites, and the like. They judged Jesus according to a system of Torah observance built up of labels, lines, and laws that defined who or what was "holy." God commanded, "Be holy, as I am holy" (Lev 11:44-45; 1 Pet 1:16). But what constitutes "holy"? Thus we must now learn the holiness code of Israel, that is, its purity system that defines what is "holy," "clean," "pure," "unspotted," and the like (Neyrey 1988b:72–82; 1996:80–104). As in the case of the model of patron-client relationships, so too the cultural model of purity and pollution is fully explained in appendix two at the end of this book. The following summary is intended to sharpen the perception of readers with knowledge of that model.

Some person, place, time, or thing was classified as "holy" in ancient Israel if it conformed to the maps that ordered and classified all that belongs to these four categories. By "map" I mean patterns of systematization, hierarchy, location, and sequencing. The Priestly account of creation in Genesis 1 tells how God put order into chaos, either by maps of place (wet separated from dry), time (night/day; a seven-day week; months and years), things (sea, air, and land creatures; plants and trees), or persons (Adam and Eve). The Priestly structure of the temple embodied this system of maps, such that whenever visitors entered the building, they were immediately socialized to these holiness maps. But pious Israelites took the system beyond the temple and into their routine lives, thus attempting to be "holy" as priests, offerings, and temple are holy. It was possible, then, for some to judge the conformity of the many according to these maps of persons, places, things, and times, thus assessing their worthiness for the presence of the temple of God.

Jesus and the "Holiness" System

Without the concepts and models just examined, we would be at a loss to understand how people in Mark's narrative assess Jesus' holiness and why they judge him the way they do. Mark records people who are strict observers of Israel's purity system constantly criticizing Jesus for his studied violation of all the maps of holiness just described. Their conclusion is potentially devastating, for, from their perspective, Jesus cannot be "holy" when he transgresses the basic maps of the purity system. He cannot be the "beloved Son in whom I am well pleased," if he does not observe the will of God. And according to the principle of contagion, Jesus would be corrupting others who join his circle. While Mark concedes that Jesus does not keep the "traditions" of the elders, he does not, on the other hand, take this to mean that Jesus lacks holiness or stands in opposition to God. What we seek, then, is Mark's narrative argument about Jesus' holiness in episodes that suggest nonobservance and even disobedience, but in which he manifests God's "holiness" in new and different ways. When we examine Mark's treatment of Jesus' observance of various maps of persons, places, times, and things, we ask three questions: What did Jesus or his disciples actually do? What warrant or authorization have they for this? What results from these actions or failure to act?

1. *Maps of time.* Mark tells two stories about how Jesus and his disciples transgress the custom of Sabbath "rest." Once when they are hungry, the disciples begin to pluck and eat grain in the field, provoking the Pharisees' censure (2:23-28). Mark does not consider Jesus ignorant of custom or casual in behavior, for he reports that Jesus justifies the disciples' actions in terms of traditional and humane extensions of Sabbath rest. Far from flagrantly dismissing Sabbath observance, these actions are justified according to humane principles: "The Sabbath was made for man, not man for the Sabbath." As further warrant, Jesus cites David as his precedent (2 Sam 15:35); although only priests were allowed to eat certain loaves, David also ate—and without censure. Jesus' warrant, then, is God's Scripture and the example of David, which allows for humane exceptions in need.

Similarly, Mark tells of Jesus in a synagogue on the Sabbath, itself a pious action suggesting ritual observance of holy time. But the scene is upset by the presence of a man with a withered arm, whose lack of wholeness becomes a trap to see what Jesus will do. Any nonobservance by Jesus will give his observant critics cause to "accuse him" (3:2). Jesus nevertheless makes the man whole, thus removing uncleanness and bringing bodily wholeness to the man with the withered arm. As for warrant, Jesus argued by means of binary opposites. What is the Sabbath for: "to do good or to do harm, to save life or to kill?" Jesus justifies his behavior because he acts on the principles of "doing good" and "saving life," actions surely endorsed by the "good" and "living" God. Therefore, not only was God not shown disrespect by Jesus' Sabbath action, but the healing made the man "whole" and so "holy." Thus despite the judgment of others, Mark does not present Jesus as nonobservant, but rather as reforming the tradition of Sabbath observance by the authority of God.

2. *Maps of persons.* Mark narrates that Jesus has dealings with a wide variety of persons whom his peers would classify according to the maps of persons examined above: observant and elite Israelites; family members who are owed loyalty; "unclean" persons subject to spirit aggression; "unclean" persons such as lepers, menstruants, the blind, and the dead; nonobservant Israelites; and non-Israelites. Put simply, "a man is told by the company he keeps," or "birds of a feather flock together." Observant people should associate with other observant folk; but clean should avoid the unclean, and Judeans should be separate from non-Judeans.

Jesus had social intercourse with all six classifications of people listed above. What does this mean? Is he out of place in dealing with some (i.e., the Jerusalem elites) and should he avoid others (the unclean and sinners)? The answers lie in the nature of the exchanges. First, Jesus engages chief priests, Sadducees, scribes, and Pharisees, who embody Israel's purity system and function as its guardians. Alas, these are they who accuse Jesus of uncleanness and nonobservance. His interaction with them, therefore, casts him as their opponent and critic. If they were truly faithful clients of God, this would tell against Jesus. As it is, Jesus is the reformer of true worship of God, not a perpetuator of decadent rites. Second, in regard to the map of his family members, Jesus not only does not obey them but disowns them in favor of other "mothers, brothers, and sisters" (3:31-35; see 10:29; Barton 1994:67–96). In the eyes of some, this speaks of rebellion and thus sinfulness. But if the blood relatives resist God's gospel, then resisting them is virtue on Jesus' part. Similarly, the residents of Nazareth perceive Jesus as inflating his status and so trying to be higher on the map of Nazareth's population (6:1-5).

Third, as regards "unclean persons," Mark presents Jesus engaging people who suffer from spirit aggression (Pilch 2000:68–70), specifically "unclean spirits." Indeed, Jesus' first public action in a synagogue on the Sabbath is to battle an "unclean" spirit (1:23-26; see also 3:11; 5:1-13; 7:25; 9:25). Here and elsewhere, he acts in power, whereby he defeats the attacking spirit because he is the "stronger one" (1:7; 3:27). Although some accuse Jesus of being in league with "unclean" spirits, and thus "unclean" himself (3:22), Mark's audience knows that God empowered Jesus with this "holy" or "clean" spirit at the baptismal commissioning (1:11), and so Jesus' commerce with "unclean" spirits is that of foe, not ally. God authorized this contact. Those freed from "unclean" spirits are liberated from the power of evil, surely a holy and noble thing. Jesus' action is honorable; his warrant comes from God himself who empowered him. Thus onlookers interpret Jesus' action correctly: "What is this? A new teaching! With authority he commands even the unclean spirits and they obey him" (1:27). Jesus, then, suffers no contagion from this contact. God wills that Jesus *not* separate himself from the unclean, but battle and defeat those spirits.

Fourth, Jesus constantly engaged people labeled by Leviticus as "unclean" because "not whole." As regards bodily surfaces, that is, skin, lepers are classified as "unclean" because they might have "too little" or "too much" skin. Skin might be flaking off of the body and so not be "in place" or be raised with boils and suppurating sores. Jesus touched a leper, commanding that he be "clean" (1:40-44), and he became "clean." No contagion here; rather Jesus healed the source of uncleanness. Later, as regards bodily structure, Jesus made whole two men with uncleannesses, one with a withered arm (3:1-6) and another with lame legs (2:1-12); both had "too little" in regard to bodily limbs. As regards bodily orifices, the menstruating woman touched Jesus (5:25-29); her flow rendered her "unclean," for menstrual blood was considered one of the "fathers of uncleanness." Like the leper, no contagion here, for Jesus healed the source of uncleanness. Two men approached Jesus, one blind and the other a deaf-mute, both of whom are unclean because their bodily orifices have "too little": blindness/eyes and deafness/ears (7:32-37; 8:23-25). Finally, Jesus took the hand of dead girl, death being the ultimate uncleanness (5:41). The degree of uncleanness varies in these examples, but the severity of contact with lepers, menstruants, and the dead is maximal; contagion inevitably results, except in these cases.

What has the "holy" God to do with this? If we consider these acts of Jesus "prophetic" after the example of Israel's prophets (8:28), then God empowers and authorizes his contact with unclean peoples. Moreover, the effect of Jesus' contact is always to restore wholeness and thus equip people for worship in Israel's temple (1:44) or for reintegration in family and society. "Holiness"-as-wholeness is, then, both a gift of God and honors God in turn, and more and more people are "holy as I am holy."

Finally, two other groups need be considered in regard to *maps of persons*, nonobservant Israelites and non-Israelites. Nonobservant Israelites include the "sinners and tax collectors" with whom Jesus shares food (2:15-16; see Donahue 1971). Of course, one could argue that Jesus' disciples too were nonobservant, both in terms of Sabbath and washing rites (7:5). Non-Israelites, however, include the crowds that gathered from "Idumea and beyond the Jordan and from about Tyre and Sidon" (3:8), as well as the Gadarene demoniac (5:1-20); Jesus traveled in "the region of Tyre and Sidon" (7:24), as well as "through the region of the Decapolis" (7:30). According to the map of places recorded in *m. Kelim* 1.6-9, cited in appendix 2, these are unholy places, to which observant Israelites should not venture. Jesus healed the sick in these non-Israelite territories, effectively bringing God's benefaction to those outside God's covenant and concern. The nonobservant Israelites were comparably blessed by the presence of Jesus, for his dealings with them consisted of invitations to discipleship and closeness to himself, which mean access to the Holy God of Israel. Thus only wholeness resulted from these contacts; certainly, the bearer of this benefaction was not made unclean by contagion with them.

Thus, as regards maps of persons, Mark interprets Jesus' actions in many striking ways. In each contact, the "unclean" person was made clean, that is, whole. Only good, then, flows from Jesus' actions. Thus one should not imagine that Jesus suffered contagion from contact when the unclean were made clean and the dead were made alive. Jesus' warrant for this, while complex, is clear. He is a "physician" sent to the sick (2:17), evidently by God, for he is able to do godly cleansings. People consider him a prophet because of the works that he does, for prophets are mighty in word and deed (6:14-15; 8:28). Jesus himself uses one of his healings as proof of God's power in him (2:10-12). Thus "with authority"—surely God's authority—he works his healings. Mark reports that the observant Pharisees and others criticized Jesus' healing only when done on the Sabbath, not otherwise; there was never an accusation of contagion. The crowds interpreted the healings as divine benefactions. Thus the God of order and holiness does not himself practice "separation" ("holy" means "separated") from unclean, nonobservant, and sinful people, but sends Jesus with a gospel calling them to change, restoring their bodily wholeness, and inclusively embracing those previously judged "separated."

3. *Maps of places.* Let us examine Jesus in four spatial contexts: temple, synagogue, house, and land outside Israel. All Israel acknowledged the temple as the most holy of all places: its courts, altar, and the holy of holies. Jesus' dealings with the temple are concentrated in the time between his entrance to Jerusalem from the Mount of Olives (11:1) and his return there (13:3). During this time, Jesus enters Jerusalem's temple (11:11), and to it he returns the next day (11:15) and the day after (11:27). All the controversies over Jesus' authorization (11:27-33), his parable about the vineyard (12:1-12), and the

four questions asked of him (12:13-36) take place in the temple. Jesus' stay ends with a final comment on the temple treasury (12:41-44). Jesus conducts his affairs in the part of the temple known as the Portico of Solomon, a place of study, discussion, and debate; he is never said to offer sacrifice or join in the temple worship. Nevertheless, God would be honored by Israelite males frequenting the holy place; and Jesus would be honored in turn as a holy person.

The fly in the ointment, however, is the controversial action of Jesus described in 11:15-19; scholars are unclear just what Jesus did and what Mark wants us to understand by it (Bauckham 1988). Mark tells us that Jesus "entered the temple," that is, he ascended the stairs to the various porticoes that surrounded the Court of the Israelites and the altar of sacrifice. He drove out those who bought and sold in this area, referring probably to those who provided offerings for sacrifice, that is, doves, and perhaps grain and wine offerings. "He would not allow any one to carry anything through the temple" (11:16). Thus in some symbolic manner, he disrupted the system of offerings to God, which in the eyes of the priests and Levites must be uniquely evil, for it interrupts the worship owed to God as prescribed in Israel's Scriptures. In the eyes of temple personnel, Jesus appears to be sinful, unholy, and thoroughly disrespectful of God, for he attacks the system of space, time, and offerings that define the holy temple.

Jesus, however, declares that God wants a different type of reverence, namely, "prayer," not sacrifice (11:17; see Isa 56:7). Mark emphasizes this focus on "prayer" by the way he continues the theme in 11:22-26 (Dowd 1988:58–66). In a summary statement about "prayer," Jesus exhorts disciples to have "faith in God" (11:22), to make petitionary prayer (11:24), to be pure of heart, and then to practice forgiveness, a logion that became associated with the Our Father (11:25). Thus, far from dishonoring God by prohibiting worship, Jesus teaches a reformed mode of worship, namely prayer. "Prayer" indeed challenges the system of the temple in the sense that one does not need priests to pray, or offerings, or special space, or calendars. Prayer can be prayed in one's home and local assembly. Thus we find competing systems of honoring God, Jesus being authorized to promote one and demote the others.

We find two opinions of Jesus' activity vis-à-vis the temple, that of Jesus' enemies, for whom he has acted shamefully, and that of the evangelist, who tells a story that vindicates Jesus' actions as authorized by God. The temple elites, "the chief priests and the scribes and the elders," immediately challenge

Jesus by demanding to know the warrant for his actions (11:27-34). Jesus answers their question with a question, asking about the authorization of John the Baptizer. Ironically, the answer to both questions is the same: God, who used John's baptism of Jesus as the occasion of the theophany in which God authorized him as "beloved Son." Thus Jesus has by no means blasphemed against God by his temple actions; in fact, God authorized them, an authorization that goes back to the beginning of the story. As Mark tells the story, Jesus' nonobservance of the map of places in regard to the temple is truly egregious, but not sinful. Acting as God's agent, he desanctifies traditional sacred space (the temple), replacing it with fluid sacred space, such as houses.

In regard to other places, synagogues might be considered local holy places. Scholars are uncertain whether in Mark's time these were mere gathering places in the village square or actual buildings (Kee 1990; McKay 1998). Nevertheless, they were the places where observant Israelites gathered for exhortation, discussion, and the like. Mark reports Jesus going to such meeting places on the Sabbath (1:21; 3:1; 6:2; see 1:39 and 5:22), and on two instances he healed an unclean person there. His nontemple behavior seems not to be out of the ordinary, except of course for healing the unclean in the synagogue. Jesus also appears in a variety of domestic settings (1:29-31; 2:15-17; 7:24-30; 14:3-9), which many scholars argue become the holy place where disciples worship without priests and offerings. Thus it is only in regard to Israel's temple that Jesus seems not to keep holy that sacred space.

4. *Maps of things.* Jesus formally raises this issue in a controversy with the Pharisees in 7:1-13 and 14-23. The language throughout this controversy contrasts the terms "defile" (7:2, 5, 15, 18, 20, 32) and "clean" (7:4, 19). At stake are two contrasting interpretations of purity, one articulated by the Pharisees and another practiced by Jesus and his disciples.

The controversy has two parts, one public (7:1-13) and one private (7:14-21). The public exchange typically contains a charge, phrased as a hostile question (7:1-5), followed by a defense, which consists of countercharges (7:6-13). The problematic issue is "washing of hands" before eating, which is replicated in washing of vessels; these "washing" rites are mandated by the "tradition of the elders." What do the disciples of Jesus signal to observant onlookers when they eat with "defiled hands"? Recall that bodily "purity" was concerned with control of the orifices, including the mouth. Nothing unclean should enter, an ideal that could be secured by attending also to the purity of the hand that brings food to the mouth (recall that the ancients ate with their fingers). Hence protection of the purity of the mouth is secured by purity of the hand. Thus the public part of the controversy over purity focuses on what goes into the mouth.

Jesus states his position on purity to the crowd: "There is nothing outside a man which by going into him can defile him; but the things which come out of a man are what defile him" (7:15). In private when the disciples ask him what this means, he repeats his public remark: "Whatever goes into a man from outside cannot defile him, since it enters not his heart but his stomach and so passes on" (7:18-19). Mark takes the remarkable step of interpreting this to mean: "Thus he declared *all foods clean*" (7:19). Yet Jesus' remarks, while declassifying what "unclean" food might enter the mouth, classifies what uncleannesses exit the eye, mouth, genitals, hands, and so on: "evil thoughts, fornication, theft, murder, adultery, envy, deceit, licentiousness, coveting. . ." (7:21-22). The conflict between the two systems of purity deserves closer attention, since Jesus' version presumably has God's warrant.

The concerns of the Pharisees are with body structure, hands, surfaces, and lips. These stand in contrast with the heart, the predominant body part for Jesus (7:2-8). Body exterior contrasts with body interior (7:15-23), and so hand washing is opposed to nonwashing (7:2-5). In terms of warrant, the Pharisees' tradition of the elders clashes with the commandment of God (7:7-8, 9-13). When schematized, the contrasting purity systems look like this:

Pharisees	Jesus and Disciples
1. *surfaces controlled*: washing of hands . . . washing of cups, pots, and vessels of bronze	1. *surfaces not controlled*: "some of his disciples ate with hands defiled, that is unwashed"
2. *purity as ritual*: washing of hands . . . honoring God with one's lips	2. *purity without ritual*: honoring God with one's heart
3. *warrant for practice of purity*: warrants in conflict: "according to the tradition of the elders . . . teaching as doctrines the precepts of men (making void the commandment of God) through your tradition which you hand on"	3. *warrant*: the commandment of God trumps all human warrants: "Honor your father and your mother"; "who speaks evil of father or mother, let him die"
4. *"outside" as important*: hands, surfaces, lips	4. *"inside" as important*: heart
5. *pollution* = what enters from outside	5. *pollution* = "nothing outside a man that by going into him can defile him"; "what comes out of a man is what defiles him"

From this we learn many things. First, Jesus operates out of a system, and so his actions and remarks are not haphazard. Moreover, he provides a sustained criticism of the reigning purity system, branding it as "tradition of the elders," but not the mandate of God. He clearly has purity concerns, but they are social and ethical; vice coming from the human heart truly pollutes men and women. Finally, the results of Jesus' remarks, if we may take 7:19 as an authentic part of Mark's Gospel, have striking social effects. If all foods are clean, then the disciples may eat at the same table with anyone; foods no longer separate. Since the purity system was a way of honoring the holy God of Israel and striving to be worthy to be in God's presence, this new system of purity says something very different about God from the old system. Holiness does not consist of strict separation as it does in the temple; rather, God warrants more commerce between different peoples and sets a table for all of them by removing the chief obstacle to their communion.

"Bread" and food are not meaningless objects for Mark because the Israelite purity system was concerned with what was eaten and with whom it was eaten. For example, the two interrelated points of Peter's experience in Acts 10 are foods and commerce with non-Israelites. Peter realizes that his triple dream tells him not simply about foods, which are all declared "clean," (10:15), but about people: "God has shown me that I should not call any man common or unclean" (10:28). In Jesus' reform, all foods are clean, and so food can no longer separate Israelite and non-Israelite. And if God acts as benefactor to non-Israelites, then they too belong at the table. For this reason scholars regularly consider the feeding in Mark 6:35-44 as directed to Israelites, and the second feeding in 8:1-10 as referring to non-Israelites; God feeds both. The contest with the Syrophoenician woman in 7:24-30 clarified this very point. She asks Jesus for God's benefaction, to which he responded with the traditional depreciation of non-Israelites: "Let the children be fed, for it is not right to take the children's bread and throw it to the dogs" (7:27). Children who sit at table and eat bread represent Israel and its sense of being elected, therefore separate, and hence holy. Thus children come before dogs, who are notoriously unclean, and bread is not shared with them. The issues, then, are food and table companions. But the woman retorts with a clever answer that brings the dogs and the table bread closer together: "Even the dogs under the table eat the children's crumbs" (7:28). Thus the Markan narrative focuses on both a map of things ("all foods clean") and the corresponding map of persons.

God's "Holiness" Redefined

What, then, does Jesus' activity in regard to Israel's maps of persons, places, times, and things tell us about God? Mark leaves no doubt that Jesus did not observe the purity system of Israel; far from trying to hide this, he makes it a major feature of his Gospel. Two judgments are possible about Jesus' behavior. The observant elites criticize Jesus' nonobservance and label him a sinner, whereas Mark and his group admire Jesus' actions and label him a holy person, the Son of God. This latter verdict means that God authorized Jesus for these actions; therefore Jesus may be said to redefine God's "holiness" in ways that clash with holiness as defined in the creation account, Leviticus, the temple, and customary observance.

In traditional piety, holiness is related to separation from all that is unclean; it requires the erection and maintenance of boundaries and surfaces, as well as the control of orifices. But according to Jesus' actions, holiness is not found in separation from what is sinful, unclean, or dead. Nor do boundaries serve to keep uncleanness at bay. Nor is control of orifices an index of holiness or uncleanness. In short, Jesus' actions point to a new definition of holiness and a new system that focuses on drawing near what was far away and extending benefaction and welcome to those previously separated. "Holiness" now has more to do with inclusivity and impartiality than with separation and boundaries. In short, the new "holiness" points to God's unrestricted benefaction to humankind, especially to those made marginal by the old system. By redefining who does or may receive God's benefaction through Jesus, Mark redefines the character of God.

Mark records a major change in understanding God and so a corresponding change in behavior. He does not tell us much about the rationale for change, such as Peter narrated in Acts 10:34-35 and 15:7-11. But Mark does perceive the systematic character of the changes wrought by Jesus. For the maps of persons, places, times, and things are interrelated and redundant. If all foods are clean and all may eat bread at the table, then the premier separation of Israelite/Gentile and clean/unclean is overcome. "Holiness" is more a gift of God and a divine benefaction than it is a studied separation from uncleanness.

To those who are observant, Jesus is too anomalous to be holy. But in God's final drawing of the map of persons, God vindicates Jesus and raises him to God's right hand. This is the same Jesus who was shamed, tortured, and crucified; but God makes whole what was not whole and honors what was shamed and makes alive what was dead. In Jesus, then, God has manifested new maps: of persons, for Jesus sits beside the holy God; of places, for God is no longer worshiped in fixed sacred space, but in the circle of Jesus' brothers and sisters; and of things, for all foods may be eaten by all disciples. God's judgments, then, tell us about God's holiness.

WHAT DO WE KNOW IF WE KNOW THIS?

1. In many ways, Mark's God-talk derives from and is intelligible to Israelite tradition. The names of the Deity ("God," "Father," and "Lord") are the traditional names used of God in Israelite writings, worship, and discourse; missing in Mark are the "many names" given to the Deity in the Greco-Roman world. God appears in theophanies, is acclaimed "one" as in the Shema, and is known as "holy" according to Israel's system.

2. The patron-client model functions as an accurate, productive, and native model for Markan God-talk. In terms of God, Patron and Father, we observe the Deity having an effect on mortals by virtue of the fourfold general symbolic media: power, commitment, influence, and inducement. God's premier client is, of course, Jesus, to whom God extends these four media and whom he equips with the same to show benefaction to others. Most importantly, God manifests *commitment* to Jesus from beginning to end of the story; and God's *power* vindicates and raises Jesus from death.

God is supremely honored by Jesus, the faithful client, and it is in articulating Jesus' loyalty to God that we find the richest seam of Markan God-talk. First, Jesus articulates how the Patron instructs him to go to Jerusalem, where shame and death await him; Jesus manifests commitment to God, expecting from the Deity commitment and power, namely, his vindication by God. Second, Jesus engages in very dangerous conflict in Jerusalem, but always in reference to God's commitment and power. Most significantly, Jesus formally explains what it means to "render to God the things that are God's" (12:13-37). He defends God's power to raise the dead as well as to call David's son "Lord." God, who is unique, must be served with wholeness, both with one's own mind, heart, and soul, and in service of one's neighbor. There is nothing new here, but the core God-talk of Israel is now on Jesus' own lips. This "love" surpasses whole burnt offerings. If sacrifice and "whole burnt offerings" have no place in the behavior of Jesus, the client, prayer does. Jesus teaches prayer by example, first in the garden (14:36-41) and then on the cross (15:34). In both instances Jesus prays sanctioned speech, that is, speech permitted and encouraged by his group. His prayers are exclusively statements of commitment and loyalty to God, expecting corresponding commitment above all else. Eventually, Jesus the client experiences God's commitment and especially his power in being vindicated, raised, and enthroned.

Part of God's benefaction entails the establishment of Jesus as mediator and broker with God's mortal clients. Thus an appreciation of all of Jesus' actions and benefactions are in effect an assessment of what God authorizes him to do. Not surprisingly, we learn of acts of power (spirit wars and healings), commitment (a physician sent to the sick), influence (mysteries and secrets revealed), and inducement (food multiplied).

3. According to Mark, the "holiness" of God is less a separation from certain classes of unclean people and more an advance toward them and an inclusion of them. By endowing Jesus with a "holy" Spirit, God effects wholeness through him and "repentance" by his word. In all of Jesus' reforms of maps of persons, places, times, and things, the old system of order is indeed relaxed, but by the same token the power of God to make others "holy" is expanded. Most dramatically, the holy God authorizes a new system of worship apart from Israel's fixed sacred space, thus devaluing the temple and its priestly courses and replacing sacrifice with prayer. God is nevertheless worshiped, but no longer according to the traditional system. Because God effects this through Jesus, who is client and agent, the Deity authorizes these changes; God's "holiness" then is not impugned.

2

PROVIDENT, BENEVOLENT, FOOLISH, AND SHAMEFUL

GOD IN MATTHEW

To you it is given to know the secrets of the kingdom of heaven.
—Matt 13:11

FINDING GOD IN MATTHEW

How do we find God in a Gospel? In the case of Matthew, we examine both its beginning and ending, because God starts the story and brings it to a fitting conclusion. Then, of course, we look within the document, paying special attention to blocks of material where God's plan and providence are described, such as the Infancy Narrative (Matthew 1–2). In the opening part of the Gospel, we begin to learn about the nature of God in the "covenants of promise" that God made, and through later references to Abraham and David in the narrative (1:1-18). Moreover, God exercises a remarkable providence over Jesus and others by protecting them and seeing them through danger and even death (2:1-23). As in the case of Mark, God's major role in Matthew is that of God-in-relationship. Hence I will consider God in relationship to Jesus and other persons in terms of the benefactor/patron-client relationship. Furthermore, Matthew records extensive remarks about God's kingdom, especially as this is revealed in the parables in Matthew 13, 18, and 20–22. Finally, I will compare and contrast Matthew's God-talk with that of his two sources, namely Mark and the Sayings Source (i.e., Q).

THE NATURE OF GOD: COVENANT AND PROVIDENCE

Many ancient philosophers talked about the "nature" of God, by which they meant God's essence (i.e., "eternal existence") and attributes. Paul also talked about the "nature of God" in a way that focused on the role that God's actions play in informing us about the character of the Deity: "Ever since the creation of the world his eternal power and divine nature, invisible though they are, have been understood and seen through the things he has made" (Rom 1:19-20). Although not writing in a Greek mode of discourse, Matthew says a similar thing when he describes God in terms of God's actions: covenant, providence, the kingdom of heaven, and God's just judgment.

God and the Covenants of Promise

Matthew begins his narrative with a genealogy for Jesus, which does what all genealogies do: it establishes the role and status of Jesus within the house of Israel as the fulfillment of the promises made to the patriarchs Abraham and David (Raymond E. Brown 1993:64–69). But 1:1-18 tells us also about the God of Jesus in that it describes a type of covenantal relationship established by God. Christian writers, when discoursing about God's covenant, compared and contrasted two types: the covenant of promises made with Abraham and David, and the covenant of law made with Moses (Clements 1967). For example, Paul affirms God's faithfulness to the ancient benefactions bestowed on the house of Israel, among which are "the glory, the covenants, the giving of the law, the worship, and the promises" (Rom 9:4). The "covenants" and the "promises" refer to God's dealings with Abraham, Isaac, and then Jacob, indicating that Paul has in mind the covenant with Abraham (9:6-13), not that with Moses. In Ephesians, before their election into the church, Gentiles were "strangers to the covenants of promise" (2:12). These "covenants of promise" surely refer to the relationship of benefaction established with Abraham and then with David in terms of God's gratuitous promise of sons as numerous as the sands on the sea and sons who would forever sit on the throne of Israel. In Galatians, to make his point, Paul conducts a *synkrisis* or comparison between the two types of covenant, and in so doing oversimplifies their differences. But that is just the point: covenantal language was shaped in controversy, and in order to make an argument, rhetorical emphasis was given to certain aspects of one type, promoting it while demoting its alternative. With this in mind, let us consider Matthew.

Matthew, I argue, has "covenants of promise" in view when his narrative begins by acclaiming Jesus as "the son of David, the son of Abraham" (1:1). The total exclusion of Moses and priests from the genealogy could imply that this type of covenant is excluded in favor of the covenant of promises made to Abraham and David. The following chart attempts to compare and contrast the two types of covenant, so as to highlight the character of God in the "covenants of promise." Historians will rightly criticize the oversimplification of this comparison, but this represents the way Paul and Matthew simplified the issue to argue that the "covenants of promise" is the earlier, better, and more favorable one.

Covenants of Promise (Abraham and David)	**Covenant of Treaty and Law (Moses)**
1. God's actions: God freely and unconditionally promises = "blessing"	1. God's actions: God strikes a contract-treaty that is entirely conditional = either "blessings" or "curses"
2. Quality of God freedom, surprise = "mercy" or "grace"	2. Quality of God fairness, reliability = "justice"
3. Israel's response to God: "Abraham believed God and it was credited to him as righteousness" (Gen 15:6; Rom 4:3) = "faith"	3. Israel's response to God: "Do this and live" (Lev 18:5; Gal 3:12); and "Cursed be every one who does not abide by all the things written in the book of the law, to do them" (Deut 27:26; Gal 3:10) = works, performance
4. Social implications: God's inclusivity: God reverses traditions re: earthly pedigree and hierarchy and embracing "the other"	4. Social implications: God's exclusivity: God chooses a certain people to be God's own, a people set apart

1. On the one hand, God's premier action in the "covenants of promise" is freely to make a gratuitous promise of blessing, which is considered unconditional and open-ended. In contrast, on Sinai God makes a contract treaty with Israel such as ancient sovereigns made with their vassals. The treaty was conditional: blessings for loyalty, but curses for rebellion.

2. The "covenants of promise" showcase God's freedom to act, even to surprise mortals; for, in dispensing favor, God is not bound by ethnic laws, birth order, or inheritance customs: the younger is regularly chosen over his older siblings. The treaty covenant, on the other hand, portrays a God of exquisite fairness, reliability, and predictability. The dynamic of this covenant is such that "the measure you give will be the measure you get" and "as you sow, so shall you reap." It contains, then, clarity of expectations and rewards. Terms such as "mercy" and "grace" characterize the promise, while "justice" describes the treaty/law.

3. The proper response to the promise is faith in God, who makes the "impossible dream." "Abraham," we are told, "*believed* God, and it was credited to him as righteousness" (Gen 15:6; see Hab 2:4). In contrast, performance constitutes the appropriate response to the treaty covenant: "Do this and live" (Lev 18:5). In the New Testament simplification of the two types of covenant, the response to the first is "faith," while the response to the other is "works" or "obedience."

4. Each type of covenant contains differing social implications. The covenants of promise, because they were made with outsiders (Abraham) or with people at the bottom of the sibling ladder (David), suggest God's inclusiveness by investing unlikely outsiders with special favor. The treaty covenant, in contrast, was made with Israel alone, God's chosen people; as such this alliance was exclusive: no one but Israel had such a covenant.

Does Matthew employ this stereotype of the "covenants of promise" in his Gospel? I argue that the opening line of the Gospel and genealogy, "Jesus Christ, the son of David, the son of Abraham," expresses this unmistakably. All who know Scripture would link the mention of David and Abraham with "covenants of promise," which is characteristic of what anthropologists call a "high context society" (Hall 1976:105–16). Moreover, sprinkled throughout the first block of ancestors are four females, Tamar, Rahab, Ruth, and the wife of Uriah. Their place in any Israelite genealogy seems strange, if not offensive, because some are clearly not Israelites and others lack sexual exclusivity, which indicates shamelessness (Raymond E. Brown 1993:71–74; Wainwright 1991:63–67). Whereas such figures would be totally out of place in the genealogies of Ezra and Nehemiah, in this kind of genealogy God's blessing worked through these disqualifications, because God is free to choose whom God wishes.

Balancing the genealogy, Matthew tells of the birth of Jesus, which is another instance of unusual divine favor. Like the four females in the genealogy, Jesus' pregnant mother at first seems to be disqualified because of her sexual irregularity. She is clearly pregnant, but her espoused husband is not the father. God's messenger clarifies the matter, even as he declares God's election of and favor on the child. A gift of God's Spirit has made Mary pregnant. Both the mother and child are blessed by this; both have God as unique covenant Patron. The angel declares the name and role of the child: "You shall call his name 'Jesus,' for he will save his people from their sins" (1:21). Jesus' election is confirmed by appeal to Isa 7:14, which both honors his mother and declares Jesus as the abiding presence of the God of promises.

While Jesus fulfills the promises made to Abraham and David, his role is to broker the inclusivity of this covenant. In the middle of the story, Jesus declares that "many will come from east and west" (8:11), which functions to illustrate powerfully this aspect of the "covenants of promise." First many come from the east, namely, magi, to seek out Jesus. They are blessed with special revelation by God, both the new star and the astrological conclusion that it heralds a new king. God leads them to Jerusalem, Bethlehem, and then home. But they and not the Jerusalem elites or Herod believe the promise in Mic 5:2 ("for from you shall come a ruler who will govern my people Israel"), which all admit refers to David and so to the covenant of promise made with David.

The hallmark of the "covenants of promise" is manifested in its social inclusivity, that is, "many from the east" but also from the territories surrounding Israel. Matthew establishes the locus of Jesus' labors right at the beginning by narrating that he travels to the "land of Zebulun and the land of Naphtali," which by appeal to Isaiah's interpretation of these lands are also "Galilee of the Gentiles" (Matt 4:15; cf. Isa 9:1-2). Very shortly, Jesus' reputation spreads far and wide: "His fame spread throughout all Syria . . . great crowds followed from Galilee and the Decapolis and Jerusalem and Judea and beyond the Jordan" (4:24-25). From a narrative point of view, these people heard that God's surprising benefaction was available in Jesus, a type of "hearing" related to "faith." Matthew tells us that all these peoples shared impartially in God's blessings: "healing every disease and every infirmity . . . they brought to him all the sick, those afflicted with various diseases and pains, demoniacs, epileptics, and paralytics, and he healed them all"

(4:23-24). God's gracious impartiality, then, is amply displayed in the actions of Jesus.

If the magi came from the east, does anyone come from the west? The stories of the centurion with the dying slave and the centurion at the cross best exemplify this. When a resident centurion comes to Jesus for a favor, according to Matthew's version (8:5-13), he has done nothing to warrant a kindness. Indeed, as part of the Roman army occupying Israel, he would qualify as the last person deserving a favor from the God of Israel. But he shows trust that God's agent Jesus can "say but a word and my servant will be healed" (8:8). Jesus makes much of this acceptance of himself as God's agent and declares: "Many will come from east and west" (8:12). From the context Matthew indicates that the "centurion" represents the "west." Such people will sit at table with "Abraham, Isaac, and Jacob," all exemplars of the "covenants of promise." The westerner, we are told, will sit at table with the patriarchs of promise. On the principle that "likes eat with likes," the centurion has become a member of these "covenants of promise." His table fellowship does not depend on circumcision or dietary observance, but on faith. Similarly, at the cross of Jesus, another centurion presided over his execution (27:27-50). The narrative does not tell us his judgment of Jesus, but we may conjecture that as Jesus' executioner he judged him deserving of such a death. He is, then, a most unlikely figure to have a conversion or change of heart. But after seeing the posthumous events described in 27:51-53, he and his cohort make the unique confession about God and Jesus in the Gospel: "Truly this was the Son of God" (27:54). The centurion and the Roman army, presumably from the west, are favored by God—and what unlikely people.

Divine Providence

The God-talk of the Greco-Roman world generally contained materials about divine "providence," which is readily found in both Stoic philosophers as well as Hellenistic Jewish writers such as Philo and Josephus. By "providence" such authors meant the divine ordering of the world, its working according to God's wisdom and power, and God's care for individuals. The technical term for "providence," *pronoia,* meant "knowledge before the fact." New Testament authors use this word, though not in the sense of God's ordering (Acts 24:2; Rom 13:14). But they know the concept, which was highly compatible with Israelite piety (see discussion of Acts in chap. 3 below). Thus the absence of the technical term for "providence" in Matthew hardly means that God is not understood in that manner. What, then, would providence look like in Matthew? Where shall we search?

"Providence" in Matthew can be found in the divine care and protection of Jesus from womb to tomb—and beyond. It is likewise evident in the elaborate pattern of "prophecy-fulfillment" that stretches through Matthew's narrative. Concerning the first meaning of divine providence in regard to Jesus, it is regularly noted that Matthew 1–2 bears structural similarity with Matthew 26–28 (Nolan 1979:104–7; Malina and Neyrey 1988:115–16).

If we were to focus exclusively on Jesus, we would see striking parallels between the public acclamation of Jesus as "king of the Judeans" first by the magi (2:2) and then by his Roman executioners (27:11, 29, 37). Similarly, of Jesus God declares that "out of Egypt I have brought my son" (2:15; see 3:17 and 17:5), a relationship first mocked by passersby, who declare that Jesus cannot be "the Son of God" (27:40, 43), but then acknowledged by the Roman cohort (28:54). Just as "all Jerusalem was troubled along with the chief priests and scribes" (2:3-4) at the birth of the new king, so too all of Jerusalem (27:25), including its chief priests, scribes, and elders (26:65), gathered against Jesus to kill him.

But let us refocus the story on God's providential care and rescue of Jesus. God's providence first rescued the honor of Jesus' mother by means of an angel, and then delivered the son from death by means of other angels (2:13-14, 20). That others were slaughtered while Jesus escaped (2:16-18) only proves that Jesus enjoyed unique providential protection. Although God did not rescue Jesus from death on the cross, God acted immediately to render a most favorable judgment about him, namely, the posthumous honors given to Jesus (27:51-54; see Neyrey 1998a:140–48), including God's vindication, raising, and enthroning of Jesus.

Generally in the Greco-Roman world, "posthumous honors" refer to respect accorded the deceased by means of "divine honors, posthumous votes of thanks, or statues erected at the public expense" (Quintilian, *Inst.* 3.7.17), as well as formal games and an official eulogy over the grave. While none of these accompanied Jesus' death, God performed certain things that confirmed Jesus' words and anticipated his vindication, thus truly honoring Jesus posthumously (see Senior 1977:29–51; Witherup 1987:578–85).

First, the temple veil was rent from top to bottom, an achievement possible only by God. Moreover, this action validated Jesus' criticisms of the temple, thus indicating divine pleasure in them. Second, the earth shook, which the ancients normally took as a sign of God's presence. This quake did not level the high priest's house, the Fortress Antonia, or any other place in Jerusalem, for its purpose was not vengeance for Jesus' death so much as manifestation of the divine presence, honoring Jesus' dying words that called for God to be present and act. Third, tombs were opened, from which the bodies of the saints were raised. The importance of this lies not only in the confirmation of Jesus' argument that God raises the dead, but in the timing of this event. Occurring immediately after Jesus' death, the resurrection of the saints is proof of God's power and pleasure to raise and enthrone Jesus. God's providence, then, honors Jesus in death by a series of actions that declare God's plan and pleasure in his death and vindication (Neyrey 1998a:140–48).

Moreover, God acted to vindicate Jesus first by raising him from death (28:6) and then by raising him to his throne and ascribing him maximum honor (28:18). The Fourth Gospel records that Martha criticized Jesus for delaying to come and save her brother Lazarus: "Lord, if you had been here, my brother would not have died" (John 11:21), which any bystander could have said of God and the crucified Jesus. Yet we know that Jesus kept declaring that it was the will of God that he travel to Jerusalem, be handed over, killed, and raised. Divine providence, then, did not prevent his death, but oddly orchestrated it. In the providential career of Jesus, however, the key element always lay in the prediction of God's vindication of Jesus, either in the triple passion prediction just noted or in psalms predicting it (on Matt 21:42 cf. Ps 118:22-23; on Matt 22:44 and 26:64 cf. Ps 110:1). Yet providence demands that prophecies be fulfilled, which takes us to the most perfect of posthumous honors, God's raising of Jesus. It had long been part of Israel's theology that those who died faithful to God would be vindicated by God. So it is with Jesus: God raised him to life (i.e., resurrection), but God also raised him up on high and seated him at God's right hand (i.e., enthronement, Matt 22:44).

When the ancients debated providence, one of the bitterest fights was waged over prophecy. For if prophecies come true, they prove God knew the future and so controlled their fulfillment, whereas unfulfilled ones invalidate providence (Neyrey 1980:409). While Matthew does not clearly participate in that scholarly conflict over prophecy and providence, he argues that the Scriptures contain divine providence, which is fulfilled in the events of Jesus' life. Thus the oft-repeated formula, "this was to fulfill what was spoken through the prophet" (1:22; 2:15, 17, 23; 4:14; 8:17; etc.), affirms God's providence in these ways. First, in the past God "prophesied" future events, which when they occur then have divine sanction. Second, especially the negative and shameful things that happen to Jesus are divinely sanctioned, precisely because they fulfill God's prophecies. God, then, knows the future and controls events; moreover, God shared knowledge of this future through the prophets—a double act of providence.

GOD-IN-RELATIONSHIP: PATRON AND BENEFACTOR

In examining the role of God in Mark's Gospel, I employed the model of patron-client relations to understand the vertical relationships between the Immortal One and mortals. I return to that model to understand Matthew's understanding of God-in-relationship. To begin consideration of Matthew's version of benefactor/patron-client relationships, let us pay closer attention to the various titles that are synonyms for "benefactor" and which ones Matthew employs and emphasizes.

Benefactors Titles

The following list, which encompasses both Greco-Roman and Israelite usage, contains the most frequently used titles describing the benevolent relationship of God with mortals: Benefactor, Creator, Father, God, King, Lord, Master, and Savior. No sympathetic treatment of God-as-Benefactor is complete without consideration of them.

1. *Benefactor.* This term enjoyed a wide range of meanings, as has been noted: "Gods and heroes, kings and statesmen, philosophers, inventors and physicians are hailed as benefactors because of their contributions to the development of the race" (Bertram 1964:654). Kings and statesmen exercise power to order things aright; philosophers and inventors convey influence or knowledge. What identified a benefactor were the material benefits bestowed. "Benefactor" is never used of God in the New Testament, only of benevolent

mortals (Luke 22:25), but the actions of a benevolent heavenly patron are found everywhere.

2. *Creator.* First we should note that whereas "Creator" (*dēmiourgos*) commonly described a Greek deity's creative activity, the LXX totally avoided it and chose instead another term for "Creator" (*ktistes,* Foerster 1964a: 1026). Although *dēmiourgos* ripened in meaning over the years, it never lost its sense of builder or workman (i.e., "God builds the city," Heb 11:10). "Creator" often appears in combination with other benefactor terms, as in: "All of these things did the great Creator and Master of the universe ordain to be in peace" (*1 Clem.* 20.11). Although Matthew never calls God by this title, the Christian God is generally said to act in this manner (see Acts 17:24; 1 Cor 8:6).

3. *Father.* We find frequent reference to God as "Father" in both Semitic and Greco-Roman literature. Dio Chrysostom states: "At that time, the Creator and Father of the World, beholding the work of his hands . . ." (*Or.* 36.60); and "Zeus is the father, not only of gods but of men as well" (*Or.* 4.22). The meaning of the title must derive from consideration of the rights and duties of earthly fathers. The duties of a father include socialization of his children, their protection, nurture, and the like (Neyrey 1996:315–19). His rights center around his children acknowledging him, as in: "Honor your father and your mother." Scholars point out how Caesar described himself as the "Father of the Fatherland" (*Pater Patriae*), extending the notion of domestic benefactor to that of a political one (D'Angelo 1992a; Stevenson 1992:425–31). In Matthew, the "Father" "rewards" those who practice piety in secret (6:1-18) and honors those who feed the hungry and clothe the naked (25:34). He provides food and clothing to those who have lost it for the sake of Jesus (6:26-33), special knowledge to the disciples in general (11:25) and to Peter in particular (16:17), and power both in the possibility of legions of angels to protect Jesus (26:53) and in his actual resurrection.

4. *God.* While this is not strictly a synonym for "benefactor" as are the other titles here, its use in Matthew suggests that it is a beneficent title. God's spirit that descends on Jesus at the Jordan commissions him for a special role and status, and empowers him for this work. Thus Jesus' victory in healings and battles with demons depends on God's spirit at work in him (see 12:28). When people see Jesus' power at work, they rightly conclude that it is God's, and so "they glorified God who had given such authority to men" (9:8; see

also 15:31). Whereas mortals find Jesus' teaching on possessions "impossible," Jesus claims that God's benefaction will empower them: "With God all things are possible" (19:26). Most importantly, this Deity is "the God of Abraham, the God of Isaac, and the God of Jacob . . . the God of the living" (22:32).

5. *King*. Dio Chrysostom explained "king" in terms of dominion and power: "He [Zeus] is addressed as 'King' because of his dominion and power" (*Or.* 1.39), which refer not to tyrannical behavior but to beneficial results when wisely and benevolently employed. Similarly, Dio calls Zeus "king," referring explicitly to the positive results of his rule: "In like manner do the gods act, and especially the great King of kings, Zeus, who is the common protector and father of men and gods" (*Or.* 2.75). Matthew, while he never uses the title "king" for God, regularly speaks of the "kingdom of heaven," probably a circumlocution for the title. This "kingdom is near" (3:2; 4:17; 10:7), that is, the benefaction of God is now available through Jesus. Disciples pray, "your kingdom come" (6:10), in other words, that God's power nourish the just but requite the wicked. If one seeks "first the kingdom of heaven," then all forms of food and clothing will be provided in abundance (6:33; 19:29). In that kingdom, benefaction will be distributed to those "from east and west" (8:11). The secrets of this kingdom are bestowed uniquely on the disciples (13:10).

6. *Lord*. Like "God," this too is technically not a benefactor title, but Matthew uses it in this sense. For example, when God communicates with mortals, it tends to be through messengers such as "the angel of the Lord" (1:20; 2:13, 19). Moreover, Matthew makes frequent appeal to the Scriptures to illuminate or give value to certain events; he expresses this often by stating, "all this took place to fulfill what the Lord had spoken through (such-and-such a prophet)" (1:22). Similarly, the "Lord of heaven and earth" hides his wisdom from others, but bestows it uniquely on Jesus' disciples (11:25). This "Lord" shows a benefactor's loyalty to Jesus by making the rejected stone into the cornerstone (20:42). In response to this "Lord," Jesus himself shows perfect client loyalty: "You shall not tempt the Lord your God" (4:7), and requires perfect loyalty of others: "You shall worship the Lord your God and him only you shall serve" (4:10); "you shall love the Lord your God with all your heart, with all your soul, and with all your mind" (22:37).

7. *Master.* This unusual term for a benefactor/patron often describes the relation of master to slave, and expresses above all power and fear. Yet it is frequent in Hellenistic prayers, perhaps because it emphasizes the dependence of the persons petitioning the deity. The Judean historian Josephus favors it as his typical address to God: "Master of all the ages and Creator of universal being . . . confirm these promises" (*Ant.* 1.272; see 4.40; 5.41; 11.64). Other writers link it with other benefactor terms, thus softening its hard edges in association with terms expressing genuine benevolence. Matthew does not use it, but Luke does, both in his Gospel and in Acts. For example, Simeon prays as he blesses the infant Jesus, "Master, now let your servant depart in peace . . . for my eyes have seen your salvation" (Luke 2:29). Similarly, the persecuted disciples prayed: "Sovereign Lord, who did make the heavens and the earth, and the sea and everything in them . . ." (Acts 4:24). The clearest use of the benevolent quality of *despotēs* (occurs in *1 Clement;* for example, "Let us learn that in generation after generation the Master has given a place of repentance to those who turn to him" (7.5; see also 9.4; 11.1; 36.2).

8. *Savior.* This title embodies a wide range of meaning. A savior is one who rescues another from dangers and serious perils, such as war, illness, judicial condemnation, and devastations of nature (e.g., floods, famines); protects and preserves the polis and its citizens or keeps them in good condition; inaugurates a golden age; and benefits others. In this vein Foerster cites an inscription how on the annual feast of Zeus, "Savior of the City," the priests of Magnesia prayed for "the [salvation] of the city, country, citizens, wives, children and other residents, for peace, for wealth, for the growth of the grain and other fruits and cattle" (1964b:967). Matthew never calls God "Savior," a title used only in Luke 1:47 and 1 Tim 1:1 for the Deity. Instead, he indicates that Jesus acts in God's "savior" role, saving people from their sins (1:21) as well as from demon possession.

What Does God-Benefactor Bestow?

I use once more the four general symbolic media (GSM)—power, commitment, inducement, and influence—as a convenient way to summarize and digest the vast data of benefaction contained in Matthew. The following chart indicates what specific materials in Matthew belong under each classification.

Power	Commitment
rescue of Jesus in Matt 2 Spirit of "power" descends upon Jesus at Jordan (3:16-17) all miracles of Jesus = God's power, especially when evil spirits are silenced and expelled power to raise the dead (22:23-33) twelve legions of God's angels available (26:53) vindication of Jesus (21:42ff.; 22:44; 27:50-54)	covenant of promises: "son of David, the son of Abraham" (1:1) election of Jesus and support of him: baptism, transfiguration, death, resurrection clients worth more than sparrows (10:32- 33) "I desire mercy, not sacrifice" (9:13; 12:8; cf. Hos 6:6) forgiveness by God (6:13-14; 9:2-8; 18:22-35) praise and honor from God (5:1-12); reward of honor from God (6:1, 4, 6, 14, 18) recipients of God's benefaction: magi, "Galilee of the Gentiles," Syrophoenician woman, "all nations" (28:19)
Inducement	**Influence**
daily bread ("Our Father," 6:9-13) seek first the kingdom; food and clothing will be provided (6:25-33) multiplication of loaves and fishes (14:13-21; 15:32-39) promise of "hundredfold" (19:29) eating at the table of God (22:1-10)	knowledge and secrets revealed (11:25-27; 13:10-17; 16:17; 24:36) dreams (1:18-25; 2:12, 13, 19; 27:19) stars (2:1ff., 9) hidden prophetic meaning of the Scriptures, esp. Isaiah (1:22-23; 2:6, 17, 23; 4:14-16; 8:17; 12:18-21; 13:14, 35; 21:4-5; 27:9) special speech revealed (10:19-20) parables (13:3-9, 31-32, 33, 44-50)

1. *Power.* As regards God's power, we see it exercised both toward Jesus and by Jesus, the mediator of God's benefaction. As noted above, both at the beginning and ending of Jesus' life, God acts to rescue him from death. In 2:13-23 God sends angelic messengers to alert the child's father to flee from the power of the rival king of the Judeans, Herod. Balancing this, we read of

God's vindication of Jesus at his death by raising him to life. Acts of this sort are manifestations of power, for death was understood as an enemy who thus far proved invincible (see 1 Cor 15:24-26; Heb 2:14-15). Jesus himself declared the raising of the dead to be a unique "power of God" (Matt 22:29). Moreover, God's raising of Jesus was understood as God's power to give a fitting riposte to the challenges made to God by slaying God's agent (e.g., 21:40-41). Thus, as well as a manifestation of commitment to Jesus, God's resurrection of him is likewise an act of power that belongs to God alone. Finally, although he declines to invoke the power of God at his arrest, Jesus is confident that he could "appeal to my Father, and he will at once send me more than twelve legions of angels" (26:53).

As regards God's power in the actions of Jesus-the-broker, all of his healing miracles should be understood as mediations of God's power to his client people. I repeat what I said in regard to miracles in Mark, that they were understood as acts of power since it was popularly thought that illness was caused by spirit aggression (Pilch 2000:68–70, 80–81). Hence healing means a defeat for the aggressor but a liberation or rescue from slavery for the one healed. For example, after Jesus heals a "blind and dumb demoniac" (12:22-23), the crowds acknowledge that his power comes from God, and so they acclaim him "son of David," that is, someone authorized by God with power for these actions. His power, they claim, is that of God, which equips him to battle evil spirits. But the Pharisees contest the source of Jesus' power, claiming, "It is only by Beelzebul, the prince of demons, that this man casts out demons" (12:24). The opposing judgments of friends and foes focus on the issue at hand: Whence Jesus' power, from God or from Beelzebul? Calmings of storms are similarly to be thought of as acts of power, inasmuch as the storm was considered a malevolent spirit (8:23-27; Kee 1968:15).

2. *Commitment.* This summarizes a range of personal relationships often labeled individually as loyalty, commitment, faithfulness, or dutifulness. It effects in the recipient a "personalized sense of obligation, sense of duty or sense of belonging"; and rather than the use of power to compel, it "urges loyalty by means of internalized sanctions such as guilt feelings, feelings of shame and disloyalty, or fear of disapproval" (Malina 1986a:78). God's commitment may take the form of the "covenants of promises" as expressed in God's dealings with Abraham and David, a fragment of which is found at the opening of Matthew's Gospel, "The genealogy of Jesus Christ, the son of

David, the son of Abraham" (1:1). God's kindness toward his people is expressed in a variety of ways, such as God's "mercy," "forgiveness," and "honor." For example, Matthew twice quotes "I desire mercy, not sacrifice" (9:13; 12:8; cf. Hos 6:6) as a response to criticism of Jesus' actions; commitment, not inducement, best describes God's relationship. In this prophetic logion, we are told much about God's mode of commitment: God shows "mercy" to those in need, and expects others to do likewise. Similarly, "forgiveness" is another mark of God's commitment: God shows it to those in debt to him and requires that those who receive God's forgiveness extend it to others (6:13-14; 18:22-35). God has declared that Jesus' task is as his name suggests, "to save his people from their sins" (1:21); for this purpose, God endows him with authority to declare sins forgiven (9:2-8). Finally, God honors and rewards those who show faithfulness to him. Certain people suffered specifically for adhering to the gospel of God that Jesus preached; they lost the commitment of their family and close friends. Jesus declares that God will manifest divine commitment to them and honor them (5:1-12). If, as has been argued, "blessed" (*makarios*) belongs to the realm of honor (and shame), then God honors those dishonored for his sake (Neyrey 1995:144–50). Similarly, disciples of Jesus, who practice piety as he enjoins it, will lose honor because they no longer perform their piety in public or in the synagogue. But, we are assured, God's commitment will be a "reward" of honor and respect to those who have practiced their piety in secret (6:1-18; Neyrey 1998a:212–21).

To whom does God show this commitment? Were this a story from traditional Israelite literature, we would likely hear that God is showing favoritism to Israel, who is called God's "chosen people." Indeed, twice in Matthew Jesus says the same thing. When sending out his own disciples "with authority over unclean spirits, to cast them out and to heal every disease and every infirmity," Jesus restricts them to Israel only: "Go nowhere among the Gentiles, and enter no town of the Samaritans, but go rather to the lost sheep of the house of Israel" (10:5-6). Despite his own peregrinations in Galilee of the Gentiles and his own dealings with people "from Galilee and the Decapolis and Jerusalem . . . and from beyond the Jordan" (4:25), he seems to show favoritism here. This is formally discarded, however, in the challenge/riposte exchange with the Syrophoenician woman. Initially Jesus refuses her request: "I was sent only to the lost sheep of the house of Israel"

(15:24). All understand "was sent" to refer to God's will; and so the favoritism implied is God's. Moreover, Jesus expressed this same sense of favoritism when he insulted the woman with the remark: "It is not fair to take the children's bread and throw it to the dogs" (15:26). But the woman responds that the dogs also eat from the table, even if only crumbs. Thus she functions in the narrative to puncture the traditional and narrow sense of God's commitment. There are no favorites!

Although an audience has to wait until the middle of Matthew's story to hear this formal rebuttal of divine favoritism, there were already instances of God's inclusivity from the beginning of the story. Jesus is of the stock of Abraham and of David (1:1), who, in terms of the type of covenant they represent to New Testament authors, stand for a commitment of God to all and everyone; the covenants of promise are based not on ethnic background or practice but on election and faith. "Wise men from the east" are shown God's favor by being led to the new king of the Jews (2:1). In contrast, the elites of Jerusalem have knowledge of the same; thus they too are potential clients of God's benefaction. No distinction, then, is made between Israelites and Gentiles. The inaugural heralding of the "gospel of the kingdom" by Jesus begins in Galilee, which curiously contains for Matthew both Israelites and Gentiles. He says that Jesus left Nazareth and dwelt in Capernaum, which is in the territory of Zebulun and Naphtali; and he interprets this territory with a reference to Isaiah: "The land of Zebulun and the land of Naphtali . . . Galilee of the Gentiles" (4:15; cf. Isa 9:1). No favoritism here: both Israelites and Gentiles are in view as objects of God's favor. After this we learn that Jesus went about "all Galilee, teaching in their synagogues and preaching the gospel of the kingdom and healing every disease and every infirmity" (4:23). Again, this would seem to preclude any sense of favoritism or of "a chosen people." Confirmation of this inclusivity comes from the next remarks: "his fame spread throughout all Syria . . . and great crowds followed from Galilee, the Decapolis, Jerusalem, Judea, and from beyond the Jordan" (4:24-25). It is to be understood that the sick and the ill from Syria, the Decapolis, and beyond the Jordan were healed as well as those from Galilee, Jerusalem, and Judea.

3. *Inducement.* This symbolic medium refers to material benefaction, such as gifts of food, clothing, money, property, dowries, and the like. We have a striking example of just such patronage shown by Roman elites and emperors

Titus, Vespasian, and Domitian to Josephus, which can sharpen our perception of this GSM. When in Rome, he "received large gifts from Poppaea," Nero's wife (*Life* 16). Moreover,

> [Titus] gave me another parcel of ground in the plain. On his departure for Rome, he took me with him on board, treating me with every mark of respect. In Rome I met with great consideration from Vespasian. He gave me a lodging in the house which he had occupied before he became Emperor; he honored me with the privilege of Roman citizenship; and he assigned me a pension. He continued to honor me up to the time of this departure from this life, without any abatement in his kindness toward me. (*Life* 422-23)

This friendship was extended by Domitian, who exempted Josephus's property in Judea from taxation, "a mark of the highest honor to the privileged individual" (*Life* 429). Moreover, the benefaction of inducement might be considered all the more valuable when it comes from a high-ranking person, more so from Roman emperors, and infinitely more so from God.

Matthew's expositions of the inducements of God all treat the basic peasant necessities of life: bread, clothing, family, and land. "Bread," of course, is one of the three benefits petitioned for in the Our Father (6:11). In a subsistence peasant world, this is no minor benefaction, given both the ruinous taxation and the famines that devastated the land (see Josephus, *Ant.* 20.51-53). All the more is the satiety of bread and fish provided by God's mediator, Jesus, to massive audiences on two occasions. Matthew expresses the prodigious character of this heavenly largesse in the remark: "And they all ate and were satisfied" (14:20; 15:37), and even then "twelve baskets full of broken pieces" remained in one case and seven baskets in another.

In another instance, a male and a female (married?) are counseled not to worry what to eat and what to wear (Matt 6:25//Luke 12:22). When the male looks at the birds of the air, he "sees" fields, which in the gender-divided world of antiquity were male places, for males did the task of farming. Birds, however, do not perform the tasks typically done by males, that is, "sowing, reaping, gathering into barns or storehouses" (Matt 6:26//Luke 12:24). Yet God gives them subsistence food. The issue is food production, the proper concern of a male peasant. Alternately a female concerns herself about "what to wear," that is, "clothing," which was produced by females in the household. Like the male, she is told to "see" the lilies of the field. In both cases, the male and the female are concerned about peasant necessities, which, we are told, God provides to both birds and flowers. God's benefaction here seems to step in when the natural sources of food and clothing are in doubt. Hence they are exhorted: "Do not be concerned about what to wear and what to eat." Their heavenly Patron-Father "knows that you need them all" (6:32); and if they "seek first his kingdom and his righteousness," then "all these things shall be yours as well" (6:33). Despite all the scholarly questions that might be raised about 6:25-33, one thing stands out as indisputable: the heavenly Father readily bestows the inducement of "what to eat and what to wear" on his faithful clients.

Next, in the discourse after the failure of the rich young man to become Jesus' disciple, we find an exchange between Peter and Jesus over what they have sacrificed to follow him. The benefaction exchanged for the disciples' loyalty to Jesus and so to God consists of inducement as well as other GSM. "Every one who has left houses or brothers or sisters or father or mother or children or lands, for my name's sake, will receive a hundredfold, and inherit eternal life" (19:29). To simplify, disciples who "left" or were "dispossessed" of "houses . . . lands," have lost the basic source of foods and other necessities of life. Patronal loyalty to them will be the astronomical "hundredfold."

Finally, Jesus tells a parable about a king who prepared a banquet for his son's marriage. Of the many aspects of the parable, only the fact that the king uses the inducement of royal food, first to high-status clients and then to no-status clients, interests us here. Whether "food" is but a symbol here of patronage or is to be understood more literally in line with the "bread" and "loaves" and "what to eat" mentioned earlier, I understand it as the GSM of inducement.

4. *Influence.* Whether esoteric knowledge, secrets, or revelations, influence constitutes a significant symbolic medium in Matthew. The best place to begin our inquiry is Jesus' prayer of thanksgiving to the God of influence: "I thank you, Father, Lord of heaven and earth, because you have hidden these things from the wise and the intelligent and have revealed them to infants; yes, Father, for such was your gracious will. All things have been handed over to me by my Father . . . no one knows the Father except the Son and anyone to whom the Son chooses to reveal him." (11:25-27). God "hides" and "reveals," and so by this manifests a kind of favoritism. The "wise and understanding" do not receive this benefaction of influence, but the unlikely "babes" do. What secret or knowledge is revealed? Presumably something to

do with the identity, role, and status of Jesus, who is allied with the poor, the nonelite, and the foolish of this world. Moreover, we are told that Jesus receives God's influence maximally: "All things [certainly knowledge] have been delivered to me by my Father." As God's favorite client, Jesus brokers this benefaction to others, again in terms of a certain form of favoritism: "No one knows the Father except the Son and anyone to whom the Son chooses to reveal him" (11:27). These remarks should be read alongside the interchange between Jesus and his disciples about the parables (13:10-17).

"Why do you speak to them in parables?" (13:10). As in 11:25-27, Jesus indicates that God's benefaction of influence manifests favoritism: "To you it has been given to know the secrets of the kingdom of heaven, but to them it has not been given" (13:11). "You" are given by God ("It has been given" is a circumlocution for "God gives"), but others are not (Kingsbury 1969:42–47, 92–125). Why? Most commentators advise us to concentrate on the positive, not the negative, remarks here. Obviously Matthew argues the benefit of being attached to Jesus, one element of which is exclusive knowledge of God's will; and if they "have" some, then "more will be given, and they will have abundance" (13:12). But why not others? When Jesus cites Isa 6:9-10, it would seem that he argues that even this phenomenon of "knowing the mysteries" and "parables" is itself a secret revealed: current events are foreknown and guided by the plan of God (Evans 1989:107–13). This is one more secret given the insiders. Finally, Jesus returns to the unique benefaction of influence given the disciples: "But blessed are your eyes, for they see, and your ears, for they hear. Truly, I say to you, many prophets and righteous men longed to see what you see, and did not see it, and to hear what you hear, and did not hear it" (13:16-17).

Continuing his celebration of the unique benefaction given the disciples through himself, Jesus contrasts the nonreceiving eyes and ears of those who receive "parables" with the disciples who are "blessed" or "honored" by God with eyes that see and ears that hear. The rhetorical climax to 13:11-17 makes a similar emphasis by comparing these same disciples with "many prophets and righteous men." Not only did unworthy people not see and hear (13:14-15), but truly worthy people likewise did not see and hear as the disciples have been privileged to. Thus the benefaction of influence shown the disciples surpasses all others given by God. By contrast and comparison, they are shown to be favorite clients of their God-Father (J. Marcus 1986:89–110).

With this "theory of revelation" clearly in mind, we can rapidly note four examples of God's benefaction of influence: dreams and stars, Peter as favored recipient of revelation, special revelation for special circumstances, and secret interpretation of the Scriptures. Dreams constitute a special class of secrets revealed. The honorable status of Joseph's wife and of her child are confirmed by a dream (1:19-25). Dreams instruct Joseph to flee from Herod (2:13) and return when it is safe (2:20). Wise men from the east see a star that leads them eventually to the crib of the Son of God, surely a unique secret revealed to them (2:1-12). A dream warns them to escape Herod and return home in a secret manner (2:12). Finally, the innocence of Jesus is revealed in a dream to Pilate's wife (27:6).

According to Matthew's portrait of Peter, this disciple is the favored recipient of secrets and special information, above and beyond the "blessed" character of the typical disciple. Peter, of course, regularly hears Jesus' privileged words to the inner core of disciples (10:5-42; 13:10-17; 28:16-20), but he is singled out to receive revelation, secrets, and special information. For example, Peter seeks clarification of Jesus' words about the issue of purity and hand washing (15:15), and thus becomes the conduit of this to the group. He is schooled by Jesus about the payment of the temple tax by the disciples (17:24-27); he asks Jesus about the reward for disciples who have left all for Jesus' sake (19:27). In each instance, he receives privileged information. But the most significant example of Peter's status as the recipient of unique knowledge is his confession at Caesarea Philippi: "You are the Christ, the Son of the living God" (16:16). This, Jesus tells him, is unique knowledge, not available from anyone on earth: "Flesh and blood has not revealed this to you, but my Father who is in heaven" (16:17). As a result of this unique benefaction, Peter is made the mediator or broker of Jesus' church.

Jesus informs the inner circle that in difficult times to come, they will be given unique speech: "Do not be anxious how you are to speak or what you are to say; for what you are to say will be given you in that hour; for it is not you who speak, but the Spirit of your Father speaking through you" (10:19-20). The bold apologetic speech of the disciples, then, will be a revelation from God.

Finally, as noted, in a number of places Matthew cites the Scriptures, often with some introductory tag such as: "this was to fulfill what was said by the prophet" (1:22-23; 2:6, 17, 23; 4:14-16; etc.). One surmises that

Pharisees and other Israelites would not find the same meaning in these passages that the disciples of Jesus do. Thus their "spiritual" or "messianic" meaning represents another example of the heavenly benefaction of influence, that is, the gift of esoteric information.

GOD, BENEFACTOR-PATRON, AND JESUS, FAVORITE AND FAITHFUL CLIENT

Earlier I listed the benefactions of God-Patron to Israel and to Jesus, the favorite client. Now for several reasons it is worthwhile to examine Jesus' response to his Patron-Father. First, throughout Matthew, Jesus speaks constantly about God-Patron, the range of which discourse one immediately sees as privileged discourse about God. Second, Jesus' remarks about his God-Patron also illustrate the proper response to the Patron by all genuine disciples of Jesus. Matthew's Gospel contains most of the discourse of Jesus about God that we found in Mark's story, especially the material after Jesus' entry into Jerusalem and in particular the "four questions" found in Matt 22:15-44, all of which is relevant to Jesus' God-talk in Matthew. This we already know. Furthermore, Matthew contains other material about God that is particularly rich and worthy of consideration because it expresses Jesus-the-client's response to God his Patron: the desert temptations (4:1-11), the reform of piety (6:1-18), remarks on the "kingdom of heaven" and the "kingdom of God," and a cluster of parables (20:1-16; 21:33—22:11) that express unique and shocking aspects of God's character.

If You Are God's Son

Immediately after God ascribes the role and status of "beloved Son" to Jesus, God's foe challenges this honorable status. Twice the challenger attacks the loyalty of Jesus-the-client with the phrase, "If you are the Son of God . . ." (4:3, 6), urging Jesus to divide his loyalty and serve himself as well as God ("command these stones to become loaves of bread . . . throw yourself down"). In a third test, the challenger seeks to have Jesus change his allegiance, abandoning God as his Patron and taking him in God's place: "All these will I give you, if you will fall down and worship me" (4:9). The crux, then, is Jesus' role as client, whether he loyally and totally serves his Patron or abandons him for another. The responses of Jesus demonstrate his total faithfulness as a client to God, his Patron:

> Man does not live by bread alone, but by every word that comes out of the mouth of God. (4:4; Deut 8:3)
> You shall not tempt the Lord your God. (4:7; Deut 6:16)
> You shall worship the Lord your God, and him only shall you serve. (4:10; Deut 6:13)

As has often been noticed, the text of each of Jesus' remarks comes from Deuteronomy, a document celebrating covenant fidelity, and affirms his Patron's exclusive rights: "Every word that comes from the mouth of God . . . not tempt the Lord your God . . . him only shall you serve." Matthew's Gospel, then, begins with the patronage of God to Jesus the client (3:16-17), which benefaction is balanced by Jesus' subsequent manifestation of loyalty to his Patron (4:1-11; see Rohrbaugh 1995:188–92).

Honor God "in Secret"

Later Jesus defends his Patron in the face of the village practice of traditional, public acts of piety, almsgiving, prayer, and fasting (6:1-18). Perceiving that many are not truly honoring their Patron by their practice, Jesus, the client, steps forward to defend God's interests. The root of disloyalty consists of "practicing your piety before men to be seen by them" (6:1); piety, whose aim is the honor and praise of God, has been diverted instead to the client. God, then, loses honor and respect from these clients; the debt of justice owed the Patron is not being paid. As a result of this insulting behavior, the heavenly Patron will no long respond with commitment to this client: "You will have no reward from your Father who is in heaven" (6:1b). The issue, then, touches Patron-client relationships and the "debt" of justice that clients owe the Patron. Thus, on behalf of his Patron, Jesus challenges the disloyal behavior of certain clients:

Taking Honor due the Patron	do not blow a trumpet as the hypocrites do in the synagogues or on the streets to be given glory by men	do not be as the hypocrites, for they love to stand in the synagogues and on the corners of the streets to be seen by them	do not look dismal like the hypocrites, they disfigure their faces so as to appear fasting
End of Patron's Benefaction	they have lost their reward (6:2)	they have lost their reward (6:5)	they have lost their reward (6:16-17)

What, then, do loyal clients do? Jesus prescribes that piety be practiced for the sake of God alone. Hence, he enjoins that true clients do what they do "in secret."

True Honor for the Patron: "In Private":	do not let your right hand know what your left hand is doing : your alms will be "in secret"	enter your room and shut the door and pray to your Father "in secret"	anoint your head and wash your face so that you may not appear to men to fast, but to your Father "in secret"
Patron's Benefaction	and your Father who sees "in secret" will reward you (6:3-4)	and your Father who sees "in secret" will reward you (6:6)	and your Father who sees "in secret" will reward you (6:17)

Jesus, then, defends the Patron's honor, manifests loyalty to him, and instructs other to do so.

THE KINGDOM IN MATTHEW

No consensus exists among scholars about the meaning(s) of the "kingdom" in Jesus' speech (Chilton 1994b:255–80). Nor do I intend to revisit the topic using old categories. Rather, within the framework of patron-client relationships, I seek to classify references to "kingdom" in terms of the model of patron-client relations, examine what is said about the Patron/Householder/King/Father, and consider what benefaction looks like in this context. In terms of the categories of patron-client relations, the classification of Matthew's material on "kingdom" looks like this:

1. Patron	farmer, householder, king, father	13:3-9, 31-33; 18:23-35; 20:1-16; 21:28-32, 33-44; 22:1-10
2. Client	Who is in/who is out of the kingdom; how is one included/excluded; rank and status in the kingdom	(a) entering into/exclusion from kingdom: 5:20; 7:21; 8:11; 16:19; 19:12, 23-24; (b) ranking in kingdom: 5:19; 11:11-12; 18:1, 4; 20:21-23
3. Broker	John the Baptizer, Jesus, scribes, Peter	3:2; 4:17; 10:7; 13:52; 16:16-20
4. Benefaction	power, commitment, influence	4:23; 5:3, 10; 6:10-13, 33; 9:35; 13:11

Matthew's narrative begins with John and then Jesus speaking as authorized brokers of God: "Repent, for the kingdom of heaven is at hand" (3:2; 4:17, 22; see 10:7). Their agency on God's behalf seems urgent, for the kingdom is "at hand." Later, other people will act in regard to the kingdom: scribes who have knowledge (13:52), and Peter, who has keys of power in regard to the kingdom (16:19). All of these brokers seek clients for the Patron, although it remains a contested matter who enters or does not enter the kingdom. Would-be clients who only give lip service to God do not enter (7:21); hence "complete" honoring of God makes one a true client, both "Saying 'Lord, Lord'" and "doing the will of my Father." "Righteousness" that exceeds that of the Pharisees qualifies one for entrance, as does making oneself a eunuch "for the sake of the kingdom" (19:12). In contrast, the rich who hold on to their riches (19:22) will enter only with difficulty (19:23-24). Finally, persons who accept Jesus as God's agent and broker will find a place at the table with the patriarchs, while those who do not will not (8:11-12). Clients of the patron's benefaction are distinguished in the world: certain behaviors honor the patron and so indicate they are his clients, but other postures stand in the way of a relationship of patron and client. Thus true clients on the one hand are "complete" (5:20; 7:21) or are willing to sacrifice earthly honor to the honor of the patron (19:12, 23-24).

I urge that a profitable way of understanding God's "kingdom" lies in assessing it in terms of patron-client relationships. The above data only sketch this but do not explain it. The social-science description of God's kingdom by Bruce Malina urges us to see it in larger terms:

> Jesus' proclamation of the kingdom of God, a theocracy involving political religion as well as political economy, involved government by God. But in the Jesus tradition, the God of Israel was not monarch but patron. To what sort of question/problem/situation is Jesus' attitude toward God as Father a response/solution? The answer: To a situation requiring patronage. God is and will be Father. (Malina 2001b:141)

"Kingdom" would have meant for people in Jesus' world the Roman Empire, which, while it described its role as civilizing the world, served as a brutal mechanism of colonial expansion that confiscated lands and extracted ruinous taxes. As a center in relation to the periphery of colonies, it took as much as it could and gave back little or nothing. Jesus' "kingdom," however, describes how Father-Patron bestows the benefaction of power, which wars on demons who enslave God's clients, inducement for those who suffer loss of land or family for the sake of their patron, and influence to know the secrets and mysteries of God.

God's Kingdom in Parables

I turn now to Matthew's parables, because these seem to hold the most promise for learning about God-as-Patron and the kingdom. Three clusters of parables concern us: (a) 13:3-9, 24-30, 31, 33, 44-46; (b) 18:23-35; and (c) 20:1-16; 21:28-32, 33-44; 22:1-10.

Matthew 13

Most scholarship on the parables in Matthew 13 seems to focus on the clients, either their reception of the seed, the surprising growth of their numbers, or their boldness. But let us reverse this and read them for what they tell us about the Patron. In 13:3-9, which even Matthew calls "the parable of the *sower*" (13:18), this solitary actor does very strange, even foolish, things. The sower prodigally throws his seed away: he casts three out of four seeds on ground unlikely to yield anything. What kind of farmer is this? By normal peasant standards he should starve. Indeed, he would be laughed at for his utter lack of farming skills; no honor here, only ridicule at his folly. But if the sower's actions tell us anything about the kingdom, then is God-the-Sower doing foolish things by casting seed on places or persons most unlikely to yield a return? This suggests that if the parable is about God or God's kingdom, its focus needs to shift to the Patron-Farmer's lack of favoritism in choosing his clients; by common standards he lacks judgment and so honor.

Later, another farmer intentionally plants a mustard seed in his field, which is presumably already planted (13:31). Deuteronomy 22 lists many things that must be kept separate and distinct, among which are seeds: "You shall not sow your vineyard with two kinds of seed, lest the whole yield be forfeited to the sanctuary, the crop which you have sown and the yield of the vineyard" (22:9). The sower, then, does something "unclean" and at variance with the law. If sowing two kinds of seeds is an "impurity," this reflects on the sower.

The next parable balances male tasks and places with female ones: a female puts leaven in flour, one of the three classic tasks of females in antiquity (food preparation, clothing production, and child rearing). But leaven is unclean, even a corruption (1 Cor 5:6-8; Gal 5:9). Israelites express this in their observance of the Feast of "Unleavened Bread," at which time they expel all leavened products from their houses and burn them. Plutarch makes the same equation that leaven = corruption in the Greco-Roman world: "For the leaven itself is generated out of corruption and when mixed (with flour) corrupts the mass, for it [the mass] becomes slack and powerless and in general the leavened thing appears to be putrid; then, increasing, it becomes sour and corrupts the flour" (*Quaest. rom.* 289F; see *Quaest. conv.* 659B). I see a homology between the male farmer who puts the out-of-place seed in a field and the female who inserts unclean leaven into pure flour. In both the actor does something classified as "unclean," but of whose action the reader should surely approve. "The kingdom of heaven," insofar as it is an active concept here, suggests that God sows and leavens. Nonclients will declare these illegal and unclean actions, and thus deny the Patron honor and respect. But honor follows, as it always does: the out-of-place seed grows marvelously and the little leaven causes a large measure to rise. The surprise or even shock of the actions described points to another aspect of honor, namely, the risk or cleverness or novelty of certain actions. I argue that the figure who both plants the mustard seed and puts the leaven in the flour is none other than God-Patron, who while mightily upsetting the world, is nevertheless producing wonderful results through the insertion of Jesus-the-client into the world of Israel.

Finally I consider two more "the kingdom of heaven is like . . ." parables that conclude Matthew 13. First, a man finds a treasure in a field, conceals it, and sells all he has to buy the field (13:44). Scholars tell us that this action violates the law, hence hearers are torn by the prospect of riches and the deviance of the action. In addition to the bizarre fact of a treasure in a peasant's field, the peasant, normally known to be conservative, takes a risk in selling all he has to buy this field, which if the truth were known would be considered an illegal act. In one sense, he breaks relations with the field's owner, for he is now cheating him. The "kingdom" of God, then, is a relationship of surprise or gratuitous benefaction; it requires that one act out of character and even fraudulently in the eyes of others.

Paralleling this story, a merchant goes in search of fine pearls. He does indeed find one, but like the farmer in 13:44, he "sold all that he had and bought it" (13:45). First, "merchants" were not considered favorably, unlike today's entrepreneurs. In Matthew's peasant world, success for a merchant means "buy cheap and sell dear." Peasants usually interpret this to mean that the merchant's success comes at their or their neighbors' expense. The merchant is, then, a thief. He is not a patron to anyone. His actions in this relationship seem risky and even bizarre: yes, he gets his pearl, but he has put his and his family's life in jeopardy to get it. One cannot eat a pearl, wear it for clothing, or sleep in it: it is foolish, then, for a merchant to sell "all" to acquire it. What, then, do we learn from this? Both farmer and merchant find themselves the recipients of benefaction gratuitously bestowed (they "find" treasure or pearl). By their actions they both indicate that they are opportunists who behave either illegally or foolishly on this occasion—yet they find favor, at least in the eyes of Matthew! While the parables focus on their suspect, risky, and foolish actions, it is clear that they are the kind of clients whom the heavenly Patron seeks. Thus God-Patron encourages and endorses their "illegal," "risky," and "foolish" actions, and rewards them with benefactions fit for elites. God, then, is not playing by the rules of the game as known to the audiences of Matthew and Jesus. As patron, he is establishing a new model of relationships.

Matthew 18

Here Matthew compares the kingdom of heaven to an earthly king who settles accounts with his servants (18:23-35). The king has previously acted as patron to many people, giving his inducement (wealth) in exchange for some other symbolic media, such as commitment. Now the patron-king seeks a return for his patronage ("settle account"), which means that his honor is being tested. For if clients do not repay their patron according to contract or if the patron cannot enforce this, he will lose face and be taken lightly. A client heavily indebted comes before the patron-king, who owes "ten thousand talents" (18:24). The patron does the culturally proper thing in mandating that the debtor-client, wife, and children be sold into slavery and the debt paid. In this he does the correct thing and suffers no loss of honor. But the man profoundly honored his patron: "he fell on his knees and implored him, 'Have patience with me'" (18:26). The patron does a most bizarre action in that he does not give the man time to repay the debt as requested, but rather totally cancels it: "the Lord released him and forgave him his debt" (18:27). Patron-client relationships are woven of services rendered and resulting "debts" and obligations. The patron's "foolish" action of gratuitously forgiving the debt upsets the pattern of relationships. The patron will be taken as an easy mark for anyone who whines!

This servant then confronts another servant who owes him but a fraction of what he owed the patron-king. Like the first episode, another patron-client relationship is in view: demand for payment, which is impossible, issuing in a plea for patience, which is here rejected, and ending with the debtor put in prison (18:28-30). This is nearer the reality of peasant life than the first story: patron-kings do not remit large debts. Debt prison or debt slavery is the more likely result. In this second scene, the servant-patron maintains the patron-client relationship, if only by signaling that he knows how to conduct such relationships; he knows, moreover, how to defend his honor, which he does by the socially accepted harsh treatment of debtors.

The parable resolves when the foolish patron calls the savvy client to account for not being as foolish in forgiving debts as the patron-king was. Thus the two original characters come face to face again: a patron-king who acts foolishly and with disregard for his honor (18:23-27) versus a client-patron who acts honorably and with regard for his honor to a fellow servant-client (18:28-30). The patron-king deals with large sums, the remitting of which might put the patron at serious disadvantage. The larger the debt, the greater the folly and the more perilous the risk. If the parable is about the kingdom of heaven and therefore about God, then we should take the patron-king to represent God. In 18:23-27 God would be seen as acting foolishly by remitting the debt; his vulnerability to the servant's entreaties actually suggests weakness; he is showing a misplaced favoritism in a person of whom he should be more wary. But looked at from the point of view of client-debtors, God-Patron represents a windfall of fresh benefaction: debt remitted! Yes, foolish to some, but deliciously wise or clever to debtors. It depends on one's point of view.

The Kingdom in the Parables in Matthew 20–22

As we saw in the case of Mark, Jesus' actions and discourse in Jerusalem all have to do with God. We may skip the hostile questioning of Jesus according to the four types of rabbinic questions (22:15-44), Jesus' actions in regard to the temple (21:12-17), and the chief priests' question, "By what authority are you doing these things?" (21:23-27), because Matthew basically repeats Mark here and we have already seen Mark's interpretation of this material. But in addition, Matthew contains a series of parables about householders and fathers in their dealings with their clients and sons that have to do with God and the kingdom of heaven:

20:1-16	a landowner and his clients
21:28-32	a father and his two sons
21:33-44	a father, his tenants, and his son
22:1-10	a father (king) and a wedding feast for his son

First, Matthew is responsible for collecting, editing, or composing these materials and putting them here in the narrative, at the beginning of Jesus' conflicts with the Jerusalem elites. I consider the basic characters in the episodes to be chosen precisely because they share something in common: landowners, fathers, and kings who act as patrons. Thus each of these stories focuses on patron-client relations, namely, the ways in which Jesus declares that God relates to us. In three of them, the patron works through his son, whether to effect reform of worship, secure the patron's share of the crops, or to feed people on the occasion of the son's wedding. Thus the patron relates to his clients through a mediator or broker. All of them also have a strong component of honor and shame, which is regularly bound up with patron-client relations. What, then, do these sayings tell us about the nature or character of the patron?

The first parable (20:1-16) describes "the kingdom of heaven" as a householder hiring day laborers for his estates, just as a patron would search for clients, though probably through a broker. On the use of patron-client relations to interpret the parables, see Malina and Rohrbaugh 1992:124–26; Scott 1989:205–17. The parable contains two surprising elements: the householder constantly returns to the village square and hires more and more laborers, and he pays all the laborers the same wage, despite the disparity of time labored. The latter feature might suggest that the patron-householder is foolish, giving a full day's wage to those who have not earned it; others label him as unjust in that he plays favorites. Even if all receive the same wage, the laborers know that some have been compensated better (because they worked less than others). Either way, the householder appears to be a strange patron, either foolish and prodigal or unjust and partial. The patron defends himself by claiming that he is not unjust; he is loyal to his contract with the laborers; and as patron, his goods and his generosity are his to dispense. Thus we see emerging in the parable a type of favoritism that flies in the face of expectations about first and last: while earlier the patron said: "pay them their wages, beginning with the last" (20:8), later he added, "I choose to give to this last (laborer) as I give to you" (20:14); finally he states "the last will be first, and the first last" (20:16). From this we learn that the patron is "foolish" in paying all the same wage; he does a strange thing by making the last first. He seems just when he hires workers throughout the day, but when he pays them, a disturbing element of favoritism enters. If this is about God and the kingdom of heaven, we learn that God-Patron is both just and generous; God does not play by the rules, but upsets them by favoring the last. The Patron is at once just, generous, and faithful, but also free and disturbing.

When Jesus later tells a parable about a father and his two sons (21:28-32), we recall that a father-son relationship is another example of the superior/inferior relationships that make up the patron-client system. Since Scripture requires children to honor their father and mother (Exod 20:12; Deut 5:16; Lev 20:9), we would expect in this case the issue of honor to stand out. Inasmuch as stories and parables in the ancient world consist of comparison and contrast of binary opposites, we would expect the two sons to represent completely contradictory embodiments of honoring their father. The father asks both sons, presumably in public before the household, to work in the vineyard. The first son honored his father by publicly agreeing to go and work. Thus the father has standing in the eyes of the household and neighbors because his son publicly honors him. Yet he does not go, which brings shame on the father. The second son shames his father by refusing the public command to work in the vineyard, but privately honors him by going to work. Thus in public the father is honored by one but shamed by the other son. Wherein does honor lie?

The parable resembles many other stories in Matthew that contrast true and false honor. For example, inasmuch as talk is cheap, not all who say "Lord, Lord" will enter the kingdom of heaven, but true honor lies in "doing the will of my Father" (7:22). Later Jesus makes this same distinction once more in regard to Pharisees and their washing traditions; he cites Isaiah to articulate his accusation: "This people honors me with their lips, but their heart is far from me" (15:8; cf. Isa 29:13). Other variations on this would include Jesus' criticism of his family standing outside in contrast with those inside: "Whoever does the will of my Father in heaven" is "brother, sister, and mother" (Matt 12:50). Thus what constitutes honor, especially the honor of God-Patron, is a consistent Matthean theme.

What, then, is honor in 21:28-32? Ideally, honor would be both public acknowledgment of the Patron and "doing his will." But except for Jesus, the perfect Son, Matthew's audience does not seem to be able to do both at the same time. Inasmuch as Jesus' task was to call for "repentance" and to "save people from their sins," Matthew judges the honor of the Patron in terms of these: changing one's mind and behavior according to Jesus' exhortation. Thus those who change, like the second son, honor the Patron and so come to share in his benefaction: "Tax collectors and harlots go into the kingdom of God before you" (21:31). But those who do not change, even after both John and Jesus exhorted them, give empty honor to God: "you did not believe him . . . you did not afterward repent and believe him" (21:32). Thus God-Patron, although dishonored by all players in the Gospel, is finally honored only by those who repent and "do the will of their Father in heaven." And the initial public honor of the first son is empty honor, even contempt of the Patron. How strange, then, that the Father-Patron endures shame from all; how weak of him to wait for those who shamed him to come to their senses.

We best interpret the parable of the vineyard and the wicked tenants (21:33-45) in the light of patron-client relations, an unusual interpretive strategy with most commentators (Lambrecht 1981:109–24). A patron-landlord planted a vineyard complete with hedge, winepress, and tower, evidently a smart parcel of land for a well-to-do person. As patron, he employs tenants, that is, clients, with whom he strikes an agreement to exchange his patronage to the tenants (food, land, lodging?) for their labor and a share of the harvest (wine and other produce). Key to all patron-client relationships is fair exchange of the symbolic media, especially faithfulness. The parable, however, tells us of the total failure of the patron-client agreement. The clients not only refuse to give the patron his share, but shame the patron by molesting and killing his agents (21:35). Their insult is repeated and then unimaginably compounded by the murder of the patron's son (21:39). Truly the clients are utterly shameless and wicked. But what of the patron? He might be seen as a foolish or stupid patron for many reasons. First, his initial choice of these clients would not seem to be savvy or enlightened. Second, even after his tenants insulted him by murdering his servants, he did not immediately send his troops to seek revenge and satisfaction (21:41). The honor code of the day would expect swift and decisive action against these rebels. Third, the patron seems to be utterly dumb and foolish to send his son to these tenants: "They will respect my son" (21:37) is not the calculation of a wise man. On the contrary, the data argue that they hold the patron in utter contempt by now and the patron knows this.

Yet this patron-father finally restores his honor. He takes vengeance on his tenants and replaces them with new tenant-clients, who, it is hoped, "will give him his fruits in their seasons" (21:41). Then, as Jesus tells the story, "the stone rejected by the builders [shame] has become the head of the corner [honor]" (21:42a). Who has done this? "It was the Lord's doing," and it brought honor to the stone and the builder, as the bystanders acknowledge this restoration of honor: "It is marvelous in our eyes" (21:42b).

In this light, the clients are indisputably shameless in their reaction to the patron. All would consider them base and unworthy of any relationship. But what about this patron-father? A case can be made that he is a foolish patron, to say nothing of a father utterly careless about the welfare of his son and heir. But might not this be the point? Were this a handbook on ancient patron-client relations, he might be the perfect example of how *not* to be a successful patron. But when one puts the parable into Jesus' discourse on God, then God, who is Patron and Father, acts in ways untypical of patrons but much to the benefit to clients. God is slow to anger; he gives many opportunities to repent and to make bent relationships straight. Yes, he is foolish beyond measure to send his son to his enemies. But this is the point: God's patronage gives blessings (tenure of the vineyard), patience, and opportunity of repentance, even to very shameful clients. Moreover, God-Patron stands by his Son-client, elevating him in his rejection, which might be understood as a patron's faithfulness to his client.

Matthew adds to the previous parables about patron figures a final story about a patron who is both king and father (22:1-10). Let us examine it in terms of patron-client relations and the attendant duties of honor. First, Matthew tells us that the patron is a "king who gave a wedding feast for his son" (22:2). Thus the king is patron to his nobles, who receive the invitation to the feast; he extends to them the benefaction of inducement, a royal wedding feast. He expects from them commitment, namely, respect and honor. The patron is also a father who shows commitment to his heir by honoring his royal marriage with a feast. As the parable goes on, we learn that the original clients, the nobles, return no honor to the king but instead treat him with contempt: when invited, "they would not come" (22:3); when the king ignored this slight and invited them once more, "they made light of it [the invitation] . . . while the rest treated his servants shamefully" (22:5-6). The actions of these clients fatally break the patron-client relationship. Instead of benefaction, the clients receive the vengeance of the patron-king, who utterly reduces them: "he sent his troops and destroyed those murderers and burned their city" (22:7). Thus his honor is restored, but it is not the honor due a patron.

Is this a wise and savvy patron-king? One might say that he is singularly stupid in failing to read the mood of his client-nobles. He seems utterly out of touch. Too trusting? Too naive? His various invitations to his clients could be seen as ludicrous. The first rejection seriously challenges his honor; but he does not respond as do all others in this world who give some riposte or response to an honor challenge (Neyrey 1998b:666–77). It is folly on the king's part to send other messengers, seemingly to their sure disgrace and even shameful death. Admittedly the king recovers much of his honor by the demonstration of power that now serves as his riposte. But he subsequently acts in a way we consider utterly foolish and without honor: he commands his servants to "go to the thoroughfares" where the urban nonelites live. The servants brought in "all whom they found, both bad and good" (22:10). If a man is known by the company he keeps, then our patron-king now shares table with the least and lowliest in his royal city. For these three reasons, then, one would consider the patron-king-father to be a foolish and inept person. He seems to misjudge at all turns what is honorable and accepts insults from his nobles: he neither knows what honor is nor how to maintain it.

But the parable is about the "kingdom of heaven" (22:1) and invites us to consider how God is Patron, King, and Father. How does God understand patron-client relations? How does God understand honor? As in the case of 20:1-16 and 21:33-46, so the parable in 22:1-10 tells of a patron who is strangely generous to his clients, whether it be a generous wage or tolerance of insults (21:35; 22:3). Does this reflect the attribute of God known as "mercy," that is, "merciful and gracious, slow to anger . . . forgiving iniquity and transgression of sins" (Exod 34:6-7)? What seems foolish in regard to a monarch like Herod the Great is a hallmark of the God of Israel. Finally, the invitation of the urban lowest classes to eat at the king's table is unintelligible to most, who would not judge that the king finds honor in associating with people who had no honor. But God manifests divine freedom by showing mercy where he would. In short, God is not playing by the rules of the patron-client relationship as players would in Matthew's world. Matthew is at pains to argue that God finally shows a sense of honor by destroying those who had shamed him. But the bulk of the story centers on the Patron-King's foolish ways of offering patronage to his clients and his equally bizarre sense of honor. In his eyes, last becomes first, least is greatest; might we not also say that shame is honor? Not surprisingly, the "kingdom of heaven" is not our world.

All of the remarks we have seen in this section are words of Jesus, and so we are justified in considering them as his own discourse about his Patron-Father. On the one hand, some of Jesus' statements are utterly favorable to God, such as his triple protestation of loyalty (commitment) in the temptations and his demand that worship should honor God alone. On the other hand, many of Jesus' remarks on the "kingdom of heaven/God" describe a leading figure acting foolishly or ineptly; this figure does things that might even be described as illegal and corrupting. One king inexplicably forgives a major debt, which calls into question not only the prudence of the act but also the savvy of the patron. If these materials describe God and the kingdom, then Jesus' God-talk seems completely shocking, foolish, and even silly. Finally, the four parables in Matthew 20–22 describe a patron-father who appears to be a foolish landlord, a father who cannot control his sons, and a father-king who is shamed by his nobles and forced to bring untouchables to the marriage of his son. But God should be most honorable, all powerful, and infinitely wise. Who is this God, Patron, and Father of Jesus?

MATTHEW AND HIS SOURCES: COMPARATIVE THEOLOGY

The Q source has little to say about God, as its focus seems to be on wisdom-like sayings. Nevertheless, a casual reading of the reconstructed document yields the following data about God, mainly about God's actions. (1) God sends prophets, both ancient ones as well as John the Baptizer and Jesus; thus in virtue of the message of these agents, God bestows influence. (2) These prophets generally exhort the crowds to repentance and reform (commitment) or pronounce a condemnation (power). (3) The direction of the reform is toward greater "purity" or wholeness, as in (a) wholehearted service of God: "You cannot serve God and mammon" (6:24; see 7:21); (b) only the few who walk the narrow way enter (7:13-14); (c) perfection (5:48), which includes removing the beam from one's eye (7:1-5). (4) Yet divine judgment comes upon those who reject God's prophets: winnowing wheat from chaff (3:7-10), "woes" (11:20-24; 23:37-39), judgment by Gentiles (12:38-42). (5) Prayer to God both honors God for his sovereignty and petitions God for his benefaction (6:9-13); this God providently protects his own (10:28-31) and favors them with secrets (11:25-27). (6) God honors those whom others shame; thus the "blessed" in the Beatitudes is pronounced by God on those who inherit God's kingdom, whom God satisfies in their want (inducement), and whom God greatly rewards in heaven (5:3, 4, 6, 11-12). Therefore, the Q source describes God sharply in terms of "purity" and "holiness" issues, especially the process of "separation" of wheat from chaff and saints from sinners. Except for the list of healings-as-credentials in Matt 11:2-5, God's benefaction ignores healings. God's purity or holiness attribute separates God and the disciples from uncleanness.

The following synoptic chart aims at comparing and contrasting Matthew and his sources. The categories for comparison consist primarily of those relating to patron-client relations (brokers, inclusivity or exclusivity, GSM), issues of worship, and the meanings of honor and shame.

Categories for Thinking about God	Q Source	Mark	Matthew
1. God's agents or brokers	prophets in general, John the Baptizer, Jesus	John the Baptizer Jesus his disciples	John the Baptizer Jesus his disciples
2. Inclusivity—exclusivity	exclusive: few, not many sheep among wolves	inclusive: healings performed for Israelites and non-Israelites in Galilee and Gentile Lands	inclusive: healings performed for Israelites and non-Israelites in Galilee and Gentile lands. "Make disciples of all nations"
3. GSM that the Patron distributes	a. Influence (secrets, prophecies, etc.) b. Power (rescue and judgment) c. Inducement (support for disciples disowned for loyalty to Jesus)	a. Influence (secrets, teachings, revelations, parables) b. Power (healings, rescues, raising the dead) c. Inducement (feedings) d. Commitment (call, election, faithfulness, fictive kinship)	a. Influence (secrets, five sermons, revelations, parables; exclusive knowledge) b. Power (healings, rescues, raising the dead) c. Inducement (feedings, clothing, 100% reward) d. Commitment (call, election, faithfulness, fictive kinship)
4. Worship	Nontemple piety: a. washing rites b. prayer	Nontemple piety: a. prayer: "my house shall be a house of prayer"; "Abba, Father" b. Entrance rites and ceremonial meal c. formal critique of temple system, including sacrifice	a. almsgiving, prayer, and fasting b. Prayer (petitionary and thanksgiving) c. Formal critique of temple system; unclean made whole in the temple d. Entrance rite ("baptize in the name of the Father, Son, and Spirit") e. ceremonial meal
5. Honor and shame	God acts with traditional power to requite insults and wrongs	a. While God still acts with judgment, much discourse about God's foolishness and weakness b. Least is greatest; last is first	a. God acts with judgment, but many parables tell of God's foolishness and weakness b. Thematic development of least is greatest, weakness is strength, servant is master

While Matthew's Gospel incorporates the Q source, its God-talk is distinctively less concerned with purity and holiness-as-separation. God, then, demonstrates an inclusive covenant commitment, in contrast to the exclusive stance of the Q source. God's benefaction is regularly bestowed on Israelites as well as those from "Syria . . . the Decapolis, Judea, Jerusalem, and beyond the Jordan" (4:24-25). God's healing power extends to a Canaanite woman in Tyre (15:21-28) and to demoniacs in Gadara (8:28-31). God's brokers, while prophets, call people to repentance rather than to judgment. God's benefaction, which in the Q source consists of modest instances of influence, power, and inducement, is more richly described in Matthew because the evangelist narrates so much more of Jesus' teaching, healings, acts of power, and feedings of thousands. Truly, one should call God "Benefactor" in Matthew, for that is God's premier role as God of the covenants of promise, of providence, and of "mercy, not sacrifice."

Whereas worship in the Q source centered on baptismal washing and prayer, in Matthew we learn of "secret" acts of piety, namely, almsgiving, prayer, and fasting (6:1-18). Jesus both teaches prayer, especially the Our Father (6:9-13), and models it by actually praying it (26:39, 42, 44). He likewise prays petitionary and thanksgiving prayers, as well as various psalms (26:38; cf. Ps 42:6; Matt 27:46; cf. Ps 22:1). He challenges the temple system of worship, declaring: "My house shall be called a house of prayer for all the nations" (Matt 21:13), and performing purificatory healing of the unclean even in the temple (21:14). True worship of God begins with an entrance rite (3:11; 28:19) and is confirmed during ceremonial meals (26:26-28).

Finally, God's honor in the Q source consists of a riposte to those who ignore God's law or who reject and kill God's agents. In Matthew the world of Israelite honor and shame is turned upside down. To be great, one must become honorless like a child or a servant. The first become last and the last first. Those dishonored for loyalty to Jesus and his gospel of God are declared honored in God's eyes. Moreover, in parable after parable we learn how foolish or weak or inept the farmer, the landlord, the father, and the king are. These parables, which describe the kingdom of God, thus talk about God's foolishness, weakness, or ineptness. This God allows himself to be put upon, for he does not immediately respond with violence and vengeance to insults. Moreover, this God hobnobs with the "wrong" people, namely, sinners, those on the margins, the unclean, and the expendables. Thus by comparing Matthew's theology with that of the Q source, we can see dramatic shifts in the early church's understanding of the Deity.

3

BENEFACTION, PROVIDENCE, AND THEODICY

GOD IN THE ACTS OF THE APOSTLES

God shows no partiality.
—Acts 10:34

INTRODUCTION

The Gospels singularly focus on Jesus, from baptism to cross to vindication. But when readers turn from them to the Acts of the Apostles, they note immediately that Acts begins with Jesus' ascension into heaven. Jesus remains present to his disciples and will play an important role in the narrative of Acts, but he is offstage. Correspondingly, the figure of God becomes much more evident and active in Acts than in the Gospels. More debate is given in Acts to what God is doing than in Mark or Luke; and a larger canvas of history is on display in Acts than in Matthew. Acts formally ascribes the roles of creator and final judge to God; it tries to find common ground with Israelite and Greco-Roman philosophies about the character and actions of God, in particular God's providence. As we shall see, Acts sets out to write a theology, both the history of God's actions and a celebration of God's person and plans. My inquiry into the way God is understood and presented in Acts takes up three related and overlapping models: (1) God-in-relationship: patron-client relationships; (2) the provident God; and (3) theodicy in Acts.

GOD-IN-RELATIONSHIP: PATRON/ BENEFACTOR-CLIENT RELATIONSHIPS

As I did with Mark's God-talk, here I begin with an analysis of God-in-relationship. This means not only attention to God as patron and benefactor, but also careful assessment of the various goods of God's benefaction. We must also attend to God's clients, especially Jesus, whom God made Lord and Christ. God, as always, uses brokers or mediators for God's purposes, and in this case we must consider Jesus as well as the commissioned eyewitnesses (10:40-42) and angels (1:10-11; 5:19-20; 12:7-11) as agents of divine benefaction. Of course, the clients are both traditional Israelites and also Gentiles (e.g., Cornelius, 10:1-8, 34-35). What, then, does the Patron/Benefactor bestow? On whom? Why?

God as Patron and Jesus as Client

The best way to know the character and intentions of patrons is to observe the patronage extended to their clients. Luke tells us immediately that like all patron-client relationships, the one between God and Jesus is particular, for God shows unique favoritism to him. Take, for example, Peter's description to Cornelius of the relationship between God and Jesus: "You know the word which he sent to Israel . . . how God anointed Jesus of Nazareth with the Holy Spirit and with power, how he went about doing good and healing all that were oppressed by the devil, for God was with him" (10:37-38; see also 2:22). Thus God ascribed to Jesus a unique role and status, which is expressed in the verb "anointed," a form of commissioning common to kings and prophets. As we shall shortly see, Luke did not consider Jesus as just another in a line of kings and prophets, but as a definitively superior person, both Lord and Christ.

Luke passes quickly to the death of Jesus to highlight the power and faithfulness of his Patron. The frequency with which Luke mentions this indicates its importance, for understanding both God and the crucified client, Jesus:

> This Jesus . . . you crucified and killed by the hands of lawless men, but God raised him up (2:24)
>
> This Jesus whom you crucified God has made by Lord and Christ (2:36)
>
> The God of Abraham and of Isaac and of Jacob, the God of our fathers, glorified his servant Jesus whom you delivered up and denied in the presence of Pilate (3:13)

> You killed the Author of Life whom God raised from the dead (3:15)
> In the name of Jesus Christ of Nazareth, whom you crucified, whom God raised from the dead (4:10)
> The God of our fathers raised Jesus whom you killed by hanging him on a tree (5:30)
> They put him to death hanging him on a tree, but God raised him on the third day (10:39-40)
> They asked Pilate to have him killed . . . but God raised him from the dead (13:28-30)

On display here are the Patron's power and faithfulness. We see God's power in the ability to undo human actions and intentions, and so assert God's will; moreover, raising the dead is regularly ascribed to God's "power" (Mark 12:24). In addition, each of the eight declarations of God's "raising" Jesus affirms the fidelity of the Patron to this client. Indeed, since the death of the client happens according to "the definite plan and foreknowledge of God" (2:23), the Patron is bound to some dramatic act of vindication.

But Acts tells us still more about God's actions, for Jesus was not merely raised and restored. God bestowed on him an even more exalted status and role than anything Jesus enjoyed in his life. The "raising" of Jesus should be thought of as an enthronement ritual, whereby the Patron elevates the vindicated Jesus according to Ps 110:1: "the Lord said to my Lord, 'Sit at my right hand, until I make thy enemies a stool for thy feet'" (Acts 2:34-35). As a metaphor, "the right hand" of God speaks to a most honorable and powerful position in the cosmos. At this elevation of Jesus, an enthronement took place: "Let the whole house of Israel know assuredly that God has made him both Lord and Christ, this Jesus whom you crucified" (2:36). "Lord" and "Christ" speak of a sovereign role and the highest possible status. The progress of Acts will make clear that God has given Jesus no mere honorific status, but a complex role that includes healing, acts of power, and finally judgment of the living and the dead. The Patron's particular favoritism to Jesus, the client, does not simply continue but increases and accelerates.

As is occasionally found in Israel's Scriptures, God's faithful clients who are slain because of their loyalty to their Patron experience a turning of the tables after death. Judged unjustly by God's enemies on earth, God vindicates them and makes them the ultimate judges of their earthly judges (Daniel 7). Twice Acts narrates how both Peter and then Paul declare to Gentiles the ultimate benefaction of God to Jesus. To the Roman centurion Cornelius, Peter declares that Jesus "is the one ordained by God to be the judge of the living and the dead" (10:40); and to the Greek philosophers in Athens, Paul states: "he has fixed a day on which he will judge the world in righteousness by a man whom he has appointed, and of this he has given assurance to all men by raising him from the dead" (17:31). "Ordained by God" and "appointed" clearly indicate that Jesus' Patron uniquely honors him with a power reserved to the Deity.

God's Client Becomes God's Broker

God-Patron's benefaction does not focus exclusively on Jesus-the-client. True, the heavenly Patron owed a special grace of faithfulness to the one who so fully obeyed the Patron's will and demonstrated unique loyalty to him. God showed true justice to his client by vindicating him and raising him up, a reversal of the earthly status Jesus endured in his death. Moreover, God elevated and enthroned Jesus "at his right hand" in heaven, not simply balancing earthly shame with heavenly honor, but establishing Jesus in a new and special role that we now consider in terms of the model of patron, broker/mediator, and client. God's elevation of Jesus, while showing loyalty and faithfulness to his servant, goes further, for in constituting Jesus as broker or mediator, God now makes the entire heavenly treasury of power, commitment, inducement, and influence available to all persons and every ethnic group through Jesus. Thus by examining the Patron's broker and his brokerage we discover more deeply the riches of the Patron and the plan of God for those who receive them.

Jesus as Broker and Mediator

Peter and then Paul proclaim to various audiences, mostly hostile, the significance of Jesus' new role and status in relationship to Israel. God established him as "both Lord and Christ" (2:36), a role descriptive of his new relationship to God's clients. Peter declares that God made Jesus the "Author of life" (3:15), that is, the source of wholeness of the man who was crippled and of holiness for sinners. To the Sanhedrin Peter announced that God gave a new and unique role to the rejected Jesus, namely, that he has been made "the head of the corner" (4:11); this stone either holds the walls of a building together or caps its arch and secures the structure. The "head of the corner," then, describes a most honorable stone with a most beneficial role for the whole building. In a variety of ways, the apostles proclaim Jesus as "Savior" and the one who brings salvation. Peter said it most clearly: "There is salvation in no one else, for there is no other name under heaven by which we must be saved" (4:12). God has therefore made Jesus the unique savior; there is no other broker or mediator but him. Moreover, the benefaction of salvation extends to Gentiles as well as Israelites, as Peter stated at the conference in Jerusalem: "We shall be saved through the grace of the Lord Jesus, just as they will" (15:11; see also 13:23; 16:31). Note the technical term for patronage/benefaction: "through the *grace* of the Lord Jesus" (Malina 1996:171–73). Finally, the apostles understand Jesus as a "king" or ruler (13:21-23). King David and the original son of David were known in the Hebrew Scriptures as generous benefactors; Solomon, the literal "son of David," was also known in Israel's lore for his healing powers, as Dennis Duling has shown (1975, 1978, 1985). Kings, then, were sources of power, wisdom, and inducement.

In these names and titles we grasp something of the new role and status of Jesus, Broker and Mediator. But what does he broker? What divine benefaction is extended through him? Scholars have long demonstrated a lengthy series of parallels between the actions of Jesus in the gospel story and the deeds and trials of Peter and Paul in the book of Acts (Talbert 1974:15–66; Mattill 1975). The power whereby Jesus made whole the legs of a paralyzed man (Luke 5:24) is the same power invoked by Peter in Acts 3:6-7 and 9:33-34; similarly, Jesus' power to raise from the dead the son of the widow of Nain (Luke 7:11-17) operates at the hands of Peter (Acts 9:36-42) and Paul (Acts 20:9-12). But something more is found in Acts. The passage from Isaiah that Jesus reads in his inaugural visit to the synagogue at Nazareth describes the source of his benefaction: "the Spirit of the Lord is upon me because he has anointed me . . ." (Luke 4:18). Then he tells us what his Patron has empowered him to do: "to preach good news to the poor . . . recovering of sight to the blind . . . to proclaim an acceptable year of the Lord." In the midst of this catalogue we read: "to proclaim release to the captives . . . to set at liberty those who are oppressed" (4:18). These are acts of power. Curiously, the Gospels never narrate that Jesus ever effects the release of captives, or liberates anyone, unless his casting out of evil spirits is understood as a liberation. In Acts, however, Jesus occasionally strengthens his disciples in prison by means of visions or angelic messengers (Paul in Acts 18:9-11; 22:17-21; 27:23-24). But Jesus frequently works their release from jail and imprisonment: twice Peter escapes (5:19-20; 12:1-11) and numerous times Paul is freed (16:22-34) or escapes death (23:12-24), shipwreck (27:41-44), and snakebite (28:3-4). Thus, in addition to the power of Jesus to heal and forgive sins, his empowerment to release captives and set at liberty the oppressed is manifest in Acts. Hence in Acts he continues to broker the power his Patron gave him at the beginning of his career.

Luke clarifies this extension of Jesus' powers in Acts by frequently noting how events happen "in the name of Jesus." By this expression Luke indicates that heavenly benefaction given in the Gospel for Jesus to distribute in a local and limited fashion has come to be understood as Jesus' mediation of these and an even a wider range of goods, no longer just to Israelites but to a vast new clientage of God, and no longer just in the time of Jesus' career but now and forever. For example, Peter heals a crippled man "in the name of Jesus Christ of Nazareth" (Acts 3:6); this miracle serves to attest not only to Jesus' vindication and resurrection, but to his new role and status. Jesus, the "Holy and Righteous One," was killed, but not for any evil or crime; thus the healing done in his name indicates God's renewed affirmation of him, for now those not whole are made whole by "the Author of life." Similarly Peter tells the Sanhedrin that the man they judged a sinner is proved now to be God's vindicated one, "in whose name" works of power are done (4:10-12; see 4:30; 16:18). In like manner, people are "baptized in the name of Jesus" and frequently told that their sins are forgiven (2:38; 8:16; 16:18; 19:5). As Peter proclaimed to the Jerusalem elite, "there is no other name under heaven given among men by which we must be saved" (4:12). There is no mistaking, then, that Jesus of Nazareth continues to act in Acts with power and holiness; his name is the unique source of benefaction. Disciples preach his name; Peter, as we saw, healed "in the name of Jesus" (3:6, 16); Philip preached the good news about the kingdom of God and the name of Jesus Christ (8:12); and Paul "is [sent] to carry my name before the Gentiles and kings and sons of Israel" (9:15; see 9:27). At the very least, this rhythmical repetition of "the name of Jesus" indicates that he functions in Acts as the unique source of benefaction and access to God. The capabilities with which he was endowed as God's client in the Gospel remain and are even expanded; although no signs or wonders happened in Luke "in the name of Jesus," they do in Acts. Yet all this happens *through* the Broker and Mediator of God; the benefactions are God's, not Jesus'.

Jesus, Broker of the Patron's Spirit

A careful examination of the phenomenon of the Holy Spirit in Acts can teach us much about Jesus' mediation of God's benefactions. In what should be read as a topic statement for the rest of Acts, Peter declares: "Being therefore exalted at the right hand of God, and having received from the Father the promise of the Holy Spirit, he has poured out this which you see and hear" (2:33). God, the Patron, has given to Jesus, whom we now call Broker or Mediator, the distribution of God's multifaceted "gift," the Holy Spirit. Luke frequently calls the Holy Spirit a "gift" (2:38; 10:45; 11:17; 15:8), one of the technical terms for benefaction in antiquity. Moreover, the "Spirit" summarizes a wide complex of benefactions. For example, at Pentecost when the Spirit was initially given, the apostles spoke powerfully and in the languages of diverse Israelite groups from all around the Mediterranean basin who were then in Jerusalem. Thus the Holy Spirit is associated with powerful, bold, and convincing speech (see 4:8, 31). The Holy Spirit is extended to a broad clientele; Peter's interpretation of these events indicates that now the floodgates of Spirit visions, prophecy, and dreams, as well as wonders and signs, have been opened, as Joel predicted (Acts 2:17-19; Joel 2:28-29).

Later in Acts Luke tells us that the gift of the Spirit dramatically serves to indicate God's election of new and unusual people beyond Israel into the circle of God's favor. For example, while preaching to Cornelius and his household, Peter and his circumcised associates "were amazed, because the gift of the Holy Spirit had been poured out even on the Gentiles" (10:45). As Peter said earlier, the traditional notion of God's favoritism toward Israel begins to change (10:28, 34), and the confirmation of this occurs when Peter observes the Holy Spirit poured out on Cornelius. The Jerusalem disciples who subsequently hear Peter's report of the gift of the Spirit affirm the inclusion of Gentiles into the circle of God's covenant friends (11:16-18). Later, Peter makes the same point to the disciples who discuss whether the Gentiles must keep Israelite practices: "God who knows the heart bore witness to them, giving them the Holy Spirit just as he did to us" (15:8). In addition, Peter declares that "God shows no partiality" (10:34) and that "God makes no distinction" (15:9), statements that articulate a new and broad sense of inclusivity. Yet every gift of Spirit is being channeled through Jesus, Broker and Mediator, as Acts 2:33 stated.

It will help us to process the disparate pieces of information about Spirit-as-benefaction if we classify them in terms of the four symbolic media already mentioned. *Power* is manifested in bold public speech, signs and wonders, healings, and judgment on sinners. *Influence* includes all visions, prophecies and their fulfillment, speaking in new languages and in tongues.

Commitment is represented by the inclusion of sinners and outsiders and by commissioning of members to roles and tasks. *Inducement* is oddly absent: no foods are multiplied or material necessities provided. In summary, when identified as "gift," Spirit expresses the benefaction of God in Christ.

Even the Broker Has Brokers

Thus far I have focused on Jesus as the broker-mediator of Israel's heavenly Patron. Acts, however, contains materials that indicate that some of Jesus' disciples function in the role of sub-broker to Jesus, and so occupy formal places in the classical patron-broker-client network. Two examples are pertinent here. First, on several occasions Peter declares how he and other disciples were designated as unique witnesses to the Jesus events: "not to all the people but to us who were chosen by God as witnesses. . . . He [God] commanded us to preach to the people and to testify that he is the one ordained by God to be judge of the living and the dead" (10:41-42; see 5:32). Thus God establishes him as sub-broker to Jesus, itself an act of benefaction and favoritism. In addition, Peter mediates Jesus' healing powers, the powers given him by God: "In the name of Jesus Christ of Nazareth, walk" (3:6; 4:9-10; 9:34, 40).

Second, the story of Simon in Acts 8 deserves consideration because it illustrates how a would-be client, Simon, seeks the goods of benefaction but without any corresponding duty to any patron. Philip arrives in Samaria, and as sub-broker brings to the region the power that Jesus enjoyed and that Jesus himself brokers to others through deacons and other roles. Philip casts out unclean spirits and makes whole the lame and paralyzed (8:7). A rival broker, Simon called "Great," sees that more and more people accepted Philip's "gospel about the kingdom of God and the name of Jesus" (8:12), at which "signs and great miracles" occurred. Simon "believed," but with notable qualifications; he offers Philip money to receive the Holy Spirit (8:19). He seeks a simple exchange of goods for power, but with no element of commitment or faith whatsoever. Divine benefaction is an act of altruism, not barter; God's patronage cannot be purchased by mere money. On this very point, Lucian mocked this kind of spiritual barter in his satire on sacrifice.

> So nothing that they [the gods] do is done without compensation. They sell men their blessings, and one can buy from them health for a calf, wealth for four oxen, a royal throne for a hundred, a safe return from Troy for nine

> bulls, and a fair voyage from Aulis to Troy for a king's daughter! One may imagine, too, that they have many things on sale for the price of a cock, a wreath, or nothing more than incense. (*Sacr.* 2)

Simon, in love with the benefaction of God, nevertheless shames the Benefactor. In loyalty to his Patron-Benefactor, Philip rebukes Simon:

> Your silver perish with you, because you thought you could obtain the gift of God with money! You have neither part nor lot in this matter, for your heart is not right before God. Repent, therefore, of this wickedness of yours, and pray to the Lord that, if possible, the intent of your heart may be forgiven you. (8:20-23)

The failure of patronage expressed here includes: money for the "gift" of God, a heart that eschews God, a perverted brokerage of God's benefaction for Simon's own benefit, and a wicked person attempting to swindle a holy person. Moreover, his offer would turn Philip against his Patron, selling his God for money. Brokers, too, must be faithful. Simon must instead create a genuine patron-client relationship with God by "praying to the Lord" for forgiveness.

Summary and Conclusion

The use of the patron-broker-client model for interpreting Luke's remarks about God seems to be secure in its details, accurate for that time period, productive of insight, and integrative of many seemingly diverse elements. It expresses a common pattern of relationships in antiquity, both the roles and statuses of the persons involved and a proper categorization of the elements of benefaction bestowed.

When seen as a heavenly patron, God's relationship to Jesus and then to the expanding circle of disciples of Jesus becomes clear. On the one hand, God manifests a dramatic loyalty to Jesus, his client, by vindicating him out of death and shame. But God more than simply restored Jesus, for he "raised" him up and elevated him to a heavenly, not earthly, role and status: "God made this Jesus Lord and Christ." On the other hand, God establishes Jesus not merely as favorite client of God, but now as exclusive and permanent mediator/broker of God's benefaction. Luke expresses this in the titles and roles Jesus now enjoys ("Author of life" 3:14; "Head of the corner"

4:11; "Leader and Savior" 5:31, etc.) and in the exclusive claims made on his behalf ("salvation in no one else; no other name by which he must be saved," 4:12). Thus we observe the structural choice God made of Jesus, both on earth and now in heaven, as exclusive mediator of God's benefaction.

Of what does God's benefaction consist? The categories used by Talcott Parsons and Bruce Malina to classify benefaction are particularly useful here. A fuller exposition of this material may be had in Appendix 1, but the chart below attempts to systematize the benefactions of God to provide the fullest possible summary of God's patronage.

1. Power	liberating (2:23-24; 3:14-15; 4:10) enthronement of Jesus as Lord and Christ (2:34-36) salvation from prison (5:17-21; 12:6-11; 16:25-34), stoning (14:1), shipwreck (27:39-44), snakebite (28:1-6) bold public speech (4:8-12; 5:29-32) signs and wonders (8:15-17; 10:38) healings (3:5-6; 8:4-8; 9:17; 10:38) power over devil and spirits (13:8-11; 16:16-18; 19:11-16) judgments: (a) death of Ananias for lying to the Holy Spirit (5:4-5); (b) blinding of Elymas (13:8); (c) death of Herod (12:20-22) judgment of the living and the dead (10:42; 17:31)
2. Commitment	forgiveness of sins (2:38; 15:8-9; 19:4-5) comfort (9:31) and joy (13:52) commissioning/authorization (10:38; 13:2-4) inclusion/belonging (9:17; 10:45; 14:27; 15:8)
3. Influence	prophecies fulfilled (4:25-26; 28:25); prophecies made (11:27-28; 20:23; 22:11) gift of prophecy (19:6) visions into heaven (7:55-56); visions of heavenly figures (9:4-6; 16:6-10; 22:17-21); vision of foods from heaven (10:9-16) speaking in tongues (10:46; 19:6) instruction (15:28) and directions (8:29; 16:6-10; 22:4) speaking in [new] languages (2:5-18, 33)
4. Inducement	curiously absent

Thus, when God acts as patron and benefactor, God acts with power to raise and rescue Jesus and other clients. Power is clearly the most important and most frequently bestowed gift. Forms of influence constitute the next most prevalent benefaction of God, especially prophecy-fulfillment of past Scriptures, prophecies of events forthcoming, visions, and dreams. God also manifests commitment in faithfulness to his clients, first Jesus, but then a wide variety of peoples, such as Peter, John, the new Jesus group in Jerusalem, Cornelius and household, and Paul, who in turn faithfully defends "the resurrection" worked by God. Curiously absent is any form of inducement, such as food multiplied or other material goods.

GOD AND PROVIDENCE

Scholars more and more attend to the doctrine of providence and the important role it plays in the way Luke describes the God of Israel (Squires 1993; Carroll 2002). By way of putting this into some context, I note that some give attention to the way in which providence functions in the writing of history in antiquity (e.g., Attridge 1976:71–108). Other scholars have compared Greek historians such as Diodorus Siculus and Dionysius of Halicarnassus with Hellenistic Jewish authors such as Josephus and Philo, calling attention to the tradition of portraying providence as the guide of history (Squires 1993:15–19, 37–52; Sandmel 1980; Carson 1981b). Thus the recounting of history in antiquity tends to be narrated with providence as the organizing principle of human affairs (Downing 1981, 1982).

Scholars concerned with providence in the book of Acts generally begin with Paul's speech on the Areopagus in Acts 17. Luke says that "Epicurean and Stoic philosophers" met Paul and conversed with him (17:18), which is our initial clue to the scene. Epicureans and Stoics held strongly opposing views of the nature of the deity and the deity's actions in the world. Both could not be correct. So, in scanning Paul's remarks to them, we notice that he articulates the story of God and Jesus so as to make sense to the Stoics but not to the Epicureans. He begins: "The God who made the world and everything in it" (17:24), which resonates with the Stoic doctrine of providence, but which is anathema to Epicureans. Moreover, God structured human social patterns for peace and harmony (17:26). God's purpose in this is likewise benevolent: "that all should seek God . . . and find him" (17:27). Scholars call this type of discourse "natural theology," a viewpoint that the deity may be discerned from the beauty and orderliness of created things, which discernment leads to a proper relationship with God (H. Owen 1959; Gärtner 1955:73–143). The God of the Scriptures, who is the Christian God, is the focus of Paul's speech (Dibelius 1956:22–76; Legrand 1976), a common focus in Paul's own preaching (see I Thess 1:9; 1 Cor 8:4-6). With this secure clue that Luke indeed employs the doctrine of providence, let us briefly survey the extensive use of this theology in the book of Acts.

It has long been recognized that Luke speaks the language of providence in his presentation of God in Acts. That is, he understands God's orderly and benevolent relationship to the world in a systematic way that is part of both Israelite wisdom literature and Greek Stoic philosophy. This theology might be considered the "orthodoxy" of the ancient world. But what constituted the ancient Israelite and Stoic doctrine of divine providence? Why was Luke so eager to describe the God of Israel in this way? And how does this relate to the model of patron/benefactor-broker-client discussed above?

In Hellenistic theology, God's providence typically includes the following elements. (1) God exists and is active. (2) God, who is wise and good, acts wisely and in goodness. (3) God, who is most rational, acts reasonably in the way the cosmos is ordered and structured. (4) God alone knows the future, but makes this known to mortals in portents, signs, and prophecies. (5) The actions of God can be summarized in two ways: (a) God creates, orders, and maintains the world; and (b) God exercises executive and judgmental functions over it. (6) God is both benevolent and just. (7) Providence is shown in a variety of ways in the world: (a) the order and regularity of creation, (b) the giving of oracles and revelations to mortals, (c) the protective care given to good individuals, and (d) the just judgment of evildoers (Downing 1981:548–49). Such actions befit a deity who is wise, powerful, benevolent, and just. It remains to see how much of the contents of this Hellenistic doctrine of providence we find in Acts.

I mentioned above that Paul's speech in Acts 17 formally and explicitly contains remarks about God-who-is-provident. God is creator: "God, who made the world and everything in it" (17:24); and God is benevolent orderer: "God made from one every nation of men to live on all the face of the earth, having determined allotted periods and boundaries of their habitation" (17:26). The following outline consists of as much data in Acts as we can find, which is then systematized around the native model of providence.

The Doctrine of Providence in the Acts of the Apostles

1. Creation (4:24; 14:15; 17:24)
2. Divine foreknowledge and plan
   - a. 2:23; 4:28
   - b. *dei*: 14:22; 17:3 (Cosgrove 1984)
3. Oracles of the future
   - a. prophecy-fulfillment: what God prophesied long ago has come true for Christ and his followers (2:14-21, 25-30; 3:19-22; 4:25-28; etc.)
   - b. oracles delivered during the narrative of Acts that come true (11:27-30; 21:10-14; 22:17-21; 27:23-27)
4. Benevolent control of history
   - a. the rescue of good people
     - 1) Peter (4; 5; 12:1-12)
     - 2) Stephen (7:54-56)
     - 3) Paul (16:19-39; 17:1-9, 12-15; 18:5-11; 19:23-20:1; 21:27-39; 22:22-29; 23:12-31; 27:9-44; 28:1-6)
   - b. control of natural events
     - 1) famine (11:28-30)
     - 2) storms (27:13-44)
     - 3) snakebite (28:3-6)
5. Just judgment of sinners
   - a. judgment of Ananias and Sapphira (5:1-6)
   - b. judgment of Herod (12:23)
6. Theodicy: Postmortem judgment
   - a. Jesus, judge of the living and dead (10:42; 17:31)
   - b. future judgment (24:25)

When a reader with an accurate appreciation of providence in the ancient world reads Acts according to the categories above, it becomes self-evident that Luke's God is a provident, just, and benevolent Deity. Moreover, the benevolence of this providential Deity is easily recognized as the content of the benefaction that the divine Patron/Benefactor bestows on "those who fear him."

Paul's address to Stoics and Epicureans in Acts 17 represents the favorite scholarly expression of God's providence in the document, but it is by no means the only one. The prayer offered in 4:23-31 by the young church after the release of Peter and John from custody is a remarkable study of divine faithfulness and power. The following chart contains the text of the prayer in the right column, along with in the left column the labeling of the aspect of divine providence that corresponds to it.

God of creation	Sovereign Lord, who made the heaven and the earth and the sea and everything in them
God of prophecy	who by the mouth of our father David, your servant, said by the Holy Spirit, "Why did the Gentiles rage, and the peoples imagine vain things? The kings of the earth set themselves in array, and the rulers were gathered together, against the Lord and against his Anointed"
God of fulfillment	for truly in this city there were gathered together against thy holy servant Jesus, whom thou didst anoint, both Herod and Pontius Pilate, with the Gentiles and the peoples of Israel
God of history	to do whatever thy hand and thy plan had predestined to take place
God of power and protection —Savior	Lord, look upon their threats, and grant to thy servants to speak thy word with all boldness, while thou stretchest out thy hand to heal, and signs and wonders are performed through the name of thy holy servant Jesus
God who answers prayers	And when they had prayed, the place in which they were gathered together was shaken; and they were all filled with the Holy Spirit and spoke the word of God with boldness

We should compare Luke's appeal to God's providence with that of Josephus, who created the following address of Moses to the Israelites cowering on the shores of the Red Sea in their flight from Egypt. This parallel will confirm the way I read Acts 4:23-31 and the typical theological understanding of providence among writers of history.

> To despair at this moment of the providence of God were an act of madness, seeing that from Him there has come to you everything He promised to perform through me for your salvation and deliverance from bondage,

> though far beyond your expectations. Rather ought you to expect help from God, who, in extricating you from extremities, may display both His own power and His tender care for you. Wherefore have faith in such a defender, who has power alike to make the little great and to sentence such mighty hosts as these to impotence. (Josephus, *Ant.* 2.130-33)

Although Josephus uses the technical term "providence of God," which Luke does not use, they both identify the provident God in the same ways: God's knowledge of the future expressed in promises that are fulfilled; God's power to save from death and deliver from prison; God's dual attributes, power and tender care; God's action as savior and defender of a people toward whom he shows faithfulness.

I argue that Luke's audience would appreciate this material in two ways, both as an illustration of God's providence but also in terms of God's patronage. Indeed, many of the categories overlap or, as anthropologists say, are redundant and so reinforcing. What providence adds to patron-client relations is its sense of the temporal nature of God's care, from creation to new creation; moreover, providence makes salient the pattern of prophecy-fulfillment embedded in Israel's Scriptures as words spoken long ago are now seen as prophecies fulfilled in the hearing of Luke's audience. This pattern of prophecy-fulfillment functions to confirm the commitment of the provident God whose faithfulness can be trusted. These times, then, are the best of times.

GOD AND THEODICY

In antiquity the issue of justice in the world and of God's judgment was part of the larger theological system we call theodicy. So important was this topic that we find numerous examples of a stereotype about theodicy in Greco-Roman, Israelite, and Christian literature. At stake is the issue of a moral world: Does it matter to God if mortals do good or do evil? Will the wicked eventually fare the same as the good? As mentioned above, the Stoics and the Epicureans were positioned on opposite sides of the issue. The Stoics affirmed that God is rational and just, has put order into the world, legislated reasonable laws, and allocates rewards or punishments accordingly. In contrast, the Epicureans argued that God "has no trouble and brings no trouble upon any other being; hence God is exempt from movements of anger and partiality" (Diogenes Laertius 10.139). Whereas the Stoic deity, who is justly involved in the affairs of this world, renders judgment according to one's rational behavior, Epicurus's God is not involved at all, shows neither anger nor partiality, and so does not judge.

The simple assertion of a just universe guided by a provident God runs into a major obstacle when the deity is slow to judge or when divine judgment is delayed. Philosophers formed a special argument to counteract this obstacle. We find this very debate in Plutarch's *Delay of Divine Judgment,* where we first hear standard antitheodicy polemics attributed to Epicureans, then a vigorous refutation of them. Speaking in defense of God's providence and so God's judgment, a speaker states: "It is one and the same argument that establishes both the providence of God and the survival of the human soul, and it is impossible to upset the one contention and let the other stand. But if the soul survives, we must expect that its due in honor and in punishment is awarded after death rather than before" (Plutarch, *Delay of Divine Judgment* 560F; see Neyrey 1980:411–14). From this argument and many other examples of it, I infer that traditional belief in divine theodicy entails three key, interrelated elements: (1) God as judge, (2) survival of death, and (3) postmortem retribution by God (Neyrey 1990:124–34).

If this is the positive presentation of belief in theodicy, the shape of its denial is equally important to us. Epicurus, accounted as the chief antagonist of belief in divine theodicy, makes his own three key elements against theodicy. (1) Denial of "providence": God is neither kind nor angry, for God is not moved by passions: "A blessed and eternal being has no trouble and brings no trouble upon any other being" (Diogenes Laertius 10.139). God, then, does *not* judge. (2) Epicurus declares the finality of death: "Death is nothing to us; for the body, when it has been resolved into its elements, has no feeling; and that which has no feeling is nothing to us" (Diogenes Laertius 10.139). There is, then, no survival after death. (3) Hence there is no postmortem retribution. Just as traditional theodicy affirms three items (judge, survival of death, postmortem retribution), Epicurus denied all three. We find, then, two diametrically opposed positions on whether God judges. Which one is right? Which one does Luke adopt?

Paul's presentation in the Areopagus speech of God's providential judgment fully contains the three elements of the traditional argument on theodicy we have just observed. (1) God judges: "God has fixed a day on which he will judge the world in righteousness by a man whom he has appointed" (17:31a). (2) Human survival of death: (a) We must note that Paul preached "the resurrection" (17:18), which is not simply the announcement of Jesus' resurrection but the survival of death by all people (see Acts 10:42). (b) Paul specifically states that God gave assurance of the coming judgment by raising Jesus from the dead, not simply to constitute him as judge, but also to give proof that there will be a resurrection unto judgment (17:31b). (3) Postmortem retribution: the "resurrection" that Paul proclaims is "resurrection unto judgment." On that future day, God will "judge the world in righteousness" (17:31) by Jesus, whom God has appointed to "judge the living and the dead" (Acts 10:42). Those to be judged are not just Christians who are alive and Christians who have died (see 1 Thess 4:14-17), but all people, including and especially the dead (see Acts 24:25). In summary, addressed as it is to Stoics and Epicureans, the Areopagus speech is about God's providence and theodicy, and especially the agreement between Stoic and Christian views.

But Acts 17 is by no means the only evidence of a debate over providence and theodicy in Acts. The same issues, pro and con, occur in the trials of Paul in Acts 23 and 24. Let us take the clearer example first, the trial of Paul before Governor Felix in Acts 24. Paul delivers a defense of his doctrine during a solemn trial before Felix (24:10-21). Tertullus, the spokesman for the priestly party, has already charged Paul with being a deviant ("pestilent fellow . . . agitator among all the Jews . . . ringleader of the sect of the Nazarenes," 24:5). According to him, Paul stands totally outside the mainstream of Israelite theology and propounds heterodox doctrines. Paul, however, defends his orthodoxy, in this case, his claim to be solidly loyal to the traditions about Israel's God. The focus, while on Paul's theology and his doctrine of God, is specifically on the issue of theodicy.

In the course of Paul's speech, he shapes the trial so as to make the formal "question for judgment" the general issue of "the resurrection" (Neyrey 1984:211–16): "With respect to the resurrection of the dead I am on trial before you this day" (24:21). Although one might presume that Paul alludes to Jesus' resurrection, his speech before Felix contains no explicit mention of Jesus at all. Rather, the reference to "the resurrection" is cast here in terms of traditional faith in Israel's God to raise the dead. It is, then, exclusively about the correct doctrine of God. As Paul says, "I worship the God of our fathers, believing everything laid down by the law or written in the prophets" (24:14). More specifically, Paul focuses his claim to orthodox theology on the precise issue of theodicy: "having a hope in God which these themselves accept, that there will be a resurrection of both the just and the unjust" (24:15). This "resurrection" comprises both survival of death ("resurrection") and portmortem retribution ("of the just and unjust"). Thus Paul's apologetic remarks in 24:15 contain the three traditional aspects of theodicy: (1) a judge: "justice" refers here to forensic judgment and implies a judge who dispenses this justice; (2) survival of death: "future judgment"; the future aspect of this judgment implies that all will survive death so as to be there; (3) postmortem retribution: at this "future judgment," a just forensic judgment will be rendered on the basis of the moral principle of self-control, one of the four cardinal virtues. Paul's theodicy, then, is orthodox, not heterodox.

Several more important data deserve consideration. In Acts 17 Paul spoke about his provident God to Stoics and Epicureans, an audience chosen because they hold mutually opposed views on providence and theodicy. I do not consider it accidental that the accusations against Paul, who was of the Pharisaic party, are made by the priestly party. The importance of this suggestion can be clarified by examination of Acts 23 (Neyrey 1990a:126–27).

Luke does things in twos and he favors parallels. (1) Contrasting audiences*:* Just as Stoics and Epicureans listened to Paul in Athens, so in Caesarea Paul's audience consists of Sadducees and Pharisees, two groups who disagree on most things: "One part were Sadducees and the other Pharisees" (23:6a). (2) Allies and enemies*:* Just as Paul's doctrine elicited the favor of the Stoics but the mockery of the Epicureans, so in Caesarea Paul allies himself with the Pharisees, thus ensuring rejection by the Sadducees: "I am a Pharisee, the son of Pharisees" (23:6b). (3) Resurrection: Just as the point of Paul's speech in Athens was the resurrection (he "preached . . . the resurrection," 17:18), so Paul declares to Pharisees and Sadducees "the resurrection of the dead" as the forensic point of judgment: "With respect to the . . . resurrection of the dead I am on trial" (23:6c). (4) Theodicy*:* Just as Luke could presume that his readers clearly distinguished Stoics and Epicureans on the issue of providence and theodicy, so the trial in Acts 23 works precisely because the Sadducees and Pharisees are known to hold opposite views on this central issue: "For the Sadducees say that there is no resurrection, nor angel, nor spirit; but the Pharisees acknowledge them all" (23:8). From a study of the way Luke typically presents characters and issues, then, these parallels between the contrasting reactions to Paul's speeches persuade me that Luke intends us to see Epicureans and Stoics holding contrasting views on theodicy in Acts 17, just as Sadducees and Pharisees differ on "the resurrection" in Acts 23.

Readers of the Gospels come to identify the Sadducees in terms of a stereotype, namely, their denial of "the resurrection": "And Sadducees came to him, who say that there is no resurrection" (Mark 12:18; see Matt 22:32 and Luke 20:27). Nothing suggests that they are reacting to Jesus' own resurrection, but rather are well known as denying survival after death. It is the stereotypical way in which people know the Sadducees.

This stereotypical perception of Sadducees and Pharisees is found elsewhere. When Josephus describes the Sadducees and the Pharisees to non-Israelites, he likens them to Epicureans and Stoics—precisely in terms of their stereotypical stands on theodicy. In several places, Josephus compares the Pharisees (an Israelite sect) with the Stoics (a Greco-Roman philosophy) in terms of providence and theodicy. For example, "The Pharisees, who are considered the most accurate interpreters of the laws, and hold the position of the leading sect, attribute everything to Fate and to God. . . . Every soul, they maintain, is imperishable, but the soul of the good alone passes into another body, while the souls of the wicked suffer eternal punishment" (*War* 2.162-63; see *Ant.* 13.172; 18.12-15).

In this description, we find the three familiar elements of orthodox theodicy. (1) God is judge: "Fate or God is all powerful"; (2) survival of death: the soul is "imperishable"; and (3) postmortem retribution: "the soul of the good passes into another body, while the souls of the wicked suffer eternal punishment." This text serves two purposes. First, Stoics are themselves known by their stereotypical theodicy beliefs. Second, the same stereotypical beliefs are thought adequately to describe the Pharisees.

Conversely, if Pharisees resemble Stoics, Sadducees can be likened to Epicureans. Josephus does this when he calls the Pharisees, Sadducees, and Essenes "three philosophies" (*War* 2.119), indicating that Pharisees = Stoics, Essenes = Pythagoreans, and Sadducees = Epicureans. Josephus also describes the belief system of the Sadducees in stereotypical form as those who reject theodicy. For example, "The Sadducees, the second of the orders, do away with Fate altogether, and remove God beyond, not merely the commission, but the very sight of evil. . . . As for persistence of the soul after death, penalties in the underworld, and rewards, they will have none of them" (Josephus, *War* 2.164-65).

Again, the three elements of the argument are evident: (1) no judge: "They remove God even from the sight of evil," that is, judgment; (2) no survival of death: "As for the persistence of the soul after death . . . they will have none"; and (3) no postmortem retribution: "As for . . . penalties in the underworld, they will have none." According to Josephus, Sadducees correspond exactly to Epicureans in terms of their denial of theodicy.

One more text deserves attention. In certain Targums on Gen 4:8, Cain and Abel debate the justice of God. Cain's sacrifice was not accepted, so he dismisses God's justice; Abel, whose sacrifice was accepted, defends God.

Cain said to Abel:	**Abel answered and said to Cain:**
"There is no Judgement, there is no Judge, there is no other world, there is no gift of good reward for the just and no punishment for the wicked."	"There is Judgement, there is a Judge, there is the gift of good reward for the just and punishment for the wicked" (Vermes 1975: 96–100)

The debate between Cain and Abel revolves around two issues, providence and theodicy. Like the Stoics and Epicureans, and the Pharisees and Sadducees, Abel and Cain voice stereotypical arguments for and against theodicy. In this exchange we readily discern the three key elements that comprise the doctrine on theodicy:

Theodicy Denied (Cain)	*Theodicy Affirmed (Abel)*
1. God is not a judge "There is no Judge"	1. God is a just judge: "There is a Judge"
2. No survival of death: "There is no other world"	2. Survival of death: "There is another world"
3. No postmortem retribution "There is no Judgement"	3. Postmortem retribution "There is Judgement"

Just as Josephus described Sadducees and Pharisees in terms of their opposing points of view on theodicy, so we find Cain and Abel contrasted point for point on the same topic.

Now to summarize what we have learned in this discussion of providence and theodicy. "God is the primary actor throughout Luke-Acts, for the actions of God extend throughout the whole span of history, from creation to final judgment" (Squires 1993:2). Once we know the structure of ancient thought on providence and theodicy, we can appreciate their presence and importance in Luke's presentation of God. I presented earlier a summary list of six elements of the doctrine of providence shared by Luke with Greek Stoic philosophers and Israelite wisdom and historical writings. My investigation of Luke 17, 23, and 24 surfaced a stereotype on theodicy consisting of three recurring elements: God as judge, postmortem survival, and postmortem rewards and punishments. For Christians these two aspects of God, providence and theodicy, mean the following. (1) God as provident. God is a benevolent, active deity, who created the world in orderliness and guides and governs its history. God, then, is Lord of all peoples in all places. God's will can be discerned in creation's rational patterns and in the prophetic Scriptures whereby God paved the way for the life, death, and exaltation of the Christ. (2) God's theodicy. The confession that Jesus will "judge the living and the dead" is grounded on a special aspect of God's provident rule, namely, God's just judgment. God has a definite will and plan, such that those who follow it prosper and those who forsake it falter. The postmortem nature of this judgment meshes closely with the proclamation of "the resurrection," both Christ's and the general notion of a universal survival of death. In Luke's scheme of things, God has invested Jesus, his broker, with this task.

Why does Luke employ notions of providence in describing God? What rhetorical function might he have in doing this? As regards the first question, the data suggest that Luke shared this theology of providence from the start. He did not choose this over that doctrine; the Israelite religion that he knew, as well as the Hellenistic philosophy he seems to have studied, is the common and current way of talking about God. Any right-thinking person, he might say, knows this; providence represents the orthodoxy of his day. This is not to deny that Luke sees the doctrine of providence as a most apt system of talking about Christian concerns. The fit is remarkable. Concerning the second question, scholars currently affirm that a significant function of Luke's

God-talk is apologetic (Cadbury 1958:308–16; Esler 1987:205–19; Squires 1993:40–43, 52–55) in response to certain real or perceived accusations. This apology might address any number of issues: Christianity, a "new" religion, lacks respect; members of it belong to the lowest social strata; it is highly secretive, and thus suspect; and Judeans attack it vigorously (Malherbe 1985). The language of providence and theodicy argues that the Christian Deity is not "new" but is the same Deity who made the world in wisdom. Nor is God's plan new, since it was already encoded in the prophecies of Israel's Scriptures. Nor is Christian discussion of God a secret or gnostic growth; it has much in common with the philosophy of God in the Greco-Roman and Judean worlds. Finally, Judeans have no cause to attack Christianity, because the belief of Jesus' disciples *is* the faith of Israel, as Paul insists (24:14-15). One significant benefit from Luke's conscious use of the theology of providence comes in the form of a systematic understanding of God and God's relationship to the world.

WHAT DO WE KNOW IF WE KNOW THIS?

1. *Native models.* The three models I have used to surface data and interpret it are all native patterns of perception in antiquity. Israelites and Greek alike think of God in terms of benefaction, providence, and theodicy.

2. *Ancient "orthodoxy."* Luke makes sure that his audience knows that the Christian God-talk stands in solid agreement with "orthodox" Israelite and Greco-Roman discourse. On the one hand, Luke's description of God's providence and theodicy are seen as compatible with the viewpoint of Israel's Pharisees and the Stoics of the Greco-Roman world. Similarly, it clashes with what was considered deviant theology argued by Epicureans and Sadducees.

3. *Altruistic benefaction.* The God of Jesus Christ is a most benevolent benefactor whose pleasure it is to give gifts and grant favors of every sort. God's benefaction is freely given, so it has the widest scope of places and persons. Thus traditional favoritism in benefaction is in the process of being transformed in terms of God's impartiality (10:34) and inclusivity. Moreover, God's gifts and the realms in which God works his benefaction are unlike what is found in Greco-Roman God-talk. In the latter, gods are task-, gift-, or place-specific: Ceres bestows grain; Aphrodite incites love; Mars governs

success in war; Athena inspires the arts; and Poseidon is master of the sea. The God of Jesus Christ works his pleasure in the heavens ("Sit at my right hand," 12:36), on the sea (Paul's storm and shipwreck, 27:13-44), and on land (Philip). Moreover, God's benefactions extend to the symbolic media of power, commitment, and influence. God, then, is the benefactor of all peoples, in every way, in all places.

4. *Providence.* Providence in some ways overlaps with benefaction, although they are not the same. If benefaction looks to a wide range of goods and benefits bestowed to diverse peoples in many places, the doctrine of providence reflects a concern with time past, present, and future. In both the Deity acts with kindness and generosity, but providence stresses God's plan, order, and purpose in the world. Hence God creates (4:24; 17:24-27), guides all by his will and plan (2:23; 4:28), and will preside over all human activity at its final moment (17:31). God's plan has spoken in prophecies whose fulfillment in the present indicates both divine knowledge and control of human affairs. New prophecies are made in the present that affect the future. All of this is calculated both to honor God's Christ and to lead all people to God's kingdom.

5. *Theodicy.* The God of Jesus Christ, like all "orthodox" deities, acts in profound justice in the world. While some wicked are punished in present time (5:1-11; 12:20-23) and many just people are rewarded now, the providential plan of God looks to the future when the man whom God appointed will judge the living and the dead. This future scenario contains three related elements: God indeed judges; there is postmortem existence; rewards and punishments will be allocated to the good and the wicked in the afterlife. Theodicy in one sense articulates a part of the doctrine of providence, namely, that a rational Deity made a reasonable world with clear laws and will hold people to account to know and follow them. This adds to providence the element of justice: as one sows, so shall one reap. As with other aspects of God-talk, Luke allies his gospel of God with the "orthodox" viewpoint of Pharisees and Stoics.

6. *Synoptic theology.* Finally, let us compare Mark, Matthew, and Acts to see what elements are found in each and the relative emphasis given them.

Mark	Matthew	Acts
1. ———————	1. Strong mention of "covenants of promise" (1:1-18; 8:5-13)	1. Passing reference to "covenant with David and Abraham" (13:17-26)
2. Patron-Benefactor: all four symbolic media bestowed	2. Patron-Benefactor: all four symbolic media bestowed	2. Patron-Benefactor: three symbolic media bestowed
3. Patron to Jesus, vindication of client	3. Patron to Jesus, vindication of client, supreme endowment in heavenly world	3. Patron to Jesus and then to Jesus' disciples; story begins with heavenly enthronement of Jesus as "Lord and Christ" and envisions his acting as judge
4. Spirit Benefaction: limited functions: authorization of Jesus and power to war on unclean spirits	4. Spirit Benefaction: limited functions: authorization of Jesus and power to war on unclean spirits	4. Spirit Benefaction: Jesus empowered to bestow Spirit in a range of functions: power, commitment, and influence
5. Formal defense of "the things of God" (12:13-37)	5. Formal defense of "the things of God" (22:21)	5. Formal defense of God: 17:24-30; 24:14-15
6. ———————	6. God as King and God's kingdom described	6. ———————
7. God and purity: Jesus authorized to change purity rules	7. God and purity: Jesus authorized to change purity rules	7. God and purity: visions authorize reclassification of unclean foods and persons
8. Providence: mainly vindication of Jesus after death	8. Providence: deliverance of the baby Jesus and crucified Jesus; providence manifested in prophecy-fulfillment pattern	8. Providence: formal articulation of concept (17:17-31; see 7:23-31); constant demonstration of providence
9. Resurrection: God's supreme power and patronage	9. Resurrection: God's supreme power and patronage	9. Resurrection: God's supreme power and patronage; postmortem existence as prelude to judgment
10. Prophecy-fulfillment modestly treated	10. Prophecy-fulfillment strongly emphasized	10. Prophecy-fulfillment as major element of providence
11. Inarticulated theodicy	11. Inarticulated theodicy	11. Strongly articulated theodicy, orthodox contrasted with heterodox views

What this analysis suggests is that Mark has a rich theology, but it is less conceptually articulated than Matthew's and is outclassed by that of Luke. Whereas Mark and Matthew look to God's actions primarily in the career of Jesus-the-client, Luke begins where they leave off, namely, God's heavenly enthronement of Jesus. At this point, God formally endows Jesus with the dispensation of the divine benefaction of God's Spirit, and positions him as the cosmic and eternal "Lord and Christ" and "Judge." Whereas Mark and Matthew spend much time arguing the case for "render to God what is God's," which is a distinctively Israelite matter, Luke tells of a Deity who fulfills the expectations of Israelites and Greek and Romans in terms of mainstream theology: God as Benefactor, as provident Deity, and as just Judge.

4

A SYSTEMATIC THEOLOGY

GOD IN ROMANS

The righteousness of God is revealed . . .
—Rom 1:17

The wrath of God is revealed . . .
—Rom 1:18

INTRODUCTION, TOPIC, AND DEVELOPMENT

One of the most important rules for a person learning rhetoric and public speaking is to ensure that one's audience is attentive and sympathetic to the writer or speaker. This is usually done in the beginning of a speech, the rhetorical part that the ancients called a *captatio benevolentiae* ("creating good-will"), such as we find in the speeches both of Paul (Acts 24:10-11; 26:1-3) and of Paul's accuser, Tertullus (Acts 24:2-3). A comparable thing seems to be going on in Romans, first in the letter's opening and then in its conclusion. As letter types go, Romans is variously classified as a "letter-essay" (Stirewalt 1991:147–74), a *logos protreptikos* (Aune 1997), or some other type. Some data in Romans lead many to classify it also as a letter of recommendation. In the letter's opening, Paul tells its recipients of his eager plans to come to Rome (1:10-15), uncertain whether they are equally eager to receive him. In the letter's closing, before Paul recommends Phoebe to the Romans (16:1-2), he talks further about why he is leaving his own turf and his own churches in the east and coming west: "I no longer have any room for work in these parts . . . I hope to see you in passing" (15:23). But "at present I am going to Jerusalem with aid for the saints" (15:24); then he will resume his apostolic role by seeking out lands that have not yet heard the gospel: "my ambition [is] to preach the gospel, not where Christ has already been named, lest I build on another man's foundation" (15:20). One reason for writing Romans, then, is to render the Roman churches favorable to his visit.

But is Paul leaving the east? He jealously defended his foundations; he was proud to be a "wise master builder" and "father" to the church in Corinth. He says that he is taking alms to the Jerusalem church, but is fearful whether "my service in Jerusalem may be acceptable to the saints" (15:31). We sense that in the social struggles between Paul, Jerusalem, and even his own foundations, he somehow lost the war. Scholars like Marshall (1987) have culled from his letters a list of things Paul is regularly accused of: flattery; being weak/sickly; not being eloquent or enlightened; constantly conflictual; embarrassing to his churches (2 Corinthians 11–12; all *peristasis* catalogues); runt of apostles, not worthy to be called an apostle (1 Cor 15:7-11); having persecuted the church; being fickle (2 Cor 10:10; 2 Cor 1:19ff.); holding questionable ideas about Scripture; urging a curious ethics: no laws or responsibility; being patronizing, for he taught others only the rudiments, not the real foods (milk, not meat); and engaging in honor challenges with the Jerusalem "pillars" (Gal 2:1-10). These constitute some of the grounds for understanding Paul's failure in the east. But has this reputation preceded him to Rome? Who would want to accept such a contentious and confused person? What he needs, then, is a letter of recommendation in which he deals with the most important of these issues, his "gospel," that is, the "gospel of God."

SYSTEMATIC GOD-TALK IN GRECO-ROMAN PHILOSOPHY

I argue that Paul was aware of controversial aspects of his "gospel" for which purpose he makes the elaborate and elegant presentation in Romans. He seems just as aware of the need to present this "gospel" in a traditional fashion, which in this case means using the categories that all Greco-Roman philosophers used in presenting their systematic doctrine on God: epistemology, physics, and ethics. "Epistemology" refers to the sources of our knowledge; "physics," to the nature of God; and "ethics," to the life of virtue or vice that follows from this. This schema can be found throughout the Greco-Roman world, and I will consider two examples, Diogenes Laertius's record of Epicurus, and Cicero's *On the Nature of the Gods*.

Epicurus's philosophy was "divided into three parts—Canonic, Physics, Ethics" (Diogenes Laertius 10.30). By "canonic" Epicurus meant our sources of knowledge, that is, epistemology—what we know and how we know it. "Epistemology" comprises the first part of Epicurus's doctrine (10.31-40). "Physics" deals with issues of change, the nature of the soul, and God (10.41-116). Finally, "ethics" discourses on the virtuous life that should follow from the first two, such as defining the "wise man," happiness, piety, not fearing death, and pleasure (10.117-54). These three elements form a logical unity, for depending on one's knowledge, one will affirm thus or such about God, and hence act in a specific way.

Using these three categories, Cicero describes the philosophy of Epicurus. His exposition only intends to display that this form of systematic thinking was widespread in the Greco-Roman world and readily understood. As regards Epicurus's epistemology, Cicero states:

> He alone perceived, first, that the gods exist, because nature herself has imprinted a conception of them on the minds of all mankind. What nation or what tribe of men is there but possesses untaught some "preconception" of the gods? (Cicero, *Nature of the Gods* 1.43)

Knowledge of God is innate in every soul ("nature imprinted a concept of them on the minds of all"). But it is not the prerogative of any ethnos or philosophical school, nor is it the result of investigation or logical reasoning.

Under the rubric of "physics," the nature of God is then described:

> we believe the gods to be blessed and immortal. For nature, which bestowed upon us an idea of the gods themselves, also engraved on our minds the belief that they are eternal and blessed. If this is so, the famous maxim of Epicurus truthfully enunciates that "that which is blessed and eternal can neither know trouble itself nor cause trouble to another, and accordingly cannot feel either

> anger or favor, since all such things belong only to the weak." (*Nature of the Gods* 1.45)

In regard to God's nature, the Deity is eternal; he has no beginning or ending. In relationship to mortals, because God is "blessed," the Deity is utterly untroubled and is moved neither by favor nor anger toward them.

Finally, according to the ethics of Epicurus, if God is eternally blessed and not involved in the chaos of this world, and if God shows neither anger nor favor, human behavior is at its best when it too seeks "pleasure" and avoids all disturbance.

> Their [the gods'] mode of life is the happiest conceivable, and the one most bountifully furnished with all good things. God is entirely inactive and free from all ties of occupation; he toils not, neither does he labor, but he takes delight in his own wisdom and virtue, and knows with absolute certainty that he will always enjoy pleasures at once consummate and everlasting. . . . We for our part deem happiness to consist in tranquillity of mind and entire exemption from all duties. (*Nature of the Gods* 1.51, 53)

Proper ethics, then, flows from the proper understanding of God. If God is totally "untroubled," then so should wise mortals be also. This is not an appeal to hedonism, but rather to an avoidance of slavelike toil, competition, war, and what we call stress-producing labors. The point of this is not to argue that Paul thinks like an Epicurean, but rather that he thinks like a philosopher; he understands these three key elements, and he appreciates that they constitute a system.

PAUL'S THEOLOGICAL SYSTEM: EPISTEMOLOGY, PHYSICS, AND ETHICS

Epistemology

At the beginning of Romans, Paul identifies two sources of knowledge about God. From the created world, Paul argues that all peoples can know God: "For what can be known about God is plain to them, because God has shown it to them" (1:19), a type of "natural theology" commonly held by Stoics and Hellenistic Israelites (see, e.g., Pohlenz 1949). This general source of knowledge of God is balanced by the specific source, namely, Israel's Scriptures.

The study of Paul's use of Scripture is best found in works like that of Richard Hays (1989), so I need only make some summary observations.

1. What parts of Scripture? Paul strongly relies on the Abraham/patriarchal narratives in Genesis, the prophets (especially Isaiah), and the Psalms. He avoids the Pentateuch, unless he finds useful items in it, such as Exod 33:19 (Rom 9:15) or Lev 18:5 (Rom 10:5) or Deut 9:4 and 30:12-14 (Rom 10:6-8).

2. Why are these chosen? As we shall see, these selections best express Paul's view of God and likewise provide proof of his orthodoxy.

3. Does Paul have a special hermeneutic? Most definitely, for Paul reads the Scriptures with a special lens that sees them as prophecy (not law or Torah). We can distinguish three modes of Pauline reading:

a. Scripture as prophetic word: "to God who is able to strengthen you according to my gospel and the proclamation of Jesus Christ . . . through the prophetic writings made known to all the Gentiles" (16:26).

b. Scripture containing a promise: "to them belong the adoption, the glory, the covenants . . . and the promises" (9:4); "Christ has become a servant of the circumcised on behalf of the truth of God in order that he might confirm the promises given to the patriarchs" (15:8; see also 4:13-16).

c. Mystery now revealed: "according to the revelation of the mystery that was kept secret for long ages but is now disclosed" (16:25). Thus, "It is not as though the word of God had failed" (9:6), but it needs to be filtered through the lens of prophecy/promise-fulfillment. The chart below summarizes the materials from Scripture that Paul chooses to explain or justify his view of God.

4. What does Paul's selection of Scripture say about God? The following chart, indeed, is a preview of coming attractions, but for the sake of the large picture of Paul's epistemology, I offer the three following topics as principles governing Paul's choice of scriptural materials.

1. Materials about God's two covenants	a. Covenant with David: "David pronounces a blessing on those to whom God reckons righteousness apart from works" (4:6; cf. Ps 32:1-3; see also Rom 1:3) b. Covenant with Abraham and the patriarchs: "Abraham believed God and it was credited to him as righteousness" (4:3; cf. Gen 15:6; and Rom 4:1-24; 9:6-13) c. God's covenantal inclusivity and impartiality: "The scripture says, 'No one who believes in him will be put to shame' [Isa 28:16]. For there is no distinction between Jew and Greek; the same Lord is Lord of all and is generous to all who call on him. 'Everyone who calls on the name of the Lord shall be saved' [Joel 2:32]" (Rom 10:11-13; see also 15:7-13) d. God's covenant fidelity: "It is not as though the word of God had failed: 'It is through Isaac that descendants shall be named for you' [Gen 21:12]. . . . 'The elder shall serve the younger' [Gen 25:23]. As it is written, 'I have loved Jacob, but I have hated Esau' [Mal 1:2-3]" (Rom 9:7-13)
2. Materials illustrating God's two attributes	a. Attribute of just judgment. (1) God as just judge: Although everyone is a liar, let God be proved true, as it is written, 'So that you may be justified in your words, and prevail in your judging' [Ps 116:11]. But if our injustice serves to confirm the justice of God, what should we say? That God is unjust to inflict wrath on us? By no means! For then how could God judge the world?" (Rom 3:4-6). (2) Just punishment of sinners: "For we have already charged that all, both Jews and Greeks, are under the power of sin, as it is written: 'There is no one who is righteous, not even one' [Ps 14:1-2]. . . . 'Their throats are open graves; they use their tongues to deceive' [Ps 5:9]. . . . 'There is no fear of God before their eyes' [Ps 36:1]" (Rom 3:9-18) b. Attribute of mercy: "'Blessed are those whose iniquities are forgiven, and whose sins are covered; blessed is the one against whom the Lord will not reckon sin' [Ps 32:1-2]" (Rom 4:7-8); "'I will have mercy on whom I have mercy, and I will have compassion on whom I have compassion' [Exod 33:19]" (Rom 9:15); "'Those who were not my people I will call "my people," and her who was not beloved I will call "beloved"' [Hos 2:23]" (Rom 9:25)
3. Materials celebrating superiority of "grace and faith"	"If Abraham was justified by works, he has something to boast about, but not before God. For what does the scripture say? 'Abraham believed God, and it was reckoned to him as righteousness' [Gen 15:6]. Now to one who works, wages are not reckoned as a gift but as something due. But to one who without works trusts him who justifies the ungodly, such faith is reckoned as righteousness" (Rom 4:3-6; see also 4:9, 22)

Physics or the Nature of God

As regards Paul's physics, he quickly tells his readers about the nature of God: "God's invisible nature, namely his eternal power and deity, has been clearly perceived in all things that have been made" (1:20). At this point he has not told his readers what comprises "God's invisible nature," but as we shall shortly see, the nature of God is to be "merciful" and benevolent, as well as to "judge justly." Later Paul will emphasize that God has two powers, creative and executive, an emphasis squarely on God's power to raise the dead. Thus Paul seems quite aware of articulating the nature of God from the beginning of his letter. I will return to this topic shortly.

Ethics

From this epistemology and physics Paul draws ethical conclusions. First, he condemns people who refused to acknowledge God in creation, which failure led them to moral depravity: "although they knew God they did not honor him as God or give thanks to him, but they became futile in their thinking and their senseless minds were darkened" (1:21). Similarly, although God does not judge the wicked immediately, they perversely misconstrue this as an argument that God does not judge and so do not change their ways. Thus rejection of true epistemology and physics leads to corrupt ethics. But in truth God, "whose kindness is meant to lead to repentance" (2:4), gives a special grant of time to sinners to repent. Or, when Paul declares that we are free from sin by God's grace, he quickly points out that this "freedom" is not for "slavery to sin" but for "slavery to righteousness" (6:12-22). Therefore, genuine knowledge and true understanding of God's nature lead to a reform of life and so honorable behavior. Knowing the way the ancients systematically discoursed on God or the gods, we can see that Paul too follows this scheme in the argument in Romans. In keeping with the focus of this book, I now examine in detail Paul's physics, that is, his proclamation of the nature of God.

PAUL'S SYSTEMATIC DISCUSSION OF THE NATURE OF GOD

I mentioned briefly that Paul's understanding of the nature of God is found in two arguments: first, God is both merciful and kind, but also a just judge;

second, God has two summary powers: God creates from nothing and God raises the dead and requites them. Let us now examine each in detail.

God's Two Attributes

Moses asked to see the face of God, but when God "passed by" Moses had a basically auditory revelation. When God spoke, the Deity revealed one of the most comprehensive descriptions of the nature of God: "The Lord, the Lord, a God merciful and gracious, slow to anger and abounding in steadfast love and faithfulness, forgiving iniquity and transgression and sin, but who will by no means clear the guilty, visiting the iniquity of the fathers upon the children and the children's children, to the third and fourth generation" (Exod 34:6-7). This self-revelation of God indicates two "measures" of God's activity in the world, mercy and just judgment. These attributes became a traditional way of thinking and relating to God, namely, to acknowledge the justice of God's judgment yet to beseech God's mercy (e.g., Ps 103:6-18; Jer 32:17-20).

While I identify two generic attributes here, mercy and just judgment, some rabbinic authors listed eleven or thirteen attributes. In general, they spun out the text of Exod 34:6-7 and itemized the individual terms, as Montefiore and Loewe observed:

> Famous is the enumeration of the thirteen norms, or divisions, or kinds, of God's attribute of Mercy which were found in the great passage of Exod. xxxiv, 6, 7: (1) The Lord, (2) the Lord (for Yahweh is God as the Merciful One), (3) God (usually God [Elohim] is the judge, God in his attribute of just severity, but here that usual interpretation of Elohim is ignored), (4) merciful, and (5) gracious, (6) longsuffering, and abundant in (7) lovingkindness and (8) fidelity, (9) keeping mercy to a thousand generations, forgiving (10) iniquity, (11) transgression, and (12) sin, and (13) acquitting. (Montefiore and Loewe 1974:43)

Considerable rabbinic reflection was given to these two basic attributes. At times, authors affirm the balanced presence of both attributes because the balance of the world requires both:

> The matter is like a king who had some empty goblets. The king said, "If I put hot water in them, they will burst; if I put cold water, they will crack." So the king mixed cold and hot water together, and poured it in, and the

> goblets were uninjured. Even so, God said, if I create the world with the attribute of mercy, sin will multiply; if I create it with the attribute of justice, how can it endure? So, I will create it with both, so that it may endure. (*Gen. Rab.* 12.15, as cited in Montefiore and Loewe 1974:73–74)

But more frequently authors talk about the attribute of mercy replacing the attribute of judgment. For example, a question was asked, "Why is the prayer of the righteous like a rake?" The answer has to do with the two attributes: "As the rake turns the grain from place to place, so the prayer of the righteous turns the attributes of God from the attribute of wrath to the attribute of mercy" (*b. Yeb.* 64a, as cited in Montefiore and Loewe 1974:342–43). This same idea is often related to Ps 81:3: "'Blow the Shofar on the New Moon' (Ps lxxxi, 3). 'On the New Moon,' that is, make new your deeds. God says, 'If you cleanse your deeds before me, then I will arise from the throne of Judgment, and sit upon the throne of Mercy, and have mercy upon you, and the attribute of Judgment shall be changed for you into the attribute of Mercy" (*Pes. Rab. Kah.* 154a, as cited in Montefiore and Loewe 1974:74; see also *Lev. Rab. Emor* xxix.3 and 6). Thus it is hardly surprising to find some authors claiming that the attribute of mercy is greater than the attribute of judgment: "Which attribute is greater: the attribute of goodness or the attribute of punishment? The attribute of goodness" (*Sifre Num. Naso* 8; cited in Montefiore and Loewe 1974:234; see also *Eccles. Rab.* iv.1.1).

Paul and the Attribute of God's Just Judgment

Knowing this tradition of the two attributes of God immediately pays us dividends as we examine the structure of Romans 1–8.

> The *wrath of God* is revealed against all ungodliness and wickedness. (1:18—3:20)
> The *righteousness of God* has been manifested. (3:21—8:39)

This parallelism implies that the first part of Romans (1:18—3:20) centers around the attribute of just judgment, whereas the second part (3:21—8:39) elaborates how the attribute of mercy is manifested in God's actions in Jesus. These broad strokes can now be filled in.

In regard to the parallel statements above about God's two attributes, Paul expresses in the words "wrath" and "righteousness" the terms we have been following, "mercy" and "just judgment." Recent scholars remind us that "righteousness" here has the sense of the first attribute, "merciful and kind, slow to anger" (Fitzmyer 1993b:105–7). A clever reader of Romans will expect a host of synonyms for both of these attributes, as the following table suggests.

Semantic Word Field for First Attribute: "Mercy"	**Semantic Word Field for Second Attribute: "Justice"**
1. adoption as God's offspring, 2. advocacy on trial, 3. call, 4. covenant, 5. election, 6. favor, 7. forbearance, 8. forgiveness of sins, 9. gift, 10. glory, 11. grace, 12. image and likeness of God, 13. kindness, 14. liberation, 15. love, 16. patience, 17. promise, 18. redemption, 19. resurrection, 20. righteousness, 21. save and salvation, 22. what is not earned but received as gift	1. judge, to judge, judgment, 2. all expressions of *lex talionis,* 4. patterns of crime/punishment, 5. wrath, 6. vengeance, 7. justice, 8. just, 9. descriptions of the great judgment, 10. perish, be condemned, be destroyed, 11. sinners

Returning to Paul's argument, let us take a close look at his inaugural statement. He begins in 1:18 with a topic statement that all people are sinners and thus come under God's "wrath" or just judgment. Four examples of a "crime and punishment" pattern explore and confirm the dire situation in which all find themselves, that is, sinners deserving of God's just judgment. Please note that each of these four examples is cast in the pattern of a *lex talionis,* that is, a tit-for-tat balance, such as "an eye for an eye, a tooth for a tooth."

Example 1 (1:19-24) a. crime: they did not give glory to God b. punishment: God gave them up to dishonoring their bodies	**Example 3 (1:28-32)** a. crime: they did not see fit to acknowledge God b. punishment: God gave them up to an unfit mind
Example 2 (1:25-27) a. crime: they exchanged the truth for a lie b. punishment: God gave them up to exchanging natural sex for unnatural	**Example 4 (2:1-3)** a. crime: you judge/condemn others b. punishment: you judge yourself . . . not escape the judgment of God

Thus this repetitive pattern of "crime and punishment" argues that from the beginning of creation human beings have incessantly committed "crimes" and so are justly subject to "punishment" or the judgment of God.

Following this, Paul briefly describes the final judgment scene before God's throne, stressing especially the "just" judgment of God:

> the day of wrath when God's righteous judgment will be revealed. For he will render to every man according to his works: to those who by patience in well-doing seek for glory and honor and immortality, he will give eternal life; but for those who are factious and do not obey the truth, but obey wickedness, there will be wrath and fury. There will be tribulation and distress for every human being who does evil, the Jew first and also the Greek, but glory and honor and peace for everyone who does good, the Jew first and also the Greek. For God shows no partiality. (2:6-11)

First, the "time" of this event is "the day of wrath." The norm of judgment is clear: "he will render to every man according to his works." This means both rewards: "he will give eternal life to those who by patience in well-doing seek for glory and honor and immortality," and punishments: "there will be wrath and fury for those who are factious and obey wickedness." This judgment of God is preeminently "just" for three reasons: "God shows no partiality," God extends this judgment equally to "the Jew first and also the Greek," and God delivers this judgment "according to [one's] works." This articulation of God's "just judgment" is a commonplace, that is, a traditional way of talking about God in Israelite writings. Paul is utterly orthodox here.

Then Paul takes up the issue of God's impartial judgment, which was introduced in 2:11. He makes the inclusive and impartial statement about God's just judgment: "All who have sinned without the law will also perish without the law, and all who have sinned under the law will be judged by the law" (2:12). "All" sinners, whether Israelite or Greek, will "perish . . . be judged." But here Paul argues that the law given Israel does not insure God's favor, so Israel has no privileged status before God; justice will not be bent arbitrarily in its favor. Rather, as Paul argues, "it is not the hearers of the law who are righteous before God, but the doers of the law who will be justified" (2:13). Actions, performance, deeds count, which makes for a level playing field for all people—justice will be the same for each and every person.

With this general principle in place, Paul then discusses four conditional cases:

A	conditional case 1 (Gentiles)	2:14-16	"when . . ."
B	conditional case 2 (Judeans)	2:17-24	"but if . . ."
B'	conditional case 3 (Judeans)	2:25	"if . . ."
A'	conditional case 4 (Gentiles)	2:26	"if . . ."

The four cases are arranged in chiastic form, that is, an ABB'A' pattern, which helps to organize the material. In keeping with the general statement in 2:12-13, the persons discussed are Israelites and Greeks, thus intentionally including all peoples and correspondingly arguing God's impartiality in judgment. The final part of this argument ends by repeating the theme of God's impartiality just developed. Thus there is no Israelite who automatically enjoys God's favor; to think such is a mistake: "He is not a real Jew who is one outwardly, nor is true circumcision something external and physical" (2:28). Rather anyone can be a "Judean" "who is one inwardly, and real circumcision is a matter of the heart, spiritual, not literal" (2:29).

Paul then defends God's just judgment. First, he argues from Scripture, citing a psalm: "That you may be justified in your words and prevail when you are judged" (3:4 on Ps 51:4). This citation, which plays with the root words "justify" and "judge," affirms the justice of God's judgment. Second, he raises a false conclusion about God's justice: does human sinfulness (i.e., "unfaithfulness" [3:3] or "wickedness" [3:5] or "my falsehood" [3:7]) exist to "show the justice of God"? Does it "abound to God's glory"? In other words, are sinful mortals merely serving to amplify God's power? Could the justice of God really be "unjust" (3:5) because humans have no freedom to do otherwise than sin and so let God flex the divine power of judgment? No, because God throughout remains virtuous: God is always "faithful" and "truthful," and therefore "just." Thus one should correctly conclude that "God is justified in his words" when he shows "justice" and "judges the world."

Finally, the exposition of the judgmental power of God concludes by returning to Paul's argument that all human beings are sinners, no exceptions, and so all stand under the judgment of God: "all men . . . are under the power of sin" (3:10). He draws his argument from the Hebrew Scriptures, a bit here, a bit there. I print it in full, but alert the reader to follow the extensive repetition of terms for inclusivity ("none," "all"):

> None is righteous, no, not one; no one understands, no one seeks for God. All have turned aside, together they have gone wrong; no one does good, not even one. (3:10-12)

Paul then continues this declaration of inclusivity in evil, but employs a different type of argument. Some have observed that the Hebrew Scriptures describe human beings in a distinctive way, which those who use this material call the "3-zone model" (Pilch 1991:203–4; Malina 2001a:68–71). In brief, all persons—God included—are said to have three zones of activity: eyes-heart, ears-mouth, and hands-feet. Information comes through the eyes and is processed in the heart; speech enters through the ears and exits from the mouth; finally, hands and feet perform purposeful activity. I cite one of many examples of this in Hebrew Scripture:

> There are six things which the Lord hates, seven which are an abomination to him: haughty eyes, a lying tongue, and hands that shed innocent blood, a heart that devises wicked plans, feet that make haste to run to evil, a false witness who breathes out lies, and a man who sows discord among brothers. (Prov 6:16-19, cited in Malina 2001a:70)

The zone of thought is represented by "eyes" and "heart . . . devises"; the zone of speech by "lying tongue," "lies," and "false witness"; and the zone of purposeful action by "hands," "feet," and "sows discord." Similarly, in Christian writings we find examples such as: "That which was from the beginning, which we have heard, which we have seen with our eyes, which we have looked upon and touched with our hands" (1 John 1:1). All three zones are in view: "heard," "seen," and "touched."

For present purposes I focus on how completeness is expressed when all three zones are evident at the same time. Paul's proof that all mortals are sinners and so stand under God's just judgment is expressed in the complete depravity of all three zones. "Their throat is an open grave, they use their tongues to deceive. . . . The venom of asps is under their lips. . . . Their mouth is full of curses and bitterness. . . . Their feet are swift to shed blood, in their paths are ruin and misery, and the way of peace they do not know. . . . There is no fear of God before their eyes" (Rom 3:10-18). Paul thus argues that evil is found in zones one ("eyes"), two ("throat," "tongues to deceive," "venom of asps under their lips," "mouths full of curses"), and three ("feet swift to shed blood" and "in their paths [= feet]"). All people are totally evil—and so justly come under God's judgment.

One can draw several conclusions from this survey. First, 1:18—3:20 formally discourses on the second attribute of God, just judgment. Second, Paul states this topic in 1:18 ("the wrath of God is revealed"), then demonstrates the "justness" of God's judgment in 1:19—2:3 by showing how it works: crime, then just punishment. Third, he subsequently calls attention to what all know, namely, the clear understanding that this "just" judgment is strictly proportional to our actions: "he [God] will render to every one according to his works." Four, but is the playing field level? Do Israelites have an advantage? Is there bias in their favor and so "unjustness" in God? No, for in 2:12-29 Paul argues that God is impartial, and so "just" in judgment. Five, this "just" quality of God's judgment is argued still further in 3:1-8. Finally, in 3:10-18 Paul argues that all are sinners, and so all stand under the just judgment of God—what a dreadful place for the world to be in. But this is Paul's segue into his exposition of the other attribute of God, divine mercy.

Paul and the Attribute of God's Mercy

"But," says Paul, "the righteousness of God has been manifested" (3:21). What follows stands in opposition to what preceded: since "all sin and fall short of the glory of God," the only exit from this impasse can be a display of the attribute of mercy. In my view the argument in Romans from 3:21 through 8:39 proclaims and explains the character of this attribute of mercy, and thus tells us about the nature of God.

Although one can contend that mercy was demonstrated in creation (1:19-23), in Paul's gospel of God mercy can be pinpointed in the death of Jesus (3:21-26). Despite their sinfulness, for which all humankind deserves judgment, all are "justified by his grace as a gift" (3:24), by mercy. This happened when "God put forward Jesus Christ as an expiation" (3:25), that is, when God took the initiative and when his attribute of mercy replaced his attribute of judgment, as we saw above in the case of rabbinic writers.

Just as the justice of God's attribute of judgment included impartiality to Israelites and Greeks, so the attribute of mercy manifests the same impartiality (3:27-31). God is the God of Israelites and of Greeks, since "God is one" (3:30; Dahl 1977a). And the norm of God's mercy is the same to both: "he will justify [Israelites and Greeks] on the basis of their faith" (3:30). Thus God's mercy is just because it extends equally to Israelites and Greeks.

"Mercy" in Romans expresses Paul's theological system. God freely extends mercy to all, but as part of a system. All, he tells us, find this mercy when they are "justified by faith," which is the purposeful work of hands or feet, but which begins in our hearts by hearing the gospel and issues from our mouths as an expression of faith. In short, the correct epistemology (preaching and Scripture) teaches the nature of God, which is mercy, and expresses itself in a confession of loyalty to God and thus an act of worship. Paul argues that Jesus had such faith: "the righteousness of God is manifested . . . through the faith of Jesus Christ" (3:22), and God "justifies him who has the faith of Jesus" (3:26; see Hays 1980; 1997:282–86). By this Paul means that Jesus knew the nature of God as the Merciful One, who would be faithful to him by raising him from the dead. Paul later states that all are similarly saved, Israelite and Greek, by faith, that is, by thinking about God in the same way Jesus did.

God's Attribute of Mercy and Abraham

It is, however, in the lengthy example of Abraham that Paul describes in full detail this attribute of mercy. As regards epistemology, Paul draws on the Abrahamic narrative in Genesis 15–18. As regards God's nature, Paul begins the display about the attribute of God's mercy by raising three issues: human boasting has nothing to do with God's mercy, which is based on the "law" of faith (i.e., mercy is a gift, not a wage); God's mercy is impartial and extends to Israelites and Greeks; and this discourse on mercy does not cancel the "law," if by "law" we mean the Scriptures, especially Genesis and the story of Abraham. The next task for Paul consists in picking up these topics and arguing them from the story of Abraham in Genesis, which when correctly understood will illustrate the mercy of God.

In Romans 4 Paul describes in great detail the system of God's nature, that is, the attribute of mercy. As is his wont Paul begins with a topic statement, which I paraphrase: "Take Abraham, for example! He did not receive God's mercy because of anything he did to earn it." Proof? Gen 15:6 says: "Abraham believed God and it was reckoned to him as righteousness" (Rom 4:3). There are six items in this citation: (1) "Abraham," (2) "believed," (3) "God," (4) "reckoned," (5) "to him," and (6) "as righteousness." Paul then takes up each, although not in the order in which we read them, and teases from them a rather full description of how the attribute of divine mercy functions; he understands this argument to be a systematic exposition of the nature and actions of God, which is valid for all peoples. The overview of the expository argument in the chart below identifies the data, upon which I will briefly comment.

4:4-8 **"reckoned"**	v. 4 wages not reckoned as gift but due (hence "not reckon") v. 5 believer's faith is reckoned to him as righteousness v. 8 against whom the Lord does not reckon their sins v. 6 David pronounces a blessing v. 7 Blessed iniquities are forgiven (gift) v. 8 Blessed sins are not reckoned (gift)
4:6-8 **"righteousness"**	v. 5 God justifies the ungodly v. 6 righteousness apart from works v. 7 iniquities forgiven . . . sins covered . . . sin not reckoned
4:9-12 **"Abraham"**	v. 9 "reckoned" to "Abraham"; how do we understand "Abraham"? v. 10 before circumcision; before "obedience to law" v. 11 circumcision = sign of previous righteousness
4:13-17b **"believed"**	v. 13 "the promise" (of God) to Abraham v. 16 repetition/resume of the argument faith . . . promise . . . grace/reckon v. 17a new "word/promise" of God (to be believed): "I have made you the father of many nations" (Gen 17:5) v. 17b believe in God: (a) who gives life to the dead; (b) calls into existence the things that do not exist
4:17c-22 **"God"**	v. 17c two powers of God: creative/eschatological v. 19 Abraham = his body as good as dead (100 years old) (raise dead); Sarah = the barrenness (better translation: deadness) of Sarah's womb
4:23-25 **"to him"**	v. 23 not for his sake alone (Abraham), but for ours also v. 24 it will be reckoned "to us who believe" in God

1. *Reckoned.* By "reckoned" Paul distinguished "mercy," which is God's gift, from "wages," which one earns. When we read a passive voice such as "was reckoned," we should take this as a circumlocution for God's action; thus God "reckoned" to Abraham the gift of the promise of land and offspring. In this regard, Abraham signals how in faith believers have God's mercy "reckoned" to them—the principle is the same. Paul then describes this "mercy" in terms of "blessing," which is also a gift (4:6-7). We see in 4:7-8 that both attributes of God are in view, with the attribute of mercy replacing the attribute of judgment:

> Blessed are they whose iniquities [attribute of judgment]
> are forgiven [attribute of mercy],

> and whose sins are covered [attribute of mercy];
> blessed is the man against whom the Lord will not reckon his sin
> [attribute of mercy overcomes attribute of judgment].

The mercy that is "reckoned," then, is first and foremost a gift, and extends not only to outright blessings bestowed by God but also to the forgiveness of sins.

2. *Righteousness.* Throughout Romans I interpret "righteousness" as Paul's code word for the attribute of mercy, as argued above. In the case of Abraham, it represents the covenant that God made with Abraham, promising him a new land and numerous progeny. But when Paul extends this example to the human race, "righteousness" takes on the meaning of outright benefaction to the "ungodly" and forgiveness of sins. In 4:5-8 Paul stresses that "righteousness" is God's gift, not the labor of human actions; thus the attribute of mercy radically remains a divine benefaction.

3. *Abraham.* Paul pays close attention to the sequence of events in the story of Abraham, because his argument rises or falls on when Abraham was circumcised and what this means. "How was it [righteousness] reckoned to him? Was it before or after he was circumcised?" (4:10). In fact, the "reckoning" of righteousness to Abraham occurred first (Gen 15:6), during his covenant vision; circumcision came later (Gen 17:10). Hence he did not earn God's mercy by circumcision; he did not in any way distort the quality of "gift" emphasized earlier. The meaning of Abraham's circumcision, Paul tells us, lies in its function as "a seal of the righteousness which he had [already] while he was still uncircumcised" (4:11). Thus "Abraham" means two things for us: (a) the inclusive figure who stands for both the uncircumcised and circumcised who equally find favor with God, and (b) a person to whom righteousness was initially and always "reckoned"; his circumcision only sealed or confirmed God's attribute of mercy toward him.

4. *Believed.* Even while "believed" describes the action of Abraham, it also says much about the attribute of mercy, which Paul sees as the content of Abraham's faith. First, we know that God "promised" Abraham descendants as numerous as the sands of the shore and the stars in the sky. A "promise" of this sort expresses God's gift to Abraham, and concretizes the attribute of God's mercy. Second, the "promise" did not come through the law of Israel, which would effectively exclude most of the world; this favoritism would smack of partiality and so of injustice. As it is, Abraham symbolizes the

impartiality and inclusivity of God's mercy: "He is the father of us all, as it is written, 'I have made you the father of many nations' [Gen 17:5]" (Rom 4:17). Moreover, "believe" means receiving the gift of a promise from God, which confirms that the attribute of God's mercy is at work and humans are not claiming God's blessings as their due. Finally, "belief" also means loyalty and faithfulness to God, even when the facts argue against the content of the mercy promised him, namely, his old age: "No distrust made him waver concerning the promise of God" (4:19).

5. *God.* We learn in 4:17 the content of Abraham's faith, that is, his understanding and acknowledgment of the nature of God: "the faith of Abraham . . . in the presence of God in whom he believed, who gives life to the dead and calls into existence the things that do not exist" (4:17). Below I will unpack in detail the content of this faith, namely, the two powers of God (creative and executive). We commonly find in Israelite literature a discussion of God's powers in the world, which are reduced to two comprehensive actions of God: power to create and power to rule. "Creative" power speaks for itself; but Paul tweaks the "ruling" or "kingly" power to focus on God's end-time role as Lord and Judge, who both raises the dead and requites them. As Paul tells us, Abraham's faith in God's two powers is not a speculative theory about God, but has to do with the existential life of Abraham, Jesus, and his disciples. For example, Abraham's faith in God's power to raise the dead affected his current situation—there was death all around: Sarah's womb was "barren," which in Greek Paul called "dead"; and Abraham's body was as good as dead, for he was a century old. While Paul mentions two powers in 4:17, he elaborates on only one of them in 4:19.

This "faith of Abraham" (4:16), this understanding of the nature of God, expresses core aspects of Paul's theology, for it is essentially faith in God's word and promises. God manifested extraordinary "mercy" by the fact that Abraham and Sarah indeed produced a child. God's faithfulness endures; and God indeed "raised the dead." Paul finally argues that this is the correct theology of all disciples, a point to which I now turn.

6. *To him.* Abraham represents a type or example of how God's attribute of mercy works and what that mercy looks like in human experience. Thus Paul considers Abraham as more significant than a particular individual, for, since Abraham is the head of the clan, he sets the pattern for membership in the clan; his fortune (promises) and his response (faith) describe the universal manner of relating to God. Hence, Paul finally argues, "But the words 'It was

reckoned to him,' were written not for his sake alone, but for ours also" (4:24). The way God's mercy will be reckoned to us depends on whether we are like Abraham in his faith and whether our acknowledgment of God conforms to the content of Abraham's faith: "It will be reckoned to us who believe in him that raised from the dead Jesus our Lord" (4:24).

What, then, does Paul tell us about God's attribute of mercy in 4:1-25? First, "righteousness" is "reckoned," that is, it is entirely divine benefaction, gift, and blessing. Second, the attribute of mercy overcomes the attribute of judgment, when God forgives sins. Third, "mercy" becomes a genuine element in our lives and takes the form of blessing, forgiveness, promise of offspring, resurrection of the dead, and the like. Fourth, specific aspects of the attribute of mercy include God's powers of creation and resurrection of the dead—both benefactions on humanity. Finally, mercy extends not only to Abraham or the Israelites, but to all who have the faith of Abraham. This is the founding myth that grounds and legitimates thinking about God's attribute of mercy in this way.

God's Attribute of Mercy and Jesus

Paul's remarks in 5:1-5 and 6-11 bring the discussion of God's attribute of mercy forward in time. In the story of Abraham we learned how this attribute operated in the scriptural past. But in 5:1ff. Paul takes the reader from past to present and then to future. The mercy of God takes the form of "peace with God through our Lord Jesus Christ" (5:1). This refers back to Paul's earlier statement on "his [God's] grace as a gift through the redemption which is in Christ Jesus" (3:24); it was "God who put forward [Jesus] as an expiation by his blood" (3:25). In the present time, it is "through him that we have obtained access to this grace in which we stand" (5:2a). The attribute of mercy also extends into the future, for "we rejoice in our hope of sharing the glory of God" (5:2b). God, who manifested the attribute of mercy in these times through Christ, will faithfully extend this attribute to the end of time. Mercy is not mercy if it is fickle. It must be firmly grounded and God must be faithful. Thus Paul declares: "Hope [of sharing the glory of God] does not disappoint us, because God's love has been poured out into our hearts through the Holy Spirit which has been given to us" (5:5). Paul, therefore, presents another topic statement that will be developed piece by piece. His focus on present and future gifts of grace from God makes further explicit the wealth of benefactions we receive in the attribute of mercy.

In the next part of the letter, Paul shows that the same attribute of mercy that is revealed in the present will have a direct impact on its revelation at the end of time. Even when we were all sinners and so liable to God's attribute of judgment, God surprisingly manifested the attribute of mercy: attribute of judgment: "While we were still weak . . . the ungodly . . . while we were yet sinners"; attribute of mercy: "God shows his love for us" (5:6-8). This mercy ("love") will endure and be the basis for blessing and security at the final judgment: "Since we are now justified by his blood, much more shall we be saved by him from the wrath of God" (5:9). There must be, we saw above, a final judgment of God, when the dead are raised and rewarded or requited. But even when the attribute of judgment is exercised, it will be accompanied for the disciples of Jesus by the attribute of mercy. Paul repeats this idea: "if while we were enemies [under the attribute of judgment] we were reconciled to God [attribute of mercy], much more shall we be saved by his life [attribute of mercy]" (5:10).

Paul comes back to the two attributes of God in Romans 8 when he concludes the portion of the letter 3:21—8:39, which argues that "the righteousness of God is manifest." He begins his resume by affirming that the attribute of God's mercy is operative: "There is now no condemnation . . . the law of the Spirit of life in Christ Jesus has set me free from the law of sin and death" (8:1-2). Where the attribute of judgment applied ("condemnation," "sin and death"), God manifests the attribute of mercy ("no condemnation," "set free"). This has happened because of God's gift of mercy, which supersedes judgment: "God has done. . . ." Paul then contrasts two ways of being, "flesh" and "spirit," each of which brings the disciple under one or another attribute of God. "Flesh" leads to judgment: first, "to set the mind on the flesh is death" (8:6), which is the judgment on sin; second, "the mind set on the flesh is hostile to God . . . does not submit to God's law . . . cannot please God" (8:7-8). "Spirit," however, brings the attribute of God's mercy. Whereas "flesh" represents human choice and action, "spirit" is the gift of God, that is, a way of expressing the attribute of mercy. This "spirit" is both "the Spirit of God" (8:19) and "the Spirit of him who raised Jesus from the dead" (8:11); earlier Paul said of this spirit "the love of God has been poured . . . through the Holy Spirit which has been given to us" (5:5). Thus this Spirit is the gift of God; and if it is found within us, God has given it. Inasmuch we were all "flesh" at one time but now have the "Spirit" of

God, then the attribute of God's just judgment has been superseded by God's attribute of mercy.

The full benefits of this benefaction of "Spirit" are truly remarkable. First, all who are led by this Spirit are "sons of God" (8:14). This echoes once more the story of Abraham, who was promised "sons" as numerous as sand and stars. Since God made Abraham a wealthy man and blessed him exceedingly, becoming part of his clan means a remarkable status transformation. This "sonship" occurs because God puts within us a "spirit of sonship": "We have received the spirit of sonship" (8:15), that is, a gift representative of the attribute of mercy. And the Spirit empowers us to confess "Abba, Father," and thus to demonstrate that "we are children of God" (8:16). Second, if we are "sons" and members of the family of God, then we are also like all of Abraham's offspring, namely, "heirs" of the great promises made to him (8:17). Thus the blessing of becoming "sons" and "heirs" indicates two more aspects of God's attribute of mercy.

The next remarks fast-forward the reader to the future to show how the attribute of mercy will function then (8:18-25, 31-39). Initially Paul states that the fullness of God's mercy has not been experienced yet. There are "sufferings of this present time" (8:18), and "the whole creation has been groaning in travail together until now" (8:22). Then, looking back into the deep past and looking forward to the future, Paul contrasts them in terms of God's two attributes. "Creation," which represents the past, has long been subject to the attribute of God's judgment: "the creation was subjected to futility, not of its own will but by the will of him who subjected it in hope" (8:20); this means that God "subjected it" in justice but wills to bring it under the attribute of mercy. "The creation itself will be set free from its bondage to decay and obtain the glorious liberty of the children of God" (8:21). Mercy, then, will replace judgment. If, as scholars argue, Adam and Eve, when created in the "image and likeness of God," were thus created deathless and immortal, they subsequently sinned and died; thus the attribute of mercy was replaced by that of judgment. But in the future, the attribute of mercy ("redemption of our bodies," 8:23) will supersede the attribute of judgment.

Paul's final remarks (8:31-39) in this section of the letter look exclusively at the great judgment scene that will occur at the end of time. As he said earlier, "God will render to every man according to his works" (2:6). Indubitably there will be a judgment, but which attribute will be dominant then for believers: just judgment or mercy? The scene Paul describes is clearly a forensic or judgmental scene: "who will bring a charge against God's elect?" (8:33). In the book of Job, Satan accuses Job before the throne of God (Job 1–2); comparably, in John's Gospel Jesus declares that Moses, traditionally the advocate of Israel, will be its accuser before God (John 5:45). When Paul takes up this motif, he asks if the all-just and all-knowing God (attribute of just judgment) will bring any charge against the elect. No, for God, "who did not spare his own Son but gave him up for us all, will he not also give us all things with him?" (Rom 8:32). God, then, is "for us," and the attribute of mercy will not melt and vanish at this time. Then is there an accuser? "Is it Christ Jesus who died [for us], yes who was raised from the dead, and who indeed intercedes for us at the right hand of God?" (8:34). Again, no! Then, at the great judgment, "God's elect" will continue to experience the attribute of mercy. Nothing, Paul says, "will be able to separate us from the love of God in Christ Jesus" (8:39).

God's Attribute of Mercy and Israel

One other section of Romans has to do with the attributes of God and the faithfulness of God's mercy, 9:1—11:36. Paul begins this section by listing nine specific benefactions that illustrate different aspects of the attribute of God's mercy: "They are *Israelites,* and to them belong the *sonship,* the *glory,* the *covenants,* the *giving of the law,* the *worship,* and the *promises*; to them belong the *patriarchs,* and of their race, according to the flesh, is the *Christ.* God who is over all be blessed for ever" (9:4-5). Immediately the question is raised whether this "mercy" shown to Israel still continues. Is the attribute of God's mercy reliable? Is God faithful? Or has Paul created a fickle deity who should not be trusted? The answer Paul gives consists in his taking each of these nine aspects of mercy individually and showing how this word of God "has not fallen to the ground."

1. *Israel (9:6-8).* Who is an Israelite? Who experiences the attribute of God's mercy? "Not all who are descended from Israel belong to Israel, and not all are children of Abraham because they are his descendants" (9:6-7). Arguing from Genesis, Paul indicates a restriction in regard to who is "Israel." Abraham begat only one free son, from whom alone all true descendants come: "Through Isaac shall your descendants be named" (9:7; cf. Gen 21:12). Later, Paul cites Isaiah to the effect that "though the number of the sons of Israel be as the sand of the sea, only a remnant will be saved"

(Rom 9:27; cf. Isa 10:22). Thus two attributes of God operate here: the attribute of judgment on sinful Israel sent into exile, but the attribute of mercy on the "remnant" who would return. Thus this "word of God," which is an act of mercy, has not fallen to the ground.

2. *Sonship (9:7-13).* Who is the legitimate son, the heir? Which son enjoyed the attribute of mercy? Abraham had two sons: Ishmael, born of a slave and "child of the flesh," and Isaac, born of the free woman and "child of the promise" (9:8). This "child of the promise" represents God's unique mercy to Abraham: "About this time I will return and Sarah will have a son" (9:9; cf. Gen 18:10). Later the conflict over the correct son is repeated in the case of Isaac's twin sons. The unique object of mercy of election was Jacob: "Jacob I loved, but Esau I hated" (Rom 9:13; cf. Mal 1:2-3). Mercy, then, is continually extended to a patriarch's son; it does not fail.

3. *Promises (9:8-9).* The "promises" must be those made to Abraham that Paul discussed in 4:13-17 and 20. Thus "promise," a gift of God, exemplifies the attribute of mercy; it too does not fall to the ground.

4. *Fathers (9:7-13).* Throughout Israel's literature we read of the patriarchs "Abraham, Isaac, and Jacob," who are noteworthy for the remarkable blessings and favors shown to them. Each patriarch received from God a covenant, which included the promise of descendants and land. Patriarchs function as heads of the clan; and their attributes, skills, and fortunes flow down to their descendants. Thus God's covenant patronage to Abraham, Isaac, and Jacob would pass from generation to generation. This aspect of the attribute of mercy has not fallen to the ground, since Jesus' disciples are Abraham's children and heirs of his inheritance.

5. *Covenants (9:10-13, 24-29).* First, note the plural, "covenants," which most take to mean the covenants with patriarchs or the covenants of promise with Abraham and David. Second, in Romans 9 one best interprets "covenant" as God's gracious "call" or "election." For example, Paul singles out a classic example of "covenant" in the figure of Jacob. Rebecca was pregnant with twins who were "not yet born and had done nothing either good or bad" (9:11). Yet God "elected" Jacob as patriarch and "called" him most favored (9:11a). Covenant, then, means mercy freely and generously shown; and such mercy has not fallen to the ground.

Paul shortly returns to the issue of "covenant," indicating how God graciously extends this mercy to new peoples. The attribute of mercy here manifests God acting in freedom to bless even the most unlikely, namely non-Israelites: "'Those who were not my people I will call "my people," and her who was not beloved I will call "my beloved."' And in the very place where it was said to them, 'You are not my people,' they will be called 'sons of the living God'" (9:24-26). Hosea describes the shape of a future covenant in which God brings favor and mercy to a group who were not "sons" or heirs of the "promises." Thus the attribute of mercy has not fallen to the ground.

6. *Glory.* I argue that throughout Romans, when Paul mentions "glory," he has in mind the nature of God as immortal and deathless. When God made Adam and Eve in the divine likeness, God made them immortal as well (attribute of mercy). But Adam and offspring died because they sinned and so "fall short of the glory of God" (attribute of judgment). In time, God acted to demonstrate the attribute of mercy by setting forth Jesus on a cross. As the detailed comparison of Adam and Jesus in 5:12-21 tells us, the inheritance of death that all received from Adam was overcome by the inheritance of eternal life through Jesus. Thus the attribute of mercy has overtaken the attribute of judgment. As a result, "glory" or immortality again becomes part of the attribute of mercy. It is, however, still in the future, as Paul compares the "sufferings of this present time" with "the glory that is to be revealed to us" (8:18). "Glory," then, is Paul's code word for Adam's immortality, that is, his being made in the image and likeness of God. Glory lost in Adam is restored in Christ, whom God has raised from the dead. This "word of God" from Gen 1:26, which describes another aspect of the attribute of mercy, has not fallen to the ground.

7. *Giving of the law.* Paul surely does not mean by this the Mosaic law given on Sinai, for of this law he has little good to say here. What is "law"? How is it an aspect of the attribute of mercy? Why not allow "law" to fall to the ground? In Romans 7 a false conclusion is raised about his use of the term "law" (7:8) when he compares a widow now free from marriage law with disciples who "have died to the law through the body of Christ" (7:4). Prior to Christ's death we "were living in the flesh, our sinful passions aroused by the law" (7:5). This state of passion and sinfulness brought us under the attribute of judgment. But inasmuch as in Christ's death we are "discharged from the law, dead to that which held us captive" (7:6), we find ourselves blessedly under the attribute of mercy. Thus if being "discharged from the law" is mercy, then being enslaved to it means judgment. Should not this "law" fall to the ground?

There was, however, another "law," not the law governed by the attribute of judgment, but one that was part of the original and primary attribute of mercy: "The law is holy, and the commandment is holy and just and good" (7:12). By this, Paul refers to the first law given by God: "You may eat freely of every tree of the garden; but of the tree of knowledge of good and evil you shall not eat, for in the day you eat it you shall die" (Gen 2:16-17). The purpose of this law was pure blessing: to preserve Adam in the image and likeness of God in which he was made (1:26), that is, immortality or deathlessness. This law, if obeyed, would maintain the attribute of mercy in which Adam was made; it had no other purpose than to protect Adam in God's greatest of all possible blessings.

Has this "law" fallen to the ground? By no means! The answer is found in the Adam-Jesus comparison in Romans 5. If Adam's trespass (failure to keep Gen 2:17) leads to death for all (judgment), so the obedience of one man leads many to righteousness (mercy). Despite the trespass (judgment), the free gift, which is the grace of God (mercy), abounds for many. If death reigned through the trespass (judgment), there is a reign of life through the abundant grace and free gift of righteousness (mercy) (paraphrase of Rom 5:14-21). That which this "law" sought to protect has been restored: life and glory. Now it functions once more to inform and defend the offspring of the new Adam and so to keep them in the mercy of the "glory" and eternal life promised them. Of all blessings, this has not fallen to the ground.

8. The worship. What is worship? If we cannot define it, we cannot recognize it. Earlier Paul described Jesus as the redemption "whom God put forward as an expiation by his blood" (3:25), using sacrificial metaphors to interpret the meaning of Jesus' death. Later he talks about "presenting your bodies as a living sacrifice, holy and acceptable to God, which is your spiritual worship" (12:1). But Paul nowhere intends his audience to imagine that they have a system of temple, priests, and sacrifices such as constitute Israel's worship in Jerusalem. What, then, might this "worship" be that "has not fallen to the ground"? I offer the following definition of worship from anthropological communication theory: "a socially meaningful symbolic act of communication, bearing directly upon persons perceived as somehow supporting, maintaining, and controlling the order of existence of the one praying, and performed with the purpose of getting results from or in the interaction of communication" (Malina 1980:215).

This definition contains five elements: (a) a *sender,* who sends a (b) *message,* (c) by means of some *channel,* (d) to a *receiver,* (e) for a *purpose,* or to have *some effect.* Malina's definition indicates that this communication extends in two directions. Communication to God contains: (a) worshipers (senders), (b) who send a communication (message), (c) in language, gesture, or sacrifice (channel), (d) to God, the object of worship (receiver), (e) in order to have some effect on God (purpose). Yet worship is also communication from God, in which (a) God (sender), (b) sends a communication (message), (c) using certain mediating figures (channels), (d) to worshipers (receivers), (e) for a purpose, or to have an effect (bless, inform, exhort, etc.). The two directional flows of worship, then, look like this:

Worship as speaking to God	sender: mortals	message: petitions, confessions, doxologies	channel: voiced prayer; incense burned; sacrifice offered	receiver: God	effect: request benefaction; give honor and praise
Worship as listening to God	sender: God	message: information, exhortation, rebuke, etc.	channel: Jesus or Holy Spirit or group prophet	receiver: Christian	group effect: reform of behavior; inform; confirm; exhort

Paul expresses these two directions of "worship" in Rom 10:4-13. First, we are told of God's communication with Israel (10:8-10). "The 'word' is near you, on your lips and in your hearts" (10:8), which as Paul says is a word from God, "the word of faith which we preach." Thus, like Abraham, God communicates to us a "word" that is a declaration of mercy and a proclamation of grace. What effect does God seek by this word? Indubitably mercy, grace, and benefaction should purify the hearts of hearers and lead them to covenant commitment.

Second, the appropriate worship response is the communication of prayer that acknowledges God's "word" of blessing (10:9-13). Prayer may be usefully classified into many types (Malina 1980; Neyrey 2001:351–53), only two of which seem relevant here: petitionary prayer, and confessional prayer or doxology. "Calling upon the name of the Lord" may be both types of prayer, for one may petition God's mercy ("call" = request) as well as glorify God's name ("call" = "hallowed be thy name"). But 10:12-13 seems to be petitionary prayer: "The same Lord is Lord of all, and bestows his riches upon all who call upon him. For 'everyone who calls upon the name of the Lord will be saved'" (10:12-13). "Call" in 10:12 petitions God for "his riches"; and when the prayer is answered, the pray-er is "saved." Thus I assume that "call" in v. 13 carries the same sense: "call upon the name of the Lord" means petition some benefaction.

Yet 10:8-10 reflects the other type of prayer mentioned, confessional or doxological. Those who confess with their lips that Jesus is Lord and believe in their hearts that God raised him from the dead have an effect on God, namely, he saves them. Prayer, then, is both on the lips and in the heart. As we saw above in the three-zone model of the human person, such a pray-er gives no mere lip service to God, but is wholly devoted, body and soul, heart and lips. A comparable prayer extolling God's "inscrutable ways" comes at the end of this section, 11:33-36a, after which we find a modest doxology (11:36b). The whole document concludes with a prayer, a doxology of weight and wisdom (16:25-27). Thus the "worship" with which Israel was graced has not fallen to the ground, but is expressed both in God's word to Israel (10:4-10) and in Israel's prayer to God (10:11-13). "Worship," which is communication to God and from God, clearly manifests God's attribute of mercy.

9. The Christ. The final blessing is "of their race, according to the flesh, the Christ" (9:5). In one sense, Paul has all along been talking about the blessing of God, who is the Christ, so we do not find any lengthy reference to Jesus in Romans 9–11. Has the promise of "the Christ" fallen to the ground? No, of course not. In the letter's opening, Paul declared of the Christ two things: God's promise of the Christ, made through the prophets, is fulfilled; and God designated Jesus as Son of God in power according to the Spirit of holiness by his resurrection from the dead (1:1-4). The gospel, which is "concerning his Son," is the same message that God promised long ago by the prophets; thus God's attribute of mercy was active in the past when the divine promise of a blessing was given. The promise of the Christ and his exaltation from death illustrate God's attribute of mercy, and "the Christ" has by no means fallen to the ground.

In summary, it may seem that everything in Romans is an aspect of either the attribute of mercy or that of just judgment. Frankly, this is the appropriate conclusion from an author who consciously structured his argument in terms of "the wrath of God is revealed" (1:18—3:20) and "the righteousness of God is manifested" (3:21—8:39; 9:1—11:36). What, then, have we learned from this survey? First, many ancient authors saw the revelation of God in Exod 34:6-7 as a significant text about God's "nature." The tradition that developed in seeing here God's two attributes became widespread, common, and fixed. Second, Paul uses the tradition in all its permutations: (a) each attribute has its own time and place; (b) at times, one attribute, usually mercy, supersedes the other; and (c) both can exist at the same time, as when God shows "patience" prior to punishment (2:4-5; 9:22-23). Third, like a genus, each attribute contains many different species. Of importance here is the appreciation that the paramount aspect of "mercy" is God's promise to raise the dead and give life that never ends. Fourth, if God's kindnesses and blessings were a matter of human initiative and effort, they would belong under the attribute of just judgment. But as it is, gift, promise, forgiveness of sins, salvation, and the like are all benefactions from God, and so belong under the attribute of mercy. Finally, Paul understands that God's mercy, which was manifested in Jesus, who died and was raised, took place in the past, continues now in the present, and will still be faithful and operative at the final judgment at the throne of God. Thus mercy, to be reliable, must endure over time.

GOD'S TWO POWERS: CREATION AND JUST JUDGMENT

Although I focus on Rom 4:17, it is advantageous to familiarize oneself with the Israelite-Christian discussion of God's two powers. Thus one can appreciate the significant and traditional character of Paul's way of speaking about God. Many Judean authors mention two powers of God, the creative and the executive. Faced with classifying the infinite number of God's actions, ancient thinkers began to summarize them into two categories, which were generally linked together, that is, God's creative and executive actions. For example, in

3 Maccabees Simon the high priest prays to God, "For you, the *creator* of all things [creative power], are a just *ruler* [executive power]; and you judge those who have done anything in insolence and arrogance" (2:3, see also 2 Macc 7:23, 28-29). We should not take this summary remark for granted. Recall that in Acts 17 Paul discourses to Epicureans and Stoics about God, beginning with creation and ending with resurrection and judgment, these same two powers.

Philo, a contemporary of Paul, is the clearest and most prolific user of this concept of God's two powers. In general, he surveys all of God's operations in the world and summarizes them in terms of two comprehensive powers, creative power and ruling power. These two powers include all of God's other actions, a point Philo makes repeatedly (e.g., *Plant.* 85-89; *Abr.* 121-25; *Flight* 95, 100). It is through one power that God "creates and operates the world" (*QG* 4.2), and by the other power God "rules what has come into being" (*QG* 4.2). These two powers, therefore, represent the fundamental and complete activity of the Deity, creation and judgment.

Philo visualizes these powers in terms of the ark described in Exod 25:22. The ark, which contains the ordinances of God, has two cherubim atop it, who face each other and bend low; and above the cherubim is the mercy seat, the throne of God. In Philo's allegory, the two cherubim symbolize the two powers of God. Of these "cherubim" he says: "His creative power is called 'God' *(theos),* because through it He placed and made and ordered this universe, and the kingly is called 'Lord' *(kyrios),* being that with which He governs what has come into being and rules it steadfastly with justice" (*Mos.* 2.99; see *Flight* 101 and *Q.Ex.* 2.68). God's actions and powers, then, may be summarized in the shorthand of "creation" and "ruling." Even God's names correspond to these two powers: creation = "God" (*theos*) and ruling = "Lord" (*kyrios*). While Philo is the clearest and most prolific exponent of this theological idea, it is by no means confined to him. Other authors, including New Testament writers, speak of the two powers of God, such as Hebrews 1 (Neyrey 1991:450–52), John 5 (Neyrey 1988:22–29, 34), Acts 17, and of course, Romans.

Paul describes Abraham as "the father of us all" (Rom 4:17a), indicating that he is the founding father of our clan and that his actions and thoughts are a legacy to and pattern for his descendants. Those who are children of Abraham "share the faith of Abraham" (4:16), that is, they think about God the way Abraham did. Abraham's "faith" in God contains two aspects: the creative and executive powers of God. Explaining this faith, Paul says, "in the presence of the God in whom he believed, who gives life to the dead [ruling or eschatological power] and calls into existence the things that do not exist [creative power]" (4:17b). While commentators readily indicate Israelite parallels to each individual power, they ignore the important linkages of the two (Fitzmyer 1993b:386; Dunn 1988:217–18). But the data above on the two powers of God should persuade us about the joined and composite nature of the two powers in Paul's mode of God-talk (Neyrey 1987a:266–72).

We must proceed cautiously, however, for after this Paul collapses the two powers into one: his emphasis in the letter is solidly on resurrection, not creation. We might think that "call into existence the things that do not exist" refers to the *creation* of a child in Sarah's womb. For example, in 4:19 the RSV reads: "he considered the barrenness of Sarah's womb." But "barrenness" is misleading, for the Greek text speaks about the "deadness" (*nekrosin*) of Sarah's womb; thus God heals "deadness" in Sarah, exercising over her the same power as over Abraham. Moreover, Paul clearly has in mind God's second power when he says of Abraham: "he considered his own body, which was as good as dead because he was about a hundred years old" (4:19). God, who raises the dead, raises to life Abraham's aged body. Thus, although Abraham's faith is in God's two powers (4:17), both Sarah and Abraham would seem in Paul's mind to be a double illustration of God's second power to raise the dead.

Two points need be made here. First, whereas Philo talked about God's "executive" or "kingly" power (*basilike*), Paul modifies this notion. As we saw above in regard to the theodicy of the book of Acts, God is both creator as well as the one who raises the dead and rewards/requites them. Thus Paul reconfigures the "ruling" or "executive" power of God to be God's eschatological power, when God on the day of wrath will raise the dead and judge them. Second, although Paul mentions creation in several places, such as 1:19-20 and 8:19-21, this theme plays a minor role in the letter's logic. His emphasis rests on the second power of God, and with good reason.

The following table, which identifies the major aspects of the eschatological power of God, sharpens our appreciation of the two elements in it.

Power to Raise the Dead	Power to Judge the Dead
"designated Son of God in power according to the Spirit of holiness by his resurrection from the dead" (1:4)	"You are storing up for yourself on the day of wrath when God's righteous judgment will be revealed. For he will render to every man according to his works" (2:5-6; see also 7-11)
"God, who gives life to the dead . . . he [Abraham] considered his own body which was as good as dead . . . the 'deadness' of Sarah's womb" (4:17, 19) "It will be reckoned to us who believe in him that raised Jesus from the dead, Jesus our Lord . . . who was raised for our justification" (4:24-25)	"on that day when, according to my gospel, God judges the secrets of men by Christ Jesus" (2:16) "Christ died for the ungodly. . . . Since we are now justified by his blood, much more shall we be saved by him from the wrath of God" (5:6-9)
"as Christ was raised from the dead by the glory of the father . . . if we have been united with him in a death like his, we will certainly be united with him in a resurrection like his" (6:4-5)	"He who did not spare his own Son, but gave him up for us all, will he not give us all things with him? Who will bring a charge against God's elect? It is God who justifies, who is to condemn? Is it Christ Jesus . . . who is at the right hand of God and who intercedes for us?" (8:31-34)
"He who raised Christ Jesus from the dead will give life to your mortal bodies" (8:11)	
"If you confess with your lips that Jesus is Lord and believe in your heart that God raised him from the dead, you will be saved" (10:9)	

In sum, then, first we learn of a commonplace in Israelite and Greco-Roman God-talk that summarized the activities of God conveniently into two generic powers, creative and ruling. Second, as Rom 4:17 illustrates, Paul knows this tradition and uses it creatively in his argument. Third, Paul makes two major redactions of the doctrine of God's two powers: (a) he redacts the "ruling" power to include eschatological actions, especially raising the dead and judging them; and (b) he overwhelmingly attends to this eschatological power in his argument. Fourth, the reason for his adoption of the second power and his extensive use of it lies in the resurrection of Jesus from death and proclamation that this is also the destiny of his disciples. Finally, there is *some* overlap between the two attributes and the two powers. While it is easy to see how "mercy" corresponds with "creation," the same is not entirely the case with "judgment" and "eschatological" power. In the letter, Paul sees God's eschatological power more in line with "mercy" than with "judgment." Raising Jesus and raising his disciples is "mercy" pure and simple. It is hoped and expected that disciples will also experience "mercy" at the final judgment (8:31-35).

IMPARTIALITY AND INCLUSIVITY

Several striking aspects of Paul's God-talk touch upon God's "impartiality" and "inclusivity." When Paul formally declares that "God shows no impartiality" (2:11) or that "there is no distinction" on God's part (3:22; 10:12), he cites a theological axiom found in Scripture (2 Chr 19:7; Deut 10:16-19), apocryphal literature (Sir 35:12-14, 18-19), noncanonical literature (*Jub.* 5:12-16; *Pss. Sol.* 2:12-13), and rabbinic writings—which is to say, that "God's impartiality" was an ancient, traditional, common axiom. Paul's use of this axiom, however, is best understood in relationship to God's two attributes discussed above.

As we saw, the argument in 1:18—3:20 pertains to the attribute of just judgment: "the wrath of God is revealed." But is this judgment fair and impartial? Paul, of course, endorses the historical sequencing of "Judean first and then Greek" (2:9), but insists on God's "impartial" judgment of all: "There will be tribulation and distress for every human being who does evil, the Jew first and also the Greek, but glory and honor and peace for every one who does good, the Judean first and also the Greek. For God shows no partiality" (Rom 2:9-11). God's judgment is just in rewarding the good and requiting the wicked; but it is also impartial in that God does not favor Israelites over Greeks. The scenario Paul envisions is that of the great judgment when "God will render to every man according to his works" (2:6)—just, impartial judgment. But balancing the attribute of God's impartial judgment is the attribute of impartial mercy, which is the thrust of 3:21—8:39.

The second part of the letter begins by asserting that the "righteousness of God is manifested" (3:21), signaling that impartial judgment is now replaced by impartial mercy, the other attribute of God. Although "all have sinned and fallen short of the grace of God, they [all] may be justified by his grace as a gift" (3:23-24). This means that "all," Israelites and Greeks, impartially receive the attribute of mercy. Later, when discoursing on "worship," Paul makes this clear: "'No one who believes in him will be put to shame.' For there is no distinction between Judean and Greek; the same Lord is Lord of all and bestows his riches upon all who call upon him. For, 'every one who calls upon the name of the Lord will be saved'" (10:11-13). This declares that the attribute of God's mercy is likewise impartial. First, "not put to shame" suggests judgment, but "no one" who believers will suffer this. On the contrary, "bestow riches" and "saved" speak clearly of the attribute of mercy. Second, the attribute of mercy, like that of just judgment, is impartial and inclusive. "No distinction" means that "*no one* will be put to shame," "upon *all* who call upon him," and "*every one* who calls . . . will be saved." Thus we see that when God acts either in the attribute of mercy or in that of judgment, God acts impartially and makes no distinction.

Finally, Paul's discourse on the olive tree makes another contribution to the appreciation of God's impartiality. He notes that Israel has been cut off of the tree because it stumbled over the gospel about Jesus. Thus, once enjoying God's attribute of mercy, Israel now comes under God's attribute of judgment. But, as Paul tells his (Gentile) audience, "if God did not spare the natural branches, neither will he spare you" (11:22). They now enjoy God's attribute of mercy, but are liable to the attribute of judgment if they prove unfaithful. Thus impartial judgment faces the Gentiles. Paul sums up: "Note then the kindness and the severity of God: severity toward those who have fallen, but God's kindness to you, provided you continue in his kindness; otherwise you too will be cut off" (11:22). "Kindness," of course, means the attribute of mercy, just as "severity" points to that of judgment. And the "severity" is impartial, for as it now extends to the unfaithful branches it could also embrace the current branches, if they too prove unfaithful. The story of the olive tree and its branches reaches a strange but impartial conclusion as Paul states: "God has consigned all men to disobedience, so that he might have mercy on all" (11:32). Again, note the two attributes: judgment ("disobedience") and mercy. But note here God impartially dealing with Israelites and Greeks: "all men" come under the attribute of judgment, whereas the attribute of mercy will supersede judgment and have mercy on "all."

DIATRIBAL FALSE QUESTIONS

The last consideration of the "nature" of God is accessible to us in the very form of discourse in the letter, the "diatribal style" (Stowers 1981). While there are two forms of diatribal style in Romans, only one of them interests us. Frequently in Paul's argument he voices an objection from an imaginary interlocutor, who raises a challenging question about what Paul has just said, albeit a false question (Stowers 1981:119–54). If the questions are "false," they imply an error in Paul's God-talk; thus we pay particular attention to them and to Paul's response, which presumably contains the correct way to think about God. Because of the challenging nature of the objections raised against Paul and his answers, we find a strong apologetic quality to this material. But it is unclear whether Paul was actually accused of bad theology or whether he uses this sophisticated manner of discourse to impress his audience.

3:1	Then, what advantage has the Jew?
3:9	Are Jews any better off?
6:1	Are we to continue in sin that grace may abound?
6:15	Are we to sin because we are not under the law but under grace?
7:7	What then shall we say? That the law is sin?
7:13	Did that which is good, then, bring death to me?
9:14	Is there injustice on God's part?
9:19	Why does he still find fault? Who can resist his will?
11:1	Has God rejected his people?
11:11	Have they stumbled so as to fall?
11:19	You will say, "Branches were broken off so that I might be grafted in."

All of these raise objections to parts of Paul's exposition of the nature of God, and so, like all challenges, they must be answered.

From what we know about Paul's exposition of God's two attributes and God's impartiality, we can grasp how these conclusions directly challenge Paul's gospel and are shown to be false conclusions.

1. "What advantage has the Jew?" (3:1). This implies that the attribute of mercy, which in this context refers to God's choice of Israel and the blessings shown it, is in jeopardy: either God showed and should continue to show partiality to Israel, or God proves unfaithful in maintaining a special relationship with Israel. The "advantage," Paul argues, lies in the attribute of mercy

whereby "Israel was entrusted with the oracles of God" (3:2), which means the Scriptures and the prophecies of salvation given Israel. Thus, since "the word of God has not fallen to the ground," God's word is eternal and God is faithful.

2. But the question is asked again: "Are we Judeans any better off?" (3:9). This involves the attribute of just judgment as well as understanding God's impartiality. For no, "all men, Jews and Greeks, are under the power of sin" (3:9). Thus God's justice is impartial: all are sinners and all fall under the attribute of just judgment.

3. Two false objections are raised in 6:1 ("Are we to continue in sin that grace may abound?") and 6:15 ("Are we to sin because we are not the law but under grace?"). Paul's response to both false conclusions involves the two attributes of God: "sin" and "law" = attribute of judgment; and "grace" = attribute of mercy. But the false conclusion lies in the assertion that although we experience the attribute of mercy (i.e., "grace"), we do not have to change our lives from sin to holiness. This would mock God, whose "mercy" means transition to a new life from death. Moreover, if we understand the correct nature of God to include the two attributes of judgment and mercy, then the correct ethics flowing from this means freedom from slavery to sin and becoming slaves of righteousness (6:15-19).

4. Paul discusses the "law" in 7:7 ("What then shall we say? That the law is sin?") and 7:13 ("Did that which is good, then, bring death to me?"). These questions falsely imply that God created a deadly device that trapped us in sin and brought us death. This would mean that God's judgment was flawed because it punished people who were impartially trapped by the law. Paul's response was to argue that "law" refers to Gen 2:17, which was to protect Adam in his likeness to God (i.e., his immortality). On the contrary, God's attribute of mercy was never more completely evident than in this benefaction.

5. Two more false conclusions call into question God's justice: 9:14 ("Is there injustice on God's part?") and 9:19 ("Why does he still find fault? Who can resist his will?"). The objection is raised because of the previous statement about God's preference of Jacob over Esau (9:13; cf. Mal 1:2-3). In refuting these false conclusions, Paul raises several other issues about the God he preaches. God must be free to do what God wills, which in this case is to show benefaction. He argues this from God's word to Moses: "I will have

mercy on whom I have mercy, and I will have compassion on whom I have compassion" (Rom 9:15; cf. Exod 33:19). Clearly Paul speaks here about the attribute of mercy. In Rom 9:14-18 we find both attributes of God operative in Israel's history: "mercy . . . compassion" (attribute of mercy) and "power . . . hardens the heart" (attribute of judgment). But the key feature here is God's freedom to bless and show mercy.

6. Two questions cast doubt on God's faithfulness: 11:1 ("Has God rejected his people?") and 11:11 ("Have they stumbled so as to fall?"). Has the attribute of mercy been withdrawn from Israel? Is Israel irrevocably under God's attribute of just judgment? Is the alternation of these attributes capricious? No, as Paul argues, the pattern of covenant benefaction in the past still holds, because God is faithful. There are major crises, however, for the "sons like the stars" are but a remnant now (11:1-6; see 9:27-29). All of this Paul argues from Scripture, the permanent word of the faithful God.

Therefore, we see how Paul structures this challenge/riposte exchange of false conclusion/correct conclusion into the fabric of this document. The false objections imply a defect in Paul's understanding of the nature of God, indicating that his discourse on God implies question God's fickleness, partiality, and injustice. But these are false conclusions, for we see that Paul affirms and defends as the core of his doctrine of God the two foundational and inclusive attributes of God and the argument that God is both inclusive and impartial. Thus Paul carefully affirms a cluster of related ideas about God: faithfulness and constancy, freedom to act in mercy as God wishes, and radical impartiality to all in terms of both just judgment and mercy.

SUMMARY AND FURTHER QUESTIONS

In this document Paul formally and consciously presents his theology. He formally argues a coherent and systematic understanding of God, which is most unusual in the Christian Scriptures. First, he follows the classical presentation of God in terms of epistemology, physics, and ethics. His emphasis rests on physics, the nature of God, which he presents in terms of the two attributes of God (mercy and just judgment) and the two powers of God (creative and eschatological). He naturally focuses on God's mercy freely given through the death of Jesus and God's eschatological power to raise the dead, first Jesus and then his disciples. Paul emphasizes that God has been, is, and will be impartial in showing either mercy or just judgment. This impartiality bleeds over into another aspect of God, inclusivity.

I need not argue the point, but I want to emphasize that Paul's discourse is very formal, highly reflective, and systematic. He knows full well what he is doing as well as the full implications of his discourse. This is made evident in his use of diatribal style, where he raises false conclusions to his argument only to answer them and prove his orthodoxy.

One topic I did not develop in this chapter is Paul's use of patron-client relationships to explain God's dealings with his audience. It seems self-evident to say that God = Patron, disciples = clients, and Paul = broker. What might be worth pursuing is consideration of God's benefaction in terms of the attributes and powers, especially mercy and eschatological power. The benefaction of mercy consists of a cornucopia of blessings, as noted earlier, but certainly "forgiveness of sins" and "resurrection of the dead" stand out as the most significant ones. Moreover, because "mercy" in all its fullness is God's benefaction, it must be taken as God's free gift and favor. It can only be received as benefaction, not earned or merited. To consider it otherwise is to shame the Patron and diminish God's goodness. We indeed are indebted to God, but not God to us, in any way at any time. We could say that God's benefaction creates a debt in us.

Finally, Paul's systematic discourse on God at every point draws on traditional materials. For, as we saw, the two attributes of mercy and judgment begin with Exod 34:6-7; the two powers of God are likewise rooted in Israelite literature, both Palestinian and Hellenistic. God's impartiality is an ancient theological axiom. At many points Paul appeals to the Scriptures to provide support for various assertions. This appeal to Scripture and common tradition functions in two ways. First, all of this material expands what I described as "epistemology" earlier: here are the sources of Paul's information and knowledge about God. Second, if this material is the orthodox heritage of Israel, then Paul's orthodoxy cannot be called into question. His doctrine of God, then, is nothing novel, defective, or deviant.

5

PATRONAGE AND HONOR, ORDER AND DISORDER

GOD IN 1 CORINTHIANS

The foolishness of God is wiser than men.
—I Cor 1:25

God arranged the organs in the body, as he chose.
—I Cor 12:18

NEW CRISIS, NEW THEOLOGY

Contemporary Pauline scholarship instructs us to read his letters "in context," that is, as situation-specific (Roetzel 1991:13–17). The rhetorical situation of each letter differs because the events within the churches addressed differ, for which differing arguments and resources are called forth. Thus in considering Paul's remarks about God in I Corinthians, we must appreciate first the social context of the letter. As Mitchell and Welborn have argued, Paul confronts what to all intents and purposes looks like civic disorder. In response to rampant factionalism, he urges conciliation (Mitchell 1991; Welborn 1997).

Paul's God-talk in the letter is never speculative, unlike the discussions of the "nature of god" in Greco-Roman philosophy. Here his remarks about God are crafted to settle issues of conflict and disorder, generally in Paul's favor. I will examine Paul's discussion of four aspects of God's actions.

1. *God ascribes differing roles and statuses.* Some of Paul's personal conflicts with others in Corinth involve God's ascription of a special role and status to cer-

tain members of the church. While there are many gifts, services, and workings (12:4-6), Paul maintains that he has been appointed "apostle," the highest role and status in the list of gifts (12:28). Even among the range of gifts that do not imply authority, he has unique wisdom (2:9-10, 16), prolific tongues (14:18), and profound prophecy (15:51-56). God's careful pyramid of rank and role puts every person in his or her place (11:3; 12:18, 24), which incidentally locates Paul very high on the structure of authorized and gifted persons.

2. *God turns the world upside down.* Inasmuch as God manifests divine "foolishness" and "weakness" through the cross of Christ (1:18-25), this locates honor and worth where they are never found in this world. Thus God upsets the values that guide mortals and establishes a new honor code (1:19-20; 3:19-20). But who imitates these values of God? Who boasts in weakness? Who disavows worldly wisdom? Paul, of course.

3. *God, Patron and Benefactor.* God acts and is described as Benefactor/Patron to the church. We need to catalogue God's benefactions and classify them in terms of the four symbolic media observed earlier. Moreover, to whom does God give which gift? Is there partiality in God's benefaction? What is the aim of these benefactions, a favorite client or an enlivened church?

4. *God of order and disorder.* Paul describes patterns of relationships that express orderly maps of persons, that is, God-established roles and statuses; but there are also actions that utterly upset many of these patterns (1:26-30). God-of-order speaks to God's holiness in separating sinners from saints, dead from alive, and other such contrasts. Hence we should examine what Paul says about God's holiness in the face of egregious sin within the group (5:1-13), bodily lack of control, which is another form of uncleanness, and commerce with demons. I begin the study of God in I Corinthians with a consideration of God-in-relationship, namely benefactor/patron-client relationships.

GOD, PAUL, JESUS, AND THE CORINTHIANS: PATRON-CLIENT RELATIONS

Like Mark, Matthew, and Acts, Paul primarily explains God's relationship with the Corinthians in terms of the common social pattern of patronage.

And like them, Paul employs this model of social interaction not as a philosopher but as a rhetorician who argues certain important points on the basis of the correct form of this relationship. Because of the potential size of this type of investigation, I narrow the focus on three areas: God-Patron in relationship to Paul, to the risen Jesus, and to the Corinthian church.

God-Patron and Paul-Client

God's relationship with Paul may be summarized under two major categories: Paul's ascribed credentials, and Paul as recipient of wisdom, secrets, and mysteries. Most of the materials on this topic occur in 1 Corinthians 1–4, the part of the letter that scholars consider to be Paul's apologetic response to criticisms of him by various people in Corinth (Dahl 1977c:40–61). Although Paul regularly states his God-given role and status at the beginning of his letters, his articulation of this in 1 Corinthians is striking. From the outset, the Corinthians must know that he is "called by the will of God to be an apostle" (1:1); thus, whatever his strength or ability, his Patron has ascribed this great honor to him. He enjoys, then, a very high role and status, all because of God's favor. Later we learn that his Patron has given him the benefaction to be a "wise master builder" (3:10). Since those who begin projects are ranked higher than those who come later, Paul claims a divinely given role superior to that given Apollos and others in Corinth. Yet later Paul confesses to the fact that he is the last, not the first, apostle: "Last of all, as to one untimely born, he appeared also to me. For I am the least of the apostles, unfit to be called an apostle, because I persecuted the church of God. But by the grace of God I am what I am, and his grace toward me was not in vain. On the contrary, I worked harder than any of them, though it was not I, but the grace of God which is with me" (15:8-10).

While admitting a host of negatives, Paul appeals to his Patron for his basic credentials as an apostle: "by the grace of God I am what I am . . . the grace of God which is with me." Thus God's benefaction has surprisingly but emphatically established Paul as apostle, master builder, father, and so on, of the Corinthian church. Why talk this way? Paul's appeal to God's patronage serves to reconfirm his role and status in the factious church at Corinth. Apology to criticism seems to be the functional reason for the fact that Paul stresses this and phrases it as he does. Nevertheless, he is God's favorite client, established as founder and father of the group. No one ranks higher, because God wills it this way.

Second, Paul's Patron makes a special benefaction of secret wisdom to him. Many suggest that a particular problem in Corinth arose because Paul appeared to have cheated them by not conveying to them the inner secrets of the Scriptures or the mysteries of knowledge to which others seem to have access. He himself admits this when he says: "But I, brethren, could not address you as spiritual men, but as men of the flesh, as babes in Christ. I fed you with milk, not solid food; for you were not ready for it; and even yet you are not ready" (3:1-2). Fragments of his defensiveness about this matter spill over into the letter. But for present purposes, I focus on his claim that whether or not he conveyed this secret knowledge, his divine Patron has indeed bestowed wisdom, secrets, and mysteries on him. For example, although Paul admits that he did not speak to them in "lofty words or wisdom" (2:2), still "among the mature we do impart wisdom, although it is not a wisdom of this age" (2:6). No question about it, he has a benefaction of heavenly wisdom, not for all, but for the few. "We impart a secret and hidden wisdom of God" (2:7). Although eye has not seen nor ear heard, "God has revealed [wisdom] to us through the spirit" (2:10). In this we hear an apologetic ring: God favors Paul with unique wisdom, and his unique version of it is superior to worldly versions of it; thus Paul is not inferior to or just on a par with his rivals, but superior to them.

In the same vein, he tells the Corinthians to honor the Patron by honoring the recipient of the Patron's gift: "This is how one should regard us, as servants of Christ and stewards of the mysteries of God" (4:1). Thus duties exist on the part of the clients. Paul owes trustworthiness to his Patron in regard to the "mysteries of God," and the Corinthians owe God respect by honoring the person commissioned as "steward" of the mysteries. Finally, note that in I Corinthians 14–15 Paul compares and contrasts two public gifts, tongues and prophecy. Paul boasted in 14:18 that he spoke in tongues more than all the rest of them; since tongues is a benefaction of God, this volubility elevates Paul's status. Later in 15:51ff. Paul plays the prophet: "Lo, I tell you a mystery." By this he likewise claims a special role and status, that of a prophet who is gifted with his Patron's secret wisdom. Why these claims? In an apologetic vein, Paul claims comparable, nay, superior benefactions of heavenly secrets and knowledge, which should confirm his social role and status in the church.

Finally, there is in Paul's articulation of the patron-client relationship between God and himself a special nuance that God reverses worldly values and expectations. Thus Paul, the persecutor of the church, becomes its apostle; and Paul, weak and foolish, nevertheless has access to power and to secret mysteries. In telling us the story of his benefaction, Paul talks about the character and plan of the Patron, who in this case acts in utterly surprising ways (see 1:18-25). This aspect of Paul's Patron-client relationship agrees with the apologetic function discussed above. Moreover, all clients, by virtue of the patron's benefaction, incur duties and debts. Paul owes God the obligation of fulfilling the role God ascribed to him; in this he is defending the interests of the Patron (see "necessity," 9:16). Those to whom Paul is apostle and father owe their Patron respect as well, which respect is shown in their treatment of God's intermediary, Paul. Thus Paul's understanding of his client-Patron relationship has specific relevance to the lively issues of disunity and conflict in the community.

God-Patron and Jesus-Client

Were this a study of Jesus the mediator between God and Corinth, I would have much to say about his role as God's broker to the client church. I would stress how God made him broker of heavenly blessings: "life in Christ Jesus, whom God made our wisdom, our righteousness and sanctification and redemption" (1:30). How frequently, Paul says, the church receives blessings "in the name of the Lord Jesus Christ": "you were washed, you were sanctified, you were justified in the name of the Lord Jesus Christ" (6:11). But I focus here on the relationship of God and Jesus, where Jesus is not mediator but client.

First Corinthians 15 provides the most profitable place to study this patron-client relationship. The whole chapter deals with Jesus' resurrection, but in differing ways; and the exposition functions in apologetic response to various questions and problems raised by members of the church. It is a rhetorical, not a theoretical or historical, argument. Of interest to us is Paul's unusual statement about the risen Jesus in 15:20-28, in which he makes three points.

First, Paul's most consistent articulation of Jesus' resurrection highlights it as God's benefaction: "Christ . . . *raised* from the dead" (15:12), and "the dead *are raised* . . . Christ *is raised*" (15:16). The passive voice here (i.e., "be raised") means that God authored this. Thus the resurrection is a God issue: "If Christ has not been raised . . . we are even found to be misrepresenting God, because we testified of God that he raised Christ, whom he did not raise if it is true that the dead are not raised" (15:14-15). Paul, then, does not tell us the meaning of Christ's resurrection (vindication, enthronement, etc.), but stresses that it is God's marvelous benefaction.

Second, it would seem that some at Corinth proclaimed that they had "already" passed from the world of flesh to that of spirit and from subjection to death to victory of life (see 2 Tim 2:16-18). Obviously this serves to create elitism in the group: the few are "already" fully into the mystery, but the masses are still mired down. Hence Paul argues a chronology that undermines this: "Christ has been raised, the first fruits of those who have fallen asleep" (15:20). All will indeed be made alive, "but each in his own order: Christ the first fruits, then at his coming those who belong to Christ" (15:23). Thus, although all are destined to have this benefaction from God, only Jesus, the first fruits, enjoys it now. The timing of this benefaction of the heavenly Patron serves to undercut the inflated claims of certain earthly clients.

Third, in time Jesus will act as God's warrior and champion, as he "destroys every rule and authority and power" (15:24) and "puts every enemy under his feet; the last enemy to be destroyed is death" (15:25-26). Thus Jesus stands tall, as "all things are in subjection under his feet" (15:27). But this victorious and glorious Jesus nevertheless remains God's client, for the "all" in "all things are put in subjection under his feet" does not include God, the Patron: "it is plain that he [God] is excepted who put all things under him [Jesus]" (15:27). The result will be a hierarchical relationship, with God in the superior position as patron, Jesus the heavenly client below the patron, and "all things" under him: "When all things are subjected to him, then the Son himself will also be subjected to him who put all things under him, that God may be everything to every one" (15:28; see 11:3). What a strange way of talking! But in light of the problems within the Corinthian church this tortured explanation of the resurrection has relevance. Many scholars argue that a problem in the church is authority: Paul's, Apollos's, and that of others. On occasion Paul tells us that his specific authority is contested or that the general authority of all teachers is challenged. With the gift of God's Spirit, who needs teachers? Who needs instruction? We frequently hear the chant "All things are lawful to me" (6:12-13; 10:23) and "Am I not free?" (9:1). Paul's response to these includes the material just seen in 15:20-28, where the risen and supremely victorious

Jesus, even in the perfect world of God's kingdom, remains God's client, with all the duties and obedience owed his Patron.

Thus the patron-client relationship between God and Jesus articulates God's superior power (over death) and God's empowerment (of Jesus the warrior). The Patron's blessings, then, do not cease with Jesus' resurrection, as God blesses him and exalts him above all things. But the client never ceases to be just that, "client," and gives reverence and respect at the feet of the one who subjected all things to him.

God-Patron and the Corinthian Church

My aim in this section remains the same as before: How does the patron-client relationship function in the specific situation of the Corinthian church that Paul addresses? Before I present the classification of benefactions from God in I Corinthians, let us briefly consider the terms Paul uses to label in a generic fashion God's actions as benefactor. The single Greek root, *char-*, produces three distinct but related terms referring to patronage and benefaction: *charis, charisma,* and *charizomai.* Malina's nuanced interpretation of them is quite useful for our inquiry: "*Charizomai* refers to showing patronage, *charis* to willingness to be a patron, and *charisma* to the outcomes of patronage" (1996:171). He goes on to explain that the verb *charizomai* means "to give in, hence to yield, donate, to bestow patronage" when petitioned to do so (1996:172). The noun *charis,* in turn, speaks to the action of giving in to someone, that is, readiness to act as patron (1996:172). And the noun *charisma* describes the result of an action of giving in, namely, patronage or a gift with strings attached. Another verb might also be considered in terms of God's benefaction, namely, "to give" (*didomi*), which only confirms what I am saying about the current terminology (see 1:4; 3:5; 12:7-8, 24; 15:38, 57).

A few examples of these terms from I Corinthians will help us grasp how these are distinctively benefaction terms. For instance, the act of giving in or acting as patron is expressed clearly when Paul says: "We have received . . . the Spirit which is from God, that we might understand the gifts bestowed (*charisthenta*) on us by God" (2:12). We "receive" because our Patron has "bestowed" benefaction on us. God, then, willingly acts as patron. God's willingness to act as patron is expressed twice in regard to Paul's reception of unique benefaction. First, Paul identifies his role in the group as a benefaction: "According to the grace (*charin*) of God given to me, like a skilled master builder I laid a foundation" (3:10). Acting as patron, God "gave" to Paul a role and status of great honor and responsibility, namely, the "grace" of church founder. Later, in an apologetic defense of his role and status, he declares: "By the grace (*chariti*) of God I am what I am, and his grace (*charis*) toward me was not in vain" (15:10). God indeed displayed benefaction (*charis*) to Paul and was faithful to that gift to Paul. Finally, the results of God's willingness to act as patron are manifested in the "gifts" or *charismata* given to the church. Paul thanks God for acting as patron so generously that "you are not lacking in any spiritual gift (*charismati*)" (1:7). Similarly, he acknowledges a universal benefaction on the church: "Each has his own special gift (*charisma*) from God, one of one kind and one of another" (7:7). Thus Paul and the church can recognize the results of God's patronage to the church. All of this, I repeat, is generic language about the phenomenon of benefactions in Corinth; it tells us *that* God acts as benefactor, although it does not give us specifics about what type of benefaction is given to whom.

Moving from generalities to specifics, I hope that the following chart adequately classifies the benefactions of God and so will serve as a roadmap for our inquiry of how God relates to Corinth as patron and benefactor.

Power	**Influence**
1. Raises the dead: 6:14; 15:20-28 2. Upsets worldly wisdom and power: 1:19-20, 26-30; 3:19-20 3. Saving power: 1:18; 10:13 4. Demonstration of power: 2:4 5. Kingdom of God: 4:20; 6:9-13	1. Testimony of God: 2:1 2. Wisdom of God: 2:6-13 3. Mysteries of God: 4:1 4. Prophecies: 14:4-12, 22-25; 15:51-56 5. Tongues: 14:2-3, 18 6. Gifts of knowledge and speech: 1:4-7; 12:8, 10, 28-30; 14:26
Commitment	**Inducement**
1. God is faithful: 1:9; 10:13 2. Election: 1:2, 26-29; 6:9-11, 19-22 3. Partner of God, not demons: 10:19-22 4. Diverse roles, statuses ascribed: 3:5-10; 12:18, 25; 12:28-30	1. All (foods) are clean: 10:23-26 2. Recompense for service: 9:3-12

1. *Power.* It is not simply a matter of God having power or being "all powerful," but of God's use of that power to benefit the church. The greatest act of the Benefactor's power is the raising of the dead, first Jesus and at the end of Jesus' battle with death, all of the faithful (15:20-28). Power is given when the Benefactor "saves" others from peril, attack, slavery, and the like. Christians are "saved" from the fate of perishing, and so experience God's power (1:18). Even when tempted, God's power "provides a way to escape it" (10:13). The "kingdom of God," we are reminded, "does not consist in talk but in power" (4:20). Hence Paul speaks in such a way that "your faith might not rest in the wisdom of men [influence], but in the power of God" (2:4). But God is also "weak" both in the crucified Christ (1:24-25) and in certain of the Corinthians who lack all earthly marks of status and importance (1:26-30). God's "weakness," of course, constitutes Paul's rhetorical ploy to attack and refute those who promote themselves at their Patron's expense. If power is manifest in weakness, this honors Jesus and Paul, but excludes others. Finally, God's power acts to refute and subvert the influential of this world (1:19-20; 3:19-20); what makes this benefaction is the way in which this power then serves to elevate and honor those lacking all worldly excellences. God's power contains a range of benefactions: resurrection from death, salvation from temptation, acts of strength expressed by the Spirit, subversion of worldly strength and wisdom. Power, I argue, is a significant benefaction to Corinth, more so than in other Pauline letters.

2. *Commitment* describes the solidarity factor between patron and client. Commitment begins with God's "election" of people, that is, their "call to be saints" (1:2). Furthermore, God "chose" those not wise, not powerful, not of noble birth to manifest his way of being patron (1:26-30). Many a sinner and evildoer were washed, sanctified, and justified by God's election of them (6:11). And what God starts, God finishes. Hence early in the letter, Paul tells us of God's commitment: "God is faithful, by whom you were called into the fellowship of his son" (1:9). God first called the Corinthians into "fellowship," thus forming a fictive-kinship bond with them; but God also maintains what he began, demonstrating a "faithfulness" that confirms commitment. Similarly, God's faithfulness confirms his relationship of favor and patronage to a disciple in temptation (10:13).

3. *Inducement,* which refers to material goods and services that a benefactor bestows, does not appear to be bestowed in Corinthians. Upon reflection, it is not clear if the two items listed above are really God's benefaction of *induce-*

ment. When Paul declares that the Corinthians may eat all foods because all foods are clean (10:23-26), God does not actually provide these foods to the Corinthians, he only declares all clean and edible—if one has them. Second, God himself does not provide Paul's food and lodging for his services, but only endorses the principle that laborers are worthy of their hiring (9:3-12). Thus God does not provide the foods that the Corinthians eat, so I refrain from claiming that God's benefaction includes inducement.

4. *Influence.* This benefaction not only embraces the mysteries, secrets, prophecies, and revelations that God imparts, but also pertains to the persons who have access to these forms of knowledge. Without a mediator, a prophet, or a priest, people have no access to God's mysteries. Corinth, of course, represents the church most taken up with influence, human rhetoric, and wisdom, as well as divine gnosis and secrets. It is not surprising, then, to observe Paul talking about the Patron's influence, especially as wisdom, knowledge, and revelations has been given to him. His initial discourse to them was the "testimony" or mystery of God (2:1), but not in a worldly manner. Having disclaimed to have earthly wisdom, Paul then discourses on secrets that "no eye has seen, nor ear heard, nor heart of man conceived" (2:9), which he claims that God has given to him: "God has revealed to us through the Spirit" (2:10). He brokers these mysteries to the church: "We impart this in words not taught by human wisdom, but taught by the Spirit" (2:13). Moreover, he claims unique access to "the mind of the Lord": "'Who has known the mind of the Lord so as to instruct him?' But we have the mind of Christ" (2:16).

The most prized benefactions of influence were prophecy and speaking in tongues. At the letter's beginning Paul thanked God for just these gifts: "I give thanks to God . . . that in every way you were enriched with all speech and knowledge" (1:4). But Paul did not give full attention to them until the section of the letter "Concerning Spiritual Persons" (12:1). First, those with truly inspired speech confess "Jesus is Lord" (12:3); all other speech must be measured against this profession of Jesus' sovereignty and authority. Subsequently, Paul conducts a contrast/comparison of the influence represented by speaking in tongues and prophecy. He ranks them in terms of utility for the group: speaking in tongues builds up only the one who speaks, whereas prophecy builds up the church (14:2-4). Paul boasts that he speaks in tongues more than all of them (14:18), and later he tells them a mystery about the end time (15:51-56), thus claiming to be a prophet as well, who shares the secret of secrets.

"Influence" also means that God localizes the benefactions of wisdom, mysteries, prophecies, and the like in certain persons, who are thereby constituted mediators of God. Paul claims this second aspect of influence, a unique role as the purveyor and conduit of mysteries and knowledge. "This is how one should regard us, as stewards of the mysteries of God" (4:1). Thus even if Paul is gifted as a "wise master architect" and a "father" to the group, he is also its premier source of God's wisdom. Later, when he considers roles and statuses in the body of Christ, Paul lists some in terms of their hierarchical significance: "God has appointed in the church first apostles, second prophets, third teachers . . ." (12:28). Paul is obviously an apostle (9:1; 15:7-11), and in his mind this role trumps all others in the church. But note that all three of these labeled roles are "speaking" roles that also depend on having access to wisdom, teaching, and the like. Therefore, I consider influence to be the most significant benefaction given to Corinth, both in terms of its internal search for esoteric knowledge and its controversy over who has access to it.

In summary, we see that Paul employs a range of terms that speak generically of benefaction. The use of the four symbolic media—power, commitment, inducement, and influence—allowed us to gather and classify specific instances of God's patronage, and so appreciate the relative emphasis Paul gives to each. Power and influence, we saw, are the dominant ones. We have also seen that the Patron employs brokers for the Corinthian group. Thus the basic elements of the patron-client relationship are clearly in view, and God's relationship to God's people is more apparent to us now.

THE HONOR OF GOD

The traditional model of honor used by social-science New Testament scholars provides an excellent way of gathering and assessing certain data about God in 1 Corinthians (Malina 2001a:27–57; Malina and Neyrey 1991: 25–66; Neyrey 1998a:1–67). As we have seen, one should consider: the source of honor, either ascribed or achieved; the acquisition of honor in challenge-riposte situations; replications of honor in family and name; the display of honor; and the gender basis of honor. Honor, which refers to the worth or precedence of someone, is first claimed in some way and then acknowledged by others, lest it become shame.

Sources of Honor

God, of course, depends on no source of honor, for God is himself the source of honor. Most ancient gods have genealogies that indicate how a deity derives from this or that stock and so enjoys proportionate respect. Not so with Paul's God, who has no mother or father or genealogy. Moreover, although we find phrases in Scripture that refer to God "gaining glory" by defeating Pharaoh or other gods, this kind of expression reflects a henotheistic worldview in which Israel chooses to serve this God, not others; thus Israel's God can gain honor by taking it from rival deities. But this does not appear in Paul, whose God is for the most part a monotheistic Deity who does not battle peoples and their deities. Paul, then, is mute on the sources of God's honor, simply because there is nothing to say here: God is God, and there is no other. Illustrative of this are the acclamations about God: "There is no God but one" (8:4), and "There is one God, the Father" (8:6) (Giblin 1975:529–37; Denaux 1996:601–5). In addition, Paul adds that God is the sourceless Source of all else: "from whom are all things and for whom we exist" (8:6). Later, when Paul states that the Spirit dispenses gifts, the Lord mediates varieties of services, and God works "workings," it is God who "inspires them in everyone" (12:6). Thus God is the ultimate source of all benefactions for every person. Hence God, who is completely sourceless as regards existence, worth, and honor, is the source of these in regard to others.

Benefaction and Honor

For mortals, benefaction begets gratitude and honor, especially the benefaction that exemplifies the civic virtues of elite Greek males. Aristotle provides a list of the premier virtues of his world that assists us in appreciating the superior quality of God's benefactions, and so the honor and praise they deserve.

Those actions are most noble and so praiseworthy that are most useful to others:

> justice: by which all have what is due to them and as the law requires
> liberality: disposition to do good with money
> magnanimity: productive of great benefits
> magnificence: in expenditures, productive of something great. (*Rhet.* 1.9.5-13)

These, of course, represent the premier civic virtues of Greece and speak to the behavior of political figures whose worth is recognized because of the *leitourgia* and other benefactions that they provide (Joubert 2000). This points us in the direction of Paul's description of God as Patron and Benefactor in I Corinthians, which includes the following: all ascribed gifts of honor, roles, and statuses that God has freely bestowed on Jesus, Paul, and Apollos; all gifts, services, and workings (12:4-6, 28-31); special blessings such as being "chosen" and "called" (1:9, 26-30; 15:9); and unique benefactions such as being "saved" and "redeemed" (6:20; 7:23). Paul began his thanksgiving prayer at the letter's beginning with proper gratitude for the flood of mercies given this church: "the grace which has been given to you in Christ Jesus . . . enriched in him with all speech and all knowledge . . . so that you are not lacking in any spiritual gift" (1:4-7). "All!" "Not lacking in any gift," indeed! How honorable is such a generous Benefactor.

Honor and Virtues

With mortals, honor was linked to "virtue," by which the ancients meant "excellence" of some sort. We look closely at Paul's description of God's virtue of justice, for which God's excellence is acknowledged. In I Corinthians Paul praises the "justice" of God in a variety of ways. Twice he notes that "God is faithful" (1:9; 10:13). From a human standpoint, "faithfulness" is understood as an aspect of the virtue of justice. The following definition of "justice" from Plutarch includes "faith[fulness]" as an aspect of this virtue: "First among the claims of righteousness are our duties to the gods, then our duties to the spirits, then those to country and parents, then those to the departed. . . . Righteousness is also accompanied by holiness and truth and loyalty (*pistis*) and hatred of wickedness" (*Virtues* 5.2-3; see *Her.* 3.3.4)

Justice has three objects, the triple duties owed to God, country, and kinship. But when God is said to be "just," we regard God's loyalty and faithfulness to his clients. What God begins, God finishes. Let us not, however, ignore the importance given to God's "faithfulness" in Israelite traditions. The Hebrew Scriptures regularly affirm God's faithfulness (Deut 7:9; 32:4; Isa 49:7; Ps 145:13); and God's covenant is governed by "steadfast love." Obviously such proclamations have to do with God's benefaction, in the sense that mortals pray and hope that God will maintain this covenant relationship. Paul and other New Testament authors declare God's faithfulness in the same sense (1 Cor 1:9; 10:13; 1 Thess 5:24; 2 Thess 3:3; Heb 10:23; 11:11; see also 2 Tim 2:19), namely, they expect that God's benefaction now begun in Christ will not fail. However, Paul's remarks in 1:9 and 10:13 about God's "faithfulness" are not petitions for this, but rather acknowledgments of it. In the world of honor, public acknowledgment of an honor claim is required, for honor claims not acknowledged are empty and vainglorious.

God's justice is also related to his judgment, which involves important notions of honor. In regard to the honor involved in the exercise of just judgment, Paul takes up the following issues: (1) God as Lawgiver, (2) God's retributive justice, and (3) the *lex talionis* norm of judgment. First, Paul rarely mentions God's law, but when he does, he seems to be citing a version of the Decalogue in 6:9-10. Before and after this list, he declares that lawbreakers "will not inherit the kingdom of God." Later he makes a passing remark that belonging in God's kingdom is not a matter of circumcision or no circumcision, "but keeping the commandments of God" (7:19). Paul may well be downplaying this aspect of God as we hear the constant chant of "freedom," which probably means a freedom from the law of Moses, all law and all authority.

When a lawmaker makes a law, then his honor is on the line, for he must enforce compliance with it or judge those who ignore or break it. Honor, then, is linked with just judgment. Although it is a long citation from a Roman author, it is the clearest example of this type of thinking.

> It has been thought that there should be three reasons for punishing crimes. One of these, which the Greeks call either *kolasis* or *nouthesia*, is the infliction of punishment for the purpose of *correction* and *reformation*, in order that one who has done wrong thoughtlessly may become more careful and scrupulous. The second is called *timoria* by those who have made a more exact differentiation between terms of this kind. That reason for punishment exists when the *dignity and prestige* of the one who is sinned against must be maintained, lest the omission of punishment bring him into *contempt* and diminish the esteem in which he is held; and therefore they think that it was given a name derived from the *preservation of honour* [Gk: *time*]. A third reason for punishment is that which is called by the Greeks *paradeigma*, when punishment is necessary for the sake of *example*, in order that others through fear of a recognized penalty may be kept from similar sins, which it is to the common interest to prevent. Therefore our forefathers used the world *exempla*, or "examples," for the severest and heaviest penalties. (Aulus Gellius, *Attic Nights* 7.14.1-4)

Paul knows of punishment whose purpose is "reform." For example, the man in the illicit sexual union is disciplined so that he might be eventually "saved in the day of the Lord Jesus" (5:5). Similarly, Paul exhorts those who "eat the bread and drink the cup in an unworthy manner" to reform themselves: "if we judged ourselves truly, we would not be judged" (11:27-32). Secondly, Paul cites the example of the Exodus generation which perished in the desert as a "warning for us," that is, as an example of God's just judgment (10:6-13). "These things happened to them as a warning, but they were written down for our instruction" (10:11). Finally, the judgment of God is intimately related to God's honor. If God makes a law that people disobey with impunity, then the prestige and respect of the Lawmaker is diminished; God will then be said to be either powerless or simply absent from the world, and so God will be shamed. In this letter, we do not find this particular type of thinking expressed by Paul, but he takes up the issue of God's honor and the need to respond in the way he perceives the challenges to God.

In the world of mortals, an endless game of challenge-riposte occurs when males are in public. Paul's endless apologetic posturing represents his response to the polemics about his reputation, wisdom, eloquence, strength, flattery, etc. (Marshall 1987). In the case of God, lawbreakers are seen as challenging God. God responds in regard to God's honor by judging in a quid-pro-quo manner or, as Paul describes it, according to the form of a *lex talionis,* "an eye for an eye, a tooth for a tooth." While this can describe the rewards of faithful service which the faithful God dispenses (3:8, 14), it generally describes the just judgments of God. For example, "If one destroys God's temple, God will destroy him" (3:17; see 14:38; see Käsemann 1969; Berger 1970). Thus, God is honorable when God judges. Often that judgment, which is inherently just, reflects divine concern for others affected by the sin of some, which is a mark of excellence, as Aristotle noted. Or it touches on the preeminence of the Lawgiver, who knows how to defend his honor, an essential component of the value of honor in antiquity (see 10:22).

Honor and Power

Power marked a reputable and honorable person, and warranted praise and respect. Cicero's list of such external qualities includes "public office, money, connexions by marriage, high birth, friends, country, and power" (Cicero, *Inv.*

2.59.177). Power means that one can impose one's will on others. Warriors and politicians exercised power, which when acknowledged by those who yielded to it also brought acknowledgment of worth and respect to the person wielding it. It is generally associated with exalted social roles such as king, pharaoh, or caesar. For I Corinthians, we will consider God's two powers, creative and eschatological.

In regard to God's creative power, we saw earlier that 8:6 declares that God alone is the source of "all things." God's creative power also establishes maps of persons such as the map of body parts in 12:18, the map of roles and statuses in 12:28, and other hierarchical relationships (11:3; 15:27-28). All such hierarchical relationships were established in God's creation of an orderly world. It is expected, we are told, that we acknowledge the social location to which God has assigned us: "Let every one lead the life which the Lord has assigned him, and in which God has called him" (7:19-24).

As regards creative power, one area receives Paul's special attention: God and foods. Did God make all foods? What do we make of Israelite food laws? The discussion of clean and unclean foods finally finds resolution when Paul states: "Eat whatever is sold in the meat market without raising any question on the ground of conscience" (10:25). Paul bases his argument for this on God's creation: "For the earth is the Lord's and everything in it" (10:26; cf. Ps 24:1; 50:12). Therefore, in creation, God constructed a map of bodily parts based on honor that is replicated in a comparable map of persons. And God's creative power erases food distinctions. God, then, is honored when the patterns of creation are acknowledged.

In regard to God's eschatological power, I focus on the elements that typically belong in any discussion of theodicy: God judges; there is an afterlife, in which rewards and punishments are justly apportioned. No data in I Corinthians suggest that anyone denies that God judges; some may imagine that the judgment has already been rendered when by baptism and the gift of Spirit they think that they have already passed beyond naive or immature notions of God as judge. But judging occurs frequently in the group, and with some vehemence. When in 4:1-5 Paul senses that he is judged by elites, he responds with an appeal to God's future, mysterious judgment. A just judgment will examine how well persons have fulfilled their triple duties: to God, country, and kin. Paul in 4:1-2 states his role according to which judgment should take place. He and Apollos, as "servants of Christ and stewards of the mysteries of God," have duties to God, who authorized them for this, and to the church for whom they labor. What matters is their "trustworthiness," that is, their fidelity and loyalty to God and the task God assigned them. Hence God alone can justly evaluate how they fulfill their duties. But, we are told, other judges are judging them, whose judgment Paul considers both wrong in principle and false in its conclusions. "It is the Lord who judges me" (4:4), whose judgment is not now, but in the future: "Do not pronounce judgment before the time, before the Lord comes." Obviously, appearances are deceiving; Paul does not appear to many at Corinth as wise, strong, eloquent, spiritual, and so on. In cases such as this, the final judgment of God is first and foremost a revelation of mysteries and secrets: disguises are unmasked; ambiguity clarified; and appearances unveiled. This, says Paul, is what God will do at the judgment: "He will bring to light the things now hidden in darkness and will disclose the purposes of the heart" (4:5). On the basis of this revelation, he will judge justly: "Then every man will receive his commendation from God" (4:5b). Therefore, Paul's doctrine of theodicy is not the speculative one we examined in Acts, but a traditional understanding that he adapts for apologetic purposes. God's judgment, which will be both informed and just, will cancel out the uninformed and unjust criticisms of members of the church. God will evaluate Paul and reward him on the basis of his duties as "servant and steward of the mysteries."

A second element in the doctrine of theodicy, survival after death, receives attention in the long discourse on the resurrection, but especially in 15:12-19. The history of the interpretation of this passage may be summarized in three distinct positions: the denial of postmortem existence, bodily resurrection, and future resurrection (Tuckett 1996). Paul has in mind in 1 Corinthians 15 a timetable that argues that Christ alone has been raised, but that all others will be raised after the defeat of the last enemy, death. Therefore no Corinthian can claim to be already in the kingdom of God (see 4:8); whether dead or still alive, all must in the future put on immortality and imperishability. The temporal factor, like so much of Paul's argument, functions as a polemic against false conceptions of God's workings. Second, scholars do not envision an Epicurean or Sadducean denial of life after death here; rather, they tend to see arguments about the nature of the resurrection, whether bodily in some sense or not. Survival after death in some form seems not to be in question. Third, postmortem retribution is not discussed in I Corinthians 15, but it appears elsewhere. For example, both before and after a list of vices, which parallels many of the laws in the Decalogue, Paul says that "the unrighteous will not inherit the kingdom of God" (6:9-10). Obviously, observant disciples will inherit, and others will not. But this determination will be made after death. While there are other references to God's judgment, I isolate these because they belong clearly to Paul's practical theodicy.

Thus Paul clearly knows and talks about God's two powers. These powers are unique to God and superior to all other powers in the cosmos. Uniqueness and superiority regularly serve as warrants for honor. By virtue of these powers, God acts in such a way that he forces all creation and human beings to do as God wills; in terms of God's creative power the cosmos was ordered and blessed and in terms of God's eschatological power all humans are treated with justice. God's powers warrant praise and honor.

Honor and Response to Challenges

I noted above that it is an essential mark of honor for a person when challenged to respond and so defend his reputation, role, and honor. We find many forms of this throughout I Corinthians that are worth examining, since the defense of God's honor is a major element of Paul's theology. Challenges to God's honor might take the form of: boasting and self-appropriation of benefactions, dismissal of God's values, dismissal of God's plans and powers, and dismissal of God's agents and their roles and tasks.

First, Paul constantly warns some Corinthians not to boast, as though achievement or success or status was in some way achieved on their part. Boasting encroaches on God's sovereignty and thus challenges the Deity. In response, Paul declares, "God chose what is foolish, weak or low and despised . . . to shame the wise and the strong, and to bring to naught things that are" as a response to boasting: "that no human being might boast in the presence of God" (1:29). Warrant for this Paul finds in Jeremiah: "Let him who boasts, boast in the Lord" (1:31; cf. Jer 9:23-24). Moreover, some in the group treat the benefaction and gifts of God as the result of their own achievement, thus tarnishing the honor of the Benefactor and impugning God's benefaction. In response, Paul defends the honor of God: "What have you that you have not received? If then you received it, why do you boast as if it were not a gift?" (4:7).

Second, God's honor seems to be attacked when some devalue what God values and mock what God holds dear. For example, in the argument in 1:18-25 we learn that some dismiss the crucified Christ, considering him "foolishness" or "a stumbling block." This, we are told, reflects the wisdom of the world, but not God's values. Thus God answers the challenge by "destroying the wisdom of the wise and thwarting the cleverness of the clever" (1:19). We learn, therefore, that "the foolishness of God is wiser than men, and the weakness of God is stronger than men" (1:25).

Third, we find a final form of challenge to God's values and plans in the contest about how gifts are evaluated and roles and statuses are accorded. For example, whenever Paul's "apostleship" is attacked, he promptly defends God's ascription of this role to him, from the letter opening ("called by the will of God to be an apostle," 1:1), well into the letter body ("Am I not an apostle? Have I not seen the Lord?" 9:1), and later ("by the grace of God I am what I am," 15:9-10). When Paul lists the roles of service in the church, he lists "first, apostles" (12:28). Thus one who rejects Paul's apostleship dishonors God, who ascribed this to him (see Luke 10:16). And one who thinks worldly thoughts rejects the thoughts of God (see Mark 8:33). As regards spiritual gifts, we observe a competition between tongues and prophecy. In Paul's comparison of them in chapter 14 he ranks prophecy as the better gift because of its utility, a factor noted earlier in Aristotle's list of virtues. Those gifts (or virtues) are greater that benefit others and not the self. In this regard, all of Paul's maps of persons, places, times, and things should be considered expressions of God's values and plans. To contest them is to challenge God. Paul insists that God responds forcefully against this false wisdom (1:19; 3:19-20).

THE GOD OF ORDER AND HOLINESS

Earlier in the exposition of Mark's understanding of God, I urged readers not familiar with the cultural notion of "purity" to consult appendix two on this topic. To that I add the following observations on Paul's appreciation and use of the same material. As an Israelite and especially a Pharisee, Paul was strongly socialized to perceive the world as an utterly orderly cosmos. He shared the same specific cultural definitions of order as found in the Bible and Jerusalem's temple (Newton 1985). Moreover, like other Israelites he frequently used the particular language of clean/unclean and pure/polluted to express his acute sense of order. Israelites in Paul's time applied "clean" to persons, places, times, or things when they fully exemplified the cultural definition of what it means to be a person or an appropriate time or a thing in its proper place. For example, Israelites are clean who have the proper bloodlines, are circumcised, keep Torah, and are not bodily mutilated. Things like foods are clean that conform to the definition of a clean animal in Leviticus; so animals failing to satisfy this definition in any way are unclean and may not be sacrificed to God or eaten at table. Sabbath is holy time on which one rests; working on this day is unclean.

The human body was particularly perceived in terms of clean/unclean in regard to its wholeness. Mutilated or deformed priests could not offer sacrifice in the temple (Lev 21:16-20). Bodily excretions were perceived as dangerous sources of pollution; hence bodies are clean that have no flow of blood, menses, semen, pus, and the like. Bodily surfaces likewise replicate purity; hence skin diseases of any sort (popularly called "leprosy," Pilch 2000:39–54) make one unclean. Excretions and flaking skin indicate material "out of place." These were no minor matters for the Israelites of Paul's world, for full membership and complete participation in the group's activities depended on being pure according to the specific popular understandings of this concept. For uncleanness there was no sympathy or toleration. The following exposition of maps of persons, place, times, and things focuses on the patterns of order, classification, and hierarchy that Paul perceives. According to Paul, these maps were made by God; thus the orderly and ordering God made the world just so. We first study the "God of order" (Neyrey 1990b:31–54).

Maps of Persons

Paul resembles others in his sense of social classification of persons, whether this is a matter of being an "insider" or "outsider" or of hierarchical ranking of persons. His sense of order in the cosmos includes "maps of persons." Paul frequently speaks of some sort of structured social relationship or hierarchy among all peoples, both those in heaven and on earth. To Paul social stratification belongs to the nature of the universe, as this is created and ordered by God. Yet his interest in these maps of persons is not an abstract passion for neatness, but functions directly in regard to the pervasive and ever-present conflicts in his churches over authority, rank, and status. To settle disputed issues of authority and social stratification, Paul appeals to maps of persons to which he was socialized as an Israelite.

Maps of Heavenly Figures

In four passages in I Corinthians Paul attempted to describe the relationship of God first to Christ, but also to Christ and Spirit (I Cor 3:21-23; 11:3; 12:3-5; 15:27-28). It remains for us to describe these maps and to see what they tell us about his orderly God.

1. *Cosmic hierarchy.* "I want you to understand that the head of every man is Christ, and the head of a woman is her husband, and the head of Christ is God" (11:3). Balancing the earthly hierarchy of woman-husband-Christ (i.e., "head" means "relationship of superiority") is the heavenly hierarchy of God as head of the exalted Christ. In heaven, even the risen Jesus, who must surely enjoy maximum freedom, power, and authority, nevertheless remains in a stratified relationship with God. In short, there exists differentiation of role and status even in heaven between God, who is patron, and Jesus, who is supreme client.

2. *Heavenly hierarchy.* In 15:27-28 Paul presents a map similar to 11:3 in which he describes a stratified relationship between God and Christ: "'For God has put all things in subjection under his feet' [Ps 8:6]. But when it says, 'All things are put in subjection under him,' it is plain that he [God] is excepted who put all things under him. When all things are subjected to him [Christ], then the Son himself will be subjected to him [God] who put all things under him, that God may be everything to every one" (15:27-28). God stands atop the pyramid of power, holiness, and purity, while Jesus is positioned at God's "feet," and then all things are under Jesus' "feet." Thus a map of heavenly persons once more positions God above Jesus.

But in the argument in 15:20-28 we find another map that excludes some persons altogether, namely, those who boasted that they had already begun to share in the resurrection (4:8) and so claimed to belong already to the heavenly world (Meeks 1983:121–22). Thus a map may include certain persons and exclude others. Parallel to this map of persons Paul describes a map of time, which explains why those boasters cannot possibly be already in the map of heavenly persons. "But each in his own order: Christ the first fruits, then at his coming those who belong to Christ. Then comes the end, when he delivers the kingdom to God the Father after destroying every rule and every authority and power. . . . The last enemy to be destroyed is death" (15:23-26). The map of time establishes Christ as the first and so far the only risen person in the heavenly realm: "Christ is the first fruits, then at his coming . . . when he delivers. . . ." And since the last enemy is death, no other person has been or will be raised until this final victory. Hence all mortals are still on earth, even if they have died and been raised with Jesus.

3. *Expanded heavenly hierarchy.* Where does the Spirit fit in the heavenly hierarchy? To some in Corinth, the Spirit seems to be the most powerful and significant heavenly figure, such that Jesus and even God seem demoted in some sense. "Now there are varieties of gifts, but the same Spirit; and there are varieties of service, but the same Lord; and there are varieties of working, but it is the same God who inspires them all in everyone" (12:4-6). The way that Paul boldly maps out the hierarchical relationships between God and Jesus also influences how we interpret this passage. Here Paul presents a balanced and parallel set of remarks about three heavenly figures: Spirit, Lord Jesus, and God. Is this an intentional map of persons? How should we read it?

First, Paul affirms unity amid the diversity of the gifts, service, and workings by the repeated use of "varieties . . . same": "varieties . . . same Spirit; varieties . . . same Lord; varieties . . . same God." This implies a harmonious relationship among the three heavenly figures mentioned; there is no rivalry or competition in heaven, despite what occurs in the Corinthian group. Scholars increasingly call attention to Paul's use of political commonplaces about dealing with factionalism and civil strife (Mitchell 1991).

Second, while harmonious, the heavenly figures do not all enjoy an equal role and status. Several reasons suggest that the three figures are listed in ascending order: God, although listed last, must surely be first in rank; God manages the distribution of all the gifts, for example, "God inspires them all in everyone." But what of the ranking of Jesus and Spirit relative to God and to each other? When the discussion of "spiritual gifts" began in 12:1-3, Paul observed that there can be good and bad spirits. The criterion for testing them rests in what they say about Jesus. One spirit declares "Jesus is accursed," whereas the other confesses "Jesus is Lord" (12:3). Thus the good spirit inspired a disciple to bend the knee to Jesus, who is Lord. The good spirit, then, serves the Lord Jesus. The problem in Corinth rests in spiritual people who consider themselves above and beyond all authority; "spirit" has been seen by them as the equivalent of freedom (2 Cor 3:17). What is striking, then, about 12:3 is that spirit inspires disciples to acknowledge the authority and sovereignty of Jesus: "Jesus is Lord." This suggests that the map of heavenly persons in 12:4-6 locates God at the top, Jesus below God, and Spirit below both of them. Paul does not allow Spirit to disrupt God's orderly world (see 1 Cor 14:32-33), and so Spirit is perceived in relationship to the other figures, even serving them. Paul, then, lists the heavenly figures in 12:4-6 in such a way as to convey a map of persons who are not equal in role or status. The function of this type of rhetoric is to describe the macrocosm of heaven in such a way that it can serve as a pattern for the microcosm of earth. In this way some corrective is offered concerning the factions and civil disunity created by some at Corinth, including pneumatic elites.

4. *When earthly folk arrive in heaven.* Will there be a map of persons in heaven? We already know that some hierarchical relationship exists among God, Christ, and Spirit. But what of disciples after they are raised? Will all be alike or identical in heaven? Paul indeed deals with this issue in 1 Corinthians 15 when he begins with examples of earthly status differentiation and argues for comparable heavenly ones. He takes his example from sowing, perhaps because of the similarity of planting with burying the dead: "What you sow is not the body which is to be, but a bare kernel, perhaps of wheat or of some other grain" (15:37). From seeds, Paul moves laterally to maps of living creatures: "For not all flesh is alike, but there is one kind for men, another for animals, another for birds, and another for fish" (15:39). And God is the author of all this earthly differentiation: "God gives it a body as he has chosen, and to each kind of seed its own body" (15:38).

But Paul then differentiates between heavenly and earthly: "There are celestial bodies and there are terrestrial bodies"; and the "glory of the celestial is one, and the glory of the terrestrial is another" (15:40). Thus heavenly glory differs; all are not equal in this glory: "There is one glory of the sun, and another glory of the moon, and another glory of the stars; for star differs from star in glory" (15:41). Maps everywhere! All made by God! But to what purpose? The immediate inference would be that in the heavenly world, all will not have the same glory or the same status.

As regards the function of this material, one would expect this sort of listing to function polemically against and apologetically for certain members of the church: polemically, to deflate those whom Paul accuses of being "puffed up"; apologetically, to raise up those of low status in the group, including

Paul himself. Thus, as regards the fate of the nonelites in the group, Paul describes their transformation into blessed and glorious figures: "So is it with the resurrection of the dead. What is sown is perishable, what is raised is imperishable. It is sown in dishonor, it is raised in glory. It is sown in weakness, it is raised in power. It is sown a physical body, it is raised a spiritual body" (15:42-44). Clearly all are transformed, but the earthly labels "perishable," "dishonor," "weakness," and "physical" would seem especially to describe the current fate of nonelites.

In summary, Paul repeatedly declares maps of persons in the heavenly realm. God, of course, sits or stands alone atop the hierarchy, as source of all creatures and blessings and gifts. The risen Jesus enjoys the role and status of heavenly mediator or broker of God's benefaction; he is located at God's "feet." Spirit, who seems to be the most troublesome figure—at least for the Corinthians—is presented as the servant of Christ ("Jesus is Lord!"). Moreover, Paul argues that this Spirit is subject to rules, such as those of tongues and prophets (14:27-31). Despite how others equate Spirit with "freedom" (2 Cor 3:17), Paul affirms what seems to be an outrageous rule: "the spirits of prophets are subject to the prophets" (1 Cor 14:32). Finally, he states the theological rationale for this: "God is not a God of confusion but of peace" (14:33). I argue that all of Paul's references to the heavenly figures of God, Christ, and Spirit are by no means speculative remarks, but model how the earthly church should think and act. If there is authority in heaven, it exists on earth as well; if there is differentiation of role and status in heaven, the same is true for earth; if there are maps of persons in heaven, there will be similar ones on earth. At bottom, then, is a pervasive understanding of God as a God of order.

5. *Heavenly maps inform earthly maps.* One map deserves attention because it seems to make a heavenly map of persons in the macrocosm the pattern for relationships in the earthly microcosm. Before Paul states his rules for how the heads of males and females should be covered or coiffed at the group's worship, he makes a map of "heads" in heaven and on earth that he intends to serve as an axiom that guarantees his remarks: "But I want you to understand that the head of every man is Christ, the head of a woman is her husband, and the head of Christ is God" (11:3). The metaphor for heaven and earth is "head," not meaning the physical bodily part but the role, status, and thus authority (Fitzmyer 1993a; D. Martin 1995:229–33). Thus we discern

parallel hierarchies: *heavenly*—God is the head of Christ; and *earthly*—husbands are the heads of their wives. But Jesus is also the "head of the husbands," mediating God's authority to the church and the worship and petitions of the church to God. Thus three classes of people find themselves in superior/inferior relationships: Christ (to God), husbands (to Christ), and wives (to husbands). As we saw above in regard to a similar map in 15:20-28, this discourse effectively tells the group's elites and those who think that by the Spirit they already share in the fullness of the new status of Christians that even in heaven "authority" exists that translates into maps of persons; thus all the more, authority of "headship" or authority exists on earth. If it is not unseemly for the risen Jesus, made Lord of all, to have a "head" over him as he sits at the feet of God, then neither is authority nor ranking unseemly for mortals.

Maps of Persons within the Church

Although my focus is on Paul's grand map of persons that reflects his thoughts about God, I note in passing how insistently Paul makes and uses maps of persons. For example, Paul lists those to whom the risen Jesus appeared: "he appeared to Cephas, then to the twelve. Then he appeared to more than five hundred brethren . . . then he appeared to James, then to all the apostles. Last of all, as to one untimely born, he appeared also to me. For I am the least of the apostles" (15:5-9). This list functions significantly for Paul, because those to whom Jesus appeared were thereby ascribed the specific role of "apostle" with specific rights and duties. This grounds Paul's own role and status: "Am I not an apostle? Have I not seen the Lord?" (9:1). The map in 15:5-9, because it is also a chronological map of time, establishes a ranking among the visionaries. Cephas is first in time (Luke 24:34); at that point the risen Jesus affirmed his leadership among the brethren (Luke 22:31-32; John 21:15-19). Paul, however, stands last, not simply because he seems to have been the last in time to receive Jesus' apparition, but also because he is "the least of the apostles, unfit to be called an apostle." He even persecuted the church. Thus a map of persons replicates a map of times. But Paul argues that God understands his last-place finish differently: "I am what I am by the grace of God, and his grace in me has not been in vain" (1 Cor 15:10). God, then, can act to change the status of the "last" and "least," warning us that maps of persons on earth are subject to God's confirmation or overthrow.

Paul presents another map that describes the ranking and status of prominent persons within the church: "And God has appointed in the church first apostles, second prophets, third teachers, then workers of miracles, then healers, helpers, administrators, speakers in various kinds of tongues. Are all apostles? Are all prophets? Are all teachers? Do all work miracles? Do all possess gifts of healing? Do all speak with tongues? Do all interpret?" (12:28-30). My reading sees this as a map of persons in the church that Paul composed in an apologetic vein to confirm the hierarchical ranking of persons and gifts in a church rife with factionalism. First, note that it is God who "appointed" these roles and statuses, and so God makes this map. Second, the highest three statuses are marked, "*first* apostles, *second* prophets, *third* teachers." This is surely not a chronology of their appearance (a map of time), but a map of ranking and so precedence. The ranking is repeated in a series of rhetorical questions that exclude the many while highlighting the few: "Are *all* apostles?" Of course not, only a few "apostles" are listed in 15:5-9. "Are *all* prophets?" No, only a few. This rhetoric reinforces that ranking encoded in "first . . . second . . . third" above. The middle of the list, which seems quite innocuous, is followed by the listing of tongues last, at the end, which is also a rhetorical strategy on Paul's part. I conclude, then, that the most important persons/gifts are listed first, while the least important (in Paul's eyes) are relegated to last place. Most importantly, Paul argues that "God appointed" this map of persons and corresponding gifts.

A complete investigation of Paul's map of persons should include his description of the body of Christ. When Paul remarked concerning the body of Christ, "one body—Judeans or Greeks, slaves or free" (12:13), he said this in support of the oneness of the body of Christ: "Just as the body is one and has many members, and all the members of the body, though many are one body, so it is with Christ" (12:12). We read such remarks in conjunction with Paul's distress at the division of the church into competing factions (1:11-12; 3:3-4; 11:18-19). But he did not mean that the one body had no appropriate map of persons/parts. Oneness does not preclude role diversity or status differentiation. "If the foot should say, 'Because I am not a hand, I do not belong to the body,' that would not make it any less a part of the body. And if the ear should say, 'Because I am not an eye, I do not belong to the body,' that would not make it any less a part of the body . . . but as it is, God arranged the organs in the body, each one of them, as he chose" (12:15-18). One way to read this would be to link people in the church with these bodily parts and organs. Then "hand" and "eye" would represent the honorable part of the body, those that are associated with power and with the face (Malina and Neyrey 1991:35–36; Neyrey 1998a:65–67); they correspond to the social and/or pneumatic elites. Those who are "not hand" or "ear," presumably those of lower social status, would represent the "weak" or "foolish" who make up the nonelites of the group. In Paul's allegory, this last category would be complaining of its low status, to whom Paul replies: "God arranged the organs of the body . . . as he chose." By this comment he means that God made the map of persons in the body of the church. The map, then, is by no means an egalitarian map, but a map or hierarchy of different roles and statuses.

Finally, Paul presents a curious description of his relationship to Apollos, presumably his rival in Corinth: "One says, 'I belong to Paul,' and another, 'I belong to Apollos'" (3:4). Clearly in the eyes of the church some sort of rearrangement is taking place about the role and status of Paul and Apollos, which seems to be discussed in the rhetorical form known as the "comparison" (or *synkrisis*). Paul joins in this comparison: "What then is Apollos? What is Paul? Servants through whom you believed, as the Lord assigned to each" (3:5). Paul implies that he and Apollos are equal in role and status: they are "servants . . . as the Lord assigned to each." Nevertheless, God's map of persons indicates that both Paul and Apollos have the same role, servant. But this word, *diakonos,* while we often associate it with table service, has as one of its prime meanings a figure such as a messenger or ambassador from kings or gods (J. N. Collins 1990:195–97). "Servant," then, would be a high-ranking person; and depending on the status of the sender, the *diakonos* would have a comparably high status.

But Paul changes the metaphor for comparison of Apollos and himself, from "servant" to "farmer" and then to "builder": "I planted, Apollos watered, but God gave the growth. So neither he who plants nor he who waters is anything, but only God who gives the growth. He who plants and he who waters are equal, and each shall receive his wages according to his labor. For we are God's fellow workers; you are God's field, God's building" (3:7-9). On the one hand, it would appear that Paul eschews role and status competition with Apollos: "neither he plants nor he who waters is anything . . . he who plants and he who waters are 'equal.'" Thus Paul does not seem to envision a map of persons that differentiates him and his rival. On the other hand, he distinguishes Apollos and himself according to a map of time, which indeed serves to construct a map of persons. Three times Paul affirmed that he was first ("I planted") and that Apollos was second ("Apollos watered"). In this letter maps of time serve to create or confirm maps of persons: Christ as "first fruits" and Paul as "last and least of the apostles." Hence we are cautioned to take seriously the priority of "planting" to "watering." God, of course, is in charge: "God gave the grown . . . neither planter nor waterer is anything, but only God." And God will pay the wages of each "according to his labor." Nevertheless, God made Paul the first figure, the planter, and Apollos the second figure, the waterer. Thus Paul and Apollos are not equal or the same, for the discoverer, founder, planter, father, and so on always enjoys more honor than all who come later. Thus, Paul implies, he has from God a divinely ascribed role and status; that is, he ranks high on the map of persons of the Corinthian group. This is God's doing, and failure to honor the agent means refusal to honor the sender.

Maps of Things

Many things might be mapped and thus classified as "in place" or "out of place" and as "clean" or "unclean." To begin with, food, the premier example of this in Second Temple Judaism, was classified by the explicit and implicit system of foods found in Genesis 1, Lev 11:1-47, and Deut 14:3-21 (Douglas 1966:41–57; Soler 1979). Despite the controversy over whether to eat meat sacrificed to idols, Paul proposes that all foods are clean, and so there is no classification of them for those in Christ (1 Cor 10:25-26). Eating and drinking, while needing regulation, were not a matter of kosher food laws. Second, note that when Paul lists related items, he arranges them in some sequence; that is, he makes a map of things that ranks or orders them. When speaking of the materials that a "wise master architect" might use to construct a building, presumably a temple, Paul enumerates the items according to a value listing: "Now if any one builds on the foundation with gold, silver, precious stone, wood, hay, straw . . ." (3:12). The map systematically arranges the most precious things first, ahead of the nonprecious materials; and, gold ranks above silver, which ranks above polished stones.

On the relative importance of spiritual gifts in Corinth, Paul labors again and again to classify them as more or less valuable and to list them in ways that suggest this classification. For example, we find a list of spiritual gifts in

I Corinthians 12: "To each is given the manifestation of the Spirit for the common good. To one is given through the Spirit the utterance of wisdom, and to another the utterance of knowledge . . . to another faith . . . to another gifts of healing . . . to another the working of miracles, to another prophecy, to another the ability to distinguish between spirits, to another various kinds of tongues, to another the interpretation of tongues" (12:7-10). In lists such as these, the beginnings and endings are important. First mentioned, and presumably most highly valued, are wisdom and knowledge, which we know were prized by this group. But last on the list are tongues and interpretation of tongues, which Paul considered disorderly and thus harmful to the group.

We might also consider the lists of gifts in I Corinthians 13 and the comparison of tongues and prophecy in chapter 14, for Paul likewise lists and classifies them in a hierarchical map of things. Although Paul does not state in regard to the materials of chapters 13–14 that God is their source and benefactor, that is a safe inference. Thus we consider that in the way "God made some apostles . . . prophets . . . teachers" (12:28), so God also gives gifts of differing excellence and significance. Excellence of gift replicates and expresses the role and status of those who receive it.

Maps of Times

Just to finish the portrait of Paul's world as an orderly, map-oriented cosmos, let us quickly examine one more basic segment of human experience that can be mapped: time. Paul understands a map of time that spans from creation at the beginning to "the end" when all are raised and judged.

As regards the beginning of time, Paul identifies God as the figure "from whom are all things and for whom all exist" (8:6). I attach to this statement of God as creator the remark about foods, "The earth is the Lord's and everything in it" (10:26; cf. Ps 24:1), which argues that all that God created is holy and good.

Time as past and present occupies much of Paul's attention; he organizes time as the superiority of either present to past or future to present. In general, the most basic time marker is some form of "then" versus "now" (Dahl 1975b:32–33):

1. "Then" versus "now" (Rom 6:17-22; 11:30; Gal 4:8-9; 3:23-27; Eph 2:11-22; 5:8)
2. "Once" but "now" (Rom 1:18—3:20; 3:21—8:39; Col 1:21-22; Eph 2:1-10)

3. "Mystery hidden" versus "mystery now revealed" (Rom 16:25-26; I Cor 2:6-10; Eph 3:4-7, 8-11)
4. "Mystery promised" versus "mystery now given" (2 Tim 1:9-11; 1 Pet 1:18-21)

The mapping of time here juxtaposes the past (sinful, ignorant, etc.) with the present (justified, enlightened, etc.). In regard to the corrupt sexual relationship in I Corinthians 5, Paul argues that the group should in the present be "unleavened" and totally free of the past, that is, "the leaven of malice and evil." The dividing moment between past and present is Christ's cross (see Gal 3:13-14; Rom 3:22-26). Because "Christ our paschal lamb is sacrificed" (I Cor 5:7), the past, characterized by leaven and sin, should be behind them, a time of evil overcome by the victory of the Lamb. Thus the present time alone is pure and holy; the past, a time of sinfulness and evil.

If Paul argues in 5:6-8 that some have slid back into the past, in other places he notes that some have not advanced from the past to the present. In Corinthians this takes the form of "childhood" versus "adulthood." Children are fed milk, not meat; adult food is for adults. Proof of their childishness is found in their behavior, "jealousy and strife among you." Thus Paul argues: "I fed you with milk, not solid food; for you were not ready for it" (3:1-2). Thus past time in this case, while not sinful or malevolent, represents something of low status, such as children have. Ideally, the babes here should be adults by now.

Similarly, in I Corinthians 13 Paul urges the group to "grow up" in Christ, that is, to outgrow its fascination with certain spiritual gifts and to behave like adults: "When I was a child, I spoke like a child, I thought like a child, I reasoned like a child; when I became an adult I gave up childish ways" (13:11). The context has to do with a contested map of gifts, "prophecy, tongues, knowledge" (13:8). According to the comparison that Paul argues, "love" surpasses all other gifts in value; it alone is the adult gift that expresses mature behavior. In addition to the child-versus-adult classification, Paul states that the contested gifts "pass away" and "cease"; and well they should, for they are "imperfect." Such things fascinate "children," but should not continue to influence "adults." Thus Paul declares in the comparison of prophecy and tongues: "Do not be children in your thinking; be babes in evil, but in thinking be mature" (14:20). The key to child versus adult lies in Paul's classification system of times and things.

In regard to present time, twice Paul reminds the group of God's immediate faithfulness to them (1:9; 10:13). Moreover, the mysteries and knowledge that God once kept secret are revealed now through Paul (2:7). And if God is the giver of all gifts, roles, and statuses, then God the Benefactor is active in the present.

Paul also describes a map of future time, whose radical distance from present time serves a polemical function in the document. We saw above that some in the group thought themselves already beyond death and evil; hence when Paul maps out a cosmic calendar for the end of time, he responds to their erroneous map of time. Jesus, the first fruits of God's resurrection, is thus far the only person to overcome death. In 15:23-26 Paul reveals a map of time that identifies who experiences the resurrection in what temporal order: "Christ the *first* fruits, *then* at his coming those who belong to Christ. *Then* comes the end. . . . The *last* enemy to be destroyed is death." The map of times replicates a map of persons, a common phenomenon. It establishes that Christ alone has already been raised, a remark deflating the claims of certain elites in the group.

The raising of the dead is the prelude to divine judgment, to rewards and punishments. This too has a significant place in Paul's map of time, probably because the same elites who considered themselves already in Christ's risen life would also deny that they face a future judgment. In several places Paul indicates that God will judge evildoers, either the temple defilers (3:16-17) or those who do evil and so do not inherit God's kingdom (6:9-10). But Paul also writes in two places about judgment in an apologetic and a polemical manner to rebuff criticism of himself (4:1-5) and to correct elitism (10:5-11), respectively. Present judgments of Paul by group members have no importance, for only the future judgment of God matters, of which Paul is confident. But the story of God's displeasure with the exodus generation that was destroyed in the desert serves as an apt example that the present favor of God that the group enjoys is no guarantee of God's future favor.

Thus God is active in all times: in the beginning and at the ending, and in past, present, and future. Indeed, God's actions in the past guarantee what God will do in the future: "God raised up the Lord and will raise us up by his power" (6:14). Although God is not measured by "first . . . second . . . third," temporal sequences for mortals are God's doing. Hence Peter and other apostles were called first, while Paul was the last and least. God made Paul "first" as planter and Apollos "second" as waterer. As with maps of persons and things, maps of time also have an argumentative function in the document, either promoting Paul's role and status or demoting the claims of some elites. Paul, the mature, wise adult, chastises his opponents for being children who eat the food of infants or who crave the toys and games of children.

Maps of Place

All know that the Jerusalem temple was spatially mapped according to a hierarchy of "holy" places. Mishnah *Kelim* 1.6-9 contains just such a map, indicating "ten degrees of holiness": from lands outside Israel, to cities, to Jerusalem, to the Temple Mount, with its Court of the Women, Court of the Israelites, and then Court of the Priests. Within the last court are the area between the porch and the altar, the sanctuary, and finally the holy of holies. Each place enjoys an increasing sense of holiness in proximity to the presence of God in the holy of holies. Moreover, we know of maps of persons that correspond to this map of places, since not all peoples enjoy the same degree of holiness to enter these spaces. Gentiles stand behind a balustrade that keeps them from Israelites; male Israelites may stand close but outside the area of the altar, which is reserved for Levites and priests; only the high priest may enter the holy of holies. The holy temple also contains maps of time and things. It enjoyed an elaborate liturgical calendar that scheduled daily, weekly, monthly, seasonal, and annual prayer and worship. Atop the south wall, a trumpeter signaled the start of the Sabbath and the beginning of the day—precise times. As regards offerings, the animals must be "clean" or "pure," which refers both to their gender and age as well as their bodily wholeness. Thus the temple functioned as the prime embodiment of a map of place, whose patterns were replicated in maps of persons, times, and things.

We turn now to Paul's remarks on the temple in 3:16-17. Paul frequently calls members of the group "saints" or holy ones (1:2; 6:1, 2; 7:14; 14:33; 16:1, 15), people who would be acceptable in the Jerusalem temple. Their suitability for entering sacred space is well expressed in the remark: "But you were washed, you were sanctified, you were justified in the name of Jesus Christ and in the Spirit of our God" (6:11). But while they may gather in a house to worship, these disciples have no fixed sacred space, that is, no temple. Yet like many other New Testament authors, Paul likens the group itself to a temple. First, "according to the grace of God," Paul himself became a "wise master builder" (3:10), who laid a foundation for a building, which I understand as preaching the gospel and thus creating the Corinthian temple.

When he asks them, "Do you not know that you are God's temple and that God's Spirit dwells in you?" (3:16), this question presupposes that he said this already and that they know it already. This simple term, "temple," evokes the sense of purity, organization, and separation of uncleanness that we saw above (Milgrom 1991:718–28). As with the Jerusalem temple, so too with Corinth, if "any one destroys God's temple, God will destroy him" (3:17). This judgment statement means that if anyone makes the temple of the holy God profane or incomplete or corrupt, then the holy God will treat them like a profanation and expel them.

Thus a basic map of space distinguishes "inside" from "outside" the group. "Inside" refers to the temple and so holiness and perfection; "outside" means people who have not been washed, sanctified, or justified. Moreover, if "inside" is holy and pure as one expects of a temple, then when uncleanness or pollution is found within, it must be expelled.

God of Purity and Holiness

We can appreciate the powerful significance of God's "holiness" in 3:16-17 by considering briefly the contagious "unholiness" described in 5:1-13. A prohibited sexual alliance is reported, which Paul labels as a contagious pollution. He likens it to leaven, which the ancients consider unclean and corrupting because it causes flour to become "too much" as it inflates and to emit an unpleasant odor. Paul, a Pharisee's Pharisee, knows well the biblical materials that prohibit any leaven in connection with sacrifices or grain offerings offered to God, as proscribed in Exod 23:18; Lev 2:11; 6:17. Leaven is also proscribed during Passover. Plutarch's remarks indicate that the symbolism of leaven as corruption was common in the Greco-Roman world as well:

> For the leaven itself is generated out of corruption and when mixed corrupts the mass, for it becomes slack and powerless and in general the leavened thing appears to be putrid; then, increasing, it becomes sour and corrupts the flour. (*Quaest. rom.* 289F)

> People say, too, that flour rises better at the time of the full moon; indeed, leavening is much the same process as putrefaction, and if the proper time limit be ignored, leavening in making dough porous and light produces the same decomposition in the end. (*Quaest. conv.* 659B)

Thus leaven connoted a spreading corruption that evoked intolerance, for it signaled a major pollution, not unlike gangrene (2 Tim 2:17). Paul convokes a judicial forum that expels from the group a man engaged in a prohibited sexual union. Paul labels it a "leaven" or corruption: "a little leaven leavens the whole batch" (I Cor 5:6). This powerful label creates a sense of threatening uncleanness. On the one hand, Christ has been sacrificed at the Feast of Unleavened Bread, so all his followers should be unleavened, that is, sinless and pure. This purity, then, is the treasure won for the group. The old leaven, if it remains, threatens their interests. On the other hand, the sense of God's holiness drawn from the Scriptures expects and requires the expulsion of this corrupting person: "Drive out the wicked person from among you" (5:13; cf. Deut 17:7; 19:19). Conversely, to allow the corrupting uncleanness to remain in the group is to show utter contempt for God's holiness.

Of course, the holiest place of all is the center of the heavens and the throne of God. Unclean sinners cannot even enter into the kingdom of God (I Cor 6:9-10). But what about the saints of Corinth who, while not unclean sinners, are still unfit for the presence of God? Paul claims to have a prophetic revelation about this situation that embodies the understanding of God's "holiness" we are considering: "I tell you this, brethren: flesh and blood cannot inherit the kingdom of God" (15:50). At first this implies that the Corinthian saints are at a serious loss, because all the saints are perishable, and "the perishable cannot inherit the imperishable" (15:50b). Obviously, the dead would seem to be at an even greater disadvantage, because God is the God of the living, and nothing unclean or corrupt like a corpse would ever appear in the presence of the God of life. But Paul tells us a prophetic mystery: "We shall not all sleep, but we shall all be changed . . . for the trumpet will sound, and the dead will be raised imperishable, and we shall be changed. For this perishable nature must put on the imperishable, and this mortal nature must put on immortality. When the perishable puts on the imperishable, and the mortal puts on immortality . . ." (15:51-54). The "trumpet," of course, is God's; thus God orchestrates the great transformation described. The dead will be resurrected as "deathless" or "imperishable" and so suitable for the presence of the God of life. "All" those living must likewise be changed, divesting themselves of perishability and mortality and vesting themselves with imperishability and immortality. Thus they become alive as God is alive; and so are fit for the presence of the living God. Thus they become "holy as I am holy."

Summary: "God Is a God of Order"

Paul indeed perceives the world as intensely ordered, an integrated system of maps of persons, things, and times. Obviously this system includes God's relationship to figures in the heavenly as well as the earthly worlds. The *heavenly* maps affirm the unqualified supremacy of God even over the risen Jesus (11:3; 15:27-28) and the Spirit (12:4-6). God, "from whom are all things and for whom we exist" (8:6), enjoys the most honorable role and status in heaven. But why does Paul talk like this? What does it tell us about the nature of God? I suspect that various members of the Corinthian group not only had favorite earthly leaders ("I am for Paul! I am for Apollos! I am for Cephas!"), but also heavenly patrons. For example, some seem obsessed with the Spirit and the gifts of this Spirit to the diminishment of the roles of God as benefactor and Jesus as heavenly sovereign. Some even apparently said, "Jesus be cursed!" (12:3), which seems to be more a discrediting of the value of his physical death than a dismissal of him, but a stumbling block and folly nonetheless (1:23). It signals that some in the group are engaged in a competition among heavenly figures parallel to that of earthly ones. The reiteration of the heavenly hierarchy in the heavenly maps of persons could be said to serve a polemical function to ensure that Spirit remains God's Spirit and does not have an independent patronage. Furthermore, if in the heavenly realm both Jesus and Spirit fit into a map of persons, such that authority, hierarchy, and differentiation exist even among them, then one might argue that this macrocosmic pattern should serve to legitimate the same structural phenomena in the microcosm.

Similarly, we find maps of *persons on earth* and *in the church*. Of significance for us is Paul's persistence in affirming that God authored these maps, hence God ascribed to individuals their rank and status.

> Paul, called by the will of God to be an apostle (1:1)
> Apollos? Paul? . . . servants as the Lord assigned to each (3:5)
> God arranged the organs of the body, each one of them as he chose (12:18)
> God has appointed in the church, first apostles, second prophets, third teachers (12:28)
> God gives it a body as he has chosen, and to each kind of seed its own body (15:38)

The God of order in the macrocosm established maps of persons in the microcosm. This serves not only to give heavenly weight to the ascribed role and status of figures like Paul versus others who seem to be achieving their status, but also to validate the authority, hierarchy, roles, and status of members of the group. Thus, although some wave the banner of freedom, proclaiming "All things are lawful to me" (6:12; 10:23) or declaring that they are so mature in the Spirit that they have graduated beyond teachers, rules, and laws, Paul's affirmation of heavenly authority in his maps of persons serves to moderate such lawless cries of absolute freedom (Malina 1978). At stake Paul sees the honor of God: those who receive Paul receive not Paul but the one who sent him. Hence the map that classifies persons is God's doing and God's will, and so God's honor is at stake.

God's order, we saw, is intimately related to God's *holiness.* Thus to be "holy as I am holy" means to side with God, who is totally separated from sin and so from death. Hence God's holiness is incompatible with sinfulness, especially sins labeled as corruptions; the sinner must be separated from the holy group before he corrupts it. The list of vices in 6:9-10 means that such people "will not inherit the kingdom of God." For earthly members of the church to enter into the presence of the heavenly Lord, they must be separated entirely from "mortality" and "perishability."

Finally, as we examine God-the-Orderer and God-Who-Is-Holy, we learn more about Paul's theology, that is, about the nature of God. In the treatment of Romans, we learned that ancient philosophy not only discussed the "nature of God" but also the "ethics" that follow from this. Clearly, the "ethics" that flow from the nature of God-as-Orderer touch upon authority, rules, and laws, as well as roles and statuses. Issues like freedom are contextualized; "love," which is the "building up of the neighbor," is the greatest of gifts. Whatever "puffs up" threatens the purity, order, and charity of the group. What could be clearer than the rules for managing prophecy and tongues? These rules are "ethics" or proper behavior that flows from the nature of God: "For God is not a God of confusion, but of peace" (14:33).

THE GOD OF DISORDER AND REVERSAL

God, however, acts in ways that create disorder and reverse human notions of order. In the course of his argument, Paul signals that God has made new maps of persons, which has to do with a heavenly reassessment of what honor, status, and worth mean. In the eyes of many this will look like disorder, a studied reversal of or rejection of the content of earthly indices of honor, even disorder of the highest rank (Neyrey 1990b:56–74). Paul will argue about the positioning of three figures on God's new map of persons: Christ Jesus, the nonelite members of the church, and Paul himself.

Christ Jesus: God's Weakness and Foolishness

According to Paul's reading of Scripture, God should be seen as acting in predictable ways in God's dealings with the world. But Paul also sees God reversing patterns of honor and turning upside down the old maps of persons. God, he perceives, reverses patterns of preference and precedence. Paul begins the letter with a discussion of the greatest example of this divine reversal, namely, the crucified Christ. According to the map of honorable persons shared by Judeans and Greeks alike, a crucified person has no place there whatsoever. The crucified Christ is "a stumbling block to Judeans and folly to Gentiles" (1:23). Yet according to God's new map of persons, Christ crucified is uniquely "the power of God and the wisdom of God" (1:24).

Paul argues in 1:18-25 about God's freedom to reverse status and honor. To begin with, he proclaims his own ascribed but strange authority to speak: "Christ . . . sent me to preach the gospel, and not with eloquent wisdom, lest the cross of Christ be emptied of his power" (1:17). How bizarre: a message of foolishness spoken by a weak speaker! Yet, as many have noted, Paul delivers a rhetorical argument in 1:18-25 of craft and persuasiveness.

Thesis: He affirms the value of the cross as a symbol as he contrasts two evaluations of it based on the results of these considerations: "For the 'word of the cross' is folly to those who are perishing, but to us who are being saved, it is the power of God" (1:18). Both cannot be true; but how then do we know that the cross is "the power of God"?

Proof: In antiquity proof may come from authority, celebrated authors, and writings; in this case, God's word as found in Isa 29:14 serves as the proof that the new heavenly map of values and persons is true: "I will destroy the wisdom of the wise, and the cleverness of the clever I will thwart" (1 Cor 1:19). At stake here is not just "the power of God," but now the "wisdom" of God. In principle, God's wisdom corrects earthly wisdom, and thus upsets or reverses what passes for honor and worth on earth.

Argument: Given that God acts in God's unique ways, what does this mean for earthly people and their values? In a series of questions Paul asserts that differing judgments about this are simply wrong, for God aggressively attacks them: "Where is the wise man . . . the scribe . . . the debater?" (1:20a). Questions for the ancients were aggressive weapons, not seeking information so much as to defeat and deflate (Neyrey 1998b:658–64). Of course, God's evaluation alone counts, and in this case it is hostile to the honor of earthly wisdom: "Has not God made foolish the wisdom of the world?" (1:20b). Up to this point, the argument has functioned abstractly, contrasting heavenly and earthly wisdom; but Paul now applies the thesis he has established in the service of the problem in Corinth. Paul admits that what he preaches, "Christ crucified," does not enjoy honor and respect in the eyes of the wise and powerful elites of Corinth. The thesis of God's aggressive criticism of earthly wisdom in 1:18-20 is now invoked in support of Paul's preaching: "For since, in the wisdom of God, the world did not know God through wisdom, it pleased God through the folly of what we preach to save those who believe" (1:21). God's criticism of earthly wisdom continues, but now in terms of how the cross of Christ is evaluated: "For Judeans demand signs and Greeks seek wisdom, but we preach Christ crucified, a stumbling block to Jews and folly to Gentiles, but to those who are called, both Judeans and Greeks, Christ the power of God and the wisdom of God" (1:22-24). Thus God's criteria for worth and honor, whereby God constructs a map of persons, sounds like earthly criteria, "wisdom" and "power." But God locates these in the crucified Christ, a person who appears utterly "shamed" by this (Heb 12:1-2) and even "cursed" by the cross (Gal 3:14). This logic, of course, makes no earthly sense, until one appreciates that the nature of God is often to be the one who turns the world upside down and reverses status and honor: "For the foolishness of God is wiser than men, and the weakness of God is stronger than men" (1 Cor 1:25).

What do we know from this? Two basic things. First, the crucified Jesus is located differently on two maps of persons. The earthly map of the elite utterly devalues his death, especially his shameful death. In turn they value his transformation by God's resurrection of him into a deathless, free, powerful, all-wise person of cosmic stature. Everything prior to the resurrection, then, looks utterly weak and foolish. But God's map of persons finds in the crucified Christ wisdom, not foolishness; power, not weakness; and honor, not shame.

Second, the dominant figure in the argument in 1:18-25 is God; we learn what God values, how God acts in the world, where God's honorable qualities lie, that is, wisdom and power. In this we learn that the God of order is also a God of disorder when it comes to human values and maps. In case any are tempted to dismiss God's ways, perish the thought! We learn that God's foolishness is wiser than human wisdom and God's weakness is stronger than human strength. Paul basically repeats this description of the God of disorder when he warns the "wise" of the group about God's wisdom: "If any one thinks that he is wise in this age, let him become a fool that he may become wise. For the wisdom of the world is folly with God" (3:18). Proof? Again an appeal to authority, in this case, Scripture: "He catches the wise in their craftiness" (Job 5:13), and "The Lord knows that the thoughts of the wise are futile" (Ps 94:11). Whereas in many places God is the author of order, which is presented by easily discerned maps, we now discover that God can be the author of disorder. The only way to know when this is the case seems to rest on an apostle and prophet like Paul who claims to have God's inspiration to understand this.

Corinth's Nonelites: Honored by God

By nonelites I mean members of the Corinthian church who do not boast of wisdom, strength, freedom, or some spiritual gift and who obviously lack recognizable marks of honor and status. This category includes artisans and slaves, who come late to the Eucharist, presumably because they have duties in the houses where they serve; and at the meetings they have meager food to eat. Nor would they eat at sacrificial meals at Corinth's temples. The human map of persons based on honor and worth would locate these nonelites at the very bottom of its hierarchies, for they have no honorable roles in society or in the group and their status is undistinguished (Meeks 1983:51–73). It would be easy for the elites, that is, the "wise" and "powerful," to "puff themselves up" in regard to them (Mitchell 1991:65–183). But, I suspect, there is another map of persons the criteria for whose status is determined by God.

Immediately following the map of God's location of the crucified Christ in 1:18-25, Paul applies the principle argued there to the status and honor of the nonelite group. All are to "consider your call, sisters and brothers" (1:26). The social fact is that "not many of you were wise according to worldly standards, not many were powerful, not many were of noble birth."

By traditional maps of persons, then, they are devoid of power and pedigree that warrant high ranking on the ladder of stratification. But,

> God chose what is foolish in the world to shame the wise,
> God chose what is weak in the world to shame the strong,
> God chose what is low and despised in the world, even things that are not,
> to bring to nothing things that are. (1:27-28)

Three times Paul tells us that "God chose" these low-status persons, making this phrase the operative focus of his argument. Furthermore, God chose to bring disorder into the world by reversing the status of elites and nonelites. God attacked the value system that undergirds the traditional map of persons ("wise," "strong," and "honorable"), and the agents of God's reversal are figures who have scant if any space on the map, "foolish," "weak," and "low and despised." God, then, raises the lowly and casts the mighty from their thrones (Luke 1:52); God makes the last to be first and the first to be last.

Paul has carefully linked 1 Cor 1:18-25 with 26-30, a rhetorical point worthy of notice. In both passages the issue is how to evaluate "wise and foolish," "strong and weak," and "honored and despised." The crucified Christ, perceived by many as foolish and weak, is in God's eyes wisdom and strength. In 1:26-30 the nonelite members of the group are "weak" and "foolish" and "despised." But just as God made Christ "the power of God and the wisdom of God" (1:24), so God chose the nonelites to challenge the status of the elites. In both passages God acts to reverse status and thus to redraw a map of persons (1:19 and 27).

Why does Paul describe God in this way? Paul seems to have both a polemical and an apologetic thrust in his articulation. First, Paul himself attacks those who would seem to disparage him because of his lack of wisdom and strength. Elites, who seem to be the referent of Paul's frequent remarks about being "puffed up" (4:18-19; 5:2; 8:1), are those very conscious of their status and position on the traditional map of persons; indeed, they seem to "boast" of this. How convenient, then, for Paul to find in the Scriptures a view of God as one who rewrites maps of persons and who reverses status. Thus this argument about the "nature of God" attacks his enemies and defends his friends.

In Paul's discussion of the social differentiation of the members of the body of Christ in 12:12-27, we saw earlier that in one section he confirms the traditional map of persons (12:14-19), which differentiates according to roles and statuses. Thus there are noble and less noble limbs and organs, that is, "eyes," "hand," and "ears." This status hierarchy is God's doing: "God arranged the organs in the body . . . as he chose" (12:18). But juxtaposed to this, Paul narrates the arrogant voice of elites who effectively devalue and dismiss nonelites to the edges of the map: "I have no need of you." Paul argues against this by claiming unique value for them: "On the contrary, the parts of the body which seem to be weaker are indispensable, and those parts of the body which we think less honorable we invest with the greater honor, and our unpresentable parts are treated with greater modesty, which our more presentable parts do not require" (12:22-24). Where does this argument come from? Paul claims that "God has composed the body, giving the greater honor to the inferior part" (12:25). These low-status folk do not overthrow those of high status, as Paul argued in 1:26-30. Rather they are acknowledged to have worth and value, "indispensable . . . greater honor . . . greater modesty."

Since the measure of worth and status is "honor," we do well to see how Paul moderates the understanding of it here. If honor traditionally resides in public body parts such as "eye," "hand," and "head" (12:14-16), here honor conversely belongs to private body parts such as the genitals and buttocks. Moreover, honor is either achieved by personal prowess (military, athletic, aesthetic) or ascribed by a high-ranking person. In both 12:14-18 and 22-24, God ascribes all honor to elites and nonelites alike. The honor understood in 12:14-18 legitimated a map of persons based on traditional rank and status, thus distancing elites from nonelites. It has a centrifugal force that pushes the nonelites to the edges of the map. In contrast, the honor in 12:21-24 displays a centripetal force that brings the periphery into the center. Thus all enjoy honor, not just the elites. As already noted, God ascribes honor to each and every member: as regards honorable parts, "God arranged the organs in the body . . . as he chose" (12:18); and as regards nonhonorable parts: "God has so composed the body, giving the greater honor to the inferior part" (12:24). God, then, is both a God of order (12:18) and of disorder (12:24).

Paul, All over the Map

At the top of God's map of persons we find the crucified Christ, despite the foolishness and weakness of the cross. Then "God chose" those in the church who like Jesus, that is, are "not wise . . . not powerful," and raised them high on God's map of persons. Third, Paul boasts that he voluntarily forewent "wisdom" so that the faith of the group may rest on the "power" of God. Paul argues that he indeed has both "wisdom" and "power," which should warrant a very high location on the map of persons. But he intentionally did not come "proclaiming to you the testimony of God in lofty words of wisdom" (2:1). Why? He chose to "know" nothing among them "except Christ, and him crucified" (2:2). We should read "know" here as "evaluate," that is, he evaluates all according to the true principle of worth and status. Thus Paul's performance left much to be desired according to earthly standards; he was with them "in weakness and in much fear and trembling; and my speech and message were not in plausible words of wisdom" (2:3-4). This value strategy, then, is Paul's choice; by it he imitates the "foolish" and "weak" crucified Christ and he ensures that the "wisdom" and "power" of his Patron-God are respected. Thus, whereas "weakness" and "foolishness" are negative criteria for worth among mortals and warrant a low or distant place on the map of persons, in the disorderly world of God they are positive markers and positively warrant a central or high place on the new map of persons.

Throughout the letter Paul defends himself against a negative understanding of "foolishness" and "weakness." Against the charge or perception that Paul is not wise, we observe him defending himself in 2:6-16 and 3:1-2; although he boasts that he does not address the Corinthians in educated discourse, the encomium to the gift of "love" in chapter 13 is indeed eloquently crafted. Furthermore, against the polemic that he is embarrassingly weak, he declares his courage and endurance in 4:8-13. I understand all of these apologetic efforts by Paul as not intended to reposition himself on the map of persons, but in terms of God's assessment of the criteria for status on the map of persons and for God's patronage.

As regards his "wisdom," Paul claims to have "a secret and hidden wisdom of God," one that "no eye has seen, nor ear heard, nor the heart of man conceived" (2:9). He enjoys this unique gift because of God's benefaction: "God has revealed to us through the Spirit" (2:10). He then claims inspiration by the Spirit, which was highly prized at Corinth: "We receive the Spirit which is from God, that we might understand the gifts bestowed on us by God" (2:12). Finally, he claims a benefaction that makes him most honorable: "We have the mind of Christ" (2:16). Evidently, we understand all of the "we" references here to speak mostly, if not exclusively, to Paul's own status. We read them in this manner because we interpret 2:1-5 and 6-16 as Paul's application of the model of the foolish and weak Christ to himself. As other places in the document indicate, he was at constant pains to force a reevaluation of himself on the map of persons, using the strategy of God's order and disorder.

As regards Paul's "weakness," his remarks in 4:8-13 are directed to elite people in the group who claim high status based on the fullness of spiritual powers. In contrast to them, Paul's experience epitomizes shamefulness. Nevertheless he catalogues his shame and even boasts of it (Fitzgerald 1988:129–48). Paul espouses disorder in the world's eyes so as to argue that his "shame" tops their "honor" on God's map of persons. Although readers already know God's criteria for honor (1:18-25), Paul begins with a statement of God's plan and purpose: "God has exhibited us apostles as last of all, like men sentenced to death" (4:9). Like the crucified Christ, Paul's shame and foolishness are God's doing, but in so doing God makes another map based on different criteria for honor. The criteria for honor are outrageous: "fools for Christ's sake," "weak," "in disrepute," "hungry and thirsty, ill-clad, buffeted, and homeless"; moreover, Paul "labors," "is reviled," "persecuted," and "slandered." In summary: "we have become, and are now, as the refuse of the world, the offscouring of all things" (4:13). What bizarre hyperbole, for the lower Paul goes in status, the higher he is in God's ranking. Thus last becomes first and least ranks as greatest.

Finally, in regard to Paul's report of his apostleship, he parades elements of his shame and dishonor, only to turn them into marks of divine respect. First, Paul tells us that he persecuted God's church (15:9; Gal 1:13, 23; Phil 3:6), which means that at one time he had no place on God's map of holy people gathered in Christ Jesus. But then he surprisingly appears on a highly significant map of "apostles," not because of any achievement on his part, but because of God's very strange taste: "I am the least of the apostles, unfit to be called an apostle, because I persecuted the church of God. But by *the grace of God* I am what I am, and his grace toward me was not in vain. On the contrary, I worked harder than any of them, though it was not I, but the *grace of God* which is with me" (15:8-10). Whatever status or role he has comes from God: "I am what I am by the grace of God," namely, an "apostle" (1:1) to whom the Lord appeared (9:1). God, then, transformed him from sinner to saint, and placed him very high on a list of highly favored people. We recall the map of persons in which "apostles" were ranked first in terms of rank and status: "God has appointed in the church first apostles . . ." (12:28).

As we know, honor is either ascribed by some high-ranking person or achieved by prowess of some sort. Paul claims both, it would seem: (a) most importantly, ascribed: "I am what I am by the grace of God . . . the grace of God which is with me"; and (b) achieved: "I worked harder than any of them." But achieved honor is fragile, for others may outlabor, outrun, outfight, and so on, the current champion. Paul reverts to the higher honor, by claiming that all his labors are indeed not his, but God's grace in him.

Thus, in the disorderly world of God, Paul finds himself all over the maps that are drawn. In the world's eyes, he belongs lower than the top, perhaps in the center, but probably on the periphery. He lacks the wisdom and power valued in Corinth; his reputation is an embarrassment to the church. By comparison with Corinth's elite, Paul rates lower in every category. But the God of disorder constructs a new map of persons, the criteria for which seem to be the opposite of earthly honor markers. And who is to argue with God? Thus, as Paul says, a sinner/outsider was transformed into a saint/insider by God's grace. Although in the eyes of many Paul's "wisdom" is either nonexistent or foolishness, in God's scheme of things it is "secret and hidden wisdom of God." Likewise with his "weakness," which in God's plan is "strength."

SUMMARY AND FURTHER QUESTIONS

The models with which we gather data about God should be clear by now. We examined God in relationship to Jesus, Paul, and the Corinthian church. God as Patron and Benefactor works acts of power in regard to Jesus, grace and favor to Paul, and gifts so numerous and plentiful to the Corinthians that "you are not lacking in any spiritual gift" (1:7). Comparably, God, who enjoys supreme honor, honors others proportionately. God raised up Jesus to life and raised him still higher to a unique heavenly position at God's feet and as head of the body of God's church. Paul was honored by God with the highest earthly roles, first apostle and then prophet.

God seems at first contradictory in terms of order and disorder. God made the various maps of persons, places, times, and things that organize and structure the world and life of the church. But God turns the world upside down and creates new maps. Weakness is strength; foolishness is wisdom; those of no honor or standing topple those of honor, wisdom, and power.

The shameful bodily parts receive honor from the honorable ones. The last, Paul, becomes the first. As in *Macbeth,* "two truths are told" that seem contradictory. My interpretation has regularly pointed to the conflicts and factions within the group, in support of which or correction of which Paul tells a specific story of how God works. The mighty are cast from their thrones and the lowly raised up.

What else might one consider in I Corinthians in regard to God? What passages or themes remain?

1. *Monotheism?* The celebrated statement in 8:4-6 deserves close reading (Giblin 1975), as well as the materials on God's jealousy (10:14-22).

2. *God's two powers.* Paul utilizes belief in the creative power of God especially in regard to foods. I argue that his remark in 8:6, "for us there is one God, the Father, from whom are all things," includes foods. For when Paul later states: "Eat whatever is sold in the meat market without raising any question on the ground of conscience" (10:25), he bases this on God's creative power: "For the earth is the Lord's and everything in it" (10:26; cf. Pss 24:1; 50:12). God's creative power appears again in Paul's legitimation of differentiated roles and statuses in regard to bodily organs and so to members of the church: "God arranged the organs in the body, each one of them, as he chose" (12:18). Therefore, in creation God constructs a map of bodily parts based on honor that is replicated in a comparable social map of persons. "Creation," then, both erases food distinctions and confirms social distinctions in the body.

God's eschatological power includes the elements that belong in a doctrine of theodicy: God judges; there is an afterlife, in which rewards and punishments are justly apportioned. No data in I Corinthians suggests that anyone denies that God judges; they may believe that the judgment has already been rendered when by baptism and the gift of Spirit they think that they have already passed beyond naive or immature notions of God as judge. But judging occurs frequently in the group, and with some vehemence. Paul senses that he is judged by elites there and responds with an appeal to God's future, just, but mysterious judgment.

Paul states in 4:1-2 the norm according to which judgment should take place. He and Apollos, as "servants of Christ and stewards of the mysteries of God," have duties to God, who authorized them, and to the church, for whom they labor. What matters is their "trustworthiness," that is, their fidelity and loyalty to God and God's task. Hence God alone can evaluate if and how they fulfilled their duties. But, we are told, other judges are judging them, whose judgment Paul considers both wrong in principle and false in conclusions. "It is the Lord who judges me" (4:4), and the judgment is not now, but future: "Do not pronounce judgment before the time, before the Lord comes." In cases such as this, the final judgment of God is first and foremost a revelation of mysteries and secrets: disguises are unmasked, ambiguity clarified, and appearances unveiled. This, says Paul, is what God will do at the judgment: "He will bring to light the things now hidden in darkness and will disclose the purposes of the heart" (4:5). On the basis of this revelation, he will judge justly: "Then every man will receive his commendation from God" (4:5b). Therefore, Paul's exposition of God's theodicy is not speculative reflection, but a flexible doctrine that functions apologetically on his behalf. God's judgment, which will be both informed and just, will cancel out the uninformed and unjust criticisms of members of the church.

Another element in the doctrine of theodicy, survival after death, receives attention in the long discourse on the resurrection. The history of the interpretation of 15:12-19 may be summarized into three distinct positions: the denial of postmortem existence, of bodily resurrection, and of future resurrection (Tuckett 1996). We saw above that Paul has in mind in I Corinthians 15 a map of time, which argues that Christ alone has been raised and that all others will be only after the defeat of the last enemy, death. Therefore no Corinthian can claim to be already in the kingdom of God; whether dead or still alive, all must in the future put on immortality and imperishability. The temporal factor, like so much of Paul's argument, functions as a polemic against false conceptions of God's workings. Second, scholars do not envision an Epicurean or Sadducean denial of life after death here; rather, they tend to see arguments about the nature of the resurrection, whether bodily in some sense or not. But survival after death seems not to be in question. Third, postmortem retribution is not discussed in I Corinthians 15, but we see it appear elsewhere. For example, both before and after a list of vices, which parallel many of the laws in the Decalogue, Paul says that "the unrighteous will not inherit the kingdom of God" (6:9-10). Obviously, observant disciples will inherit, and others will not, such as the man in the illicit sexual union (5:1-13). While there are other references to God's judgment, I isolate these because they belong clearly to Paul's practical theodicy.

3. *God and the Scriptures.* In this letter Paul infrequently cites the Scriptures, which clearly state the plan and purpose of God. I have gathered and classified the Scriptures cited by Paul in two categories: Scriptures of "reversal" and of "order." *Scriptures of reversal:* Paul portrays God defending the worth and value of Christ's crucifixion by aggressively attacking worldly folly (1:18-25); the proof of Paul's argument rests in the citation of Isaiah: "I will destroy the wisdom of the wise and the cleverness of the clever I will thwart" (1:19; cf. Isa 29:14; see also 1 Cor 3:19a). *Scriptures of order:* Paul knows of Scriptures in which God establishes an orderly world. This includes a list of laws similar to the Decalogue (6:9-10), the command that excludes a sinner from the church: "Drive out the wicked person from among you" (5:13; cf. Deut 17:7; 19:19), and a psalm that describes the last stages of the world when "God has put all things under his feet" (1 Cor 15:27; cf. Ps 8:6).

6

THEOLOGIES IN CONFLICT

PAUL'S GOD IN GALATIANS

God sent the Spirit of his son into our hearts,
crying, "Abba! Father!"
—Gal 4:6

INTRODUCTION

The models I use to gather data on God in Galatians are all familiar. First, as in the case of Romans, Paul has a type of systematic theology that structures his understanding of God in terms of epistemology, nature, and ethics. Second, by far the most significant model is God-in-relationship, namely, God as Patron and Benefactor and the appropriate response of clients (obedience, faith, praise). Third, as we have seen elsewhere, Paul compares and contrasts two types of covenants from Scripture: the benefaction covenant made with Abraham and the contractual covenant made with Moses. Fourth, Paul employs two Israelite models for interpreting God's actions, the two attributes (mercy, judgment) and the two powers (creation, execution). As always, honor plays an important role in describing God's actions to us and the debt of respect owed God. Finally, we need to consider the possibility that God is at war still with Satan and demons, who "bewitch" his people. What does this say of God's power and sovereignty?

PATTERNS OF THOUGHT AND PERSUASION: RHETORIC AND ANCIENT THEOLOGY

Most commentators on Galatians make some remarks in passing about the Deity mentioned in the letter. But very few consider "God" as a topic worthy of separate, special attention beyond passing mention in their commentaries (notable exceptions: Betz 1979:350; Martyn 1997:603). Few even list "God" in the index. As we have discovered, the same could be said of Romans and 1 Corinthians. Is it that "God" is a minor player in the argument of Paul? Or do interpreters simply fail to notice "God" in the document and so ignore what is said about the Deity? I consider it my task, then, to recover Paul's discourse on God in Galatians. But to garner this data, I bring to the task many of the resources employed in the study of other Pauline letters. We know from Romans that Paul employs a systematic manner of talking about God: (1) epistemology or knowledge about God, (2) physics or discussion of the nature of God, and (3) ethics or the appropriate behavior that flows from God's nature.

Epistemology

Whence comes Paul's and the Galatians' knowledge of God? Paul argues that the two are intertwined. Paul's own knowledge of God came immediately to him when God "revealed his Son to me, in order that I might preach him among the Gentiles" (1:16; Betz 1979:69–70). Because this immediate knowledge was correct and unique (Malina and Neyrey 1996:40–42), Paul boasts that he "did not confer with flesh and blood" (1:16b). Mediated knowledge must be considered less accurate and valuable than immediate or eyewitness knowledge. The God who enlightened Paul later authorized him to bring this immediate knowledge to others; that is, Paul became "an apostle—not from men nor through man, but through Jesus Christ and God the Father" (1:1). He also says that from the very start his knowledge of God was for the purpose of "preaching him [God] among the Gentiles" (1:16). After a revelation that instructed Paul to go to Jerusalem (2:1), Paul set before the church his gospel to the Gentiles about God, which was formally acknowledged by the Jerusalem elite (Malina and Neyrey 1996:47–50). His knowledge instructs him how to read the Scriptures of Israel in a distinctive way; the two covenants allegorize two ways of relationship to God: faith versus works of the law (3:6-29; 4:21-31). Thus what Paul knows and how he comes to know it are key elements in the argument of the letter: revelations freely given him, even when he was an enemy of God; knowledge immediately bestowed on him by God; and unique and novel ways of reading the Scriptures. Epistemology, then, constitutes a critical element of the argument of the letter.

Physics

As regards physics or the nature of God, Paul argues strenuously that God's nature is that of a benefactor, whose character it is to bestow benefaction, gift, grace, and mercy. God is not rewarding Abraham or his adopted children for their faith, for God acted first to promise blessings. It belongs to God to act freely and do what pleases God; thus God is not a God of political or financial contracts. As the relationship between God and humanity develops, whatever connection exists between God and mortals always begins with God's initiative and is always characterized by grace and gift. The initiative is God's; it is totally God's gift.

Ethics

In Cicero's *On the Nature of the Gods*, an Epicurean philosopher explained the relationship of ethics and physics, which is worthwhile to examine.

> If we sought to attain nothing else beside piety in worshiping the gods and freedom from superstition, what has been said had sufficed; since the exalted *nature of the gods*, being both eternal and supremely blessed, would receive man's pious worship; and furthermore all fear of the divine power or divine anger would have been banished (since it is understood that anger and favor alike are excluded from the *nature* of a being at once blessed and immortal). (Cicero, *Nature of the Gods* 1.45, emphasis added)

By nature, Epicurus's god is "supremely blessed," and so shows no anger to any creature. Hence the proper ethics flowing from the nature of this god entails "freedom from superstition" (about final punishments) and transcendence of all "fear of the divine power and anger." A comparable Israelite example of the relationship of God's nature and human ethics would surely be, "Be holy, as I am holy" (Lev 11:44-45). Is there such a connection in Galatians between God's nature as benefactor and human behavior?

All agree that Paul treats ethics in the last part of the letter (5:1—6:11), a section generally labeled "exhortation." I will consider three sections,

5:13-15, 16-24, and 6:1-5. If the nature of God is as we described it above, how does it correlate with this ethical material?

5:13-15. When Paul describes the nature of the Deity in 2:15—4:31, he characterizes God in terms of benefaction: generosity, benefaction, gift giving, and faithfulness. Thus when Paul exhorts group members to show benevolence toward one another, "through love be servants of one another" (5:13), "love" functions here as Paul's shorthand for a kind of altruism he associates with God (Betz 1979:274–76). The warrant in 5:14 for this exhortation derives from Lev 19:18, "You shall love your neighbor as yourself." Conversely, absence of this benevolence ("bite and devour one another") leads to mutual ruin (Gal 5:15).

5:16-24. Here Paul compares and contrasts two ways of acting. He calls one way "works of the flesh" and implies that it represents the wrong theology. "Flesh" in 5:17-21 links this material with previous mention of Hagar's conception of her son Ishmael as "according to the flesh." Paul juxtaposed Hagar with Sarah as two opposed covenants. Circumcision (5:2-12), as well as other judaizing matters (4:10-11), are likewise concerned with the "flesh." It seems likely, then, that Paul intends some parallelism between "flesh" versus "spirit" in the two covenants (3:5-28; 4:21-31) and in the two ways (5:16-24). Thus he begins by condemning behavior that contrasts with his understanding of the nature of God. In addition to vices that seem to resemble elements of the Decalogue ("fornication, impurity, licentiousness, idolatry"), Paul lists vices that destroy civic intercourse, thus totally subverting benevolence and altruism: "enmity, strife, jealousy, anger, selfishness, dissension, party spirit, envy . . ." (5:20-21). Those who do these actions cannot be imitating God. Conversely, he lauds virtues that express the benevolence and altruism of God: "love, joy, peace, patience, kindness, faithfulness, gentleness . . ." (5:22-23). To act in this way, one must have God's Spirit, and so behavior of this sort is directly related to the nature of God, who freely gave the Spirit to the church (3:1-5).

6:1-5. Paul twice commands the Galatians to act with altruism and benefaction. "If anyone is overtaken in any trespass, you should restore him in a spirit of gentleness" (6:1). We do not know if the trespasser has offended a member of the group who should then forgive the trespass without seeking vengeance; but the general condition Paul describes resembles the Matthean Our Father, especially with its codicil about "forgive trespasses" (Matt 6:9-

15). To "restore him in a spirit of gentleness" indeed sounds as though anger and retribution are absent, just as the attribute of God's mercy supersedes the attribute of just judgment.

The closest parallel in Galatians to this exhortation is Paul's statement at the letter's opening, in which he delivers a summary statement of the gospel, followed by a doxology. "Grace to you and peace from God the Father and our Lord Jesus Christ, who gave himself for our sins to deliver us from the present evil age, according to the will of our God and Father; to whom be the glory for ever and ever. Amen" (1:3-4). Here Christ "gave himself" to deliver us from an evil age; this language relates to Paul's later remark that his life is now "by the faith of the Son of God, who loved me and gave himself up for me" (2:20). It is certainly true that Paul holds up for imitation Christ's self-emptying behavior as he portrayed Jesus as the ideal model in the celebrated hymn in Phil 2:6-11.

I suggest, however, that Paul's understanding of God's nature stands behind this language of "love." First, whatever Christ did was done "according to the will of our God and Father." Thus it is God's initiative and action that "sent his Son . . . to redeem those under the law" (4:4-5). It is God's redeeming behavior that is the model for imitation. Next, Paul exhorts his audience to "bear one another's burdens and so fulfill the law of Christ" (6:2). This "law of Christ," while articulated by Jesus (e.g., Mark 12:29-31), is God's law as found in the Scriptures. Whereas the Decalogue functions to defend and protect the rights of adult male Israelites, the remarks about "bearing one another's burdens" look to a type of social relationship characterized by altruism and generosity, which constitute Paul's understanding of God's nature. Thus I consider the remark by Paul, "if a man is overtaken by any trespass, you should restore him in a spirit of gentleness" (6:1), to imitate the mercy of God that was shown to Paul and to Galatian sinners.

GOD AS PATRON AND BENEFACTOR

By now we are familiar with the classical model of God as Patron and Benefactor, Christ and Paul as brokers, and the disciples of Jesus as clients. As a well-known native model in antiquity, both Paul and the Galatians would be adept at recognizing data mentioned by Paul and classifying it immediately in this pattern of social relations. For us, the benefactor-client model proves useful in reading Galatians in two ways. First, God's benefaction is ancient, widespread, and enduring, so much so that the dominant image of God in Galatians is that of a Deity who constantly bestows grace. Second, the conflict between Paul and the Judaizers might be phrased as one that determines how God's benefaction functions. If liberation from slavery, sin, and death are gratuitous gifts of divine benefaction, then the proper response to the Benefactor is "faith" and "obedience." But if benefaction depends in any way on human observance of dietary, calendar, and other rules, the Benefactor becomes less a generous patron and more a manager of accounts. Seneca makes just this type of distinction between a benefactor who acts out of altruism and another who calculates response:

> When a man bestows a benefit, what does he aim at? To be of service and to give pleasure to the one to whom he gives. If he accomplishes what he wished, if his intention is conveyed to me and stirs in me a joyful response, he gets what he sought. For he had no wish that I should give him anything in exchange. Otherwise, it would have been, not a benefaction, but a bargaining. (*Ben.* 2.31.2)

God, the Generous Benefactor and Patron

If God is Benefactor, what range of benefactions does God bestow? The chart on the following page (197) both lists and relates the major benefactions mentioned by Paul in Galatians. There is no doubt that all eight items are different but related benefactions that God has bestowed. Since Paul himself follows a rigorous time line in narrating these benefactions, let us take his cue for seeing how these diverse benefactions relate to one another.

Earliest in time is "blessing," the promise given to Abraham that he would have heirs, not from both Ishmael and Isaac, but only from the free son: "The promises were made to Abraham and to his offspring. It does not say, 'And to your offsprings,' referring to many, but, referring to one, 'And to your offspring,' which is Christ" (3:16). This "blessing" relates to all peoples, for when the promise was made to Abraham, there was no Israel as yet. Paul, however, portrays Abraham as the source of blessing to the Gentiles: "Men of faith are the offspring of Abraham" (3:6), not men who are circumcised. Moreover, "Scripture, foreseeing that God would justify the Gentiles by faith, preached the gospel beforehand to Abraham, saying 'In you shall all nations be blessed'" (3:8-9). Thus "blessing" comes first and generously to all peoples. Second in time comes the other covenant, which Paul labels as "curse," the opposite of "blessing." Completing his contrast of the two covenants, he links "promise/faith/blessing" and contrasts it with "works/curse" (3:10-11). It is genuinely hard to see how the second covenant is in any sense a benefaction.

God's Benefactions	**Texts in Galatians**
1. "gift"	"you are so quickly deserting him who called you in the grace of Christ" (1:6); "you are severed from Christ, you who would be justified by the law; you have fallen away from grace" (5:4; see 1:3, 15; 2:9, 21; 6:18)
2. "promise"	"if the inheritance is by the law, it is no longer by promise; but God gave it to Abraham by a promise" (3:18); "the son of the slave was born according to the flesh, the son of the free woman through promise" (4:23; see 3:14-19, 29; 4:28)
3. "sonship"	"God sent forth his Son . . . so that we might receive adoption as sons. adoption" And because you are sons, God has sent the Spirit of his Son into our hearts, crying 'Abba, Father'" (4:4-6)
4. "heirs"	"If you are Christ's, then you are Abraham's offspring, heirs according to the promise" (3:29); "So through God, you are no longer a slave, but a son, and if a son then an heir" (4:7)
5. "freedom"	"spy out our freedom which we have in Christ Jesus, that they might bring us into bondage" (2:4); "you are no longer a slave, but a son" (4:7; see 4:8-9, 25; 5:1, 13)
6. "deliverance/ redemption"	"[Christ] who gave himself up to deliver us from the present evil age according to the will of our God" (1:4); "God sent his Son . . . to redeem those who were under the law" (4:5)
7. "righteousness/ justification"	"we know that no one is justified by works of the law" (2:16); "Abraham believed God and it was reckoned to him as righteousness" (3:6)
8. "blessing"	"'In you shall all the nations be blessed.' So then, those who are men of faith are blessed with Abraham who had faith" (3:8-9); "in Christ Jesus the blessing of Abraham might come upon the Gentiles" (3:14)

The third temporal moment describes how the next benefaction of God was Jesus Christ, whom God sent to redeem a people in slavery (4:5). This Jesus, "according to the will of our God and Father," delivered us from the present evil age (1:4). God's benefaction focuses on the cross and resurrection of Jesus, whom Paul identifies as "mediator" of the Benefactor's blessings (4:4-6). Although Paul does not explain the powerful efficacy of Jesus' crucifixion, he obliquely refers to it: "if justification were through the law, then Christ died to no purpose" (2:21), effectively saying that "justification" of sinful humankind was "the purpose" achieved through the cross. How did this happen? Twice in the letter Paul says that Christ entered into our state and took upon himself the "curse" owed us in justice (3:13-14); he was "born under the law" so as to free those under the law (4:4). Thus Christ achieved a great freedom: freedom from slavery to the law, to sin, and to death. But all of this is God's latest act of benefaction, "to whom be the glory for ever and ever" (1:5).

E. P. Sanders gathered terms describing the effect of Jesus' death that he called "transfer terminology" (1983:8–9). He did not evaluate any of this in terms of benefaction-client relationships, although that is an appropriate historical and social model for us to evaluate this material. Inasmuch as Jesus' achievements occurred "according to the will of our God and Father" (1:4), they are all then God's benefactions, effected through God's broker-mediator, Jesus. Here too is a catalogue of God's benefactions achieved through Jesus.

Transfer Terminology

sinners, enemies	righteoused } by death reconciled } of Christ		Rom 5:8-10
condemnation	death of Christ	acquittal *(dikaiōsis)*/life	Rom 5:18
sinners	death of Christ	righteous *(dikaioi)*	Rom 5:19
in sin	death with Christ	life	Rom 6:4
in sin	righteoused by sharing Christ's life	life	Rom 6:7
enslaved to law/flesh	death with Christ	new life in Spirit	Rom 7:4-6
condemnation /sin/death	death with Christ	in Christ no condemnation	Rom 8:1f.
unrighteous	washed, righteoused, sanctified (in baptism)	[righteous]	1 Cor 6:9-11
Jews or Gentiles (sinners)	righteoused by faith		Gal 2:16
	by faith	spirit	Gal 3:2, 14
	by faith	sons of Abraham	Gal 3:7, 14
	by law X	righteousness/life	Gal 3:21
	through faith	sons of God	Gal 3:26
righteous under the law/refuse	faith/sharing sufferings	in him/righteousness from God	Phil 3:6-11

Several observations on Sanders's chart are in order. As extensive as it seems, it omits items such as "redemption" from slavery, "expiation" from sin, new creation, "reconciliation" of enemies, and "sanctification" of uncleanness (Fitzmyer 1987:59–71). The benefactions, then, are truly quite expansive. Second, Sanders's terminology and my additions should be considered in terms of rituals of status transformation, because in each case the persons who experience the transfer or transformation are ascribed a new role and status. Transformation into the status of "freed slave" is benefaction enough, but how extraordinary to be adopted and made "son" and even "heir" in a most noble family.

In addition to the scriptural examples of divine benefaction (Abraham, Sarah, and Isaac) and historical examples such as the crucified Christ, Paul offers another consideration of God's benefaction when he takes up two recent examples: God's dealings with Paul himself (1:12-16) and with the disciples in Galatia (3:1-5). In 1:12-16, even as he describes his transformation, he likewise says much about his Transformer-Benefactor. As persecutor of the church, Paul (Saul) stood opposed to God, considering Jesus as a corruption within Israel. It did not matter to God that Paul was "advanced in Judaism beyond many of my own age" or "was extremely zealous for the traditions of my fathers" (1:14), because he violently opposed God's church and tried to destroy it. Yet God who is Benefactor showed mercy and favor to this most unlikely person, whom God indeed had "set apart" before he was born and called through his grace: "God was pleased to reveal his Son to me" (1:15-16). Paul, then, is a premier example of the way God-as-Benefactor works: Paul had no standing in God's eyes; God's free and surprising mercy turned an enemy into a servant; and God bestowed favor, even a noble role and status, on a most unlikely person. It is true that patron-client relationships are marked by favoritism, such as Israel as "chosen people" or Mary, Mother of God, as "blessed among women." Paul's account expresses a comparable sense that he enjoys a unique place in God's plans and is thus a "favorite" of God, especially in light of his original status as God's enemy. Moreover, Paul's narrative here functions rhetorically as an example of the way God-as-Benefactor works. It goes beyond an apology for Paul's embattled status in the church and manifests how God's grace and favor are gifts, not wages, and how benefaction begins the relationship, not balances or concludes it. This benefaction, then, describes the nature of God.

Rhetorical considerations of Galatians indicate that Paul stated the thesis to be argued in 2:15-21 and began the proof in 3:1 (Betz 1979:18–19). The remarks, then, in 3:1-5 function as part of the proof of "justification through the faith of Jesus Christ" (2:16). Granted, they precede the scriptural proofs related to Abraham, but they nevertheless argue from experience that the thesis is correct. Paul begins by claiming that some terminal harm is being done to the church; he calls it "witchcraft," which would mean that an evil power is drawing the group away from the fullness of divine benefaction to ruin (Neyrey 1990b:181–206). But such a remark as "Who has bewitched you?" presumes a prior blessing and benefaction. In a series of rhetorical questions, Paul forces the Galatians to examine their own experience of God's benefaction and see the truth of his claim, which is now under threat:

> Who has bewitched you?
> Did you receive the Spirit by works of the law, or by hearing with faith?
> Having begun in the Spirit, are you now ending in the flesh?
> Did you experience so many things in vain?
> Does he who supplies the Spirit to you and works miracles among you
> do so by works of the law, or by hearing with faith? (3:1-5)

All five questions speak to a time of blessing in the recent past of the Galatians, a period rich in God's benefaction. This benefaction is endangered, as though it might be destroyed or distorted ("Who has bewitched you?"). If corrupted, then a new transformation would take place that negates the benefaction: beginning in Spirit but ending in flesh. The source of ruin has to do with misconstruing the source of benefaction. Whence came the "Spirit"? By benefaction-as-gift or by labor that earns a wage? Does the Benefactor bestow the benefaction of Spirit and miracles as gift or as earned wages (see Rom 4:4-5)? The very experience of the Galatians stands as proof of Paul's thesis that justification is both gift and modeled in faith. If the Galatians truly examine their own experience, they will know that the Benefactor who supplies the Spirit and other kindnesses began the benefactor-client relationship on his own initiative and as his own free gift. Thus Paul and now the Galatians are proof alongside Abraham and Scripture of the way God's benefaction is bestowed. Their experience confirms that benefaction is the nature of God.

Paul understands the Christ event as an explosion of benefaction that is tied to the Abraham story. First, the Abraham "promise" should be understood as a "covenant," such that Hagar and Sarah represent "two covenants" (4:24). The covenant of promise looked forward to God's benefaction of a free son, Isaac, who would be Abraham's heir. The promise is fulfilled in Jesus ("'And to your offspring,' which is Christ," 3:16). Jesus is preeminently the Son, whom God sent to make more sons. God sent his Son and God sent the Spirit to allow all to be chips off the old block, that is, to bear a family resemblance with Jesus. The Spirit of his Son empowers all to be related to God just as Jesus is, and so all declare "Abba, Father" to their benefactor. And if adopted into the family, these new sons are also heirs of Abraham's blessings and promise. Thus slaves become free sons and heirs in the most noble of houses. Benefactions of this sort, while typical of Israelite in-group talk, are all the more extraordinary for non-Israelites and those with no legal claim to membership or status in Israel.

One last task remains in consideration of God's benefaction, namely, classification of it according to the four symbolic media: power, commitment, influence, and inducement. One should not presume that God's benefaction is described in the same way in each of Paul's letters.

Power	**Influence**
1. resurrection from the dead (1:1) 2. deliverance from present evil age (1:4) 3. Spirit (3:1-5) 4. deliverance from slavery (4:3-5) 5. new creation (6:15)	1. only one true gospel (1:6-10) 2. immediate revelation to Paul (1:12-16) 3. "went up by a revelation" (2:2) 4. entrusted with a gospel (2:2 and 7) 5. Spirit inspires: "Abba, Father" (4:6)
Commitment	**Inducement:**
1. gift (1:2, 6, 15; 2:9, 21; 5:4; 6:18) 2. no partiality (2:6; 3:7-8) 3. blessing (3:9, 14) 4. promise (3:16-18, 22) 5. sonship (3:7, 26; 4:4-7) 6. covenant (3:6-14; 4:24-31) 7. adoption (4:5) 8. heirs/inheritance (3:29; 4:4-7)	absent

Since this table is a classification of God's benefactions, it should tell us something about God. The premier benefaction of God in Galatians, commitment, has to do with belonging. Belonging is impartial and is extended to "all," both to Israelites and non-Israelites (see also 3:28). Belonging changes one's status from slave, sinner, or outsider to that of "son" and "heir." Belonging according to the pattern of Abraham is based on God's promise, which does not fail, and God's free gift and blessing. The technical term for this relationship of benefaction is "covenant," not just any covenant but that made with Abraham. And as Paul argues, this entire "belonging" relationship begins and ends with the gift of God's Spirit.

God's power obviously plays a role in raising the dead, the deliverance of the elect from slavery, and even deliverance from this evil age. A new creation is not possible without God's power. Yet this aspect of benefaction plays a lesser role in the argument to influence, the revelation by God to Paul. Inasmuch as the letter argues that one construal of the gospel is right and another wrong, the knowledge given by God to Paul is hardly ornamental. There is only one gospel; all others are anathema. Paul received this gospel immediately from God; he travels to Jerusalem because God reveals that he should. Thus the gospel is acknowledged by the pillars of the church, who accept it as God-authored (Malina and Neyrey 1996:43–48). Paul makes an important argument for the validity of his gospel by appealing to experience, both his own and that of the Galatians. His experience was a surprising revelation of God's Son to Paul, such that he needed no teachers and so "did not consult with flesh and blood" (1:16-17). Clearly Paul promotes this aspect of God's benefaction as a potent apologetic and polemical weapon.

GOD'S MAPS OF TIMES: THE TWO COVENANTS

Paul often perceives God as making new maps of time, which serve to organize and interpret God's action in the world. In Romans the dominant map sorted out the times of Genesis: (1) grace and immortality in creation, (2) then sin and death, but finally (3) obedient faithfulness and so restoration of grace and immortality (Rom 5:12-21; 7:7-12). The map of time contrasted the first Adam, created in God's image, with the second Adam, sinner, who lost this image and likeness, and then with the new Adam, Jesus. In I Corinthians Paul's map of time looked to the future, not the past; it indicated how the new Adam alone had been raised from the dead already; all others will eventually be raised, but not until "the end," when Jesus conquers the last enemy, death (I Cor 15:20-26). Maps, then, indicate where mortals stand at any given moment in terms of God's full benefaction. Thus they can tell us much about how Paul understands the history of that benefaction and the plan and purpose of the Benefactor.

In Galatians the map of time focuses on two covenants, each of which reflects a different aspect of the God of Israel (Gal 3:6-13 and 4:21-31). First a word of caution: Paul's understanding of these would never stand up to historical criticism; he exaggerates, simplifies, dichotomizes, and bends the stories to his purposes. Hence the chart below reflects Paul's editorializing, not the scholarly interpretation of the covenants. But then we seek Paul's understanding of God, not historical accuracy.

Gal 3:6-14—Two Covenants Contrasted

Covenant of Promise/Abraham	Covenant of Law/Moses
1. God's primary action: God freely makes a promise, which is unconditional	1. God's primary action: God strikes a contract-treaty, which is conditional
2. Aim of the covenant: blessing	2. Aim of the covenant: blessing and curse
3. Aspect of God in view: freedom, surprise, illustrative of God's attribute of mercy	3. Aspect of God in view: fairness, justice, reliability, illustrative of God's attribute of just judgment
4. Israel's ideal response: "Abraham *believed* God, and it was reckoned to him as righteousness" (Gal 3:6; cf. Gen 15:6)—"faith"	4. Israel's ideal response: "He who *does them* shall live by them" (Gal 3:12; cf. Lev 18:5)—"works"
5. Map of time: *first* covenant, found in earliest parts of Israel's history (Gen 12–18)	5. Map of time: *second* covenant: "the law, which came four hundred and thirty years afterward, does not annul a covenant previously ratified by God" (Gal 3:17)
6. Why given? Initial act of grace (3:6-8)	6. Why given? "Because of transgressions . . . custodian" (3:19, 23)
7. Social implications: inclusivity. "In you shall all the nations be blessed" (Gal 3:8; Gen 12:3; see Gal 3:28)	7. Social implications: exclusivity. God chooses a people to be his own, a people set apart

The covenant with Abraham was first in time; hence, according to the "golden age" model of time common in antiquity, it was the best and most perfect time. Everything after that represents degeneration to some degree: gold, silver, bronze (see 1 Cor 3:12). In making this "covenant of promise" with Abraham, God acted as the perfect benefactor by taking complete initiative in the relationship and freely bestowing virtual immortality to Abraham by promising him offspring as numerous as the stars and sands. God also displayed divine freedom to do something new and extraordinary. God's aim was unqualified and unconditional "blessing," which was impartial and destined to benefit all. This covenant, then, should be thought of as God's superior benefaction.

In contrast, Paul's description of the second covenant, the one made with Moses, gives a distinctively different description of God. The second covenant, temporally later and thus qualitatively inferior, came "four hundred and thirty years afterward" (3:17). Because God's purpose was to deal with "transgressions" (3:19), this covenant functioned as a "custodian" or monitor of children (3:23-24), who were "no better than slaves" (4:1). God's aim, then, was not "blessing" but "curse" (3:10-13), or discipline under a stern *paidagogos* (3:24; Longenecker 1990:146–48). The form of this second covenant consisted of a conditional contract in which observance would be followed by blessing ("He who does them shall live," 3:12) or curse ("Cursed be every one who does not abide by all things written in the book of the law to do them," 3:10). When Paul then explains why God made this second covenant, he states that God set out to correct wickedness and to discipline humanity to walk in God's ways. As Paul describes it, the covenant with Moses could hardly be called benefaction or blessing.

Can either of these two covenants be said to be benefactions of God? I argued above that Paul indeed understands God as benefactor in this document, evidence of which I showed in the classification of divine benefaction according to the four symbolic media. But is this material appropriate for the second covenant? While the first covenant clearly seems to represent an altruistic act of generosity on God's part, this is hardly the case with the second covenant, which "kept [Israel] under restraint" and subject to a "custodian." Those in this second covenant do not share in any of the benefactions that characterize the first one. Far from acting as a benefactor, God seems more of a bookkeeper or manager in the second covenant.

This reminds us of the contrast Seneca makes between types of benefactors: one generously and freely bestows benefits while another keeps a record of benefaction as a merchant keeps records: "When a man bestows a benefit, what does he aim at? To be of service and to give pleasure to the one to whom he gives. . . . Otherwise, it would have been, not a benefaction, but a bargaining" (*Ben.* 2.31.2). Similarly, "No one enters his benefactions in his account-book, or like a greedy tax-collector calls for payment upon a set day, at a set hour. Otherwise, they transform themselves into a loan" (*Ben.* 1.2.3).

The covenant with Abraham was a free gift and a benefaction; but the same cannot be said of the covenant with Moses. According to Paul, benefaction does not belong here, only discipline. Moreover, a certain calculus is established that one's keeping of the law or not is balanced in the scale of justice to yield blessing or curse. While this is not a merchant's account, it is matter of work and wages (Rom 4:3-4), a contract of balanced reciprocity such as we see later in the document: "God is not mocked, for whatever a man sows, that he will also reap" (Gal 6:7). Two entirely different notions of reciprocity are in view: altruistic (Abraham, first covenant) and balanced (Moses, second covenant). The first befits a benefactor, but not the second. "What reason have the gods for doing deeds of kindness? It is their nature" (Seneca, *Ep.* 95.48-49; see Philo, *Plant.* 130).

When did the second covenant end? How does the map of time come to a resolution compatible with God's benefaction? First, the covenant of promise with Abraham remained always in force; it was never terminated, as Paul argues by means of a comparison of an original will with subsequent codicils. "No one annuls a man's will . . . once it has been ratified" (3:15). It is a promise waiting to be fulfilled. And God is indeed faithful; the word of God will not fall to the ground (Rom 9:6). Second, God reactivated the dynamic of this covenant in the cross and resurrection of Jesus: "God sent him" to redeem us; and "God sent the Spirit of his Son" to teach us how to respond to our Benefactor as had Jesus, "Abba, Father" (4:6; Hays 2002:123–44). Inasmuch as Paul's ability to "tell time" functions in 3:17 to inform us just when the second covenant took effect, so too we can precisely reckon the end of that second covenant: when Christ become a "curse" by hanging on a tree (3:13-14). Thus Paul argues that the promise is realized because the faith and obedience of Jesus redeem us from a period of slavery and childhood, and transform us into "sons" and "heirs." "If you are Christ's, then you are

Abraham's offspring, heirs according to the promise" (3:29; see 4:7). Thus Paul's map of time has three periods: (1) covenant with Abraham, (2) covenant with Moses, and (3) covenant with Abraham realized in Jesus. Jesus' death is the dramatic point in time that ended the second covenant.

This map of time encodes much of Paul's theology in Galatians. First, God is described as the consummate benefactor, who freely bestows a promise of sons (= immortal life) to Abraham. The promise, Paul argues, belongs to the beginning of history, and so its early timing leads us to consider it as the "golden age" of God's dealings with humanity. This golden age will never fail, although it may be temporarily superseded by a lesser age. As an act of benefaction, it represents certain aspects of God as generosity, surprise, faithfulness, and the like.

Paul's doctrine of God encoded in the presentation of the first covenant functions in the letter as an argument, not a speculative investigation of the "nature of God" as we find in Greco-Roman philosophers. He selects certain things from the Scriptures, ignoring others; he weaves them into a system that supports his argument with local agitators and distant teachers. It also serves as an apologetic for Paul's own role and status in the group. Thus we lose much if we fail to appreciate the utilitarian character of the Pauline portrait of God in Galatians. First, Paul's construal of salvation history into contrasting covenants, one with Abraham and the other with Moses, leaves much to be desired by modern scholars; but it is a convenient and useful rhetorical schema in the larger argument. The common rhetorical figure called "comparison" allows Paul to celebrate Abraham and vilify Moses. If the covenants are as he describes them, then the disputed responses to covenant are equally identified and value laden: to a promise, a client owes faith(fulness) and obedience; to a contract, a client owes a certain behavior or the observance of the (disciplinary) law. Thus Paul can claim that teachers urging Israelite practices such as circumcision, diet, and Sabbath observance are enslaving those made free in Christ or dragging them back to "flesh" when in Christ they have "spirit." The contrast between Sarah and Hagar is an excellent example of this labeling (4:21-31). Finally, the description of God's ways in the first covenant serves on the local level to refurbish Paul's status, because he argues that he too was changed from persecutor to apostle, from sinner to chosen, by this Benefactor-God. Similarly, the initial experience of God's benefaction by the Galatians (3:1-5) demonstrates how God acts; and because it was the first encounter of the Galatians with God, it too is a "golden" age and hence paradigmatic of God's workings.

GOD'S ATTRIBUTES AND POWERS

Mercy, Then Just Judgment

The examples of the covenant with Abraham (3:6-29), Paul's experience (1:12-17), and that of the Galatians (3:1-5) may accurately and profitably be considered as illustrating the attribute of God's mercy. By "attribute of mercy" I mean God's grace, benefaction, gift, or promise, as well as forgiveness of sins. The covenant with Abraham stands out as the perfect example of this attribute in the argument of the letter: it is based on the earliest parts of Scripture; it represents a surprising blessing to Abraham; it promises him eternal life in the endless succession of sons; and its place as the first of blessings marks it as both golden in worth and golden in time.

Is the second covenant, then, an example of God's attribute of just judgment? So it would seem. It was given "because of transgressions" (3:19), and so supersedes the attribute of mercy for a time. It functions as discipline or corrective (3:25). It represents "just judgment" in that it renders blessings and curses: blessings to those who "do them" (3:12), and curses to those who "do not do all of them" (3:10).

Finally, when God sent his Son to redeem those under the law, God manifested again the attribute of mercy, which now supersedes the attribute of just judgment. All the benefactions mentioned earlier in this chapter illustrate this restored attribute of God. Thus the initial primacy and superiority of the attribute of mercy is celebrated.

But given the nature of the dispute with those seducing the Galatians with Judean customs, we should not lightly pass over the rhetorical importance of the attribute of just judgment in the argument. It is a regular function of the way Paul thinks to construe all reality in terms of dualistic opposites (Lloyd 1966; Martyn 1985). In Galatians we find the following redundant dualisms:

1. Covenant with Abraham characterized by promise/faith	1. Covenant with Moses characterized by law/doing
2. Free wife, Sarah; free son, Isaac	2. Slave wife, Hagar; slave son, Ishmael
3. Blessing	3. Curse
4. Isaac born of the promise	4. Ishmael born of the flesh
5. Freedom	5. Slavery
6. Home: Jerusalem above	6. Home: Jerusalem below

In Paul's evaluation all items in the left column belong under the attribute of mercy, but all on the right, under the attribute of just judgment. He warns constantly that those who choose Judean customs are in fact slipping from the attribute of mercy to that of God's just judgment. Paul's interpretation of the meaning of circumcision illustrates this: "If you receive circumcision, Christ is of no advantage to you" (5:2). This would be a catastrophic loss in and of itself; but Paul follows it up by declaring that the man who is circumcised is "severed from Christ" (5:4) with the attendant loss of all of the benefactions we have noted. He states this in a form of *lex talionis*, the measure of just judgment we have observed elsewhere in Paul: "if you are 'cut around' [i.e., circumcised], then you are 'cut off' from Christ." Or, as you cut, so shall you be cut. There can be no doubt that the attribute of mercy yields to that of just judgment for so disloyal a client.

As part of the logic of Paul's exhortation on the "two ways," he lists first vices and then virtues. Only at the end of the vice list does he give a warrant for avoiding them, which is a proclamation about the attribute of God's judgment. "I warn you, as I warned you before, that those who do such things shall not inherit the kingdom of God" (5:21). The exhortation presumes that by virtue of the death of Jesus the hearers have been redeemed from slavery and death, and so they stand under the attribute of God's mercy. But this mercy is the Galatians' to lose. If their life does not honor their Benefactor but shames him with wickedness, then they will find themselves under the attribute of just judgment.

Later in the same exhortation, Paul declares: "Do not be deceived; God is not mocked" (6:7). Evidently, he fears that some will seek to escape God's justice; if so, then they seek to deceive God and maintain their standing under the attribute of God's mercy, when they deserve to experience the attribute of judgment. Since God's judgment must be "just," Paul explains in the following metaphor of sowing and reaping that one's behavior has a direct relationship to the "harvest" one reaps. "As a man sows, so shall he reap" (6:8).

Thus, as Paul tells the history, God's attribute of mercy was manifest in the promise of eternal life made to Abraham. Because God must be faithful, the promise endured and finally matured in Jesus. Thus the attribute of mercy abides, even as God abides. This same attribute extends to all, because all can become part of Abraham's clan and family by having his faith; thus the mercy of God is impartial as well as eternal. This mercy extends to Paul and to the church: they begin their life in Christ by an act of God's gracious favor. Thus the attribute of mercy has a temporal primacy that is also a value superiority; its presence in history indicates that this is God's preferred way of acting, namely, as generous benefactor. All time and all life, then, would be lived by disciples of Jesus being blessed and enriched by God in his mercy.

Would that we could be faithful! As Paul argues against those fascinated with Judean customs, they are going back across a boundary that separated blessing from curse and freedom from slavery. The shift means that the attribute of judgment replaces that of mercy. Those who abuse their freedom in Christ and choose to live in the flesh also leave the benefaction of mercy for the attribute of judgment.

SUMMARY AND FURTHER TOPICS

Paul's God-talk in Galatians has many of the features of the Greco-Roman theological system we saw already in Romans: epistemology, physics, and ethics. As regards epistemology or knowledge of God, Paul's immediate revelation serves as his unique source of knowledge. This revelation also serves a rhetorical function in the letter, for it elevates Paul in role and status over those who learned of God and Christ from mortals; his knowledge is superior and more reliable. Why would anyone listen to other teachers? Moreover, it is the nature of God to act freely in benefaction, examples of this being Paul himself as well as the Galatians (3:1-5). Given God's benefaction in the Spirit, one's appropriate response is to walk in that Spirit, and not to return to the flesh.

As in other Pauline letters, God-in-relationship functions as the premier description of God's actions. God bestows blessing and benefit freely, impartially, and eternally, beginning with Abraham and then with all his heirs. Primarily, this benefaction may be described in terms of commitment, that is, the ways in which God creates us as new creatures, free, adult, filled with the Spirit, relating to God as Jesus did, as adopted children and heirs. The surprise and freedom of God to enter into relationship functions as a pivotal argument in the document against those urging Judean customs.

As in most of Paul's letters, he creates a map of times that rationalizes the workings of God: (1) covenant with Abraham, (2) covenant on Sinai, and (3) covenant in Jesus. The temporal priority of Abraham's relationship with God translates into theological superiority; the covenant on Sinai was only a temporary covenant, destined to pass when Christ died on the cross. The two covenants imply quite different things about God.

As regards the two attributes of God, mercy is temporarily prior and dogmatically superior. Mercy, as free benefaction extended impartially to all, legitimates Paul's role and standing as well as the status of the Galatians. To forgo this mercy or to spurn it once received means that one experiences the attribute of just judgment.

FURTHER TOPICS TO EXPLORE:

1. *Two powers.* Although one finds passing mention of "new creation" (6:15; see Martyn 1997:108–9) and raising of the dead (1:1, 4), Paul does not make much use of the doctrine of God's two powers, contrary to what we saw in Romans and 1 Corinthians.

2. *War and witchcraft.* I do not take Paul's remark in 3:1 as a metaphor: "Oh, foolish Galatians, who has bewitched you?" (Neyrey 1990b; J. H. Elliott 1990). While I am not the first to suggest that Paul sees a war occurring (Martyn 1997:533–37), the cultural shape of the description of this war suggests that Paul perceives God's holy and innocent church being seduced and poisoned by Satan and company disguised as teachers of Torah. The issue, then, is that God has enemies who seek to shame and diminish God by harming God's children and heirs of the promise. This makes for sharp remarks against those whom Paul considers as agents of the evil one, such as "Anathema" (1:8, 9). As God's warrior, Paul speaks in sarcasm, vitriol, and ironic rebuke. This discourse deserves to be examined further in terms of the rhetorical situation of Paul.

3. *Honor and shame.* The letter has only one doxology (1:4), no confessional acknowledgments of God, and no honoring of God with special titles. Nev-

ertheless, all that Paul says about God-in-relationship belongs to the category of praise by virtue of benefaction. All of God's actions expressing both mercy and just judgment are noble and honorable. Indeed, I argue that the rhetorical conflict between Paul's gospel and those urging Judean customs is basically one of honor and shame. Paul describes God's actions as free, surprising, and generous benefactions; to call them into question is to shame God. Thus the very argument, seemingly theoretical, is at the same time a struggle for honor and shame.

4. *Knowing God or being known by God.* Paul makes a correction in his text when he states that the Galatians by virtue of their grace-caused transformation "have come to know God" (4:9). In context, "know" means "acknowledge"; that is, they should show loyalty and faithfulness to God-Patron. Good enough, except that Paul fears that the Galatians are turning back to their old ways, namely "slavery" (4:8, 10). Paul qualifies the phrase to read: "rather, to be known by God," which burnishes the benefaction of the Giver and reminds the receivers of the debt they owe (see Betz 1979:215–17).

7

WHO ELSE IS CALLED "GOD"?

JESUS IN THE FOURTH GOSPEL

And the Word was God.
—John 1:2

My Lord and my God.
—John 20:28

INTRODUCTION

Although this monograph aims to attend to the neglected factor of New Testament theology, namely, God, we can still learn much about this God and Father of Jesus Christ by examining two documents in which Jesus is acclaimed "God" and "Lord" or "equal to God." When we learn why Jesus is thus labeled and described, we will discover ways of thinking about God as well. Hence in this chapter on the Gospel of John and in the next chapter on the Letter to the Hebrews, we consider how each of these clearly describes Jesus in ways always reserved to describe the God of the house of Israel, that is, divine powers, eternity, and names.

When we ask who else is called "God," we think immediately of the Fourth Gospel. At its beginning, the author declares that "the word was 'God'" (1:1); and at the end, a disciple acknowledges Jesus as "Lord and God" (20:28). In between, his enemies twice charge that Jesus "makes himself equal to God" (5:18) and "makes himself God" (10:34). Why would anyone, friend or foe, say this of Jesus? What content goes into the confession of Jesus as "Lord and God," and what is meant by claiming that Jesus is "equal to God"? In what ways is Jesus properly called "God"? Scholars call this an investigation of the "high" christology in John, as opposed to the "low" christology of the Synoptic Gospels.

JESUS, EQUAL TO GOD: GOD'S TWO POWERS

Equal to God

In John 5 Jesus works a miracle on the Sabbath (5:1-5), which leads to a charge that he "violated the Sabbath" (5:16), which charge prompts an apologetic defense of him and his action (5:30-47). At a later time in the history of the Johannine community, a new controversy develops over the exalted understanding of Jesus by the Johannine group: its confession of Jesus as a divine, heavenly figure. This later controversy is reflected in 5:17-29, where a new charge is brought against Jesus ("he makes himself equal to God," 5:18), which prompts a new apology (5:19-29; see Neyrey 1988a:9–36).

As the following synopsis shows, the new charge in 5:18 is not simply a doublet of the old charge in 5:16. The prosecution by the Jews is heightened ("they sought to kill him"), and a new and more cogent reason for this is offered ("he makes himself equal to God").

Old Charge (5:16) sinful action: violation of Sabbath	*New Charge (5:18)* sinful action: blasphemy—he makes himself equal to God
Old Apology (5:30-47) series of witnesses testifying to Jesus' obedience and sinlessness	*New Apology (5:19-29)* careful explanation of how God made Jesus "equal to God"

The key to understanding the new apology (5:19-29) lies in distinguishing two parts of the new charge against Jesus. Part of it is simply erroneous and must be rejected ("he makes himself"), but part of it is true ("equal to God") and requires defense and careful explanation.

Since Jesus enjoys the same honor as God, the same authority, and the same extraordinary powers, he is undeniably "equal to God." This equality with God is not Jesus' vainglorious self-extension; rather it is God's will and purpose that he be so recognized and honored. Refusal to honor Jesus just as one honors God is to dishonor God.

In summary, the evangelist rejects the charge that Jesus "makes himself" anything. God loves him, shows him all he does; God gives him all judgment, to have life in himself, to raise the dead and judge them. And God wills that he be honored equally with him. Contrary to the charge in 5:18, the proper statement should be: "God makes Jesus equal to himself." The contents of the claim for Jesus' equality should be familiar by now, for they embody what I earlier described as God's two basic powers, creative and eschatological power.

Jesus and God's Two Powers

The evangelist attributes to Jesus in 5:19-29 both of God's two basic powers (Dodd 1968:322–23). Raising the dead, judging, and having life in oneself refer to God's eschatological power. But the power credited to him in 5:19-20 has nothing to do with executive leadership or eschatological power. Here the evangelist refers to God's granting creative power to Jesus.

Jesus claimed: "my Father is working still and I am working" (5:17). That statement functions as an apology for not resting on the Sabbath—the initial charge against Jesus was that he worked on the Sabbath. Jesus' remark about his "Father working" implies that God also did not stop creating on the seventh day but continued working (Philo, *Cher.* 88-89; *Leg.* 1.5; *Gen. Rab.* 11.10; *Exod. Rab.* 30.6). Apropos of the healing in 5:1-9, Jesus defends himself by claiming two things: (a) God continues to work on the Sabbath, hence Jesus imitates God's continued creative work by his healing on the Sabbath; and (b) God shows him all that he does, empowering him for works of creation and providence. Indeed, all God's deeds of creation/providence Jesus also does. The Gospel has already attributed all creation to the Logos (1:1-3), and we should see 5:1-9 and 17-20 as the continuation of that theme. Jesus has God's full creative power, just as he has God's complete eschatological power.

What is the significance of insisting that Jesus has God's two powers? As we saw earlier, ancient theology dealt with God's operations in the world, and philosophers such as Philo judged that these two powers encompassed all divine actions in the world. Philo frequently argues that God has two great powers, which are inclusive of many others: creative power and executive

As regards the charge "he makes himself," Jesus disowns acting arrogantly or independently of God, much less contrary to God's law, for "of himself the Son can do nothing" (5:19). Rather he does "what he sees the Father doing," which does not mean that he spies on God and steals heavenly secrets. On the contrary, "the Father loves the Son and shows him all that he does" (5:20). Thus the charge is untrue that Jesus arrogantly assumes power or status ("makes himself"); for, as the defense argues, God loves the Son and *shows* the Son what he does. That is, *God* makes him equal. But as regards the second part of the charge, Jesus' equality with God is clearly maintained: "what the Father does, the Son does likewise" (5:19b), and the Father shows him "all that he himself does" (5:20a).

In 5:21-29 the Gospel again denies the first part of the charge while affirming the second. First, the evangelist argues that Jesus has not arrogated to himself any power, for whatever powers he enjoys have been given him by God:

5:22 The Father judges no one, but *has given* all judgment to the Son.
5:26 As the Father has life in himself, so he *has given* the Son to have life in himself.
5:27 . . . and *has given* him authority to execute judgment.

Again, it is not true that Jesus "makes himself" anything. God ascribes all honor and bestows all powers to Jesus.

Second, 5:21-29 indicates quite clearly in what sense Jesus is "equal to God": Jesus has God's full eschatological power:

1. to make alive: as the Father raises the dead and gives them life, so the Son makes alive whom he wills (5:21);
2. judgment: the Father has given all judgment to the Son (5:22);
3. honor: that all may honor the Son just as they honor the Father (5:23);
4. the dead hear and live: the dead will hear the voice of the Son of God and those who hear will live (5:25);
5. life in himself: as the Father has life in himself, so he has granted the Son also to have life in himself (5:26);
6. judgment: and has given him authority to execute judgment, because he is the Son of man (5:27);
7. the dead are raised and judged: all in the tombs will hear his voice and come forth, those who have done good to the resurrection of life, and those who have done evil to the resurrection of judgment (5:28-29).

power. I present four short texts as a sampler of this kind of thinking, two from Philo himself and two from Maccabean literature.

> The voice told me that while God is indeed one,
> His highest and chiefest powers are two, even goodness and sovereignty. Through His goodness He begat all that is, through his sovereignty He rules what He has begotten. (*Cher.* 27-28)

> . . . powers of Him who speaks the Word, their leader being creative power, in the exercise of which the Creator produced the universe by a word; second in order is the royal power, in virtue of which He that has made it governs that which has come into being. (*Flight* 95)

God's initial activity in the world was exercised by the creative power, by which God begat and produced all that is; and through the executive power God ruled over all creation and governed it. The two powers thus totally complement each other: temporally, in that creation represents the beginning of any action of God and governance carries on from them until time is no more; comprehensively, in that together all things and persons are in every way the objects of God's attention. Moreover, these two powers correlate closely with the two attributes of God expressed in Exod 34:6-7, mercy and justice. In one place Philo lists not two but four potencies of God; a careful eye can see that two are the two powers we are examining and the second pair are the two attributes:

> the leader being creative power, in the exercise of which the Creator produced the universe by a word; second in order is the royal power, in virtue of which He that has made it governs that which has come into being; third stands the gracious power, in the exercise of which the Great Artificer takes pity and compassion on his own work; fourth is the legislative power, by which He prescribes duties incumbent on us . . . prohibits those things that should not be done. (*Flight* 95)

Sometimes one senses that Philo equates creative power and gracious power, for all of creation was gift, blessing, and grace. He also seems to link, though not equate, the royal or executive power with the attribute of just judgment, which prescribes duties and proscribes evil. Although I present here but a sample of this material, it is extensive in the writings of Philo and elsewhere.

In two examples from 2 and 3 Maccabees, those facing an immediate and cruel death maintain faith in God under two aspects, Creator and postmortem Judge and Savior. The first example is the exhortation by the mother of the seven sons to the son facing death:

> Therefore, the Creator of the world, who shaped the beginning of man and who devised the origin of all things, will in his mercy give life and breath back to you again. (2 Macc 7:23)

The second example is the prayer of the high priest Simon. It balances the previous one in that formerly a female exhorts a son of her private, kinship group, whereas Simon speaks in public in his civic role of priest of the house of Israel. Both have the same theology, namely, that God begins all in creation and will conclude all after death. The strictly executive or ruling character of the second power in Philo is tailored in this literature to address postmortem issues of rewards and punishment:

> Lord, Lord, king of the heaven, and sovereign of all creation, holy among the holy ones, the only ruler, almighty, give attention to us who are suffering grievously from an impious and profane man. . . . For you, the creator of all things and the governor of all, are a just Ruler, and you judge those who have done anything in insolence and arrogance. (3 Macc 2:2-3)

These two passages express a cosmic understanding of God, who creates and shapes all (i.e., the world, all things, and even human beginning) and who governs all. Although creative power is mentioned, the two citations focus on God's executive and ruling power. But here we find a development of this power embracing the resurrection of the dead and judgment, rewards for those who faithfully died but punishments for those who killed them. This metamorphosis of executive into eschatological power is in large measure occasioned by the context of the Maccabean authors and their audiences: how will God deal with the martyrdom of Israel's faithful? Mere executive power, while important in general, is inadequate here. So attention is given to its transformation into eschatological power, such as we find in the Fourth Gospel.

These two powers, creative and executive, are equated with two names of God. Because of his creative power, the Deity is often entitled "God"; the exegesis is fanciful, but the ancients thought that "God" (*theos*) derived from a verb that means to place or order (*tithemi*). Because of his executive power, the Deity is named "Lord." Commenting on "He called upon the name of the Lord, as God eternal" (Gen 21:33), Philo says:

> The title "Lord" is the power in virtue of which He rules, that of "God" the power in virtue of which He bestows benefits. This is why the name "God" is employed throughout all of the record of Creation given by Moses. (*Plant.* 86-87)

> . . . the Father of the Universe, while on either side of Him are the senior potencies, the creative and the kingly. The title of the former is "God," since it made and ordered the All; the title of the latter is "Lord," since it is the fundamental right of the maker to rule and control what he has brought into being. (*Abr.* 121)

> His creative potency is called "God," because through it He placed and made and ordered the universe, and the kingly is called "Lord," being that with which He governs what has come into being and rules it steadfastly with justice. (*Mos.* 2.99)

The content of each potency has already been established in the examples above. What we find here is the equation of a specific name with a particular power. God-as-Creator is named "God" with reference to God's making, placing, and ordering all; a variation of this in *On Planting* extends creative power beyond the first creation to a type of providential benefaction that maintains creation: "the power in virtue of which He bestows benefits." God-as-Sovereign is known as "Lord" because of his kingly power to rule, control, and govern "steadfastly with justice."

Therefore, the content of the phrase "equal to God" in John is clear: it refers to Jesus' full possession of God's two powers. The emphasis in 5:19-29 rests on the eschatological power, in particular Jesus' equal honor, his having life in himself, and his ability to raise and judge the dead. Since these two powers were part of traditional Israelite God-talk, the evangelist could expect his audience to grasp them and appreciate what he was claiming for Jesus. Furthermore, creative and eschatological powers describe all of God's actions, thus making the claim that Jesus is "equal" to God no extrinsic label, as Moses was called "god to Pharaoh." All that could be said about God's actions should also be said about Jesus: they are equal!

The Two Powers in the Fourth Gospel

A literary evaluation of John 5:19-29 indicates that the remarks about Jesus' equality with God by virtue of having God's two powers function as a topic statement that is developed in subsequent chapters. The following survey hopes to show how seven aspects of Jesus' eschatological power are repeated and developed in the discourses that follow.

1. *Equal to God.* The charge that Jesus makes himself "equal to God" (5:18) is repeated later when Jesus states: "I and the Father are one" (10:30). As a result, the audience accuses him of blasphemy, "because you, being a man, make yourself God" (10:33). The charge rests on Jesus' claim to have one of God's two powers: in one case, creative power (5:18), and in the other, eschatological power (10:30).

2. *The Son gives life.* In defense of his "equality," Jesus claims God's power to give life: "As the Father raises the dead and *gives* them *life,* so the Son *gives life*" (5:21). Later Jesus announces himself as the bread of life. Subsequently, in a controversy over life and death, Jesus claims: "if any one keeps my word, he will never see death" (8:51).

3. *Judgment.* Despite claiming that he does not judge (8:15), Jesus later affirms that he does indeed judge (8:26). He issues a law (8:24), for which failure to comply results in "die in your sins" (8:24b). When witnesses testify that they comply with this law (8:30), Jesus as judge examines their testimony and exposes it as false.

4. *Honor.* More people dishonor Jesus than honor him, for example, some make claims which belittle Jesus's work (6:31), others "murmur" about his claims (6:42), and others drop out of his circle (6:60). Later Jesus demands honor when he uses God's unique name, "I AM" (8:28); in the same context he claims honor like that of God for existing eternally; he never came into being nor passes out of it (8:56). His explanation for being "equal to God" (10:31-39) is rejected, thus denying him honor.

5. *Dead Hear and Live.* The premier illustration of this is the summons to Lazarus, four days in the tomb, to come out at the voice of Jesus' command (11:43-44).

6. *Life in Himself.* Inasmuch as "I AM" contains the element of eternal existence, that is, uncreated in the past and imperishable in the future, then Jesus uniquely has eternal existence. Moreover, the claims in 10:17-18 argue that Jesus has a command from God and so God's power to lay down his life and take it back.

7. *Resurrection and Life.* In an abbreviated form, Jesus promises that he will raise on the last day those who eat his Bread from heaven (6:39, 40, 44, 54). Later, when Martha confronts Jesus, she speaks the traditional theodicy of resurrection on the last day (11:24). But Jesus commandeers this to himself by declaring that he is this resurrection (11:25).

Eschatological Power: 5:21-29	**John 6**	**John 8**	**John 10**	**John 11**
1. Equal to God: "he makes himself equal to God" (5:18)	--------	--------	"I and the Father are one" (10:30); "you, being a man, make yourself God" (10:33)	--------
2. The Son gives life: "As the Father raises the dead and gives them life, so also the Son gives life" (5:21)	"I am the bread of life" (6:35, 48-51, 53-54, 57-58); "everyone who sees the Son and believes in him should have eternal life" (6:40)	"If any one keeps my word, he will never see death" (8:51)	"I give them eternal life, and they shall never perish" (10:28)	"I am the resurrection and the life; he who believes in me, though he die, yet shall he live; whoever lives and believes in me shall never die" (11:25-26)
3. Judgment: "The Father has given all judgment to the Son" (5:22); "and has given him authority to execute judgment" (5:27)	--------	8:21-58 (see Neyrey 1987b:515–20)	10:22-27 (see Neyrey 1988a:66–68)	--------
4. Honor: "all may honor the Son even as they honor the Father. Who does not honor the Son does not honor the Father who sent him" (5:23-24)	--------	"believe that I AM" (8:24); "when you have lifted up the Son of man, then you will know that I AM" (8:28); "before Abraham came into being, I AM" (8:58)	nonhonor: 10:31-39	--------
5. The dead hear and live: "the dead will hear the voice of the Son of God and those who hear will live" (5:25)	--------	-----	(10:3-4)	"He cried out in a loud voice: 'Lazarus, come out.' The dead man came out" (11:43-44)
6. Life in himself	--------	content of "I AM" sayings in 8:24, 28, 58	"I lay down my life that I may take it again . . . I have power to lay it down and I have power to take it back" (10:17-18)	"I am the resurrection and the life" (11:25)
7. Resurrection and life: "All who are in the tombs will hear his voice and come forth, those who have done good to the resurrection of life, and those who have done evil, to the resurrection of judgment" (5:28-29)	"And I will raise him up on the last day" (6:39, 40, 44, 54)	--------	--------	"I am the resurrection and the life" (11:25)

The Two Powers and Their Special Names

In Philo and the rabbis, the two powers of God are associated with God's two names (Dahl and Segal 1978:1–28; Marmorstein 1932:295–306). For Philo the beneficent, creative power (*dynamis poietikē*) is called *theos* (which the LXX uses as the equivalent of the Hebrew *Elohim*) and the royal, judgmental power (*dynamis basilikē*) is called *kyrios* (which the LXX uses as the equivalent of the Tetragrammaton).

The rabbis likewise associated the two powers with God's two names, although for them the creative power was linked with the Tetragrammaton and judgment with *Elohim* (Dahl and Segal 1978:1–3). But the tradition is clear that God's two powers are linked respectively with God's two names. Is this true in John? And what might it signify?

In the Gospel prologue, where Jesus is credited with creative power, he is called *God* (*theos,* 1:1-3). *Lord,* however, is generally difficult to interpret, for while Jesus is often acclaimed *Lord* in John, this title is constantly open to the minimalist interpretation of "sir" or "master." There is one climactic confession in the Gospel in which Jesus is acclaimed "My *Lord* (*kyrios*) and my *God* (*theos*)" (20:28). Surely at this point *Lord* should be treated as a cultic title, its full force acclaiming Jesus as a divine figure (Bultmann 1971:695). But what is intended by acclaiming Jesus as *Lord* (*kyrios*) after his resurrection? Is his exercise of a certain power implied and acknowledged?

Creative power is not only claimed but demonstrated (1:1-18; 5:1-9, 19-20), and so Jesus is rightly called *God.* Eschatological power is initially only claimed in 5:21-29, and its demonstration remains the task of the rest of the Gospel, especially the next several chapters. As we saw in the table on page 220, the statement of Jesus' powers in 5:19-29 functions as a topic statement that is elaborated in subsequent discussions (Neyrey 1981:115–17).

What was claimed in 5:21-29, then, is formally discussed and finally demonstrated. Jesus proves that he has life in himself, can raise the dead, and make alive; he can lay down his life and take it back. Thus he has the fullness of God's eschatological power. It is after this demonstration that the evangelist records that the title *Lord* (*kyrios*) is properly given to Jesus, "My Lord and my God" (20:28). This confession functions as the fulfillment of the remark about enjoying God's honor: "all should honor the Son even as they honor the Father" (5:23). Therefore, not only does the evangelist claim that Jesus is "equal to God," but he also explains this by reference to God's two powers. Moreover, he confesses Jesus both as *God* and *Lord*, linking "God" with creation (1:1) and "Lord" with eschatological power (20:28).

The Fourth Gospel is unique in the many ways it speaks of the heavenly character and role of Jesus. The attribution of God's two powers and the confession of Jesus with the two names of God associated with each power are a major part of the Fourth Gospel's understanding of Jesus as a heavenly figure. To this material I add two more considerations of Jesus: (1) as the appearing Deity of the Scriptures, and (2) as "I AM."

NO ONE HAS EVER SEEN GOD—JESUS, THE APPEARING DEITY OF THE SCRIPTURES

From the Gospel's very beginning, the evangelist absolutely maintains that "no one has ever seen God" (1:18; 6:46)—except the Son, of course. Nor has anyone ever ascended to the heavens to see God or receive revelations there (3:13)—except the Son, who descended from there. This means that the Israelites neither saw God's shape nor heard his voice (5:37)—not Abraham, Jacob, Moses, Elijah, or any of Israel's patriarchs or prophets ever saw God. But Scripture says that "God" appeared to them; what does that mean? If the ancients did not see God, whom did they see? In several places, the Fourth Gospel argues that the appearing Deity was not God (whom no one has ever seen) but Jesus (Neyrey 1982:589–94).

For example, Abraham saw Jesus' day (8:56). As Dahl has shown (1975b:108–9), this refers to an experience of Abraham, such as the theophany at the covenant of the pieces (Genesis 15) or his reception of the three heavenly visitors (Genesis 18; Urban and Henry 1979:166–93). Although Abraham is credited with prophetic visions of the future, John 8:56 does not refer to his vision of Jesus-who-is-to-come-as-the-Messiah, for the text continues with the extraordinary claim that Jesus was not a mere future figure on Abraham's prophetic horizon, but rather a contemporary of Abraham, or better, an eternal divine figure: "before Abraham *came into being*, I AM" (8:58). Abraham "came into being" (8:58) and "died" (8:52), like all other mortals. Jesus, however, is of a different order, for he does not come into being nor does he perish; he is "I AM," that is, a figure who is eternal in the past and imperishable in the future. Thus, although Abraham did not see God, he had theophanies nonetheless. For in his visions he saw Jesus as the appearing Deity, as the one who bears the name of God, "I AM."

Likewise in John 12:41 the evangelist stated that Isaiah "saw his glory." As a prophet, Isaiah's role was to prophesy about forthcoming events (see Sir 48:24-25). But John 12:41 refers to a time in the prophet's life when he saw Jesus' glory, namely, Isaiah's vision in the temple (Isaiah 6). Isaiah did not see God; but since the theophany was genuine, the evangelist argues that he must have seen the heavenly Jesus, the glory of God.

A similar argument might be made apropos of John 1:51. Jesus promises his disciples that they will see a heavenly vision; for they will look into heaven, even to the throne of God, and view the Son of man there with angels ascending and descending toward him. This clearly alludes to Jacob's vision in Gen 28:12, suggesting that the disciples will see what Jacob saw: a vision of a heavenly figure appearing. But the Gospel implies that Jacob, although he never saw God, had a genuine theophany; like Abraham and Isaiah, Jacob saw Jesus, the heavenly figure.

The author of the Fourth Gospel was not the only one to engage in this type of scriptural exegesis. For example, Justin Martyr employed it in his *Dialogue with Trypho,* when he argued with his Jewish opponent that it was Jesus who appeared to the patriarchs. After systematically demonstrating that Jesus appeared to Abraham (*Dial.* 56, 59), to Moses (*Dial.* 56, 59, 60, 120), and to Jacob (*Dial.* 58, 60, 86, 126), Justin summarized his claim to have shown that "neither Abraham, nor Isaac, nor Jacob, nor any other man, saw the Father and ineffable Lord of all and of Christ, but (saw) him who was according to his will his Son, being God, and the angel because he ministered to his will" (*Dial.* 127). The structure of Justin's argument is also like that of John: no one has ever seen God; therefore the patriarchs, who received genuine theophanies according to the Scriptures, saw Jesus, who is properly called God.

For completely other reasons, Philo likewise argues that the theophanies in the Scriptures were not visions of God (material persons cannot see the immaterial God). Therefore, they were revelations of God's Logos or of a power of God. In Gen 17:1, for example, Abraham did not see God but only a power of God (*Names* 15, 17). Despite his request to God to "show me thyself"

(Exod 33:13 LXX), Moses saw only "the back of God," which is one of "the powers that keep guard around you" (*Spec. Laws* 1.45-46). In Gen 28:12 Jacob saw one of the powers of God (*Dreams* 1.70). But in another theophany (Gen 31:13), Jacob is told that the appearing figure is not God but "god who appeared to you in place of God" (*Dreams* 1.228). Are there two gods? No, Philo can distinguish between "god" and "lord": "Accordingly the holy word in the present instance has indicated Him who is truly God by means of the article, saying 'I am the God' (Gen 31:13) while it omits the article when mentioning him who is improperly so called, saying 'Who appeared to you in one place' not 'of the God,' but simply 'of God'" (*Dreams* 1.229). The point is that according to Philo "*god*" appears in theophanies, for no one can see *God*.

The appearing figure is *god*, one of God's powers, even the Logos, who is "improperly" called "god." In summary, John considers Jesus as a heavenly, eternal figure in virtue of the fact that Jesus was active throughout Israel's history, functioning as the one who gave theophanies to Israel's patriarchs and prophets.

JESUS AS "I AM"

In 8:24, 28, and 58, Jesus uses the name "I AM" of himself. Later in 17:6 and 11-12 he honorably confesses that he received this name from God and dutifully manifested it to his disciples. Scholars agree that the "name" in John 17 is not "God" or "Lord," but "I AM" (R. E. Brown 1970:756). What is meant by "I AM," and what does it tell us of the role and status of Jesus? It is a commonplace of Johannine scholarship to argue that "I AM" reflects the usage of the Greek version of Isaiah, which in turn is a condensed version of the name manifested to Moses at the burning bush in Exod 3:14 (Harner 1970; R. E. Brown 1965:533–38). But what does "I AM" mean? To learn this, we must inquire how "I AM" was popularly interpreted by ancient Israelite authors. To begin with, the Greek translation of the Scriptures interpreted the name of God in Exod 3:14 to mean "the Existent One," indicating that this name refers to a divine mode of being, which is eternal in past and future, and so not contingent.

Exod 3:14 (MT)	**Exod 3:14 (LXX)**
God said to Moses: "I AM WHO I AM."	God said to Moses: "I AM THE EXISTENT ONE"
And he said: "Say this to the children of Israel,	And he said: "Say this to the children of Israel,
'I AM has sent me to you.'"	'THE EXISTENT ONE has sent me to you.'"

Second, Philo repeats this interpretation of "I AM" as "the Existent One," always drawing a distinction between God's eternal existence and that of creatures who exist with contingent existence only. Philo's version of the conversation between Moses and God over "the name" of God makes these distinctions and so emphasizes God's eternal existence. "'If I ask the name of him who sent me, and I cannot myself tell them, will they not think me a deceiver?' God replied: 'First tell them that I am He Who Is, that they may learn the difference between what is and what is not, and also the further lesson that no name at all can properly be used of me, to whom alone existence belongs'" (*Mos.* 1.74-76). In one sense God does not have a name, such as we have. Our names indicate our parentage, profession, and personal eccentricities; none of these applies to God. Nor can we know God's essence. But we can know in a negative way that God is utterly different from mortals, for "He Who Is" belongs only to God, whereas all mortals are born and die.

In another version of this conversation between God and Moses, Philo again interprets "I AM" as referring to God's unique existence. True deities are uncreated (no past) and imperishable (no future)—they "are" without beginning or ending. All others come into being and pass away; they do not have divine existence, which was, is, and will be. "For, among the virtues, that of God really is, actually existing, inasmuch as God alone has veritable being. That is why Moses will say of Him as best he may in human speech, 'I am He that is' (Exod iii.14), implying that all others lesser than He have not being, as being indeed is, but exist in semblance only, and are conventionally said to exist" (*Worse* 160; see *Names* 11; *Dreams* 1.230-31). As Hengel observed, a genuine Hellenistic influence is already introduced into the interpretation of the sacred name, in which noncontingent being is contrasted with contingent being, and eternal with temporal existence (Hengel 1974:255–67; Morton Smith 1958).

Another source of interpretation of "I AM" can be found in the Targums of Exodus. The following figure lays out the data, from which I will draw some conclusions (McNamara 1966).

Exod 3:14	*Tg. Yerushalmi* I	*Tg. Yer.* II Polyglots *Tg. Yer.* II Paris	*Tg. Neofiti*	*Tg. Neof.* gl I
(a) God said to Moses,	(a) And the Lord said to Moses,	(a) The Memra of the Lord said to Moses,	(a) And the Lord said to Moses,	(a) And the Lord said to Moses,
(b) "I AM WHO I AM"	(b) "He who spoke and the world was; who spoke and all things were"	(b) "He who said to the world 'Be!' and it was; and who shall yet say to it 'Be!' and it will be"	(b) "I AM WHO I AM"	(b) "I have existed before the world was created; and I have existed after the world was created; I am he who was your support during the captivity of Egypt; and I am he who will be your support during all generations"
(c) And he said: "Say this to the children of Israel":	(c) And he said: "Thus shall you say to the children of Israel":	(c) And he said: "Thus shall you say to the children of Israel":	(c) And he said to him:	(c) And he said: "Thus shall you say to the children of Israel":
(d) "'I AM' has sent me to you"	(d) "'I AM HE WHO IS AND WHO WILL BE' has sent me to you"	(d) "I AM"	(d) "He who spoke and the world was from the beginning and shall again to it 'Be!' and it shall be. He has sent me to you"	(d) "'I AM' has sent me to you"

All the Targums in some way contrast the creator God with contingent creation, thus saying that God's "existence" is from of old and eternal. Moreover, God will be in the future to make a new creation, hence God exists imperishably. Thus "I AM" includes God's eternity in the past and imperishability in the future. "I AM," then, refers to divine duration.

A cursory examination of these texts suggests two lines of interpretation. All the Targums understand "I AM" to refer to a special quality of God's being, viz., God's past and future eternity. And they all link the special name with God's actions or powers: creation in the past and eschatological new creation in the future. Thus the "I AM" of Exod 3:14 was popularly understood to contain remarks about God's two powers as well as God's eternity both past and future.

CONCLUSION

1. *Johannine Christians are monotheists:* this Gospel does not claim that Jesus is Yahweh or that he replaces God. Jesus himself seems to endorse monotheism, echoing the Shema (Deut 6:4-5), when he addresses Israel's Deity, "This is eternal life, that they know thee, *the only true God*" (17:3). Yet the Johannine community also calls Jesus "God."

2. *Jesus is not blaspheming* when he claims to be "equal to God." It is God who "makes him" what he is: (a) God commissioned him to reveal his name; (b) God gave him his two powers; and (c) God sent him into the world as his apostle and agent, equal to himself (Borgen 1968).

3. *Jesus is not a rival of Yahweh, a pretender to the throne.* All that he says and does is done in obedience to the will of God who sent him (see 5:23; 7:16-18; 8:38; 17:4).

4. *Jesus is not a recent invention* of Christian imagination; he is not a new figure in cosmic or national history. He was face to face with God in the beginning, before anything was created. Although in glory, he was continuously active in Israel's salvation history: he created the cosmos, and he gave theophanies to Israel's patriarchs. Therefore his current appearance in our midst is continuous with his past activity.

The exalted confession of Jesus, then, was born in controversy and came to maturity as a point of conflict. It was never a neutral dogma, but served continually as a formal boundary line distinguishing elite Johannine Christians from synagogue members and certain apostolic Christians as well (see 8:24).

8

WHO ELSE IS CALLED "GOD"?

JESUS IN HEBREWS

Without father or mother or genealogy,
he has neither beginning of days nor end of life.
—Heb 7:3

FOCUS AND HYPOTHESIS

In addition to the Fourth Gospel, which calls Jesus "God," the author of Hebrews interprets Melchizedek in terms of characteristics reserved for God alone. The author of Heb 7:3 affirms of Melchizedek: "He is without father or mother or genealogy; he has neither beginning of days nor end of life . . . he continues a priest forever." The author draws on Gen 14:17-20, which introduces Melchizedek without the customary identification of his clan or lineage. Because Scripture itself is silent on these matters, the author of Hebrews interprets this silence as a positive quality: if Melchizedek is "without father or mother or genealogy," then he has no beginning. And of his ending, the author turns to Ps 110:4, "You are a priest *forever* . . . ," to deduce Melchizedek's eternal priesthood. The focus, then, is on the temporal qualities of having no beginning or ending, which in ancient thought was a characteristic of a true deity.

The points made in 7:3 correspond exactly to the commonplaces in Hellenistic thought that describe a true deity. Paraphrased in terms of Greek philosophy, the author states three things of Melchizedek: he is (1) ungenerated, (2) uncreated in the past and imperishable in the future, and (3) eternal or immortal. This chapter focuses on the Greco-Roman background of the language and concepts in Heb 7:3. Because Melchizedek serves as a type for Jesus, then he too should also be described in these three ways, which would mean that the author of Hebrews was consciously declaring Jesus a true deity.

THE SHAPE OF HELLENISTIC GOD-TALK

To discover what specific commonplaces are the appropriate background for understanding Heb 7:3, we turn to the Greco-Roman world for comparative parallels (Spicq 1953:183–84; Attridge 1989:189–91). First we note the form in which the remarks about Melchizedek are cast, namely "negative theology." He is "*without* father, *without* mother, *without* genealogy," and therefore he is totally unlike all mortals, each of whom has father, mother, and genealogy. Unlike mortals, who all were created and came into being, Melchizedek has no beginning; hence he must be eternal in the past. Moreover, whereas all mortal creatures have both a beginning and end, Melchizedek, like a true deity, has neither beginning nor end. Thus philosophers negate from a true deity what is characteristic of mortals. Historians find this type of negative predication in the God-talk of the Greek philosophers and in Christian writers (H. A. Wolfson 1952:115–30; 1957:145–56; Whittaker 1969; Young 1979:53–54).

Frequently Greco-Roman authors use a cluster of terms to describe the eternal past and future of true deities. Most of these attend to the future imperishability of a deity; some, however, describe the deity's past, uncreated being.

> 1. eternal in the past: *un*created (*agenētos*); *un*generated (*agennētos*); *without* beginning (*anarchos*)
> 2. eternal in the future: *ever*lasting (*aidios*); *ever*lasting (*aiōnios*); *im*perishable (*aphthartos*); death*less*, *im*mortal (*athanatos*); not ruined (*anolethros*); *without* end (*ateleutētos*)

I am particularly interested in the way the terms for past and future eternity are often linked together to express a timeless existence for the gods. For example, Theophilus writes of the Christian God: "He is *without* beginning because He is *un*created, and He is *un*changeable because He is *im*mortal" (*Autol.* I.3). The task now is to examine the frequency and the permutations of this kind of God-talk in three distinct modes: (I) eternal in past and future, (2) remains forever, and (3) without mother or father.

Eternal in the Past/Imperishable in the Future

True deities are defined precisely in contrast with mortals, for they are uncreated and imperishable, whereas mortals come into being and pass out of existence (Neyrey 1991:440–45). Greco-Roman God-talk expressed this concept in many different linguistic configurations, which I will now briefly survey. I focus on the various forms of "eternal in the past/imperishable in the future" with a view toward comparing them with what is said in Heb 7:3.

I. *Eternal (aidios)-imperishable (aphthartos).* Philosophers commonly express God's past and future eternity in these two terms. For example, Diodorus Siculus compares and contrasts true gods with mortals made gods after death. His distinguishing characteristic of a true god is eternity of existence, eternity both in the past and in the future: "As regards the gods, men of ancient times have handed down to later generations two different conceptions: Certain of the gods, they say, are eternal and imperishable . . . for each of these genesis and duration are from everlasting to everlasting" (6.I.2). While the term "eternal" (*aidios*) normally means "everlasting" with a view to the future, here it refers to "eternity in the past" because it explains "genesis from everlasting." Plutarch provides a corroborative example of this in his contrast between heavenly beings and the true deity; here "eternal" refers to what is not subject to generation: "the sun and the moon and the rest of the gods, since they have a similar principle of constitution, are subject to generation, but Zeus is everlasting (*aidios*)" (*Stoic. rep.* 1052A). In another place, Plutarch concludes his discussion of Egyptian gods with the remark: "So far as the celestial gods are concerned whose genesis is from eternity, this is the account given by the Egyptians" (Diodorus, *History* I.12.10).

2. *Uncreated (agenētos)-imperishable (aphthartos).* Diogenes Laertius cites Zeno's doctrine of God: "(God) is indestructible (*aphthartos*) and ingenerable (*agenētos*)" (7.137). This pair of predicates frequently describes God in the writings of Philo. He speaks of how creatures reflect divine qualities: "For the good and beautiful things in the world could never have been what they are, save

that they were made in the image of the archetype, which is truly good and beautiful, even the *Un*created, the Blessed, the *Im*perishable" (*Cher.* 86). Moreover, with regard to Epicurus's view of the eternity of the world, Plutarch remarks: "the universe is infinite, *un*generated, and *im*perishable" (*Adv. Col.* 1114A), an idea found frequently in Aristotle (*Cael.* 1.12) and Philo (*Eternity* 7, 10-12, 20, 69, 93; *Dreams* 2.283).

3. *Unbegotten (agennētos)-imperishable (aphthartos).* There was considerable confusion in the ancient world over the terms *agenētos* (uncreated) and *agennētos* (unbegotten), which differ by a single *n*. Thus it is not accidental to find variations of this formula in which God is said to be not just uncreated but unbegotten, as well as imperishable. For example, Plutarch spoke of Isis and Osiris as true gods because of their eternity: "In regard not only to these gods [Isis and Osiris], but in regard to the other gods, save only those whose existence had no begetting (*agennētoi*) and shall have no end (*aphthartoi*), the priests say . . ." (*Is. Os.* 359C). Likewise, Christian theologians proclaim of God: "God alone is unbegotten and incorruptible" (Justin, *Dial.* 5).

4. *Uncreated (agenētos) or unbegotten (agennētos)-eternal (aidios).* The pagan writer Plutarch sings the praises of the true god Apollos by contrasting him with heroic mortals who were subsequently divinized. The essential difference is that true gods are eternal in the past as well as eternal in the future: "My native tradition removes this god from among those deities who were changed from mortals into immortals, like Heracles and Dionysus, whose virtues enabled them to cast off mortality and suffering; but he is one of those deities who are unbegotten (*agennēton*) and eternal (*aidion*)" (*Pel.* 16). Similarly, the Christian apologist Athenagoras distinguishes God from matter because "the Deity is unbegotten and imperishable," whereas matter is created and perishes (*Leg.* 4; see 6.2; 10.1; 19.1; 22.2, 3; 30.3).

Philo commonly speaks of God as "uncreated and eternal" (*agenētos kai aidios*). Judean worshipers of the true God corrected the error common among others by "passing over all created objects because they were created and naturally liable to destruction and chose the service only of the Uncreated and Eternal" (*Spec. Laws* 2.166). Defending Moses, who gave the Israelites the truest conception of God, Josephus tells how Moses described God as "One, uncreated and immutable to all eternity" (*Ag. Ap.* 2.167).

Occasionally we find not just two terms expressing the fullness of divine eternity, but three. Philo spoke in this manner several times, for example: "the uncreated (*agenēton*) Father, the Imperishable (*aphtharton*), the Eternal (*aidion*)" (*Joseph* 265; see *Decalogue* 41; *Alleg. Interp.* 1.51; 3.31).

5. *Unbegotten (agennētos) or uncreated (agenētos)-without ruin (anōlethros).* At the beginning of a small treatise, "On How Many Heads Ought We to Praise God," Alexander Rhetor said: "God is unbegotten (*agennēton*) and indestructible (*anōlethron*)." Clement of Alexandria quotes Parmenides in Plato's *Sophist* describing god as "uncreated (*agenēton*) and indestructible (*anōlethron*)" (*Strom.* 5.14). Plato makes the same claims for the soul, namely, that it is "uncreated (*agennēton*) and indestructible (*anōlethron*)" (*Tim.* 52A).

6. *No beginning/no end.* God's eternity may just was well be expressed in other terms that claim the same eternity of past and future. For example, one may speak of God as having neither beginning nor end. In discussing whether gods were made of atoms, Cicero recorded a discussion that argued that this would be impossible, for it would imply that gods were not eternal in the past, much less imperishable in the future: "Suppose we allow that the gods are made of atoms: then it follows that they are not eternal. For what is made of atoms came into being at some time; and if gods came into being, before they came into existence there were no gods; and if the gods had a beginning they must also have an end" (*Nature of the Gods* 1.24.68).

Writing nearly two centuries after the period we are studying, Tertullian reflects traditional God-talk when he speaks of the eternity of the true God: "I give that definition [of God] which all men's common sense will accept, that God is supremely great, firmly established in eternity, unbegotten, uncreated, without beginning and without end (*sine initio, sine fine*)" (*Adv. Marc.* 1.3). Three terms explicitly refer to eternity in the past: "unbegotten," "uncreated," and "without beginning," which are balanced with notions of eternity in the future: "without end."

Philo described "Fate" as something that has neither beginning nor end: "Fate has no beginning (*anarchos*) or end (*ateleutētos*)" (*Eternity* 75). Theophilus, listing the attributes of God, states that the Deity is "without beginning (*anarchos*) because he is unbegotten (*agennētos*); and he is unchangeable, because he is immortal" (*Autol.* 1.4). In addition to describing God in this fashion, ancient writers applied the same sense of eternity to the concept of time.

In summary, the specific linguistic formulae may differ, but all six variations noted above describe eternity in the past and imperishability in the future as a key, constant characteristic of a true god. Hence, when Heb 7:3

speaks of a figure as having "no beginning and no end," this formula immediately and necessarily suggests that such a figure must be divine, a true god.

Remains Forever

Not only is Melchizedek "without beginning of days and end of life," he "remains forever" (7:3). This is the second of three notices in Hebrews that someone "remains." When in Heb 1:11-12 the author quotes Ps 102:25-27 apropos of Jesus, he makes a sharp contrast between things perishable/imperishable and things changeable/unchanging: "They will perish, but you remain . . . they will be changed, but you are the same and your years will never end." In this context "remaining" must refer to future immortality, imperishability, and eternity inasmuch as it is contrasted with what "perishes," "changes," and "ends." The same meaning should be understood in 7:24 when the author states that Jesus "remains forever." This statement about Jesus' "permanent priesthood" functions precisely in terms of the contrast with the priesthood of the Levitical priests, who are "prevented by death from remaining in office" (7:23; see 7:15-16). Again, Jesus' "remaining forever" must be understood in contrast with "perishing" and "dying." Thus, when the author describes Melchizedek as "remaining forever" (7:3), this too must be understood in terms of some sort of deathlessness, imperishability, unchangeableness, and eternity, all characteristics of a true deity (Neyrey 1991:445–46). This becomes clearer when we examine further the ways in which the ancients described gods.

In one sense, by surveying the Greco-Roman formulae for God's past and future eternity, we have already surfaced five of the key predicates that explain "remain forever." A true god must be "eternal" (*aidios*), "imperishable" (*aphthartos*), "indestructible" (*anōlethros*), "everlasting" (*aiōnios*), and "endless" (*ateleutētos*). Each of these compares and contrasts a true god with human beings, who are called "mortals," those who die. Moreover, a true god must be "deathless" (*athanatos*), and so gods are regularly called "the *im*mortals." Similarly, when the true gods are contrasted with idols, the latter perish, but the gods remain (see Cicero, *Nature of the Gods* 1.11.27; Philo, *Cher.* 51; *Mos.* 2.171).

But true gods "remain forever" because it belongs to their nature not to change. Hence Philo contrasts the immortal god with mortals and the unchanging god with things mutable: "Separate, therefore, my soul, all that is created, mortal, mutable, profane from thy conception of God the 'uncreated,' the 'unchangeable,' the 'immortal,' the holy and solely blessed" (*Sacrifices* 101; see McLelland 1976:37–40). As well as calling God "uncreated," "eternal," "imperishable," and "deathless," Philo regularly calls the Deity "unchanging" (*atreptos;* see *Alleg. Interp.* 1.51; 2.33, 89; *Cher.* 52, 90; *Names* 28, 54, 175).

Thus it belongs to a true god to be "eternal" in the sense of enduring forever in the future, imperishable, without end, and without change, that is, to "remain forever." Hence, when the author of Hebrews says of the figure in 7:3 that he "remains forever," he is using a commonplace about the future eternity of a true god.

Without Father or Mother or Genealogy

The terms "without father" and "without mother" most commonly refer in negative fashion to honorless children, either illegitimate, orphaned, or abandoned. But these same terms are positively applied to Greco-Roman deities in an honorable manner. From the ancient world we learn that the goddess Athena was "without mother" (*amētōr*), but not "without a father," who was Zeus (Plato, *Sym.* 180D). Hephaistos was "without a father," but had a mother (Pollux, *Onom.* 3.26). Finally, commenting on the number "7," Philo indicates it is honorable and perfect because it is neither begotten nor begets: "This number is likened to the 'motherless' (*amētori*) and virgin Nike, who is said to have appeared out of the head of Zeus" (*Creation* 100).

As rare as it is to find "without mother" or "without father" applied to a deity, two authors did describe the true deity in this fulsome fashion. Lactantius quotes an ancient oracle of Apollo about god: "Self-produced, untaught, without a mother, unshaken." He then quotes Mercury to the effect that a true god must be without both mother and father: "Mercury, that thrice greatest . . . not only speaks of God as 'without a mother,' as Apollo does, but also as 'without a father' because He has no origin from any other source but Himself" (*Div. Inst.* 1.7.1). Lactantius repeats this in another place: "For God the Father Himself, who is the origin and source of all things, inasmuch as He is without parents, is most truly named by Trismegistus 'fatherless' (*apatôr*) and 'motherless' (*amētôr*), because He was born from no one" (*Div. Inst.* 4.13.1). Mercury, the heavenly messenger, says that God's perfection lies precisely in God's having no source, that is, "without mother, without father, without genealogy."

A comparable passage occurs in the *Apocalypse of Abraham*, in which we find the following acclamation of God:

> Eternal One, Mighty One, Holy El, God autocrat
> self-originate, incorruptible, immaculate,
> unbegotten, spotless, immortal,
> self-perfected, self-devised,
> without mother, without father, ungenerated.
> (17:8-11; Rubinkiewicz 1983:697)

The form is clearly "negative theology," even if some of the terms suggest a certain transcendence, such as "self-originate," "self-perfected," and "self-devised." We easily recognize phrases about the true eternity of this god—(a) eternal in the past: "unbegotten," "self-originate"; and (b) imperishable in the future: "incorruptible" and "immortal." In addition, this god is "without mother, without father, ungenerated," that is, sourceless. Both Lactantius's citations from Greek theology and the *Apocalypse of Abraham* suggest that when some figure is acclaimed "without father or mother or genealogy," such a one is a true god.

It is not uncommon to find the claim that God is "self-begotten" (*autogenētos*). For example, Justin cites an ancient Greek oracle, which he claims is prophetic of the true god of the Christians: "Only the Chaldaeans have obtained wisdom, and the Hebrews, who worship God Himself, the self-begotten (*autogenēton*) King" (*Cohort.* 11). Examples of this abound (see Whittaker 1975, 1980).

In summary, a full and convincing appreciation of the background of Heb 7:3 requires that we note both the diversity of expression and the consistency of concept in regard to the eternity of a true deity. A true god must be completely "eternal" in past and future.

Hellenistic Terminology	*Heb 7:3*
1. ungenerated	1. no father, mother, or genealogy
2. uncreated in past, imperishable in future	2. without beginning of days or end of life
3. continuous existence	3. remains forever

The description of Melchizedek in Heb 7:3, when understood against this background, immediately and cogently suggests that we are hearing popular and common characterization of a true god. But when the author of Hebrews presents Melchizedek in terms used to describe a true god, he does not exalt Melchizedek for his own sake, but only to promote his antitype, Jesus; for, as the author says, Melchizedek, "resembling the Son of God, remains a priest forever" (7:3). All this discussion of eternity, then, should be seen in function of the author's clear and nuanced acclamation of Jesus as a true God.

JESUS, TRUE GOD OR HEROIZED MORTAL?

Alongside the commonplaces just surveyed, I put others that compare and contrast true gods with heroized mortals, who were made gods after their deaths because of their benefaction to humankind. This material has a bearing on how we understand the remarks about Jesus. Did Hebrews acclaim Jesus a hero divinized after his death because of his benefactions to humankind, or did the author consider him a true god, fully eternal in past and future?

Two classical authors discussed the nature of true gods by contrasting genuine gods, who are eternal in the past and imperishable in the future, with heroes, who were made immortal after death because of their benefactions. Diodorus Siculus wrote under Caesar and Augustus in the waning days of the first century BCE, and Plutarch flourished in the late first century CE. Their writings offer a discussion of a true deity that bears on the figure of Jesus in Hebrews.

When Diodorus Siculus distinguishes true gods from divinized heroes, he sees that the differences lie exclusively in the fact that true gods are fully eternal, that is, uncreated in the past and imperishable in the future. Divinized heroes, however, were born as mere mortals but attained to "immortality" because of their benefactions to humankind:

> As regards the gods, men of ancient times have handed down to later generations two different conceptions: Certain of the gods, they say, are *eternal and imperishable* . . . for each of these *genesis and duration* are from everlasting to everlasting. But the other gods, we are told, were terrestrial beings who attained to immortal honors and fame because of their benefactions to mankind, such as Heracles, Dionysus, Aristaeus, and the others who were like them. (6.1.2; see Talbert 1977:26–35)

He says the same thing about the way Ethiopians think about god/gods: "The Ethiopians entertain two opinions: they believe that some of them . . . have a nature which is *eternal* and *imperishable*, but others of them, they think, share a mortal nature and have come to receive immortal honors because of their virtue and the benefactions which they have bestowed on all mankind" (3.9.1).

Plutarch echoes just this sort of stereotypical description of the gods when he acclaims the excellence of Apollos Tegyraeus: "My native tradition removes this god from among those deities who were changed from mortals into immortals. Like Heracles and Dionysus, whose virtues enabled them to cast off mortality and suffering; but he is one of those deities who are *unbegotten* and *eternal*, if we may judge by what the most ancient and wisest men have said on such matters" (*Pel.* 16).

From these examples, one can sketch the differences between true gods and divinized benefactor-heroes:

True Gods	*Divinized Benefactor-Heroes*
1. ancient	1. recent, new
2. celestial	2. terrestrial
3. without a beginning and ungenerated	3. came into being and born in time
4. imperishable	4. died, translated in death
5. eternal	5. made immortal

According to this commonplace, then, what type of deity is Jesus? Is he a true god or a divinized benefactor-hero? From what I have noted in regard to Heb 7:3 and other passages in the document, I must conclude that the author of Hebrews acclaims Jesus as a "true god" because of his full eternity in the past and imperishability in the future. Granted that other documents acclaim his death as a benefaction to us, the author of Hebrews never states that God exalted him for his benefaction. After all, he was a "priest forever."

CONFIRMATION IN HEBREWS

My reading of Heb 7:3 can be confirmed by a careful examination of the remarks about Jesus in the document's beginning and ending, the premier rhetorical places in a text. In beginnings authors initially shape the audience's imagination, while in endings clear conclusions may be drawn or initial themes repeated. Such rhetorical emphasis seems to hold true both for the beginning and the ending of Hebrews.

Opening: Past and Future Eternity

In chapter 1 the author states the most honorable and exalted things that he possibly can about Jesus. The audience is thus conditioned how to label Jesus or acclaim him. In the traditional culture of the author, appeal is regularly made to authority, in this case the most solemn of authorities, the Scriptures. In a chain of quotations from the Psalms and other biblical writings (Meier 1985), the author unmistakably calls Jesus "God" (1:8; cf. Ps 45:6) and predicates of him divine eternity, both eternity in the past and imperishability in the future.

Citing Ps 102:25-27, the author first acclaims Jesus' *eternity in the past.* We have already been told that it is Jesus "through whom God made the world" (1:2b). Of him the psalm says: "Thou, Lord, founded the earth in the beginning, and the heavens are the work of your hands" (1:10). Thus biblical texts (Psalm 102 in Heb 1:10 and Psalm 2 in Heb 1:5) speak to Jesus' past, namely, to his eternity before creation. The author balances this with further remarks from Psalm 102 about his eternity in the future.

> They will perish, but you remain,
> they will grow old like a garment
> (like a mantle) you will roll them up.
> And they will be changed.
> But you are the same
> and your years are without end.
> (Heb 1:11-12; cf. Ps 102:26-27)

Unlike the perishable world, which is subject to change, Jesus is imperishable and will not change. He "remains" and his "years are without end."

Eternity in both past and future would seem to be the plain meaning of Psalm 102. If so, it speaks unmistakably of Jesus as a true god according to commonplace Hellenistic characteristics of a true deity. This may be confirmed by noting another commonplace about a true god that is here predicated of Jesus: he is said to have the two basic powers of God, creative and executive, a concept discussed earlier in regard to Romans. As we have seen in Heb 1:2 and 10, Jesus exercises "creative power," whereby he caused the world to be.

Likewise 1:8 tells us that Jesus enjoys "executive power": "Your throne, O God, is for ever and ever, the righteous scepter is the scepter of your kingdom." The author expresses this sense of Jesus' complete sovereignty in other terms, calling him "the heir of all things" (1:2) who is "seated at the right hand of the Majesty on high" (1:3).

Yet one quickly notes that the author of Hebrews seems considerably more interested in Jesus' imperishability and eternity in the future than he is in his eternity in the past. Using Ps 110:4 as another indisputable authority, the author argues that Jesus' future existence is proclaimed: "You are a priest forever" (Heb 5:6; 7:3, 17, 21). God's oath establishes Jesus' future eternity in the precise role of a priest according to the order of Melchizedek. Yet as this study has shown, Melchizedek is himself described in the terms used of a true god, uncreated/ungenerated in the past and imperishable in the future (7:3).

Document Ending: "The Same"—Eternally Existing

At the end of the document, the author makes one final predication of Jesus: "Jesus Christ is the same, yesterday, today, and forever" (13:8). This remark seems to repeat what was said about Jesus in the first chapter.

> You are the same (*autos*) and your years will never end. (1:12)
>
> Jesus Christ is the same (*autos*) yesterday, today, and forever. (13:8)

In 1:12 the author cited Ps 102:28, a psalm used in the early church primarily to affirm the unchangeableness and imperishability of the true God against pagan and gnostic gods (see Irenaeus, *Haer.* 4.3.1; Origen, *Cels.* 1.21). Hebrews likewise understands the psalm in the same way, but applies it to Jesus, implying that he too is a true deity because he is eternal and imperishable.

The relevant background for understanding Heb 13:8 comes to us in a variety of ways in which the ancients discourse on the eternal existence of a deity. For example, many ancient philosophers describe God as the unique being who was, is, and will be. Yet Plato refined this by stating that it is improper to speak in terms of God's past, present, and future. Properly, God simply "is" (*Tim.* 37e-38a). Philo too reflects this when he says that God's life is not a time, but an eternity: "in eternity there is no past or future, but only present existence" (*Unchangeable* 32). Moreover, Philo frequently names the true God as the "Existent One" whose existence is only "now." Like the commonplaces about a true deity in Heb 7:3, this continuous existence was expressed in many ways.

1. *First and last.* Eusebius cites in his *Praeparatio evangelica* an ancient hymn to Zeus in which this supreme god was acclaimed: "Zeus first, Zeus last" (3.9). Of course, if God was "first" and will be "last," then God "is." This statement makes a striking parallel with the remarks about God as "first and last" in Isa 41:4; 44:6; and 48:12. A variation of this appears in Revelation, which uses a progressive formula to describe the heavenly being: first, "I am the Alpha and the Omega" (1:8); then, "I am the Alpha and the Omega, the beginning and the end" (21:6); and finally, "I am the Alpha and the Omega, the first and the last, the beginning and the end" (22:13).

2. *Beginning, middle, end.* We occasionally find statements about divine activity that parallel the remarks about God's eternity. For example, an inscription on the statue of Aion at Eleusis reads: "who has no beginning, middle, end" (Dittenberger 1960:3.1125). Likewise Plato remarked: "God, as the old tradition declares, holds in his hands the beginning, the middle, and the end of all that is" (*Laws* 715e; see *Tim.* 37b). But Josephus contains the clearest example of this formula. Discussing the first commandment in the Decalogue, he speaks of God's perfection: "God is the beginning, the middle, and the end of all things" (*Ag. Ap.* 2.190). Who holds the beginning, middle, and end of all things must himself be eternal in past, present, and future.

3. *Is, was, and will be.* Although the data are not numerous, over the years scholars have pointed out statements about gods that explicitly describe the divine eternity in terms of past, present, and future. For example, Pausanias records a fragment of a hymn that acclaims Zeus's eternity: "Zeus was, Zeus is, and Zeus will be" (*Descr.* 10.12.10). In the Hermetic Corpus there is a very fulsome description of God's eternity: "God is everlasting, God is eternal. That he should come into being or should ever have come into being is impossible. He is, he was, he will be forever" (*Asclepius* 2.14b; see also Plutarch, *Is. Os.* 354C). At the beginning of the third book of the *Sibylline Oracles* a summary statement about God is made, in which we find the phrase: "as existing now, and formerly and again in the future" (3.16). This type of remark resembles God's own confession in the book of Revelation: "I am the Alpha and the Omega, who is and who was and who is to come" (1:8; see 1:4; 4:8; 11:17).

Thus, just as the author acclaimed Jesus' past eternity and future imperishability in Heb 1:10-12, so he repeats it in 13:8. The repetition seems consciously intended, with Ps 102:28 ("you are the same") being the common link. Yet beyond the citation of a Jewish psalm, the predication contains the same material found in Hellenistic commonplaces on true gods in terms of their timeless existence. Moreover, these materials confirm the hypothesis of this study that the predications in Heb 7:3 of eternity in the past and imperishability in the future were truly acclamations about Jesus' status as a divine figure. For 1:10-12 and 13:8 confess the same thing of Jesus, although in different terms. Yet the author seems to use popular topoi on the nature of a true deity, giving further salience to these predications.

SUMMARY AND CONCLUSIONS

First, by examining the Hellenistic parallels to the statements made in Heb 7:3, we know that its language originates in and reflects the mode of thought found in Greco-Roman philosophical speculation about a true deity. Unmistakably, the author of Hebrews intends his readers to understand the figure described in 7:3 as a true deity, completely in accord with the commonplaces that describe true gods as fully eternal: uncreated or ungenerated in the past and imperishable in the future.

Heb 7:3	*Greek Philosophy*
1. "without father or mother or genealogy"	1. ungenerated (*agennētos*)
2. "without beginning . . . or ending"	2. eternal in the past; imperishable in the future
3. "remains forever"	3. eternal (*aidios*); always existing (*aion*)

Second, this fixation on past and future eternity, while concentrated in Heb 7:3, appears both at the beginning and ending of the document.

Eternity in the Past	*Imperishability in the Future*
Heb 1 "through whom he created the world," 1:2 "you founded the earth in the beginning," 1:10	Heb 1 "They perish, but you remain . . . they will be changed, but you are the same and your years will never end," 1:11-12
Heb 7 "without father, without mother, without genealogy," 7:3a "without beginning of days," 7:3b	Heb 7 "without end of life," 7:3b "he remains forever," 7:3c "a priest forever, according to the order of Melchizedek," 5:6; 7:17, 21
Heb 13 "Jesus Christ yesterday, today, . . ." 13:8	Heb 13 ". . . and tomorrow," 13:8

Third, whatever the author says of Melchizedek must be understood as stated in service of Jesus. The assertions about complete eternity in Heb 7:3 are made apropos of Jesus in the rhetorically significant places of the document, its beginning and end.

Fourth, Jesus is called "God" because he enjoys the primary characteristics of a true deity: he is (1) uncreated and ungenerated in the past, without mother or father or genealogy; and (2) imperishable, without end, and eternal. Since these temporal characteristics are unique to true deities, we learn that the author of Hebrews consciously knows what he is doing; the designation of Jesus as "God" has substance.

Fifth, when the author acclaimed Jesus as "God" in Heb 1:8, he intended that title to have specific content. Jesus may properly be called a divine figure because he enjoys God's two basic powers, ruling power (1:8) and creative power (1:11). Similarly, Jesus is a divine figure because he fulfills the category of a genuine deity by his full eternity, a point made explicit both in the first and last chapters, as well as the typology of Melchizedek in 7:3. In this the author of Hebrews begins to make ontological and not just functional statements about Jesus.

9

CONCLUSION

To the only God, our Savior, be glory, majesty, dominion and authority, before all time and now and for ever. Amen.
—Jude 25

SUMMARY

I gather the major concepts and models used in this study of God, the neglected factor in New Testament study, to provide readers with an extensive checklist of ways of reading documents and gathering data.

1. *Names.* What names are given to the Deity and what significance might each have? Common titles and names of God in the New Testament are: "God," "Lord," "Father," "Savior," "Sovereign," and "Judge." What benefaction is associated with each?

2. *Two Attributes.* According to Exod 34:6-7, God has two basic attributes, which summarize all his other aspects: mercy and just judgment. Allowing for synonyms, are both functioning or might one have precedence over another (Rom 1:18 and 3:21)?

3. *Two Powers.* God's actions in the world were similarly summarized into two powers, creation and executive/eschatological power. These are often associated with a specific name of God: "creation" with "God" and "executive"

with "Lord." God's eschatological power to raise the dead is much more frequently discussed than creative power (Rom 4:17-25; John 5:19-29).

4. *Covenants.* Many New Testament authors use a stereotype of two types of covenants found in Scripture (covenant of Abraham and David, covenant of Moses). In each, God is seen working in a distinctive manner, creating a distinctive relationship between God and the receivers of the covenant. Each, in turn, portrays God acting in very different ways and representing quite different values (Gal 3:6-14; 4:20-30; Matt 1:1; Eph 2:12).

5. *Theodicy.* We know that Stoics and Epicureans disagreed over whether God judges at all, but especially whether he judges those who have died; similarly Pharisees and Sadducees stood on opposites sides of this debate (Acts 17 and 23–24). But God has made Jesus "judge of the living and the dead," thus bringing Christians into the conversation in support of theodicy.

6. *Providence.* Like theodicy, the doctrine of providence served as a chief issue in Greco-Roman and Israelite God-talk. This material is often looked at under the rubric of "natural theology," learning about God from creation (Acts 17:16-32; Rom 1:18-24). The issue for Jesus and his disciples is fast-forwarded from the creation of the world to the current providence of God in his dealings with Jesus and the disciples of Jesus. Does God give and fulfill prophecies? Does God rescue from death, stoning, shipwreck, and the like? Does God have a "will" or "plan" or "purpose"?

7. *Systematic Theology.* Greco-Roman philosophy uses a pattern to structure God-talk: (a) epistemology, (b) physics/nature, and (c) ethics. Paul uses this pattern, I argue, in Romans and to a lesser extent in Galatians. But it may well be found in other documents. Moreover, I noted that Paul used the technique of diatribal style in Romans to surface false theological conclusions so as systematically to correct them and leave the reader with a comprehensive statement of his understanding of God.

8. *Eternity.* The investigation of Heb 7:3 uncovered many ways in which the ancients expressed a pivotal characteristic of a true god, namely, full eternity: uncreated and ungenerated eternity in the past as well as imperishable and deathlessness in the future. This concept also informs the name of God, "I AM," used in a text such as John 8:58.

9. *Negative Theology.* As theological thinking became more sophisticated in antiquity, authors began insisting that we cannot know God's essence, but only his actions in the world. Moreover, in an effort to purge God-talk of

anthropomorphisms, authors began using language about God that removed from the Deity things that characterize mortals. Hence we find God described as "without father, without mother, without genealogy, without beginning or ending." Theophilus says: "The appearance of God is ineffable and indescribable, and cannot be seen by eyes of flesh, in glory, incomprehensible, in greatness unfathomable, in height inconceivable, in wisdom unrivaled, in goodness inimitable, in kindness unutterable" *(Autol.* 1.3). This type of God-talk will be helpful in examining the doxologies in 1 Timothy.

10. *Holy As God Is Holy.* On the one hand, readers will appeal to God as the maker and defender of order in the world and the church; God's holiness, then, is linked to respect for God's order. But we also find God reforming previous patterns of order or reversing them entirely (1 Cor 1:18-25, 26-29; 3:19-20; 12:22-25). Holiness, in this case, means to accept God's new drawings of lines. This concept is essential for understanding both Jesus' behavior and the reactions to it by the rule enforcers of his day. It will have its most important effect in sorting out the food rules practiced by Paul's churches. Moreover, the dead do not come into the presence of the living God; they must become like God and put on incorruptibility and immortality (1 Cor 15:50-55). Nor may sinners come before the sinless and perfect God (1 Cor 6:9-10). "This is the will of God, your sanctification: that you abstain from unchastity" (1 Thess 4:3). For the aim of knowing God's "holiness" is to be "holy as I am holy" (1 Pet 1:14-19).

11. *God's Honor and Glory.* Honor, the pivotal value of the ancient world, describes the only item that humans can offer God, since God does not need sacrifice. God's honor is attached first and foremost to God's role as benefactor and patron, then to God's power to create and raise the dead. God defends the divine honor when challenged (Matt 21:33-46; 24:45-51), and requites sinners with a *lex talionis* or quid pro quo punishment (1 Cor 3:17). The honor of the Patron is at stake when God sends an agent, prophet, or Son with a task: anyone who receives Jesus receives not Jesus but God who sent him. Thus God's honor is equated with the honor of his agent: "All may honor the Son even as they honor the Father" (John 5:23).

12. *God-in-Relationship.* Unlike the god of Epicurus who in his perfect blessedness has no relationship whatsoever with mortals, the God of Jesus Christ is first and foremost a provident Deity who relates to mortals as the consummate patron and benefactor. Among the names of God listed above

are the common ones also used in Greco-Roman God-talk to label the deity under some aspect of benefaction. In patron-client relations, moreover, a most important element is God's "faithfulness," without which the relationship cannot survive (I Cor 1:9; I Thess 5:23-24; Rom 9:4ff.). To aid in recovering this material in a document, I employed the model of four symbolic media (power, commitment, influence, inducement) to assess which types of benefaction are bestowed and among them which ones have greater significance.

13. *Monotheism.* Although two chapters in this book consciously acclaim Jesus as "God," "Lord," or "equal to God," the New Testament still insists in a number of texts on the traditional Israelite monotheistic confession (Mark 12:28-34, 35-38; John 17:3; Rom 3:29-30; I Cor 8:4). This is particularly noteworthy in places when the "one God" is associated with the "mediator Jesus Christ": "There is one God and there is one mediator between God and mortals, the man Jesus Christ" (I Tim 2:5). See also I Tim 1:17; 6:16; and Jude 24-25.

14. *Freedom.* Occasionally, especially when Paul wishes to argue that God may do new and different things, he vigorously defends the freedom of God. Like a potter, God may make whatever vessel God wishes (Rom 9:14-17). Similarly, God is free to choose Jacob over Esau (Rom 9:11-13).

15. *Impartiality and Inclusivity.* Fortunately for readers, Paul and also Luke use the very expression "God is impartial" (Rom 2:11; 3:22-24; 10:10-13; 11:32; Gal 2:6; Acts 10:35; also I Pet 1:17). This characteristic affects our understanding of God's two attributes, for God is impartial in judgment, just as God shows no favoritism. It also belongs in the consideration of God-in-relation, where divine impartiality cancels out the popular notion of favoritism for the elect few in patronage.

16. *Prayer and Worship.* Using communication theory, I examined how worship communicates in two directions: (a) mortals in prayer or sacrifice communicate with God, and (b) God by means of oracles, revelations, dreams, and portents communicates with mortals. Unlike Judeans, Christian worship of God occurs in fluid, not sacred, space; it has no hereditary priesthood or system of sacrifices; rather, it is characterized by prayer of many types, especially prayers of praise and petition.

WHERE DO WE GO FROM HERE?

Good books do not end investigation and inquiry, but indeed suggest where a reader might go with the materials in the book to read on one's own and conduct one's own research. These remarks, then, are like the last class in a seminar that summarizes, but especially excites students to continue learning.

1. *Other Documents.* This book examined the God-talk in but eight of the twenty-seven documents of the New Testament. Obviously much more remains to be done, but where are the most suggestive places? It is only my opinion, but I consider these particularly worthwhile documents to examine: the Gospel of Luke, Ephesians, Colossians, Jude, and Revelation. Going beyond the New Testament period, one should examine the *Didache, 1 Clement,* and the great writers of the second century, Justin and Irenaeus.

2. *Greco-Roman God-Talk.* I have found the most stimulus by reading various works of the ancients in which the deity is described or debated. Of particular significance are Diogenes Laertius's *Lives of the Philosophers,* Lucian's satires, Cicero's *Nature of the Gods,* Plutarch's tractates such as *Delay of the Divine Judgment,* the cluster of materials on Greek oracles, the arguments with Stoics and Epicureans, and finally the tractates of Philo Judaeus.

3. *Praise of God.* Many writers on rhetoric in antiquity included a special part of their treatment of epideictic rhetoric dedicated to the praise of God. The canons of praise are generally those found in the rhetoric of praise and blame, but they represent nevertheless a clear sense of conventional understanding of God. Among the important sources of "praise of God" are Quintilian (*Inst.* 3.7.6-9), Alexander of Numenius (*Rhetores Graeci* 3.4-6), and Menander Rhetor (1.333-44). Equally helpful in this regard would be the investigation of hymns composed to honor and praise the gods, such as one finds in J. H. Charlesworth 1994, Fiensy 1985, and Foster 1995.

4. *Who Else?* Although we studied how Jesus is acclaimed a true god in both the Gospel of John and Hebrews, still others in the Israelite lore were likewise declared "god." For example, according to Exod 7:1, God sent Moses to Pharaoh as god: "I send you as god to Pharaoh." Because of the apparent scandal of this remark in Scripture, considerable effort was brought to bear on an interpretation that did not compromise Israelite monotheism. In at least six places Philo examines this (*Alleg. Interp.* 1.40; *Sacr.* 9; *Worse* 161f; *Migr.* 84; *Names* 19; and *Dreams* 2.189). No study of this material would be complete without

the commentary on these passages by Carl Holladay (1977:103–33; see Meeks 1968:354–61). In John 10:34 Jesus offers a defense to those accusing him of making himself God; according to Israel's own Scriptures, other persons have been called "gods": "I said, 'You are gods, sons of the Most High'" (Ps 82:6). An investigation of the midrash on this psalm indicates that many people, from Adam on and including the Israelites at Sinai, were made supremely holy and thus deathless (Neyrey 1989:655–59).

APPENDIX 1

GOD-IN-RELATIONSHIP

PATRON-BROKER-CLIENT

BASIC FEATURES OF PATRON-CLIENT RELATIONSHIPS

Students of antiquity already pay much attention to the phenomenon of patron-client relations (Saller 1982; Veyne 1990; Wallace-Hadrill 1989). Frederick Danker's *Benefactor* brought it to the attention of New Testament scholars (1981, 1982). Bruce Malina contributed by bringing to the interpreters of early Christian writings the formal use of the anthropology of patron-client relations (1996:143–49; see Moxnes 1991). What is a patron-client relationship? As one anthropologist stated: "Patronage is a model or analytic construct which the social scientist applies in order to understand and explain a range of apparent different social relationships: father-son, God-man, saint-devotee, godfather-godchild, lord-vassal, landlord-tenant, politician-voter, professor-assistant, and so forth" (Blok 1969:366). Thus patron-client relationships describe the vertical dimension of exchange between higher and lower-status persons.

The standard features of a patron-client relationship are as follows (Eisenstadt and Roniger 1984:43–64; Wallace-Hadrill 1989:1–8; Joubert 2000: 17–72):

1. The relationship is *asymmetrical,* that is, between parties of different status; thus it represents a vertical dimension of superior and inferior relationships (Gellner and Waterbury 1977:4; Saller 1982:1–2). Dionysius of Halicarnassus's description of Roman patron-client relations begins with acknowledgment of the unequal status of the two members: "After Romulus had distinguished those of superior rank from their inferiors, he next established laws by which the duties of each were prescribed" (2.9.10).

2. A strong element of *unconditionality* and long-range credit is built into these relationships. A son would likely inherit his father's and mother's patrons. Hence Israelites spoke of "the God of our fathers."

3. A strong element of *interpersonal obligation* is prevalent in these relationships; it is couched in terms of personal loyalty or attachment between patrons and clients. John Rich (1990:128) describes the importance of loyalty/faithfulness in the patron-client relation: "In one of the most important of its many uses *fides* means 'protection.' The weaker party is said 'to be in the *fides*' of the stronger. At the formation of such a relationship, the weaker party is said to give himself into or entrust himself to the *fides* of the stronger and the stronger to receive the weaker into his *fides*."

4. Despite their long-range, almost lifelong, endurance, patron-clients relations are entered into *voluntarily* and can be abandoned voluntarily.

5. It frequently contains a strong element of *favoritism*. For example, Plutarch states: "There are favors that involve causing no offense, such as giving a friend preferential help in obtaining a post, putting some prestigious administrative function into his hands, or a friendly embassy" (*Precepts for Politicians* 19-20).

6. In it basic goods and services are *exchanged,* with clear notions of *reciprocity*; thus a *debt* in incurred by the client who then has obligations to the patron (Saller 1982:21, 27–29).

7. The relationship often has a "*kinship glaze*" over it, which reduces the crassness of the exchange while it heightens the commitment and loyalty of the client. The patron is "father" to the client. Dionysius of Halicarnassus narrates that Romulus did not wish the patron-client relations in Rome to resemble the harshness shown earlier by the Greeks: "The Athenians called their clients '*thetes*' or 'hirelings,' because they served for hire, and the Thessalians called theirs '*penestai*' or 'toilers,' by the very name reproaching them with their condition" (2.9). So he recommended that the poor and lowly be described by a "handsome designation," namely "patronage."

8. *Honor,* both given and received, features significantly in these relationships (Veyne 1990:124–30).

Human patron-client relationships will tend to be asymmetrical, reciprocal, voluntary, often expressing favoritism, focused on honor and respect, and held together by "goodwill" or faithfulness. As we shall see, changes occur when this social scheme is applied to the relationship of God/gods and mortals. But at least this serves as a reliable template for examining God's patron-benefactor relations with mortals.

A CLASSIC NEW TESTAMENT EXAMPLE

This model of patron-client relations is well known to New Testament scholars. The Q account of Jesus and the centurion provides a clear understanding of the process, even if no technical terms are present (Matt 8:5-13//Luke 7:1-10). In phase one of the story, the centurion has shown himself a patron to the town, because, as his clients say: "He loves our nation and he built us our synagogue" (Luke 7:5). As indebted clients, "the elders of the Judeans" come to Jesus and mediate on their patron's behalf for Jesus' favor: patron = centurion; clients = elders. But in the second phase of the narrative, Jesus becomes the patron with power to aid his petitioner, and so new roles appear: patron = Jesus; client = centurion. The elders, once clients of the centurion, continue to serve as mediators. Luke also refers to patrons/benefactors in 22:25 when Jesus describes the typical practice of high-status persons: "those in authority over them are called benefactors *(euergetai)*." Even if the technical term "patron" or "benefactor" does not appear in a document, the phenomenon is common (Mott 1975; Malina 1996; Joubert 2000).

WHAT DO PATRONS AND CLIENTS EXCHANGE?

If patron/benefactor-client relationships entail an exchange, what is exchanged and what are the expectations of the parties involved? Roman patronage included in it a client's duty to show gratitude to his patrons

(Cicero, *Duties* 1.47; Seneca, *Ben.* 1.4.2); similarly, in Greek benefaction (Dio Chrysostom, *Or.* 75.6). What is exchanged? Malina has systematized the model of Talcott Parsons that describes four basic media of social exchange (Malina 1986a:77–87). At a high level of abstraction, we find four general or symbolic media of communication: power, commitment, inducement, and influence. The following chart indicates what is included under each heading.

Power: generally reflects the collective effectiveness system, that is, government in all its forms; the capacity to produce conformity or to get results by simply requiring the performance of some obligation or duty. The wielder of power must have a right to do so with a corresponding duty for others to perform.	***Commitment:*** reflects belonging to family, extended family, circle of friends, fictive family; this appeals to loyalty, faithfulness, covenant of some kind. Operative here is an internal sense of obligation, duty, and belonging. Instead of power to force compliance, commitment produces loyalty by guilt or shame.
Inducement: specific to the economic system and to wealth, goods, services that might be exchanged. Examples of this include meals, dinners, and the like (e.g., Matt 25:35-36). Gifts, such as meals, must be reciprocated (Luke 14:12).	***Influence:*** specific to who has access to the other media; who has clout or "pull." While it may refer to information (secrets, revelations), it is less knowledge of some information and more knowledge of whom to go to or who has access.

Generally, these are linked, such that if the patron bestows inducement (grain, bride-price), the client will know that the patron's commitment is also offered. To come back to an earlier example, the centurion-as-patron in Luke 7:1-10 has produced both commitment ("he loves our nation") and inducement ("he built our synagogue"). In return, he activates the commitment of the elders of that town to use their influence with Jesus to help his slave. The elders know to whom to turn, namely, Jesus. They presume that Jesus has power, the ability to command spirit-caused diseases to yield. Thus we find in this example all four media being exchanged: power (Jesus' ability to heal), commitment (centurion's "love," elders' loyalty), inducement (he built our synagogue), and influence (elders' know to whom to turn).

TYPES OF RECIPROCITY

Why do people engage in patron-client exchange? What, if anything, do they expect to get? Malina (1986a:98–106) mediates for us anthropological theories of exchange, which identify three types of reciprocity pertinent to the ancient Mediterranean: (1) *Generalized reciprocity* describes "altruistic" interactions whereby the interests of "the other are primary" (i.e., "solidarity extreme"). It is generally extended to kin-group members (i.e., "charity begins at home"). (2) *Balanced reciprocity* looks to mutual interests, in a balanced fashion (i.e., quid pro quo exchange). It has one's neighbors and villagers in view. (3) *Negative reciprocity* seeks self-interest at the expense of "the other," who is probably a stranger or an enemy; hence it is the "unsocial extreme." A schematic view of the model is suggested in the following diagram (Malina 1986a:101–4).

Types of Reciprocity	Comparative Aspects
Generalized reciprocity	1. characteristic: give without expectation of return 2. forms: child rearing, hospitality 3. recipients: parents, children, kin 4. biblical examples: Matt 7:11//Luke 11:11-13; Luke 10:33-35
Balanced reciprocity	1. characteristic: tit for tat, quid pro quo 2. forms: barter, assistance agreements 3. recipients: neighbors 4. biblical examples: 1 Cor 9:3-12; Matt 10:10//Luke 10:7
Negative reciprocity	1. characteristic: exploitation; reap where one has not sown 2. forms: robbery; buy cheap, sell dear 3. recipients: strangers, enemies 4. biblical examples: Luke 10:30; 19:22

Philo provides an excellent illustration of these abstract types of reciprocity when he asks: "Why did God create?" Philo began with a text, "Noah found grace with the Lord God" (Gen 6:8), then asked about this "grace," whether it is something earned or deserved, and thus expressive of a balanced reciprocity between God and Noah. He rejected any notion of "balance" here, and offered another explanation: "The second explanation ('he was thought worthy of grace') is founded on a not unreasonable idea, that the Cause judges those worthy of His gifts, who do not deface with base practices the coin within them which bears the stamp of God, even the sacred mind. And yet perhaps that explanation is not the true one" (*Unchangeable* 105).

Since no balanced reciprocity whatsoever is appropriate between God and mortals, Philo offers a third explanation, which turns to a different form of reciprocity, not balanced, but generalized:

> the man of worth . . . in all his inquiries found this to be the highest truth, that all things are the grace or gift of God—earth, water, air, fire, sun, stars, heaven, all plants and animals. . . . But God has given His good things in abundance to the All and its parts, not because He judged anything worthy of grace, but looking to His eternal goodness, and thinking that to be beneficent was incumbent upon His blessed and happy nature. So that if anyone should ask me what was the motive for the creation of the world, I will answer that it was the goodness of the Existent, that goodness which is the oldest of His bounties and itself the source of others. (*Unchangeable* 107-8)

Thus creation was a singular act of generalized reciprocity, which most appropriately suits God: "to be beneficent was incumbent upon His blessed and happy nature." Thus to be God means to bestow unmerited blessings and to act according to the "solidarity extreme."

DRAMATIS PERSONAE

1. *Patron.* Obviously we seek to examine how God plays the premier role of patron and benefactor. The following chart lists six of the major titles of God-as-Patron as found in Greco-Roman theology. I correlate them with the typical benefactions that such a figure bestows. Here is a summary of what New Testament and early church authors would understand by describing God as patron and/or benefactor.

"King"	power (wage war; defend) inducement commitment (as father)	"Benefactor"	power (king, statesman) inducement (material benefits) commitment influence (inventors, philosophers)
"Father"	power (protect, defend) commitment inducement (nurture) influence (socialization)	"Creator"	power (creator) inducement (food, animals for humans) commitment (faithfulness in maintaining creation for mortals) influence (wisdom in creation)
"Savior"	power (protect, defend) inducement (golden age, grain, fruits, and cattle	"Sovereign"	power commitment (faithfulness, forgiveness)

Patron-benefactors, then, are the high-ranking persons whose pleasure and purpose it is to benefit their clients in a wide variety of ways.

2. *Clients,* we have seen, are the lower-ranking persons who receive patronage and benefaction. They owe primarily loyalty, faithfulness, and commitment to their patrons.

3. *Broker or mediator* describes the role of a person perfectly positioned between God-Patron and people-clients to intercede on their behalf or to convey a heavenly revelation. This broker must himself prove faithful to the Patron, for he is first and foremost the client of God. Then he must be assessed in terms of his success in his mediation of prayers and sacrifices to the Patron and the Patron's benefactions to the clients (Malina 1996:149–57). Thus in considering God as patron and benefactor, we must also examine divine benefaction first to Jesus-the-broker and then to God's clients through Jesus.

APPENDIX 2

"BE HOLY, AS I AM HOLY": GOD, PURITY, AND ORDER

In cultural terms, purity means "that which is in place." Some persons, places, things, and times are "in place" or separated from what is "out of place." Thus they are "pure" or "holy." This presumes that people know the system of being "in place," that is, the order that human minds impose on reality. This is easily seen in the way we "map" persons, places, times, and things.

1. *Persons.* In *t. Meg.* 2.7 we find an ancient "map of persons" concerning who might listen to the scroll of Esther: "Priests, Levites, Israelites, Converts, Freed Slaves, Disqualified Priests, Temple Slaves, Bastards, Those with Damaged Testicles, and Those without a Penis" (Malina 2001a:197; Neyrey 1991:279). This "map" has several principles of ordering: (1) proximity to the altar and then (2) a hierarchical system of rank and status based on Temple function. Priests and Levites are at the top, followed by Israelite males, converts, and freed slaves. These are followed by disqualified priests only; then those with damaged bloodlines follow next (i.e., bastards). (3) Another principle of ordering is present, namely, whole or damaged bodies, especially those body parts, which promote or prevent creation of new life (those with

crushed testicles . . . without a penis). As a map, this locates and positions people in relative degrees of wholeness or social status, and so conveys a sense of "holiness" in its orderliness and perfection. Lesser-ranked people should not try to climb higher, nor should higher-ranked people allow themselves to be put lower, lest order be broken and uncleanness or chaos prevail. Moreover, all listed on this map are in some sense "insiders," as opposed to Gentiles, who, while allowed in the temple, must stand behind a balustrade and be separate from those mentioned above. Thus purity means wholeness or perfection; therefore a bodily defect, especially of the genitals, means that its sufferer lacks purity and thus holiness.

2. *Places.* As regards maps of places, Israel and its temple were, of course, the holiest of places. We have in *m. Kelim* 1.6-9 an excellent map of the purity of places. The rubric is "ten degrees of holiness":

> There are ten degrees of holiness: the *Land of Israel* is holier than any other land. . . . The *walled cities* [of the Land of Israel] are still more holy. . . . *Within the walls* [of Jerusalem] is still more holy. . . . The *Temple Mount* is still more holy. . . . The *Rampart* is still more holy. . . . The *Court of the Women* is still more holy. . . . The *Court of the Israelites* is still more holy. . . . The *Court of the Priests* is still more holy. . . . *Between the Porch and the Altar* is still more holy. . . . The *Sanctuary* is still more holy. . . . The *Holy of Holies* is still more holy.

The order of the map is clear: one moves from the perimeter to the center. As one approaches Jerusalem and the temple, the "holiness" quotient increases. Hence the temple is the measure of holiness of space. This correlates with the "map of persons" observed above, for "priests" and "Levites" attend the altar and the sanctuary (with only the high priest entering the holy of holies). Israelite males remain outside in their court, with Israelite females behind them in their court. When all persons function in their proper spaces, purity reigns because order is preserved. But if Gentiles entered the Court of the Israelites, they would be liable to death. One thinks of the perception by observant Israelites about Paul's presence in the temple; he is labeled "unclean" and "out of order": "This is the man who is teaching against the people and the law and this place; he has also brought Greeks into the temple and thus defiled this place" (Acts 21:28). He is perceived as radically out of place and so must be removed from the holy place: "they dragged him out of the temple and at once the gates were shut" (21:30).

3. *Things.* As for a map of things, one of the most regulated things appears to have been foods. The following summary remark by Jacob Neusner best expresses this concern over foods by pre-70 Pharisees, whom the Gospels say found fault with Jesus' map of things.

> The Houses' rulings pertaining either immediately or ultimately to table-fellowship involve preparation of food, ritual purity relating directly to food or indirectly to the need to keep food ritually clean, and agricultural rules concerning the proper growing, tithing, and preparation of agricultural produce for table use. The agricultural laws relate to producing or preparing food for consumption, assuring either that tithes and offerings have been set aside as the law requires, or that conditions for the nurture of crops have conformed to biblical taboos. Of the 341 individual Houses' legal pericopae, no fewer than 229, approximately 67 per cent of the whole, directly or indirectly concern table-fellowship. . . . The Houses' laws of ritual cleanness apply in the main to the ritual cleanness of foods, and of people, dishes, and implements involved in its preparation. Pharisaic laws regarding Sabbath and festivals, moreover, involve in large measure the preparation and preservation of food. (1973b:86)

Note that "leaven", too, is classified as "unclean," for before the Feast of Unleavened Bread, all leavened foods must be taken out and burned, so that the Passover may be celebrated "pure" and "holy." This is the background of Paul's declaration that in regard to a social sin in the community, "a little leaven leavens the whole lump"; thus we should "cleanse out the old leaven that you may be a new lump . . . unleavened" (I Cor 5:6-7).

This notion of leaven as unclean is found several times in the writings of Plutarch, suggesting that it was known as well to the Greco-Roman world: "For the leaven itself is generated out of corruption and when mixed (with flour) corrupts the mass, for it (the mass) becomes slack and powerless and in general the leavened thing appears to be putrid; then, increasing, it becomes sour and corrupts the flour" (*Quaest. rom.* 289F; see also *Quaest. conv.* 659B).

4. *Times.* A map of times would indicate which days are ordinary and which are holy, for example, the Sabbath, the public fast days, as well as pilgrimage feast days. Indeed, a map of times such as that operative in the temple would map the course of the day (daily morning and evening sacrifices and prayers), weekly Sabbaths, seasonal feasts such as New Year, Tabernacles,

Dedication, Passover, and the like (see Gal 4:10). We have archeological evidence that a temple functionary blew a trumpet to signal sunrise and sunset, which was essential for a holy celebration of the Sabbath: one needed to know the exact moment that the Sabbath began and ended.

5. *Human Body*. Finally, the human body was mapped, in the sense that it was subject to control and ordering. Ideally, the human body should be the perfect container, in which only pure foods enter, but from which nothing would exit. Because this is impossible, great attention was then paid to the body's orifices and surface in an attempt to impose order and control. Mouths should speak only truth, not lies or blasphemies, and ingest only clean foods. Eyes should be protected from evil, such as lust, and ears guarded against gossip and slander. Finally, the genitals, because of their contribution to the making of life, were carefully scrutinized and regulated. Males are defiled by seminal emission, even if for only a day; hence the high priest was kept awake the night before Yom Kippur lest he slumber and soil himself (*m. Yoma* 1.1-7). Females' monthly menstruation was a time of taboo for them, and males may not have sexual intercourse with them. Women must be purified after childbirth, once all fluids in their wombs have dried. Control, then, means "order," which means "purity."

As regards bodily surface, most scrutiny was given to the skin, the outer "garment" of the body. Hence any skin blemish creates a problem. Boils or suppurating sores are "too much" and so render the person unclean; flaking skin suggests that things are "out of place," hence unclean. Leviticus 13 provides an exhaustive list of possible uncleannesses of the skin, especially the one labeled "leprosy" (see Pilch 2000:50–53).

Finally, a body is "pure" when it is "whole," that is, not "too much" or "too little." This applies to animals to be ordered in sacrifice: they must be whole and unblemished. So too with humans: priests who are not bodily whole may not function in the temple, as Lev 21:17-21 states:

> Say to Aaron, None of your descendants who has a blemish may approach to offer the bread of his God. For no one who has a blemish shall draw near, a man blind or lame, or one who has a mutilated face or a limb too long, or a man who has an injured foot or an injured hand, or a hunchback, or a dwarf, or a man with a defect in his sight or an itching disease or scabs or crushed testicles; no man of the descendants of Aaron the priest who has a blemish shall come near to offer the Lord's offerings by fire.

The principle of "too much" or "too little" is evident here. Those with "too little" include the blind, lame, those with injured foot or hand, a dwarf, those with defective sight, and those with crushed testicles; those with "too much" include the hunchback or those with a limb too long. These principles served as strategy when certain priests engaged in combat: "Hyrcanus threw himself at the feet of Antigonus, who with his own teeth lacerated his suppliant's ears, in order to disqualify him for ever, under any change of circumstances, from resuming the high priesthood; since freedom from physical defect is essential to the holder of that office" (Josephus, *War* 1.269-70). By having his ear mutilated, Hyrcanus became "too little," and so he was forever disqualified to function as high priest.

Thus as we examine New Testament documents we should be aware of the following. (a) God is the *author of all of these maps,* which may be found in Genesis 1, the Priestly account of creation, or in the layout and functioning of the Jerusalem temple. (b) In making these maps, God makes *separations* or *divisions,* as Gen 1:7, 8, 14 indicate. In the Habdalah prayer on the Sabbath, we read of God's "separations" or "divisions" as characteristic of the Deity: "Blessed are you, Lord our God, king of the world, who divides between holy and profane, between light and darkness, between Israel and the peoples, between the seventh day and the six days of work. Blessed are you, Lord, who divides between sacred and profane." (c) God is himself *completely holy,* that is, "separated" from all that is unclean, corrupt, dead, and the like. And God demands, "Be ye holy as I am holy." (d) God's maps have a distinct *moral quality* to them: they are not optional but obligatory. Their observance brings blessing, but their nonobservance entails separation and even destruction. (e) *People knew these maps.* Both the traditions discussed and observed in local synagogues and pilgrimages to Jerusalem's temple would inform even peasants of the basics of the system of order and thus purity.

APPENDIX 3

HONOR AND SHAME

Defining Honor. Honor may be abstractly defined as a person's worth, standing, or the respect shown him or her. But synonyms of honor may clarify the matter: "honor" = "fame," "glory," "praise," "acclaim" and the like. It is recognized as the "pivotal value" of the ancient Mediterranean world, and "love of honor" (*philotimia*) was valued as the source of ambition to greatness. Xenophon described the Athenians as passionate for praise: "Athenians excel all others not so much in singing or in stature or in strength, as in love of honour, which is the strongest incentive to deeds of honour and renown" (*Mem.* 3.3.13). Later, Augustine commented on how the Romans were utterly obsessed with the love of praise and renown: "For the glory that the Romans burned to possess is the favourable judgment of men who think well of other men" (*City of God* 5.12). And he noted that love of honor need not be self-centered: "He [God] granted supremacy to men who for the sake of honor, praise and glory served the country in which they were seeking their own glory, and did not hesitate to prefer her safety to their own. Thus for one vice, that is, love of praise, they overcame the love of money and many other vices"

(5.13). Hence, in both East and West, the ancients held honor and praise in highest esteem. How does one get honor?

Sources of Honor. One may actively acquire it or have it passively ascribed. Ascribed honor describes how a person passively through birth, family connections, or endowment by notable persons of power is considered to be worthy of respect or of a certain status and role. It resembles, therefore, inherited wealth that comes to a person through birth. Thus ascribed honor means the standing or worth that a person enjoys because of kinship or endowment, not because of any effort or achievement. Most commonly, ascribed honor derives from birth into an honorable family (Joseph is of the "house of David," Matt 1:20; Luke 1:27). Thus, offspring have the same honor as parents ("like mother, like daughter," Ezek 16:44; "like father, like son," Matt 13:55). Birth into an honorable family makes one honorable, since the family is the repository of the honor of past illustrious ancestors and their accumulated acquired honor. One of the major purposes of genealogies in the Bible is to set out a person's honor lines and thus to situate them socially on a scale of prominence (see Luke 3:23-38). Finally, a nobleman might adopt a commoner, thus bestowing honor on him; or Caesar might appoint a procurator to a province, thus endowing him with honorable status.

Acquired honor, on the other hand, rests entirely on efforts and achievements, that is, a person's "excellence" or prowess. In antiquity a "lover of honor" might achieve it by military prowess (i.e., David and his "ten thousands," I Sam 21:11), athletic exploits, and aesthetic superiority in drama or poetry. One might also achieve honor by benefactions; Danker, for example, has gathered many benefaction inscriptions in which cities honor So-and-So for his benefaction (1982). Achieved honor, moreover, derives from virtue, especially the famous four: courage, justice, temperance, and wisdom. In the rules for encomia, students are told to find praise for a person in his "deeds of the soul," that is, in his exercise of virtue.

The ordinary means of achieving honor whether in symposia, learned discourses or in village social intercourse was the game of challenge and riposte. The choreography was regular and predictable: a person makes a *claim,* which others *challenge,* in response to which the claimant must give a *riposte*; when the dust settles, the observing *public signals victory* to one of the combatants. This too is an exercise taught in the progymnasmata, namely, the *chreia.*

It is important to note that challenges may be negative (overtly hostile) or positive (merely imposing). Positive challenges include 1. gift giving, 2. compliments, 3. volunteering, and 4. requesting. These challenge either by putting a person on the spot (volunteering, requesting) or by creating a debt of sorts (gift given means gift must be returned; compliment paid means praise is due). Since the rule of the game was to "owe no one anything" (Rom 13:8), then all attempts to make another one's debtor in any fashion carry a risk. Now concerning the negative challenges, why are they made? What is at stake? In antiquity, most people viewed the world in terms of limited good; that is, there is only so much strength, beauty, success, happiness, wealth, etc. in the world and the supply cannot be increased, except by God's specific action. Hence all see the world in terms of a zero-sum game, such that if someone is perceived as having or increasing in a valued, but limited good, others will tend to see themselves as losing precisely what the other person is gaining. Hence, envy awakens; challenges are made to cut the increasing person down to size (Hagedorn and Neyrey 1988; Neyrey and Rohrbaugh 2001).

Honor and Blood. Honor, both ascribed and acquired, is often symbolized by blood. Blood means one's own blood, i.e., oneself as a living human being, as well as that of all members of the same biological or fictive family ("Blood is thicker than water"; "Blood will out."). Honor is always presumed to exist within one's own family of blood, i.e., among all of one's blood relatives. A person can always trust his blood relatives. J. K. Campbell provides an excellent summary of how honor is related to "blood":

> The honour of the family, and its solidarity, are symbolized in the idea of blood. In marriage a man and woman mix their different blood to produce "one blood" which is the blood of their children. Relationships in the family are a participation in this common blood. . . . Blood is intimately related to courage. And it is a matter of common observation that as a man loses blood, he loses strength. Since courage and physical strength are particularly the qualities that men require in order to defend the reputation of their families, it is entirely consistent that for the Sarakatsani the honour of the family is literally the honour of its blood. (1964:144, see also 185–86, 268–69)

Honor and Name. Iago told Othello: "Good name, my Lord, is the immediate jewel of the soul. Who steals my purse steals trash. . .who filches from me my good name, steals that which not enriches him, but makes me poor indeed." Getting and keeping a "good name" is an essential part of honor in antiquity. And since honor is replicated in "blood," the good name of one's family also signals that honor. Hence, males are known by the name of their fathers and their kinship groups. For example, Peter is "Simon, son of John"

(Matt 16:17); James and John are always known as "the sons of Zebedee" (Luke 5:10). To know the family name is to know the honor rating of an individual.

Again, a good name was a concern of people in every context of public action for it gave purpose and meaning to their lives, much as money does in our society. A good name fundamentally means honor adequate to carry on the social interactions necessary for decent human existence, especially for contracting marriages. Oaths are taken on the honor capital stored in family names: "I swear by my father's name." From another point of view, the good name that stands for family honor is equally central. For example, individuals inherited not just their father's name and reputation, but also his trade and status. Josephus reflects how worth and status are family affairs and become the legacy of children born into those families. Speaking of the Hasmoneans, he remarked: "Theirs [the Hasmoneans] was a splendid and renowned house because of both their lineage and their priestly office, as well as the things which its founders achieved on behalf of the nation" (*Ant.* 14.490; see *Ant.* 11.309). Thus Hasmonean children by virtue of their "blood and name" inherited royal status and even special offices, such as the priesthood. Moreover, they inherited as well the family credit rating which was earned through "the things achieved on behalf of the nation." What was true of elite families proved true also for nonelites: sons of carpenters became carpenters, inheriting whatever standing and respect the paternal family enjoyed.

Honor Displayed: Wealth and Honor. Kings and aristocrats in antiquity practiced what we call "conspicuous consumption," which was a way of displaying one's "worth" by means of fine clothing, elegant dinners, villas, horses and the like (Kautsky 1982:187–94).

Herod, we are told, celebrated his birthday with a banquet for the elite (Mark 6:21), to be sure no mean event. Agrippa had tailored for himself a robe "completely woven of silver," which he wore at the theater at Caesarea, with the desired effect. With sunrise the king's robe "was wondrously radiant and by its glitter inspired fear and awe on those who gazed intently upon it" (*Ant.* 19.344; see also Acts 12:21). Plutarch may not know the term "conspicuous consumption," but he recognizes the phenomenon:

> With no one to look on, wealth becomes sightless indeed and bereft of radiance. For when the rich man dines with his wife or intimates he lets his

> tables of citrus-wood and golden beakers rest in peace and uses common furnishings, and his wife attends it without her gold and purple and dressed in plain attire. But when a banquet—*that is, a spectacle and a show*—is got up and the drama of wealth brought on, "out of the ships he fetches the urns and tripods" (*Il.* 23.259); the repositories of the lamps are given no rest, the cups are changed, the cup-bearers are made to put on new attire, nothing is left undisturbed, gold, silver, or jeweled plate, the owners thus confessing that their wealth is for others. (Plutarch, *On Love of Wealth* 528B; see *Table-Talk* 679B)

The wealthy man has the trappings of wealth, but they are not productive in the game of honor until displayed. Inasmuch as his "wealth is for others," it claims honor only when on display, not in a closet or chest..

Finally, we have illustrations of how honor might be ascribed a person by virtue of a monarch's benefaction which is signaled entirely in terms of luxury goods, golden chain, and mount. Josephus tells us in his account of Esther that the plot by Haman to shame Mordecai failed and that Haman became agent of the monarch's favor and respect for Mordecai:

> He [Mordecai] put on the purple robe that the king always used to wear, placed the [golden] chain around his neck, mounting the horse, went the round of the city, with Haman going before him and proclaiming that this should be the reward given by the king to him whom he cherished and held worthy of honor. (*Ant.* 11.257-58; see Philo, *Joseph* 120)

Honor Displayed: The Physical Body. One's physical body itself contains a system of honor, for it serves as the constant stage on which honor was displayed and claimed. The most important part of a person's physical presence is the front, namely, head, face, and eyes. Courtiers crawled with faces bowed to the ground toward sovereigns and retreated the same way: the worth of the monarch was thus symbolized by the fact that lesser people did not see the monarch's face, much less look him in the eye. Honorable heads were anointed and crowned as marks of respect. Yet the eyes may be the most important bodily organ in the way in which honor is claimed and acknowledged; for it is one's standing "in the eyes of" others which constitutes worth and honor. For example, "affronts" occur *in the front,* that is, before the very eye of the person being insulted; and, of course, they must occur in public, that is, in the eyes of others. One might "find favor in the eyes" of others (Gen 6:8; 1 Sam 26:21) which translates as acknowledgment of worth which leads to favorable marriage alliances (Gen 34:11), singular benefactions (Gen 50:4), and food to sustain life (Ruth 2:10). Conversely, when people look with contempt, they have clearly withdrawn their respect (Gen 16:4-5); a wife can be divorced by her husband "if she finds no favor in his eyes because he has found some indecency in her" (Deut 24:1).Worth and value, then, are signaled in the eyes of another.

Other body parts likewise symbolized worth and value. The right arm and hand were generally honored, probably because they wielded weapons of war, a sure way to reputation. The penis and testicles, which express a male's fertility and his power to extend himself in time, were also honorable parts. The feet were generally not considered honorable, unless they belonged to a person of such status that others fell to the ground at them, washed, or anointed them (Luke 7:38) or unless these feet trampled on the necks and backs of enemies. Hence, God assured the enthroned king of Israel of great status by putting his enemies under his feet: "I make your enemies your footstool" (Ps 110:1).

Acknowledgment of Honor. The ancients truly refined the art of recognition of honor. Crowns of glory were given winners at games and odes and poems were written to celebrate these exploits. As noted above, the many benefaction inscriptions indicate how cities knew the necessity and art of honoring those who built their theaters, aqueducts and the like. Recognition of worth could be done at public expense. Aristotle, for example, catalogues the sorts of things whereby a city recognized and celebrated someone's excellence:

> The components of honor are sacrifices [made to the benefactor after death], memorial inscriptions in verse or prose, receipt of special awards, grants of land, front seats at festivals, burial at public expense, statues, free food in the state dining room, among barbarians such things as *proskynesis* and rights of precedence, and gifts that are held in honor in each society. (*Rhet.* 1.5.9)

Indeed an outstanding warrior, athlete, benefactor, etc., would rightly feel slighted if his excellence was not thus publicly recognized and memorialized. All of these "components of honor," moreover, are public acknowledgments of worth which all in the city can observe.

Gender and Honor. It is axiomatic that the ancient world was fundamentally gender divided. This means that as part of the way males and females understood their specific gender, they perceived that human beings were two different species of human (Malina and Neyrey 1996:104–5, 111–13). This, of course, is a social construction and represents only a culturally defined way of considering gender. The ancients, of course, would claim that such a point of view is rooted in nature and ordained by God. When Aristotle compares males with rulers and females with slaves, he reflects the gender stereotype of his cultural world that they were two entirely different species of human being. This citation comes from his discussion of the origin of the political institution in antiquity, which is based on simpler forms of social organization, especially the family.

> In the first place there must be a union of those who cannot exist without each other; namely, of male and female, that the race may continue . . . and of natural ruler and subject, that both may be preserved. For that which can foresee by the exercise of mind [i.e., male] is by nature intended to be lord and master, and that which can with its body give effect to such foresight [i.e., female] is a subject, and by nature a slave; hence master and slave have the same interest. (*Pol.* 1.2)

Since male and female are two different species of human, maleness and femaleness must likewise be completely distinct. As such, males were thought to belong to the public world and females to the private world. This means that most things in the world could be conceptualized as either male or female, that is, as appropriate to the stereotype of maleness and femaleness, such as space, roles, tasks, and objects. Furthermore, the two genders should be separate and not mix or overlap. Hence, to be a male meant *not* being a female, *not* keeping to female space (private or household world), *not* assuming female roles such as mother or recipient sexual partner, *not* performing female tasks (clothing production, food preparation, and child rearing), and *not* using female tools (spindle, pots).

We take the following remark of Xenophon to be a clear example of the gender stereotype that is found often the Hellenistic world.

> Human beings live not in the open air, like beasts, but obviously need shelter. Those who mean to win store to fill the covered space, have need of someone to work at the open-air occupations; since ploughing, sowing, planting and grazing are all such open-air employments . . . again, as soon as this is stored in the covered place, there is need of someone to keep it and to work at the things that must be done under cover. Cover is needed for the nursing of the infants; cover is needed for the making of the corn into bread, and likewise for the manufacture of clothes from the wool." (Xenophon, *Oeconomicus* 7:20-21)

Males and females are distinguished in terms of space (males: open air; females: shelter, cover). In their respective spaces they perform gender-specific tasks: males = ploughing, sowing, planting, and grazing, whereas females = nursing of the infants, making of the corn into bread, and manufacture of clothes from the wool. Implied are the gender-specific tools pertinent to each task, and even animals. For goats needed no pasture and provided milk for the family, and so was a household or woman's animal; but sheep, which need distant pasture, were the man's care.

BIBLIOGRAPHY

Albrektson, Bertil

1967 *History and the Gods: An Essay on the Idea of Historical Events as Divine Manifestations in the Ancient Near East and in Israel.* ConBOT 1. Lund: Gleerup.

Alcock, Susan E., and Robin Osborne, editors

1994 *Placing the Gods: Sanctuaries and Sacred Space in Ancient Greece.* Oxford: Oxford Univ. Press.

Altmann, A.

1968 "*Homo Imago Dei* in Jewish and Christian Theology." *JR* 48:235–39.

Amir, Yehoshua

1978 "Die Begegnung des biblischen und des philosophischen Monotheismus als Grundthema des jüdischen Hellenismus." *EvT* 38:2–19.

Appold, Mark

1976 *The Oneness Motif in the Fourth Gospel: Motif Analysis and Exegetical Probe into the Theology of John.* WUNT 2/1. Tübingen: Mohr/Siebeck.

Argyle, Aubrey William

1965 *God in the New Testament.* London: Hodder & Stoughton.

Attridge, Harold W.

1976 *The Interpretation of Biblical History in the Antiquitates Judaicae of Flavius Josephus.* Harvard Dissertations in Religion 7. Missoula, Mont.: Scholars.

1978 "The Philosophical Critique of Religion under the Early Empire." In *ANRW* II.16.1.46–78.

1989 *The Epistle of the Hebrews.* Hermeneia. Philadelphia: Fotress Press.

Aune, David E.

1972 *The Cultic Setting of Realized Eschatology in Early Christianity.* NovTSup 28. Leiden: Brill.

1981 "The Problem of the Genre of the Gospels: A Critique of C. H. Talbert's *What Is a Gospel?*" In *Gospel Perspectives: Studies of History and Tradition in the Four Gospels,* edited by R. T. France and David Wenham, 2.9–60. Sheffield: JSOT Press.

1983 *Prophecy in Early Christianity and the Ancient Mediterranean World.* Grand Rapids: Eerdmans.

1992 "Worship, Early Christian." In *ABD* 6.973–89.

1993 "The Phenomenology of Greco-Roman Prayer." In *SBLSP 1993,* 787–95.

1997 "Romans as a *Logos Protreptikos.*" In *The Romans Debate: Revised and Expanded Edition,* edited by Karl P. Donfried, 278–98. Peabody, Mass.: Hendrickson.

2001 "Prayer in the Greco-Roman World." In *Introduction to God's Presence: Prayer in the New Testament,* edited by Richard N. Longenecker, 23–42. Grand Rapids: Eerdmans.

Balentine, Samuel E.

1983 *The Hidden God: The Hiding of the Face of God in the Old Testament.* Oxford: Oxford Univ. Press.

1993 *Prayer in the Hebrew Bible: The Drama of Divine-Human Dialogue.* OBT. Minneapolis: Fortress Press.

Ball, David M.

1996 *The "I Am" in John's Gospel: Literary Function, Background and Theological Implications.* JSNTSup 124. Sheffield: Sheffield Academic.

Barker, Margaret

1992 *The Great Angel: A Study of Israel's Second God.* Louisville: Westminster John Knox.

Barr, James

1988 "Abba Isn't Daddy." *JTS* 39:28–47.

Barré, Michael

1981 "'Fear of God' and the World of Wisdom." *BTB* 11:41–43.

Bartchy, S. Scott

1995 "*Agnostos Theos*: Luke's Message to the 'Nations' about Israel's God." In *SBLSP 1995,* 304–20.

Barton, Stephen C.

1994 *Discipleship and Family Ties in Mark and Matthew.* SNTSMS 80. Cambridge: Cambridge Univ. Press.

Bassler, Jouette

1982 *Divine Impartiality: Paul and a Theological Axiom.* SBLDS 59. Chico, Calif.: Scholars Press.

1984 "Divine Impartiality in Paul's Letter to the Romans." *NovT* 26:43–58.

1986 "Luke and Paul on Impartiality." *Bib* 66:546–52.

1993 "God in the New Testament." In *ABD* 2.1049–55.

Bauckham, Richard

1981 "Worship of Jesus in Apocalyptic Christianity." *NTS* 27:322–41.

1988 "Jesus' Demonstration in the Temple." In *Law and Religion: Essays on the Place of the Law in Israel and Early Christianity,* edited by Barnabas Lindars, 72–89. Cambridge: Clarke.

Beckwith, Roger T.

1987 "The Unity and Diversity of God's Covenants." *TynB* 38:93–118.

Benin, Stephen D.

1991 *The Footprints of God: Divine Accommodation in Jewish and Christian Thought.* SUNY Series in Judaica. Albany: SUNY Press.

Berger, Klaus

1970 "Zu den sogennanten Sätze heiligen Rechts." *NTS* 17:10–40.

Bernstein, Alan E.

1993 *The Formation of Hell: Death and Retribution in the Ancient and Early Christian Worlds.* Ithaca, N.Y.: Cornell Univ. Press.

Bertram, Georg

1964 "*euergasia.*" In *TDNT* 2.654–55.

Betz, Hans Dieter

1979 *Galatians. A Commentary on Paul's Letter to the Churches of Galatia.* Hermeneia. Philadelphia: Fortress Press.

Bickerman, Elias

1962 "The Civic Prayer of Jerusalem." *HTR* 55:163–85.

1979 *The God of the Maccabees: Studies on the Meaning and Origin of the Maccabean Revolt.* Translated by Horst R. Moehring. SJLA 32. Leiden: Brill.

Birnbaum, Ellen

1995 "What Does Philo Mean by 'Seeing God'? Some Methodological Considerations." In *SBLSP 1995,* 535–52.

Blenkinsopp, Joseph

1986 "Yahweh and Other Deities: Conflict and Accommodation in Ancient Israel." *Int* 40:354–66.

1990 "The Judge of All the Earth: Theodicy in the Midrash on Genesis 18:22-33." *JJS* 41:1–12.

Blok, Anton

1969 "Variations in Patronage." *Sociologische Gids* 16:365–78.

Borgen, Peder

1968 "God's Agent in the Fourth Gospel." In *Religions in Antiquity: Essays in Memory of Erwin Ramsdell Goodenough,* edited by Jacob Neusner, 137–48. SHR 14. Leiden: Brill.

Boring, M. Eugene

1996 "Names of God in the New Testament." In *HBD* 734–36.

Bossmann, David M.

1988 "Images of God in the Letters of Paul." *BTB* 18:67–76.

Bousset, Wilhelm

1903 *Die Religion des Judentums.* Berlin: Reuther & Reichard.

Bovon, François

1981 "Le Dieu du Luc." *RSR* 69:279–300.

Bremer, J. M.

1981 "Greek Hymns." In *Faith, Hope, and Worship: Aspects of Religious Mentality in the Ancient World,* edited by H. S. Versnel, 193–215. SGRR 2. Leiden: Brill.

Brown, John Pairman

1993 "From Divine Kingship to Dispersal of Power in the Mediterranean City-State." *ZAW* 105:62–86.

Brown, Raymond E.

1965 *The Gospel according to John I–XII.* AB 29. Garden City, N.Y.: Doubleday.

1970 *The Gospel according to John XIII–XXI.* AB 29A. Garden City, N.Y.: Doubleday.

1993 *The Birth of the Messiah: A Commentary on the Infancy Narratives in the Gospels of Matthew and Luke.* ABRL. New York: Doubleday.

Brown, Tricia Gates

1999 "Spirit in the Johannine Writings: Johannine Pneumatology in Social-Science Perspective." Ph.D. diss., Univ. of St. Andrews, Scotland.

Bruce, F. F.

1963 "'Our God and Saviour': A Recurring Biblical Pattern." In *The Savior God,* edited by S. G. F. Brandon, 51–66. Manchester: Manchester Univ. Press.

Buchanan, George W.

1986 "Apostolic Christology." In *SBLSP 1986,* 172–82.

Bultmann, Rudolf

1971 *The Gospel of John: A Commentary.* Translated by G. R. Beasley-Murray et al. Philadelphia: Westminster.

Burkert, Walter

1985 *Greek Religion.* Translated by John Raffan. Cambridge: Harvard Univ. Press.

Cadbury, Henry J.

1958 *The Making of Luke-Acts.* Rev. ed. London: SPCK.

Caird, G. B.

1969 "The Glory of God in the Fourth Gospel: An Exercise in Biblical Semantics." *NTS* 15:265–77.

Campbell, J. K.

1964 *Honour, Family and Patronage. A Study of Institutions and Moral Values in a Greek Mountain Community.* Oxford: Oxford Univ. Press.

Carroll, John T.

2002 "The God of Israel and the Salvation of the Nations." In *The Forgotten God: Perspectives in Biblical Theology,* edited by A. Andrew Das and Frank J. Matera, 91–106. Louisville: Westminster John Knox.

Carson, D. A.

1981 *Divine Sovereignty and Human Responsibility: Biblical Perspectives in Tension.* New Foundations Theological Library. Atlanta: John Knox.

Casey, Maurice

1991 *From Jewish Prophet to Gentile God: The Origins and Development of New Testament Christology.* Louisville: Westminster John Knox.

Charlesworth, James H.

1982 "A Prolegomena to a New Study of the Jewish Background of the Hymns and Prayers in the New Testament." *JJS* 33:265–85.

1986 "Jewish Hymns, Odes, and Prayers (ca. 167 B.C.E.–135 C.E.)." In *Early Judaism and Its Modern Interpreters,* edited by R. A. Kraft and G. W. E. Nickelsburg, 411–36. Atlanta: Scholars.

1993 "Prayer in the New Testament in Light of Contemporary Jewish Prayers." In *SBLSP 1993,* 773–86.

1994 *The Lord's Prayer and Other Prayer Texts from the Greco-Roman Era.* Valley Forge, Pa.: Trinity.

Charlesworth, Martin P.

1935 "Some Observations on Ruler-Cult Especially in Rome." *HTR* 28:5–43.

Chazon, E. Glickler

1993 "Prayers from Qumran: Issues and Methods." In *SBLSP 1993,* 758–72.

Chernus, I.

1982 "Visions of God in Merkabah Mysticism." *JSJ* 13:123–46.

Childs, Brevard S.

1970 "The God of Israel and the Church." In *Biblical Theology in Crisis,* 201–46. Philadelphia: Westminster.

Chilton, Bruce

1987 *God in Strength: Jesus' Announcement of the Kingdom.* Sheffield: JSOT Press.

1994a "God as 'Father' in the Targumim, in Non-Canonical Literature of Early Judaism and Primitive Christianity, and in Matthew." In *Judaic Approaches to the Gospels,* 39–73. Atlanta: Scholars.

1994b "The Kingdom of God in Recent Discussion." In *Studying the Historical Jesus,* edited by Bruce Chilton and Craig A. Evans, 254–80. NTTS 19. Leiden: Brill.

1996 *Pure Kingdom: Jesus' Vision of God.* Grand Rapids: Eerdmans.

Clements, Ronald E.

1965 "Deuteronomy and the Jerusalem Cult Tradition." *VT* 15:300–312.

1967 *Abraham and David: Genesis XV and Its Meaning for Israelite Tradition.* SBT 2/5. Naperville, Ill.: Allenson.

Cohon, Samuel S.

1955 "The Unity of God: A Study in Hellenistic and Rabbinic Theology." *HUCA* 26:25–79.

Collins, John J.

1977 "Cosmos and Salvation: Jewish Wisdom and Apocalyptic in the Hellenistic Age." *HR* 17:121–42.

Collins, John N.

1990 *Diakonia: Re-interpreting the Ancient Sources.* Oxford: Oxford Univ. Press.

Collins, Raymond F.

1977 "The Theology of Paul's First Letter to the Thessalonians." *Louvain Studies* 6:315–37.

Cope, Lamar

1973 "Jesus' Radical Concept of God." *Christian Century* 90:448–50.

Coppens, J.

1976 *Le Notion biblique de Dieu.* BETL 41. Gembloux: Duculot.

Cosgrove, Charles H.

1984 "The Divine DEI in Luke-Acts: Investigations into the Lukan Understanding of God's Providence." *NovT* 26:168–90.

Crenshaw, James L.

1984 *A Whirlpool of Torment: Israelite Traditions of God as an Oppressive Presence.* OBT. Philadelphia: Fortress Press.

Crenshaw, James L., editor

1983 *Theodicy in the Old Testament.* IRT. Philadelphia: Fortress Press.

Cullmann, Oscar

1953 *Early Christian Worship.* Translated by A. Stewart Todd and James B. Torrance. Philadelphia: Westminster.

Cuss, Dominique

1974 *Imperial Cult and Honorary Terms in the New Testament.* PBGALT 23. Fribourg: Univ. of Fribourg Press.

Dahl, Nils A.

1951 "A New and Living Way. The Approach to God according to Hebrews 10:19–25." *Int* 5:401–12.

1975a "The Neglected Factor in New Testament Theology." *Reflections* 73:5–8.

1975b *Jesus in the Memory of the Early Church.* Minneapolis: Augsburg.

1977a "The One God of Jew and Gentiles (Rom 3:29-30)." In *Studies in Paul,* 178–91. Minneapolis: Augsburg.

1977b "Contradictions in the Scriptures." In *Studies in Paul,* 159–77. Minneapolis: Augsburg.

1977c "Paul and the Church at Corinth." In *Studies in Paul,* 40–61. Minneapolis: Augsburg.

Dahl, Nils A., and Alan Segal

1978 "Philo and the Rabbis on the Names of God." *JSJ* 9:1–23.

D'Angelo, Mary Rose

1992a "Abba and 'Father': Imperial Theology and the Jesus Traditions." *JBL* 111:611–30.

1992b "Theology in Mark and Q: Abba and 'Father' in Context." *HTR* 85:149–74.

1999 "Intimating Deity in the Gospel of John: Theological Language and 'Father' in the Prayers of Jesus." *Semeia* 85:59–82.

Daniélou, Jean

1964 *The Theology of Jewish Christianity.* Translated and edited by John A. Baker. Chicago: Regnery.

1973 *Gospel Message and Hellenistic Culture.* Translated by John A. Baker. Philadelphia: Westminster.

Danker, Frederick W.

1981 "The Endangered Benefactor of Luke-Acts." In *SBLSP 1981,* 39–48.

1982 *Benefactor: Epigraphic Study of a Graeco-Roman and New Testament Semantic Field.* St. Louis: Clayton.

1988 "Bridging St. Paul and the Apostolic Fathers: A Study in Reciprocity." *CurTM* 15:84–94.

1992 "Benefactor." In *ABD* 1.669–71.

Das, A. Andrew, and Frank J. Matera, editors

2002 *The Forgotten God: Perspectives in Biblical Theology. Essays in Honor of Paul J. Achtemeier on His Seventy-fifth Birthday*. Louisville: Westminster John Knox.

Daube, David

1959 "A Prayer Pattern in Judaism." *SE* I (*TU* 73):539–45.

1973 *The New Testament and Rabbinic Judaism*. New York: Arno.

Davies, G. Henton

1962 "Worship in the Old Testament." In *IDB* 4.879–83.

Deichgräber, Reinhard

1967 *Gotteshymnus und Christushymnus der frühen Christenheit*. SUNT 5. Göttingen: Vandenhoek & Ruprecht.

Delling, Gerhard

1952 "Monos Theos." *TLZ* 77:469–76.

1962 *Worship in the New Testament*. Translated by Percy Scott. Philadelphia: Westminster.

1970 *Studien zum Neuen Testament und zum hellenistischen Judentum: Gesammelte Aufsätze 1950–1968*. Edited by Ferdinand Hahn. Göttingen: Vandenhoeck & Ruprecht.

Demke, C.

1976 "'Ein Gott und viele Herren': Die Verkündigung des einen Gott in den Briefen des Paulus." *EvT* 36:473–84.

Denaux, Adelbert

1996 "Theology and Christology in 1 Cor 8,4-6." In *The Corinthian Correspondence*, edited by R. Bieringer, 593–606. BETL 125. Leuven: Leuven Univ. Press.

Dibelius, Martin

1956 *Studies in the Acts of the Apostles*. Translated by Mary Ling. London: SCM.

DiLella, Alexander A.

1986 "Sirach 51:1-12: Poetic Structure and Analysis of Ben Sira's Psalm." *CBQ* 48:395–407.

Dittenberger, Wilhelm

1960 *Sylloge Inscriptionum Graecarum*. 4 vols. Hildesheim: Olms.

Dillon, John M.

1975 *The Transcendence of God in Philo: Some Possible Sources*. Center for Hermeneutical Studies. Protocol 16. Berkeley: Center for Hermeneutical Studies in Hellenistic and Modern Culture.

1992 "Providence." In *ABD* 5.520–21.

Dobschütz, Ernst von

1931 "Zwei- und Dreigliedrige Formeln: Ein Beitrag zur Vorgeschichte der Trinitätsformel." *JBL* 50:117–47.

Dodd, C.H.

1968 *The Interpretation of the Fourth Gospel*. Cambridge: Cambridge Univ. Press.

Dodds, E. R.

1963 *Proclus: The Elements of Theology*. Oxford: Clarendon.

Donahue, John R.

1971 "Tax Collectors and Sinners: An Attempt at Identification." *CBQ* 33:39–61.

1982 "A Neglected Factor in the Gospel of Mark." *JBL* 101:563–94.

Donfried, Karl P.

1997 "The Imperial Cults of Thessalonika and Political Conflict in 1 Thessalonians." In *Paul and Empire: Religion and Power in Roman Imperial Society,* edited by Richard Horsley, 215–23. Harrisburg: Trinity.

Douglas, Mary

1966 *Purity and Danger.* London: Routledge and Kegan Paul.

1982 *Natural Symbols. Explorations in Cosmology.* New York. Pantheon.

Dowd, Sharyn E.

1988 *Prayer, Power, and the Problem of Suffering: Mark 11:22-25 in the Context of Markan Theology.* SBLDS 105. Atlanta: Scholars.

Downing, F. Gerald

1981 "Ethical Pagan Theism and the Speeches of Acts." *NTS* 27:544–63.

1982 "Common Ground with Paganism in Luke and in Josephus." *NTS* 28:546–59.

1992 "The Ambiguity of 'The Pharisee and the Toll-Collector' (Luke 18:9-14) in the Greco-Roman World of Late Antiquity." *CBQ* 54:80–99.

Duling, Dennis C.

1975 "Solomon, Exorcism, and the Son of David." *HTR* 68:235–52.

1978 "The Therapeutic Son of David." *NTS* 24:392–410.

1985 "The Eleazar Miracle and Solomon's Magical Wisdom in Flavius Josephus' *Antiquitates Judaicae* 8.42-48." *HTR* 78:1–25.

1992 "Matthew's Plurisignificant 'Son of David' in Social Science Perspective: Kinship, Kingship, Magic, and Miracle." *BTB* 22:99–116.

Dunn, James D. G.

1980 *Christology in the Making.* Philadelphia: Westminster.

1982 "Was Christianity a Monotheistic Faith from the Beginning?" *SJT* 35:303–36.

1988 *Romans 1–8.* WBC 38A. Dallas: Word.

Dupont, Jacques

1946 "*MONOI SOPHOI THEOI* (Rom. xvi, 27)." *ETL* 22:362–75.

1980 "Le Magnificat comme discours sur Dieu." *La nouvelle revue théologique* 102:321–43.

Eickelman, Dale

1989 *The Middle East: An Anthropological Approach.* Englewood Cliffs, N.J.: Prentice Hall.

Eilberg-Schwartz, Howard

1987 "Creation and Classification in Judaism: From Priestly to Rabbinic Conceptions." *HR* 26:357–81.

Eisenstadt, M.

1974 "Xenophanes' Proposed Reform of Greek Religion." *Hermes* 102:142–50.

Eisenstadt, Shlomo, and Louis Roniger

1984 *Patrons, Clients, and Friends: Interpersonal Relations and the Structure of Trust in Society.* Cambridge: Cambridge Univ. Press.

Elior, R.

1990 "Merkabah Mysticism. A Critical Review." *Numen* 37:233–49.

Elliott, John H.

1988 "The Fear of the Leer: The Evil Eye from the Bible to Li'l Abner." *Forum* 4.4:42–71.

1990 "Paul, Galatians, and the Evil Eye." *CurTM* 17:262–73.

1996 "Patronage and Clientage." In *The Social Sciences and New Testament Interpretation*, edited by Richard L. Rohrbaugh, 144–56. Peabody, Mass.: Hendrickson.

Elliott, J. K.

1981 "The Language and Style of the Concluding Doxology to the Epistle to the Romans." *ZNW* 72:124–30.

Esler, Philip F.

1987 *Community and Gospel in Luke-Acts. The Social and Political Motivations of Lucan Theology*. SNTSMS. Cambridge: Cambridge Univ. Press.

Evans, Craig A.

1989 *To See and Not Perceive: Isaiah 6.9-10 in Early Jewish and Christian Interpretation*. JSOTSup 64. Sheffield: JSOT Press.

Farnell, Lewis R.

1921 *Greek Hero Cults and Ideas of Immortality*. Oxford: Oxford Univ. Press.

Fears, J. R.

1981 "The Theology of Victory at Rome." In *ANRW* II.17.2:736–826.

Ferguson, Everett

1980 "Spiritual Sacrifice in Early Christianity and Its Environment." In *ANRW* II.23.2:1151–89.

Fiensy, David

1985 *Prayers Alleged to Be Jewish: An Examination of the Constitutiones Apostolorum*. BJS 65. Atlanta: Scholars.

1989 "The Hellenistic Synagogal Prayers: One Hundred Years of Discussion." *JSP* 5:17–27.

1991 *The Social History of Palestine in the Herodian Period: The Land Is Mine*. SBEC 20. Lewiston, N.Y.: Mellen.

Finkel, Asher

1981 "The Prayer of Jesus in Matthew." In *Standing Before God*, edited by Asher Finkel and Lawrence Frizzell, 131–70. New York: Ktav.

1987 "God's Attributes in Jewish Prayer: Their Meaning and Use." Paper presented at the SBL annual meeting.

1993 "Prayer of Early Rabbinic Tradition: Representative Texts." In *SBLSP 1993*, 796–807.

Fischel, Henry A.

1973 *Rabbinic Literature and Greco-Roman Philosoph* . SPB 21. Leiden: Brill.

Fitzgerald, John T.

1988 *Cracks in an Earthen Vessel: An Examination of the Catalogues of Hardships in the Corinthian Correspondence*. SBLDS 99. Atlanta: Scholars.

Fitzmyer, Joseph A.

1985 "*Abba* and Jesus' Relation to God." In *A cause de l'Évangile: Étude sur les Synoptiques et Actes,* edited by F. Neirynck, 14–38. LD 123. Paris: Cerf.

1987 *Pauline Theology: A Brief Sketch.* Englewood Cliffs, N.J.: Prentice-Hall.

1993a "*Kephalē* in I Corinthians 11:3." *Int* 47:52–59.

1993b *Romans.* AB 33. New York: Doubleday.

Flusser, David

1984 "Psalms, Hymns, and Prayers." In *Jewish Writings of the Second Temple Period,* vol. 2, edited by Michael E. Stone, 551–78. Philadelphia: Fortress Press.

Foerster, Werner

1964a "*ktizō.*" In *TDNT* 3.1001–35.

1964b "*sozō.*" In *TDNT* 7.967–1002.

Fohrer, Georg

1964 "*sōtēr.*" In *TDNT* 7.1003–23.

Fossum, Jarl

1985 *The Name of God and the Angel of the Lord: Samaritan and Jewish Concepts of Intermediation and the Origins of Gnosticism.* WUNT 36. Tübingen: Mohr/Siebeck.

Foster, John L.

1995 *Hymns, Prayers and Songs: An Anthology of Ancient Egyptian Lyric Poetry.* SBLWAW 8. Atlanta: Scholars.

France, R. T.

1982 "The Worship of Jesus: A Neglected Factor in Christological Debate." In *Christ the Lord: Studies in Christology Presented to Donald Guthrie,* edited by H. H. Rowdon, 17–36. Leicester: InterVarsity.

Fritsch, C. T.

1943 *The Anti-Anthropomorphisms of the Greek Pentateuch.* POT 10. Princeton: Princeton Univ. Press.

Gammie, John G.

1989 *Holiness in Israel.* OBT. Minneapolis: Fortress Press.

Garnsey, Peter, and Greg Woolf

1990 "Patronage of the Rural Poor in the Roman World." In *Patronage in Ancient Society,* edited by Andrew Wallace-Hadrill, 153–70. LNSAS 1. London: Routledge.

Gärtner, Bertil

1955 *The Areopagus Speech and Natural Revelation.* ASNU 21. Uppsala: Gleerup.

1968 "The Pauline and Johannine Idea of 'To know God' against the Hellenistic Background: The Greek Philosophical Principle 'Like by Like' in Paul and John." *NTS* 14:209–31.

Gellner, Ernst, and John Waterbury, editors

1977 *Patrons and Clients in Mediterranean Societies.* London: Duckworth.

Georgi, Dieter

1986 "The God Question." In idem, *The Opponents of Paul in Second Corinthians,* 120–51. Philadelphia: Fortress Press.

1997 "God Turned Upside Down." In *Paul and Empire: Religion and Power in Roman Imperial Society,* edited by Richard Horsley, 148–57. Harrisburg, Pa.: Trinity.

Gerson, Lloyd P.

1990 *God and Greek Philosophy: Studies in the Early History of Natural Theology.* New York: Routledge.

Giblin, Charles H.

1971 "'The Things of God' in the Question Concerning Tribute to Caesar." *CBQ* 33:510–27.

1975 "Three Monotheistic Texts in Paul." *CBQ* 37:527–47.

Glatt, M. J.

1986 "Midrash: The Defender of God." *Judaism* 35:87–97.

Glover, W. W.

1978 "The 'Kingdom of God' in Luke." *BT* 29:213–37.

Goldin, Judah

1986 "The Freedom and Restraint of Haggadah." In *Midrash and Literature,* edited by G. H. Hartman and S. Budick, 57–76. New Haven: Yale Univ. Press.

Goodenough, Erwin R.

1953 *Jewish Symbols in the Greco-Roman Period.* New York: Pantheon.

Gordon, Cyrus H.

1977 "Paternity at Two Levels." *JBL* 96:101.

1978 "The Double Paternity of Jesus." *BAR* 4:26–27.

Gräbe, Petrus J.

2000 *The Power of God in Paul's Letters.* WUNT 2/123. Tübingen: Mohr/Siebeck.

Grant, Robert M.

1966 *The Early Christian Doctrine of God.* Charlottesville: Univ. of Virginia Press.

1986 *Gods and the One God.* LEC 1. Philadelphia: Westminster.

Gray, John

1979 *The Biblical Doctrine of the Reign of God.* Edinburgh: T. & T. Clark.

Griffiths, J. Gwyn

1991 *The Divine Verdict: A Study of Divine Judgement in the Ancient Religions.* SHR 52. Leiden: Brill.

Guthrie, Donald, and Ralph P. Martin

1993 "God." In *Dictionary of Paul and His Letters,* edited by Gerald Hawthorne et al., 354–69. Downers Grove, Ill.: InterVarsity.

Habel, Norman

1965 "The Form and Significance of the Call Narrative." *ZAW* 77:297–323.

Hagedorn, Anselm C., and Jerome H. Neyrey

1988 "'It Was Out of Envy that They Handed Jesus Over' (Mark 15:10): The Anatomy of Envy and the Gospel of Mark." *JSNT* 69:15–56.

Hagner, Donald A.

1971 "The Vision of God in Philo and John: A Comparative Study." *JETS* 14:81–93.

Hahn, Ferdinand

1980 "The Confession of the One God in the New Testament." *HBT* 2:69–84.

Hall, Edward T.

1976 *Beyond Culture.* New York: Doubleday.

Hamerton-Kelly, Robert

1979 *God the Father: Theology and Patriarchy in the Teaching of Jesus.* OBT. Philadelphia: Fortress Press.

1981 "God the Father in the Bible and in the Experience of Jesus: The State of the Question." In *God as Father?* edited by Johannes-Baptist Metz and Eduard Schillebeeckx, 95–102. Concilium 143. Edinburgh: T. & T. Clark.

Harner, Philip B.

1970 *The "I Am" of the Fourth Gospel: A Study in Johannine Usage and Thought.* Facet Books 26. Philadelphia: Fortress Press.

Harrington, Hannah K.

1993 *The Impurity Systems of Qumran and the Rabbis: Biblical Foundations.* SBLDS 143. Atlanta: Scholars.

Harris, Horton

1992 *Jesus as God: The New Testament Use of THEOS in Reference to Jesus.* Grand Rapids: Baker.

Harris, Murray J.

1980 "Titus 2:13 and the Deity of Christ." In *Pauline Studies,* edited by D. A. Hagner and M. J. Harris, 262–77. Grand Rapids: Eerdmans.

Harvey, A. E.

1982 "Son of God: The Constraints of Monotheism." In idem, *Jesus and the Constraints of History,* 154–77. Philadelphia: Westminster.

Hayman, Peter

1989 "Was God a Magician? Sefer Yesir and Jewish Magic." *JJS* 40:225–57.

1991 "Monotheism—A Misused Word in Jewish Studies." *JJS* 42:1–15.

Hays, Richard B.

1980 "Psalm 143 and the Logic of Romans." *JBL* 99:107–15.

1989 *Echoes of Scripture in the Letters of Paul.* New Haven: Yale Univ. Press.

1997 *The Faith of Jesus Christ: The Narrative Substructure of Galatians 3:1—4:11.* Grand Rapids: Eerdmans.

2002 "The God of Mercy Who Rescues Us from the Present Evil Age: Romans and Galatians." In *The Forgotten God: Perspectives in Biblical Theology. Essays in Honor of Paul J. Achtemeier on His Seventy-Fifth Birthday,* edited by A. Andrew Das and Frank J. Matera, 123–44. Louisville: Westminster John Knox.

Helm, Paul, and Carl R. Trueman, editors

2002 *The Trustworthiness of God: Perspectives on the Nature of Scripture.* Grand Rapids: Eerdmans.

Hendrix, Holland

1992 "Benefactor/Patron Networks in the Urban Environment. Evidence from Thessalonika." *Semeia* 56:39–58.

Hengel, Martin

1974 *Judaism and Hellenism: Studies in Their Encounter in Palestine during the Early Hellenistic Period.* Translated by John Bowden. Philadelphia: Fortress Press.

Hermann, Johannes

1964 "*euchomai*." In *TDNT* 2.775–808.

Hickson, Frances V.

1993 *Roman Prayer Language: Livy and the "Aeneid" of Vergil.* BAK 30. Stuttgart: Teubner.

Hochstaffel, Josef

1976 *Negative Theologie: Ein Versuch zur Vermittlung des patristischen Begriffs.* Munich: Kösel.

Hodgson, Robert

1989 "Valerius Maximus and the Social World of the New Testament." *CBQ* 51:683–93.

Holladay, Carl R.

1977 *THEIOS ANĒR in Hellenistic Judaism: A Critique of the Use of This Category in New Testament Christology.* SBLDS 40. Missoula, Mont.: Scholars.

Hophius, O.

1971 "Eine Altjüdische Parallele zu Röm. IV.17b." *NTS* 18:93–94.

1973 "Die Unabänderlichkeit des göttischen Heilsratschlusses." *ZNW* 64:135–45.

Horsley, Richard A.

1978 "The Background of the Confessional Formula in 1 Cor 8:6." *ZNW* 69: 130–35.

Horst, P. W. van der

1989 "The Altar of the 'Unknown God' in Athens (Acts 17:23) and the Cult of 'Unknown Gods' in Hellenistic and Roman Periods." In *ANRW* II.18.2:1426–56.

Houston, Walter

1993 *Purity and Monotheism: Clean and Unclean Animals in Biblical Law.* JSOTSup 140. Sheffield: JSOT Press.

Howard, G.

1977 "The Tetragrammaton and the New Testament." *JBL* 96:63–83.

Hummel, Horace D.

1984 "The Image of God." *Concordia Journal* 10:83–93.

Hurtado, Larry W.

1988 *One God, One Lord: Early Christian Devotion and Ancient Jewish Monotheism.* Philadelphia: Fortress Press.

1993 "What Do We Mean by 'First-Century Jewish Monotheism'?" In *SBLSP 1993,* 348–68.

2003 *Lord Jesus Christ: Devotion to Jesus in Earliest Christianity.* Grand Rapids: Eerdmans.

Husser, Jean-Marie

1999 *Dreams and Dream Narratives in the Biblical World.* Translated by Jill M. Munro. Biblical Seminar 63. Sheffield: Sheffield Academic.

Isenberg, Sheldon

1970 "An Anti-Sadducee Polemic in the Palestinian Targum Tradition." *HTR* 63:433–44.

Jacobs, I.

1990 "Kingship and Holiness in the Third Benediction of the Amidah and in the Yozer." *JJS* 41:62–74.

Jeremias, Joachim

1969 *Jerusalem in the Time of Jesus.* Translated by F. H. Cave and C. H. Cave. Philadelphia: Fortress Press.

Jervell, Jacob

1960 *Imago Dei: Gen 1,26f im Spätjudentum, in der Gnosis, und in den paulinischen Briefen.* FRLANT 58. Göttingen: Vandenhoeck & Ruprecht.

Johnson, N. B.

1948 *Prayer in the Apocrypha and Pseudepigrapha: A Study of the Jewish Concept of God.* SBLMS 2. Philadelphia: Society of Biblical Literature.

Jones, D. L.

1980 "Christianity and the Roman Imperial Cult." In *ANRW* II.23.2:1023–54.

Jónsson, Gunnlaugur A.

1988 *The Image of God: Genesis 1:26-28 in a Century of Old Testament Research.* ConBOT 26. Stockholm: Almqvist & Wiksell.

Joubert, Stephan

2000 *Paul as Benefactor: Reciprocity, Strategy and Theological Reflection in Paul's Collection.* WUNT 2/124. Tübingen: Mohr/Siebeck.

2001 "One Form of Social Exchange or Two? 'Euergetism,' Patronage, and New Testament Studies." *BTB* 31:17–25.

Kajanto, Iiro

1981 "Fortuna." In *ANRW* II.17.1:503–58.

Käsemann, Ernst

1968 *The Testament of Jesus: A Study of John in the Light of Chapter 17.* Translated by Gerhard Krodel. Philadelphia: Fortress Press.

1969 "Sentences of Holy Law in the New Testament." In *New Testament Questions of Today,* 66–81. Translated by W. J. Montague. Philadelphia: Fortress Press.

Keck, Leander E.

1996 "God the Other Who Acts Otherwise: An Exegetical Essay on 1 Cor 1:26-31." *WW* 16:437–43.

Kee, Howard Clark

1968 "The Terminology of Mark's Exorcism Stories." *NTS* 14:232–46.

1990 "The Transformation of the Synagogue after 70 C.E.: Its Import for Early Christianity." *NTS* 36:1–24.

Kennedy, J. P.

1982 "Plotinus and the Via Antiqua: A Study of Philosophical Theology." Ph.D. diss., Brown Univ..

Kimelman, Reuven

1988 "The Daily *'Amidah* and the Rhetoric of Redemption." *JQR* 79:165–97.

King, Karen L.

1994 *Revelation of the Unknowable God: Introduction, Text, Translation, and Notes.* California Classical Library. Santa Rosa, Calif.: Polebridge.

Kingsbury, Jack Dean

1969 *The Parables of Jesus in Matthew 13: A Study in Redaction-Criticism.* London: SPCK.

2002 "'God' within the Narrative World of Mark." In *The Forgotten God: Perspectives in Biblical Theology. Essays in Honor of Paul J. Achtemeier on His Seventy-Fifth Birthday,* edited by A. Andrew Das and Frank J. Matera, 75–90. Louisville: Westminster John Knox.

Kautsky, John H.

1982 *The Politics of Aristocratic Empires.* Chapel Hill: Univ. of North Carolina Press.

Kraus, Hans-Joachim

1971 "The Living God: A Chapter in Biblical Theology." In *Theology of the Liberating Word,* edited by Frederick Herzog, 76–107. Nashville: Abingdon.

Krentz, Edgar M.

1989 "God in the New Testament." In *Our Naming of God: Problems and Prospects of God-talk Today,* edited by Carl E. Braaten, 75–90. Minneapolis: Fortress Press.

Kümmel, Werner Georg

1945 "Die Gottesverkündigung Jesu und der Gottesgedanke des Spätjudentums." *Judaica* 1:40–68.

Ladouceur, David

1980 "Hellenistic Preconceptions of Shipwreck and Pollution as a Context for Acts 27–28." *HTR* 73:435–49.

Lamberton, Robert

1986 *Homer the Theologian: Neoplatonist Allegorical Reading and the Growth of the Epic.* Transformation of the Classical Heritage 9. Berkeley: Univ. of California Press.

Lambrecht, Jan

1981 *Once More Astonished: The Parables of Jesus.* New York: Crossroad.

Legrand, L.

1976 "The Areopagus Speech, Its Theological Kerygma and Its Missionary Significance." In *La Notion biblique de Dieu: Le dieu de la Bible et le dieu des philosophes,* edited by J. Coppens et al., 337–50. BETL 41. Gembloux: Duculot.

1981 "The Unknown God of Athens: Acts 17 and the Religion of the Gentiles." *IJT* 30:158–67.

Levine, Baruch

1968 "On the Presence of God in Biblical Religion." In *Religions in Antiquity: Essays in Memory of Erwin Ramsdell Goodenough,* edited by Jacob Neusner, 71–87. SHR 14. Leiden: Brill.

Lindsay, Dennis R.

1993 *Josephus and Faith. Pistis and Pisteuein as Faith Terminology in the Writings of Flavius Josephus and in the New Testament.* AGAJU 19. Leiden: Brill.

Lindström, Fredrik

1994 *Suffering and Sin: Interpretations of Illness in the Individual Complaint Psalms.* ConBOT 37. Stockholm: Almqvist & Wiksell.

Lloyd, Alan B., editor

1997 *What Is a God? Studies in the Nature of Greek Divinity.* London: Duckworth.

Lloyd, G. E. R.

1966 *Polarity and Analogy: Two Types of Argumentation in Early Greek Thought.* Cambridge: Cambridge Univ. Press.

Loewe, H.

1993 "The Concept of Blessing." *SIDIC* (Rome) 26:2–9.

Long, C. R.

1989 "The Gods of the Months in Ancient Art." *AJA* 93:589–95.

Longenecker, Richard N.

1990 *Galatians*. WBC 41. Dallas: Word.

Malherbe, Abraham J.

1986 "Not in a Corner: Early Christian Apologetic in Acts 26:26. *Second Century* 5: 193–210.

Malina, Bruce J.

1978 "Freedom: A Theological Inquiry into the Dimensions of a Symbol." *BTB* 8: 62–76.

1980 "What Is Prayer?" *TBT* 18:214–20.

1986a *Christian Origins and Cultural Anthropology: Practical Models for Biblical Interpretation*. Atlanta: John Knox.

1986b "'Religion' in the World of Paul." *BTB* 16:92–101.

1996 "Patron and Client: The Analogy Behind Synoptic Theology." In *The Social World of Jesus and the Gospels*, 143–78. London: Routledge.

2001a *The New Testament World: Insights from Cultural Anthropology*. 3d ed. Louisville: Westminster John Knox.

2001b *The Social Gospel of Jesus: The Kingdom of God in Mediterranean Perspective*. Minneapolis: Fortress Press.

Malina, Bruce J., and Jerome H. Neyrey

1988 *Calling Jesus Names: The Social Value of Labels in Matthew*. Social Facets. Sonoma, Calif.: Polebridge.

1991 "Honor and Shame in Luke-Acts: Pivotal Values of the Mediterranean." In *The Social World of Luke-Acts*, edited by Jerome H. Neyrey, 25–66. Peabody, Mass.: Hendrickson.

1996 *Portraits of Paul: An Archaeology of Ancient Personality*. Louisville: Westminster John Knox.

Malina, Bruce J., and Richard L. Rohrbaugh

1992 *Social-Science Commentary on the Synoptic Gospels*. Minneapolis: Fortress Press.

2003 *Social-Science Commentary on the Synoptic Gospels*. Rev. ed. Minneapolis: Fortress Press.

Marcus, Joel

1986 *The Mystery of the Kingdom of God*. SBLDS 90. Atlanta: Scholars.

1988 "Entering into the Kingly Power of God." *JBL* 107:663–75.

Marcus, Ralph

1932 "Divine Names and Attributes in Hellenistic Jewish Literature." In *Proceedings of the American Academy of Jewish Research*, 43–120. Philadelphia: Jewish Publication Society of America.

Marmorstein, A.

1932 "Philo and the Names of God." *JQR* 22:295–306.

1968 *The Old Rabbinic Doctrine of God*. 2 vols. New York: Ktav.

Marshall, Peter

1987 *Enmity in Corinth: Social Conventions in Paul's Relations with the Corinthians.* WUNT 2/23. Tübingen: Mohr/Siebeck.

Martens, John

1994 "Romans 2:14-16: A Stoic Reading." *NTS* 40:55–67.

Martin, Dale

1995 *The Corinthian Body.* New Haven: Yale Univ. Press.

Martin, Ralph P.

1964 *Worship in the Early Church.* Grand Rapids: Eerdmans.

Martin, Troy W.

2002 "*The Good* as God (Romans 5,7)." *JSNT* 25:55–70.

Martyn, J. Louis

1985 "Apocalyptic Antinomies in Paul's Letter to the Galatians." *NTS* 31: 410–24.

1997 *Galatians.* AB 33A. New York: Doubleday.

Mastin, B. A.

1976 "A Neglected Feature of the Christology of the Fourth Gospel." *NTS* 22:32–51.

Mattill, A. J.

1975 "The Paul-Jesus Parallels and the Purpose of Luke-Acts: H. H. Evans Reconsidered." *NovT* 17:15–45.

McKay, Heather

1998 "Ancient Synagogues: The Continuing Dialectic between Two Major Views." *CRBS* 6:103–42.

McLelland, Joseph C.

1976 *God the Anonymous: A Study in Alexandrian Philosophical Theology.* PMS 4. Philadelphia: Philadelphia Patristics Foundation.

McNamara, Martin

1966 "The Divine Name and the 'Second Death' in the Apocalypse and in the Targums." In *The New Testament and the Palestinian Targum to the Pentateuch,* 97–112. AnBib 27. Rome: Pontifical Biblical Institute Press.

Meeks, Wayne A.

1968 "Moses as God and King." In *Religions in Antiquity: Essays in Memory of Erwin Ramsdell Goodenough,* edited by Jacob Neusner, 354–71. SHR 14. Leiden: Brill.

1976 "The Divine Agent and His Counterfeit in Philo and the Fourth Gospel." In *Aspects of Religious Propaganda in Judaism and Early Christianity,* edited by Elisabeth Schüssler Fiorenza, 43–67. Notre Dame: Univ. of Notre Dame Press.

1983 *The First Urban Christians: The Social World of the Apostle Paul.* New Haven: Yale Univ. Press.

Meier, John P.

1985 "Structure and Theology in Heb 1,1-4." *Bib* 66:168–89.

Meijer, P. A.

1981 "Philosophers, Intellectuals and Religion in Hellas." In *Faith, Hope, and Worship: Aspects of Religious Mentality in the Ancient World,* edited by H. S. Versnel, 193–215. SGRR 2. Leiden: Brill.

Mettinger, Tryggve N. D.

1988 *In Search of God: The Meaning and Message of the Everlasting Names.* Translated by Frederick H. Cryer. Philadelphia: Fortress Press.

Mikalson, Jon D.

1983 *Athenian Popular Religion.* Chapel Hill: Univ. of North Carolina Press.

1991 *Honor Thy Gods: Popular Religion in Greek Tragedy.* Chapel Hill: Univ. of North Carolina Press.

Miles, Gary B., and Garry Trompf

1976 "Luke and Antiphon: The Theology of Acts 27–28 in the Light of Pagan Beliefs about Divine Retribution, Pollution, and Shipwreck." *HTR* 69:259–67.

Milgrom, Jacob

1991 *Leviticus 1–16.* AB 3. New York: Doubleday.

Miller, Ed. L.

1981 "The *Logos* Was God." *EvQ* 53:65–77.

Miller, Patrick D.

1994 *They Cried to the Lord: The Form and Theology of Biblical Prayer.* Minneapolis: Fortress Press.

Minear, Paul S.

1988 *The God of the Gospels: A Theological Workbook.* Atlanta: John Knox.

Mitchell, Margaret M.

1991 *Paul and the Rhetoric of Reconciliation: An Exegetical Investigation of the Language and Composition of 1 Corinthians.* Louisville: Westminster John Knox.

Momigliano, Arnoldo

1956 "How Roman Emperors Became Gods." *American Scholar* 55:181–93.

Montgomery, J. A.

1920 "The Religion of Flavius Josephus." *JQR* 11:277–305.

Montefiore, C. G., and H. Loewe

1974 *A Rabbinic Anthology.* New York: Schocken.

Moore, George Foote

1958 *Judaism in the First Centuries of the Christian Era.* 2 vols. New York: Schocken.

Morray-Jones, C. R. A.

1992 "Transformational Mysticism in the Apocalyptic-Merkabah Tradition." *JJS* 43:1–31.

Mott, Stephen Charles

1971 "The Greek Benefactor and Deliverance from Moral Distress." Ph.D. diss., Harvard Univ..

1975 "The Power of Giving and Receiving: Reciprocity in Hellenistic Benevolence." In *Current Issues in Biblical and Patristic Interpretation: Studies in Honor of Merrill C. Tenney Presented by His Former Students,* edited by Gerald F. Hawthorne, 60–72. Grand Rapids: Eerdmans.

1978 "Greek Ethics and Christian Conversion: The Philonic Background of Titus II.10-14 and III.3-7." *NovT* 20:22–48.

Mowery, Robert L.

1995 "Lord, God, and Father: Theological Language in Luke-Acts." In *SBLSP 1995,* 82–101.

Moxnes, Halvor

1980 *Theology in Conflict: Studies in Paul's Understanding of God in Romans.* NovTSup 53. Leiden: Brill.

1991 "Patron-Client Relations and the New Community in Luke-Acts." In *The Social World of Luke-Acts: Models for Interpretation,* edited by Jerome H. Neyrey, 241–68. Peabody, Mass.: Hendrickson.

Neusner, Jacob

1972 "Judaism in a Time of Crisis. Four Responses to the Destruction of the Second Temple." *Judaism* 21:313–27.

1973a *The Idea of Purity in Ancient Judaism.* SJLA 1. Leiden: Brill.

1973b *From Politics to Piety: The Emergence of Pharisaic Judaism.* Englewood Cliffs, N.J.: Prentice-Hall.

1975 "The Idea of Purity in Ancient Judaism." *JAAR* 43:15–26.

1976 "'First Cleanse the Inside': The 'Halakhic' Background of a Controversy Saying." *NTS* 22:486–95.

1978 "History and Purity in First-Century Judaism." *HR* 18:1–17.

1979 "Map Without Territory: Mishnah's System of Sacrifices and Sanctuary." *HR* 19:103–27.

Neville, Robert C.

1992 *God the Creator: On the Transcendence and Presence of God.* Albany: SUNY Press.

Newman, Carey C.

1992 *Paul's Glory-Christology: Tradition and Rhetoric.* NovTSup 69. Leiden: Brill.

Newton, Michael

1985 *The Concept of Purity at Qumran and in the Letters of Paul.* SNTSMS 53. Cambridge: Cambridge Univ. Press.

Neyrey, Jerome H.

1980 "The Form and Background of the Polemic in 2 Peter." *JBL* 99:407–31.

1981 "The Debate in John III: Sectarian Epistemology and Christology." *NovT* 23:115–27.

1982 "The Jacob Allusions in John 1:51." *CBQ* 44:586–605.

1984 "The Forensic Defense Speech and Paul's Trial Speeches in Act 22-26: Form and Function."In *Luke-Acts: New Perspectives from the Society of Biblical Literature Seminar,* edited by Charles H. Talbert, 210–24. New York: Crossroads.

1986 "'My Lord and My God': The Divinity of Jesus in John's Gospel." In *SBLSP 1986,* 152–71.

1987a "Hope against Hope." *The Way* 27:264–73.

1987b "Jesus the Judge: Forensic Process in John 8:21-59." *Bib* 68:509–42.

1988a *An Ideology of Revolt: John's Christology in Social Science Perspective.* Philadelphia: Fortress Press.

1988b "A Symbolic Approach to Mark 7." *Forum* 4.3:63–91.

1989 "'I Said: You Are God': Psalm 82:6 and John 10." *CBQ* 108:647–63.

1990a "Acts 17, Epicureans and Theodicy: A Study in Stereotypes." In *Greeks, Romans, and Christians: Essays in Honor of Abraham J. Malherbe,* edited by David Balch and Wayne Meeks, 118–34. Minneapolis: Fortress Press.

1990b *Paul, In Other Words: A Cultural Reading of His Letters.* Louisville: Westminster John Knox.

1991 "'Without Beginning of Days or End of Life' (Hebrews 7:3): Topos for a True Deity." *CBQ* 53:439–55.

1993 *2 Peter, Jude.* AB 37C. New York: Doubleday.

1995 "Loss of Wealth, Loss of Family and Loss of Honor: A Cultural Interpretation of the Original Four Makarisms." In *Modelling Early Christianity: Social-scientific Studies of the New Testament in Its Context,* edited by Philip F. Esler, 139–58. London: Routledge.

1996 "Father." In *The Collegeville Pastoral Dictionary of Biblical Theology,* edited by Carroll Stuhlmuller, 315–19. Collegeville, Minn.: Liturgical.

1998a *Honor and Shame in the Gospel of Matthew.* Louisville: Westminster John Knox.

1998b "Questions, Chreiai, and Challenges to Honor. The Interface of Rhetoric and Culture in Mark's Gospel." *CBQ* 60:657–81.

1998c "Wholeness." In *Handbook of Biblical Social Values,* edited by John J. Pilch and Bruce J. Malina, 204–8. Peabody, Mass.: Hendrickson.

2001 "Prayer, in Other Words: New Testament Prayers in Social-Science Perspective." In *Social Scientific Models for Interpreting the Bible: Essays by the Context Group in Honor of Bruce J. Malina,* edited by John J. Pilch, 349–80. BibInterSer 53. Leiden: Brill.

Neyrey, Jerome H., and Richard L. Rohrbaugh

2001 "'He must increase, I must decrease' (John 3:30): Cultural and Social Interpretation." *CBQ* 63:464–83.

Nilsson, M. P.

1963 "The High God and the Mediator." *HTR* 56:101–20.

Nock, Arthur Darby

1972 *Essays on Religion and the Ancient World.* Cambridge: Harvard Univ. Press.

Nolan, Brian M.

1979 *The Royal Son of God: The Christology in Matthew 1–2 in the Setting of the Gospel.* Orbis biblicus et orientalis 23. Göttingen: Vandenhoeck & Ruprecht.

Nolan, Patrick, and Gerhard Lenski

1999 *Human Societies: An Introduction to Macrosociology.* 8th ed. New York: McGraw-Hill.

Obbink, Dirk

1995 *Philodemus on Piety: Critical Text with Commentary.* Oxford: Clarendon.

O'Brien, Peter T.

1980 "Thanksgiving within the Structure of Pauline Theology." In *Pauline Studies: Essays Presented to Professor F. F. Bruce on His Seventieth Birthday,* edited by D. A. Hagner and M. J. Harris, 50–66. Grand Rapids: Eerdmans.

Oepke, A.

1967 "*mesitēs.*" In *TDNT* 4:598–624.

Old, H. O.

1985 "Psalms of Praise in the Worship of the New Testament Church." *Int* 39:20–33.

Olyan, Saul M.

1993 *A Thousand Thousands Served Him: Exegesis and the Naming of the Angels in Ancient Judaism.* TSAJ 36. Tübingen: Mohr/Siebeck.

Orr, David G.

1978 "Roman Domestic Religion: The Evidence of the Household Shrines." In *ANRW* II.16.2:1557–91.

O'Toole, Robert

1982 "Paul at Athens and Luke's Notion of Worship." *RB* 89:185–97.

Owen, H. P.

1959 "The Scope of Natural Revelation in Rom I and Acts XVII." *NTS* 5:133–43.

Owen, J. M.

1973 "Jesus and God." *Colloquium* 6:19–35.

Pao, David W.

2002 *Thanksgiving: An Investigation of a Pauline Theme.* New Studies in Biblical Theology 13. Downers Grove, Ill.: InterVarsity.

Parker, Robert

1983 *Miasma: Pollution and Purification in Early Greek Religion.* Oxford: Clarendon.

Patterson, Stephen J.

1998 *The God of Jesus Christ: The Historical Jesus and the Search for Meaning.* Harrisburg: Trinity.

Peels, H. G. L.

1995 *The Vengeance of God: The Meaning of the Root NQM and the Function of the NQM-Texts in the Context of Divine Revelation in the Old Testament.* OtSt 31. Leiden: Brill.

Perkins, Pheme

1985 "God in the New Testament: Preliminary Soundings." *ThTo* 42:332–41.

Perrin, Norman

1969 *What Is Redaction Criticism?* Guides to Biblical Scholarship. Philadelphia: Fortress Press.

Pétrement, Simone

1990 *A Separate God: The Christian Origins of Gnosticism.* Translated by Carol Harrison. San Francisco: Harper & Row.

Pickett, Raymond W.

1993 "The Death of Christ as Divine Patronage." In *SBLSP 1993,* 726–39.

Pilch, John J.

1991 "Sickness and Healing in Luke-Acts." In *Social World of Luke-Acts: Models for Interpretation,* edited by Jerome H. Neyrey, 181–209. Peabody, Mass.: Hendrickson.

2000 *Healing in the New Testament. Insights from Medical and Mediterranean Anthropology.* Minneapolis: Fortress Press.

Piper, John

1983 *The Justification of God: An Exegetical and Theological Study of Romans 9:1-23.* Grand Rapids: Baker.

Plymale, Steven F.

1990 "Luke's Theology of Prayer." In *SBLSP 1990,* 529–51.

1991 *The Prayer Texts of Luke-Acts.* AUSTR 118. New York: Lang.

Pohlenz, Max

1949 "Paulus und die Stoa." *ZNW* 42:69–104.

Porter, Barbara Nevling, editor

2000 *One God or Many? Concepts of Divinity in the Ancient World.* Transactions of the Casco Bay Assyriological Institute 1. Chebeauge, Maine: Casco Bay Assyriological Institute.

Prestige, G. L.

1952 *God in Patristic Thought.* London: SPCK.

Price, S. R. F.

1984 "Gods and Emperors: The Greek Language of the Imperial Cult." *JHS* 104:79–95.

Purdue, Leo G.

1996 "Names of God in the Old Testament." In *HBD,* 685–87.

Quere, R.

1985 "'Naming' God 'Father.'" *CurTM* 12:5–14.

Qimron, Elisha

1990 "Times for Praising God: A Fragment of a Scroll from Qumran (4Q409)." *JQR* 80:341–47.

Rainbow, Paul

1991 "Jewish Monotheism as the Matrix for New Testament Christology: A Review Article." *NovT* 33:78–91.

Räisänen, Heikki

1988 "Paul, God, and Israel: Romans 9–11 in Recent Research." In *The Social World of Formative Christianity and Judaism: Essays in Tribute to Howard Clark Kee,* edited by Jacob Neusner et al., 178–206. Philadelphia: Fortress Press.

Reese, James M.

1978 "The Principal Model of God in the New Testament." *BTB* 8:126–31.

Reinhartz, Adele, editor

1999 *God the Father in the Gospel of John. Semeia* 85.

Rengstorf, Karl

1964 "*dēspotēs.*" In *TDNT* 2.44–45.

Reumann, John

1974 "Psalm 22 at the Cross: Lament and Thanksgiving for Jesus Christ." *Int* 28:39–58.

1982 *Righteousness in the New Testament: Justification in the Lutheran-Roman Catholic Dialogue.* Philadelphia: Fortress Press.

Rice, David G., and John E. Stambaugh

1979 *Sources for the Study of Greek Religion.* SBLSBS 14. Missoula, Mont.: Scholars.

Rich, John

1990 "Patronage and Interstate Relations in the Roman Republic." In *Patronage in Ancient Society,* edited by Andrew Wallace-Hadrill, 117–36. London: Routledge.

Richardson, C. C.

1962 "Worship in New Testament Times, Christian." In *IDB* 4.883–94.

Richardson, Neil

1994 *Paul's Language about God.* JSNTSup 99. Sheffield: Sheffield Academic.

1999 *God in the New Testament.* Peterborough: Epworth.

Roetzel, Calvin J.

1991 *The Letters of Paul: Conversations in Context.* Louisville: Westminster John Knox.

Rohrbaugh, Richard L.

1995 "Legitimating Sonship—A Test of Honour. A Social-Scientific Study of Luke 4:1-30." In *Modelling Early Christianity. Social-Scientific Studies of the New Testament in Its Context,* edited by Philip F. Esler, 183–97. London: Routledge.

Rubinkiewicz, R.

1983 "The Apocalypse of Abraham." In *The Old Testament Pseudepigrapha,* edited by James H. Charlesworth, 2.685–709. Garden City, N.Y.: Doubleday.

Runia, David T.

1988 "Naming and Knowing: Themes in Philonic Theology with Special Reference to *De Mutatione Nominum.*" In *Knowledge of God in the Greco-Roman World,* edited by R. van den Broek, 69–91. EPROER 112. Leiden: Brill.

1995 "God of the Philosophers, God of the Patriarchs: Exegetical Backgrounds in Philo of Alexandria." In *Philo and the Church Fathers: A Collection of Papers,* 2–17. VCSup 32. Leiden: Brill.

Russell, D. A., and N. G. Wilson

1981 *Menander Rhetor.* Oxford: Clarendon.

Saller, Richard P.

1982 *Personal Patronage under the Early Empire.* Cambridge: Cambridge Univ. Press.

Sanders, E. P.

1983 *Paul, the Law, and the Jewish People.* Philadelphia: Fortress Press.

1992 "Observing the Law of God I: General Characteristics, Worship and Sabbath." In *Judaism: Practice and Belief 63 BCE–66 CE,* 190–208. Philadelphia: Trinity.

Sandmel, Samuel

1980 "Some Comments on Providence in Philo." In *The Divine Helmsman: Studies in God's Control of Human Events, Presented to Lou H. Silberman,* edited by James L. Crenshaw and Samuel Sandmel, 79–85. New York: Ktav.

Saunders, Trevor J.

1994 *Plato's Penal Code: Tradition, Controversy, and Reform in Greek Penology.* Oxford: Oxford Univ. Press.

Schäfer, K.

1972 "Jesus on God." *Concilium* 76:58–66.

Schäfer, P.

1984 "Merkabah Mysticism and Rabbinic Judaism." *JAOS* 104:537–41.

Schiffren, Mara

1997 "Biblical Hypostases and the Concept of God." In *SBLSP 1997,* 194–223.

Schillebeeckx, Edward

1974 "The 'God of Jesus' and the 'Jesus of God.'" *Concilium* 93:110–26.

Schineller, Peter

1976 "Christ and Church: A Spectrum of Views." *TS* 37:545–66.

Schoedel, William R.

1979 "Enclosing, Not Enclosed: The Early Christian Doctrine of God." In *Early Christian Literature and the Classical Intellectual Tradition in Honorem Robert M. Grant,* edited by William R. Schoedel and Robert L. Wilken, 75–86. Théologie historique 53. Paris: Beauchesne.

Scott, Jamie, and Paul Simpson-Housley, editors

1991 *Sacred Places and Profane Spaces: Essays in the Geographics of Judaism, Christianity, and Islam.* Contributions to the Study of Religion 30. New York: Greenwood.

Scott, Bernard Brandon

1989 *Hear Then the Parable: A Commentary on the Parables of Jesus.* Philadelphia: Fortress Press.

Scroggs, Robin

1993 "The *Theo*centrism of Paul." In *The Text and the Times: New Testament Essays for Today,* 192–211. Minneapolis: Fortress Press.

Schwartz, Seth

1994 "Josephus in Galilee: Rural Patronage and Social Breakdown." In *Josephus and the History of the Greco-Roman Periods,* edited by F. Parente and Joseph Siever, 290–306. StPB 41. Leiden: Brill.

Schweizer, Eduard

1939 *Ego Eimi: Die religionsgeschichtliche Herkunft und theologische Bedeutung der johanneischen Bildreden.* FRLANT 56. Göttingen: Vandenhoeck & Ruprecht.

Scullion, John J.

1992 "God in the Old Testament." In *ABD* 2.1041–48.

Segal, Alan

1977 *Two Powers in Heaven: Early Rabbinic Reports about Christianity and Gnosticism.* SJLA 25. Leiden: Brill.

Senior, Donald P.

1977 "The Death of God's Son and the Beginning of the New Age." In *The Language of the Cross,* edited by Aelred Lacomara, 29–51. Chicago: Franciscan Herald.

1984 "The Struggle to Be Universal: Mission as a Vantage Point for New Testament Investigation." *CBQ* 46:63–81.

Shutt, R. J. H.

1980 "The Concept of God in the Works of Flavius Josephus." *JJS* 31:171–87.

Smith, Jonathan Z.

1968 "The Prayer of Joseph." In *Religions in Antiquity: Essays in Memory of Erwin Ramsdell Goodenough,* edited by Jacob Neusner, 253–94. SHR 14. Leiden: Brill.

Smith, Mark S.

2002 *The Early History of God.* 2d ed. Grand Rapids: Eerdmans.

Smith, Morton

1952 "The Common Theology of the Ancient Near East." *JBL* 71:135–47.

1958 "The Image of God: Notes on the Hellenization of Judaism, with Especial Reference to Goodenough's Work on Jewish Symbols." *BJRL* 40:473–512.

1968 "On the Shape of God and the Humanity of the Gentiles." In *Religions in Antiquity: Essays in Memory of Erwin Ramsdell Goodenough,* edited by Jacob Neusner, 315–26. SHR 14. Leiden: Brill.

Soards, Marion

1985 "The Righteousness of God in the Writings of the Apostle Paul." *BTB* 15:104–9.

Soler, Jean

1979 "The Dietary Prohibitions of the Hebrews." In *Food and Drink in History,* edited by Robert Forster and Orest Ranum, 126–38. Baltimore: Johns Hopkins Univ. Press.

Spicq, C.

1953 *L'Épître aux Hébreux.* Sources bibliques. Paris: Gabalda.

1960 *"Ametamelētos* dans Rom 11:29." *RB* 67:210–19.

Squires, John

1993 *The Plan of God in Luke-Acts.* SNTSMS 76. Cambridge: Cambridge Univ. Press.

Stauffer, Ethelbert

1964 "*theos.*" In *TDNT* 3.65–119.

Stern, D.

1992 "*Imitatio Hominis*: Anthropomorphism and the Character(s) of God in Rabbinic Literature." *Prooftexts* 12:151–74.

Stirewalt, Martin Luther

1991 "The Form and Function of the Greek Letter-Essay." In *The Romans Debate,* edited by Karl P. Donfried, 147–74. Rev. ed. Peabody, Mass.: Hendrickson.

Stevenson, T. R.

1992 "The Ideal Benefactor and the Father Analogy in Greek and Roman Thought." *CQ* 42:421–36.

1996 "Social and Psychological Interpretations of Graeco-Roman Religions: Some Thoughts on the Ideal Benefactor." *Antichthon* 30:1–18.

Stowers, Stanley K.

1981 *The Diatribe and Paul's Letter to the Romans.* SBLDS 57. Chico, Calif.: Scholars.

Straten, F. T. van

1981 "Gifts for the Gods." In *Faith, Hope, and Worship: Aspects of Religious Mentality in the Ancient World,* edited by H. S. Versnel, 65–151. SGRR 2. Leiden: Brill.

Swain, S.

1989 "Plutarch: Chance, Providence and History." *AJP* 110:272–302.

Talbert, Charles H.

1974 *Literary Patterns, Theological Themes and the Genre of Luke-Acts.* SBLMS 20. Missoula, Mont.: Scholars.

1975 "The Concept of Immortals in Mediterranean Antiquity." *JBL* 94:419–36.

1977 *What Is a Gospel? The Genre of the Canonical Gospels.* Philadelphia: Fortress Press.

Talbert, Charles H., and J. H. Hayes

1995 "A Theology of Sea Storms in Luke-Acts." In *SBLSP 1995,* 321–36.

Taylor, Lily Ross

1975 *The Divinity of the Roman Emperor.* Philological Monographs 1. Philadelphia: Porcupine.

Teixidor, Javier

1977 *The Pagan God: Popular Religion in the Greco-Roman Near East.* Princeton: Princeton Univ. Press.

Thompson, Marianne Meye

1993 "'God's Voice You Have Not Heard, God's Form You Have Never Seen': Characterization of God in the Gospel of John." *Semeia* 63:177–205.

2000 *The Promise of the Father: Jesus and God in the New Testament.* Louisville: Westminster John Knox.

2001 *The God of the Gospel of John.* Grand Rapids: Eerdmans.

Thüsing, Wilhelm

1986 *Per Christum in Deum*. Neutestamentliche Abhandlungen 1. Münster: Aschendorff.

Tolmie, D. François

1998 "The Characterization of God in the Fourth Gospel." *JSNT* 69:57–75.

Trompf, G. W.

1971 "The Conception of God in Hebrews 4:12-13." *ST* 25:123–32.

Tuckett, Christopher M.

1996 "The Corinthians Who Say 'There Is No Resurrection of the Dead' (1 Cor 15,12)." In *The Corinthian Correspondence,* edited by R. Bieringer, 247–75. BETL 125. Leuven: Leuven Univ. Press.

Unnik, W. C. van

1959 "*Dominus Vobiscum*: The Background of a Liturgical Phrase." In *New Testament Essays: Studies in Memory of T. W. Manson,* edited by Angus John Brockhurst Higgins, 270–305. Manchester: Univ. of Manchester Press.

1970 "'Alles ist dir möglich' (Mk 14:36)." In *Verborum Veritas: Festschrift für Gustav Stählin zum 70. Geburstag,* edited by Otto Böcher and Klaus Haacker, 27–36. Wuppertal: Theologischer Verlag.

Urban, L., and P. Henry

1979 "'Before Abraham Was I AM': Does Philo Explain John 8:56-58?" *Studia philonica* 6:157–93.

Vermes, Geza

1975 *Post-Biblical Jewish Studies.* SJLA 8. Leiden: Brill.

Vernant, Jean-Pierre

1991 *Mortals and Immortals: Collected Essays,* edited by Froma I. Zeitlin. Princeton: Princeton Univ. Press.

Versnel, H. S.

1981 "Religious Mentality in Ancient Prayer." In *Faith, Hope, and Worship: Aspects of Religious Mentality in the Ancient World,* edited by H. S. Versnel, 1–64. SGRR 2. Leiden: Brill.

2000 "Thrice One: Three Greek Experiments in Oneness." In *One God or Many? Concepts of Divinity in the Ancient World,* edited by Barbara Porter, 79–163. Chebeauge, Maine: Casco Bay Assyriological Institute.

Veyne, Paul

1990 *Bread and Circuses: Historical Sociology and Political Pluralism.* Translated by Brian Pearce. London: Penguin.

Wainwright, Elaine Mary

1991 *Towards a Feminist Critical Reading of the Gospel according to Matthew.* BZNW 60. Berlin: de Gruyter.

Wald, Stephen G.

1988 *The Doctrine of the Divine Name: An Introduction to Classical Kabbalistic Theology.* BJS 149. Atlanta: Scholars.

Walker, William O.

1982 "The Lord's Prayer in Matthew and John." *NTS* 28:237–56.

Wallace-Hadrill, Andrew, editor

1989 *Patronage in Ancient Society.* LNSAS 1. London: Routledge.

Walsh, J. J.

1991 "On Christian Atheism." *VC* 45:255–77.

Wasden, J.

1976 "Scenes from the Graeco-Roman Underworld." *Crux* 13:23–28.

Welborn, L. L.

1997 *Politics and Rhetoric in the Corinthian Epistles.* Macon, Ga.: Mercer Univ. Press.

Wendland, Paul

1904 "*Sōtēr.*" *ZNW* 5:335–53.

Westermann, Claus

1980 *The Psalms: Structure, Content, and Message.* Translated by Ralph D. Gehrke. Minneapolis: Augsburg.

Whittaker, John

1969 "Neopythagoreanism and Negative Theology." *Symbolae Osloenses* 44:109–25.

1970 "A Hellenistic Context for John 10,29." *VC* 24:246–60.

1975 "The Historical Background of Proclus' Doctrine of *authupostata.*" In *De Jamblique à Proclus,* edited by B. D. Larsen, 193–210. Fondation Hardt, Entretiens 21. Geneva: Vandoeuvres.

1980 "Self-Generating Principles in Second-Century Gnostic Systems." In *The Rediscovery of Gnosticism: Proceedings of the International Conference on Gnosticism at Yale, 1978,* edited by Bentley Layton, 176–89. SHR 41. Leiden: Brill.

Wicks, Henry J.

1980 "The Doctrine of God in the Works of Flavius Josephus." *JJS* 31:171–87.

Wifall, Walter

1979 "Models of God in the Old Testament." *BTB* 9:179–86.

Williams, Michael A.

1997 "Negative Theology and Demiurgical Myths in Late Antiquity." In *SBLSP 1997,* 20–46.

Williams, Sam K.

1980 "The Righteousness of God in Romans." *JBL* 99:241–90.

Wills, Lawrence

1984 "The Form of the Sermon in Hellenistic Judaism and Early Christianity." *HTR* 77:277–99.

Witherup, Ronald D.

1987 "The Death of Jesus and the Raising of the Saints: Matthew 27:51-54 in Context." In *SBLSP 1987*, 574–85.

Wolfson, E. R.

1992 "Images of God's Feet: Some Observations on the Divine Body in Judaism." In *People of the Body: Jews and Judaism from an Embodied Perspective*, edited by Howard Eilberg-Schwartz, 143–81. The Body in Culture, History, and Religion. Albany: SUNY Press.

Wolfson, H. A.

1947 *Philo: Foundations of Religious Philosophy in Judaism, Christianity, and Islam*. 2 vols. Cambridge: Harvard Univ. Press.

1952 "Albinus and Plotinus on Divine Attributes." *HTR* 45:115–30.

1957 "Negative Attributes in the Church Fathers and the Gnostic Basilides." *HTR* 50:145–56.

Wright, N. T.

1996 "A Biblical Portrait of God." In *The Changing Face of God: Lincoln Lectures in Theology*, 9–29. Lincoln, England: Lincoln Cathedral Publications.

York, John O.

1990 *The Last Shall Be First: The Rhetoric of Reversal in Luke*. JSNTSup 46. Sheffield: Sheffield Academic.

Young, Francis M.

1979 "The God of the Greeks and the Nature of Religious Language." In *Early Christian Literature and the Classical Intellectual Tradition in Honorem Robert M. Grant*, edited by R. Schoedel and Robert L. Wilken, 45–74. Théologie histoique 53. Paris: Beauchesne.

INDEX OF SUBJECTS

INDEX OF SCRIPTURE AND LITERATURE

GRECO-ROMAN LITERATURE